The Use
and Development
of the Xinkan Languages

Published through the Recovering Languages and Literacies of the Americas initiative, supported by the Andrew W. Mellon Foundation

The Use
and Development
of the Xinkan Languages

Chris Rogers

University of Texas Press : Austin

This book is a part of the Recovering Languages and Literacies of the Americas publication initiative, funded by a grant from the Andrew W. Mellon Foundation.

Requests for permission to reproduce material from this work should be sent to:

    Permissions
    University of Texas Press
    P.O. Box 7819
    Austin, TX 78713-7819
    http://utpress.utexas.edu/index.php/rp-form

♾ The paper used in this book meets the minimum requirements of ANSI/NISO Z39.48-1992 (R1997) (Permanence of Paper).

Library of Congress Cataloging-in-Publication Data
Rogers, Chris, 1977– author.
    The use and development of the Xinkan languages / Chris Rogers. — First edition.
       pages cm — (Recovering languages and literacies of the Americas Mellon Foundation Initiative)
    Includes bibliographical references and index.
    ISBN 978-1-4773-0831-8 (cloth)
    ISBN 978-1-4773-0832-5 (pbk.)
    ISBN 978-1-4773-0833-2 (library e-book)
    ISBN 978-1-4773-0834-9 (non-library e-book)
1. Xinca language—Grammar, Historical.   2. Extinct languages—Guatemala.
3. Indians of South America—Guatemala—Languages.   4. Guatemala—Languages.
I. Title.   II. Series: Recovering languages and literacies of the Americas.
    PM4498.X31R64 2016
    497'.9—dc23
                                               2015030234

This grammar is dedicated to the Xinkan community of Guatemala

and especially to the last speakers of these languages

and those involved in efforts toward language revitalization.

Contents

List of figures and tables

Acknowledgements

A grammatical description of a language (let alone of four languages) is never an individual achievement. It is only possible through collaboration with and assistance from language speakers, language communities, scholars, publishers, colleagues, friends, and family. This grammar is no different. I am indebted to those who shared ideas, emails, and presentations, and I am grateful to students and audiences who have improved my thinking and analysis.

First, this grammar would not be possible without Terrence Kaufman and Lyle Campbell, who granted me permission to use, analyze, and interpret their unpublished field notes on Xinkan; they have both been very helpful.

Many discussions and emails with them have shaped, influenced, and improved my analysis. Their data set was organized and analyzed as part of National Science Foundation grant 0513449, 'Xinkan, Pipil and Mochó: Bringing three endangered language documentation projects to completion.' Lyle also served as the chair of my dissertation committee, where he gave extensive feedback on an earlier version of this grammar. His comments have been invaluable. He has been a dedicated mentor and friend and has guided this research thoughtfully and helpfully. I owe much of my current thinking about Xinkan, and linguistics in general, to him.

I cannot stress enough that without the significant contributions of Lyle and Terry, we would know next to nothing about the Xinkan languages or how they have changed over the last three hundred years. Moreover, I imagine that the current speakers would have experienced much more difficulty recalling their languages without the recorded information. The work that Lyle and Terry initiated should be applauded as an ideal in language documentation projects.

In addition, I could not have completed this work without the support of the Xinkan community in Guatemala. Of utmost importance, I specifically would like to thank each of the last speakers of the Xinkan languages for allowing me to record them and for teaching me about their language and culture. Thank you Carlos Méndez, Juan Santos Benito, Nicolás Vásquez Hernández, Félix Hernández, Herlindo Pablo García, Pablo Esquite García (fallecido), Raymundo Hernández Godínez, Ángel Vásquez, Ignacio Pérez Realejo, and Jorge Pérez Gonzáles.

Many other individuals associated with the Xinkan community also were instrumental in the writing of this grammar. Carlos Marcial López played a vital role in building my relationship with the Xinkan community; his hospitality and interest in seeing this work completed are greatly appreciated. I would also like to thank the Parlamento del Pueblo Xinkan de Guatemala (PAPXIG), the Consejo del Pueblo Xinkan de Guatemala (COPXIG), and all of the members of these organizations for supporting and participating in revitalization workshops and giving me feedback on the grammatical sketch that served as a preliminary outline of Xinkan grammar. Among this group I would especially like to thank Zulma Bibiana Esquite López, Espectación García Pérez (Chonito), Allan Antonio Hernández, and Ever Benito for helping me get to know the Xinkan speakers and accompanying me on my visits.

I would also like to acknowledge the other colleagues who read earlier versions of this grammar: Mauricio Mixco, Rachel Hayes-Harb, MaryAnn Christison, John Robertson, and Andrew Garrett, who read my dissertation; and Frauke Sasche and Nora England, who reviewed the current manuscript. I recognize the work and time they gave in support of this project; their helpful feedback and cooperation have improved this book and have been invaluable in the writing and revisions of this grammar. Of course, all errors are mine alone.

Finally, I want to thank my family (Sarah, Alexis, Jacob, Joseph, and Elizabeth) for supporting me as I prepared these materials.

List of abbreviations

*	reconstructed form		DUR	durative (temporal duration)
**	ungrammatical form		EPIST	epistemic modal
%	uncommon, but grammatical		EQUAL	equational
<	comes from		EX	example from database
>	changes into		EXCL	exclusive
⟨...⟩	orthographic representation of an original source		EXIST	existence
			FORM	formal
→	becomes, is pronounced as		FUT	future
1PL	first person plural		FUTEXP	future expectation
1SG	first person singular		G	Guazacapán Xinka
2PL	second person plural		GEN	genitive
2SG	second person singular		GENPOSS	indirect object possession
3PL	third person plural		ICOMP	incompletive
3SG	third person singular		IDUR	imperfective durative (temporal duration)
ADJ	adjective			
AFF	affective		IMPV	imperative
AGR	agreement		INCH	inchoative
AGT	agent(ive)		INCL	inclusive
AN	agent noun		INFORM	informal
ANTIP	antipassive		INSTR	instrument noun
ART	article		INTR	intransitivizer
BEN	benefactive case		INTS	intensifier
C	consonant		IPERF	imperfective
CAUS	causative		IRR/COIRR	irrealis
Ch	Chiquimulilla Xinka		IV	intransitive verb
COMP	completive		lit.	literally
CON	conditional		J	Jumaytepeque Xinka
CONJ	conjunction		LOC	locative
CONTR	contrastive emphasis		MOD	modal particle
DEM	demonstrative		N	noun
DEP	dependent		NEG.IMPV	negative.imperative
DIM	diminutive		NOM/ACC	nominative-accuative
DIR	direct object		OBJ	object

OPT	optative		S	subject
PART	participle		SG	singular
PERF	perfective		Sp.	Spanish
PL	plural		SUBJ	subject
PN	patient noun		TEMP.DUR	temporal duration
PNT	patient		TV	transitive verb
POSS	possessive		V	verb
PRED	predicate		V	vowel
PRES.PART	present participle		VN	verbal noun
PST	past		VOC	vocative
QP	question particle		VP	verb phrase
REFL	reflexive		XP	place holder for any phrase type
REL	relativizer		Y	Yupiltepeque Xinka

The Use
and Development
of the Xinkan Languages

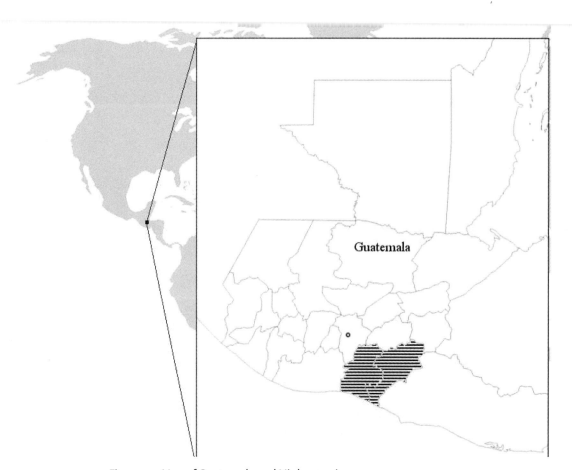

Figure 1.1 Map of Guatemala and Xinkan region

ONE

Introduction to the languages and their speakers

A reference grammar is a special achievement for a field linguist. It represents a solution to a complex linguistic puzzle. It records both the rocky and the zenlike individual relationship the linguist has had with the language(s) as appropriate analyses are tested. It represents the discovery of a new perspective on the shared human experience. It highlights the areas of investigation that need more discovery.

However, for a language community a reference grammar is much more. A grammar represents a shared culture and identity. It can provide members of the community justification for their collective and individual histories by affording authenticity in the eyes of the national and international communities. A grammar can become a tool for developing learning materials and encouraging cultural preservation. It can be the most defining feature of a language community.

I have written this reference grammar to reflect my own scientific relationship with Xinkan as a linguistic family. I expect this will mean that those readers interested in the history and languages of Central America will find interesting new ideas. In this regard, it will add to the scholarly knowledge of this area.

However, this grammar also reflects my interest in supporting the community. I have written it to give the Xinkas a stepping-stone in the (re)discovery of their history and culture. I expect this to lead to a sense of their language history and to provide them with at least some of the tools necessary to carry on the cultural, and especially linguistic, revitalization efforts currently underway.

1.1   The Xinkan linguistic context

Xinkan is a language family of at least four closely related languages. Speakers were once spread throughout southeastern Guatemala. Currently speakers of these languages live solely within the department of Santa Rosa in the southeastern portion of the country. These languages are unique within Mesoamerica as they are unrelated to any of the other languages or language groups used or spoken within this cultural and geographic area. Figure 1.1 shows the Xinkan area of Guatemala (shaded).

There has never been a community of individuals united linguistically, geographically, or politically called Xinkas. This has resulted in some confusion among scholars and community members about the appropriate label for these languages. In the past most community members who claimed Xinkan heritage referred to themselves as 'Pipil' (the name of a Uto-Aztecan language once spoken widely in this geographical area). However, the term 'Xinka' has been used to refer to these languages since at least 1770, and the term has become significant in the contemporary environment of indigenous cultural reaffirmation in Guatemala.[1] The practice has carried over into the everyday conversations of many community members, who choose to refer to themselves as Xinka. Interestingly, this label does not coincide etymologically with any known Xinkan word.[2]

In light of the fact that there are clear linguistic differences between at least four Xinkan varieties, it has become standard practice among scholars to refer to these individual languages by the towns where they were, or are, spoken.[3] I follow this practice and call the four varieties discussed in this grammar Guazacapán Xinka, Chiquimulilla Xinka, Jumaytepeque Xinka, and Yupiltepeque Xinka. Elsewhere in this grammar, I use just the town names to refer to a specific variety of Xinkan. The repetitive term Xinka is dropped. Nevertheless, the community members do not provide unique labels for each of these varieties. Among community members and some scholars interested in Central American languages, the lack of individual labels for each language has led to confusion regarding the nature of the relationship between the assorted linguistic varieties. One of the linguistic benefits of this grammar is the ample evidence it offers that each variety represents an independent, though closely related, language.

The town of Guazacapán lies at the intersection of the Guatemalan highlands and the Pacific coastal plains. Chiquimulilla is approximately five kilometers to the east, Jumaytepeque thirty-five kilometers to the north, and Yupiltepeque sixty-nine kilometers to the northeast. Past documentation has briefly mentioned other towns that were most likely Xinkan-speaking at one time, including Taxisco, Sinacatán, and Jutiapa. (A second variety spoken in the town of Chiquimulilla has also been mentioned.)[4] Since there is little information on these additional languages, conclusions about their relationship to the other four Xinkan languages are not discussed here. In the Maya Pre-Classic era (2000 BC–AD 250) this area was on the trade route that connected Mesoamerica and lower Central America.[5] Figure 1.2 shows the geographical relationship between the four Xinkan towns.

Often a reference grammar will focus on a single linguistic variety. In this regard, this book is quite different. However, since I envision this grammar will serve the needs of the community and because I follow their practice of treating the linguistic varieties of Xinkan equally, I believe it is necessary and appropriate to include all the varieties. This grammar thus considers Xinkan as a language group while still acknowledging the differences between its varieties.

Another benefit of this grammar is that it shows the course of development these varieties have followed as they diverged from a common mother tongue. The individual diversification of each of the Xinkan varieties from its common source has resulted in mutual unintelligibility between the speakers of each variety. This diver-

Figure 1.2 Map of Xinkan towns represented in the grammar

sification is especially unique since speakers of these languages are believed to have occupied, and still do occupy, a relatively small geographical region of Guatemala.

Currently there are no fluent native speakers of any of the Xinkan languages or varieties (see below). Yupiltepeque Xinka was the first language to be lost as its speakers shifted to Spanish, and it has not been used as a language of communication since around the turn of the twentieth century (after 1908).[6] Fortunately, prior to this shift a few small grammatical descriptions and vocabulary lists were published. All of the information about Yupiltepeque Xinka in this grammar come from these sources. Consequently, it may be painfully obvious that there are large gaps in the information on Yupiltepeque Xinka in this work. This is unavoidable. However, the available information does provide a significant look into the patterns and structures of this variety.

Similarly, speakers of Chiquimulilla Xinka, Guazacapán Xinka, and Jumaytepeque Xinka only used the language as a means of wider communication until the 1960s and late 1970s. Speakers of these linguistic varieties can still be found, but most have gone through a period of extreme linguistic attrition that naturally affects their grammatical competence in the Xinkan languages. They have not used their languages for more than forty years, opting instead for the national language of Guatemala: Spanish. Those speakers still able to use one of the languages are elderly and speak Xinkan only with much difficulty, though with practice each is able to remember aspects of his individual variety of the language. Fortunately, in the 1970s Terrence Kaufman and Lyle Campbell conducted extensive fieldwork with the last fully fluent and competent speakers of these three then-surviving Xinkan languages. A significant portion of the data in this grammar comes from their unpublished materials.

Occasionally, relationships between the Xinkan varieties and other languages in Mesoamerica have been proposed.[7] However, these relationships have all been discredited, in spite of occasionally receiving a relatively widespread reception. Nevertheless, over the languages' long history it is true that Xinkan speakers have been in contact with the speakers of many other languages. They have borrowed words and grammatical structures in the process, making the language group a record of their unique cultural history and development.[8] Without a doubt, given the nature of language contact in the area, the Xinkan languages also left their own traces on the languages of the area.[9]

The Mesoamerican languages that are geographically closest to the Xinkan languages are Poqomam (Mayan: Greater K'ichean) to the north and west, Ch'orti' (Mayan: Cholan) to the far northeast, and Pipil (Uto-Aztecan: Nahua branch) to the immediate southeast. Kaqchikel (Mayan: K'ichean) is also nearby, though not contiguous. Evidence of the contact between Xinkan speakers and the speakers of these languages is seen in the loanwords used in each of the Xinkan languages. For example, the word *wünak* (Guazacapán), *winak* (Chiquimulilla) 'witch, sorcerer' (not available in either Jumaytepeque or Yupltepeque Xinka), is a borrowing from Mayan *winaq* 'person'.[10] There are also some Mixe-Zoquean loanwords in Xinkan that are diffused throughout the majority of the Mesoamerican linguistic area.[11] Other languages may have once been active in this geographical area and influenced the Xinkan languages. There is some evidence for this additional contact, but the resolution to that question lies beyond the descriptive scope of this grammar.

Geographically, the archeological site at Chalchuapa, El Salvador, lies directly to the east and adjacent to the Xinkan region. This site was Poqomam-speaking at the time of the Spanish invasion, although Poqomam reached Chalchuapa very late, and some scholars associate the site with speakers of the Cholan-Tzeltalan branch of Mayan. This site is considered to be one of the two largest Pre-Classic architectural sites; La Blanca is the second.[12] Undoubtedly, the importance of the region in the archeological record suggests cultural contact and borrowed linguistic elements between the languages involved.

1.2   Past work with the Xinkan languages

Only rarely does a grammatical description of a language exist in isolation. More often, it builds on the shoulders of previous ideas and analyses. Such is the case with this reference grammar. It finds linguistic and cultural importance as only one step in the Xinkan descriptive linguistic tradition. It is especially significant in this regard, as it adds more detail and understanding to the previous descriptions and offers the most comprehensive information to date.

Nevertheless, while a reference grammar is a rewarding accomplishment, there is a chance it will serve the community very little. For example, previous grammatical descriptions of Xinkan are stored in locations far removed from the Xinkan community. While these previous descriptions would benefit the community, members simply have no access to them or are entirely unaware of them. Consequently, I have opted to include a brief synopsis of the past descriptions of the language to benefit the community and to give the appropriate background for this work.

The oldest description of a Xinkan language depicts Guazacapán Xinka and was written by a priest named Manuel Maldonado Matos around the year 1770. Entitled *El Arte de la lengua Szinca*, it was exceptionally well written for the time, although this grammar also has some significant shortcomings. The description of the language in the *Arte* is incomplete. For example, many of the unique aspects of Xinkan grammar, such as the alignment patterns, vowel patterns, and characterization of the consonants, are left undescribed.

Yet, the *Arte* is useful in many other ways. The information in Maldonado's work is very important for a clear picture of the grammatical development of these languages. It has merit in what it does provide, not in what it lacks. It does provide a measure of understanding of how a fluent Spanish speaker in the 1700s viewed the linguistic structures of one of the Xinkan languages. The original handwritten manuscript contains a 108-page grammatical description and a 1,300-item vocabulary list. Frauke Sachse (2004 & 2010) provides a superb analysis of this colonial document, supplemented by her own fieldwork with Xinkan.

In 1908 Eustorjio Calderón provided a short comparative description of Yupiltepeque and Chiquimulilla Xinka, with a few passing notes on another possible variety of Xinkan (North Chiquimulilla Xinka). A large amount of what is known about Yupiltepeque Xinka comes from Calderón's description. His work focuses on vocabulary, however, which means the scant grammatical information it contains is insufficient for a complete description of the language. Furthermore, it is written using a premodern Spanish orthography that leaves the characterization of the sounds of Xinkan vague and often ambiguous. I completed a complete philological analysis of Calderón's work in order to glean as much grammatical information as possible about Yupiltepeque Xinka, and the outcomes of that study are included here.

Walter Lehmann's 1920 summary of Xinkan languages, found in *Zentral-Amerika*, is of measured value as a grammatical description. His goal seems to have been to gather all the known information about Xinkan (similar to the goal of this grammar) and to suggest some ideas about the origin of the language family. In this regard, Lehmann's work is significant, since so little is known about the history of the Xinkan languages. He republished much of Calderón's description, with a few corrections to the orthography that were the result of typographical errors. Lehmann also provides some historical anecdotes and assumptions about the development of Xinkan culture. Finally, he included word lists garnered from various other individuals who had spent time learning the Xinkan languages. One major drawback of Lehmann's work is that it is partially written in German, a language nobody in the modern Xinkan community understands. Aside from the language barrier, the information presented in this grammar should be very useful in comprehending aspects of Xinkan grammar. From my understanding of the current Xinkan sociolinguistic context (see section 1.3 below and Rogers 2016 for more details), this work has the potential of being very important for the community in their efforts to revalue Xinkan identity.

In 1967 Otto Schumann wrote a grammatical sketch of Guazacapán Xinka as a small part of his ethnographic work on the Xinkan culture. *Xinca de Guazacapán* was part of his licentiate program, although he never published his writings widely. Similar to the previous works on Xinkan, this short description is linguistically incomplete when compared to some of the other resources. However, it is important as a record of the development of Guazacapán Xinka and as a vignette into Xinkan life during the 1960s.

Between 1972 and 1979 Terrence Kaufman and Lyle Campbell worked with the last speakers of the three Xinkan languages still in use: Guazacapán Xinka, Chiquimulilla Xinka, and Jumaytepeque Xinka. Yupiltepeque Xinka had already become extinct before this time. While their field notes, comprising audio recordings and handwritten linguistic examples, are relatively exhaustive and complete, they were never published. In fact, until recently nobody in the community had ever seen them. A practical grammatical sketch has been completed and delivered to the community with information taken from these field notes, but it remains unpublished. Digital copies of these notes have also been left with community members, but they contain some difficult linguistic terminology that might impede their usefulness to the community. In its entirety, the information in Kaufman and Campbell's field notes fills thirteen large file boxes with information contained on 8 × 11 sheets of paper or on 3 × 5 note cards, digital copies of which are archived at AILLA (Archive of the Indigenous Languages of South America). These resources were organized and systematically reviewed by a team of researchers that I led at the University of Utah. This research team, supported by a National Science Foundation grant, created a database from the field notes that contains all of the vocabulary items and their definitions, example sentences, texts, and linguistic comparisons. This database was vetted by both Kaufman and Campbell for accuracy and completeness, and it became the starting point for the analyses below and for interactions with the last speakers of these languages in my own fieldwork. (See section 1.4.1 for a more detailed discussion of this database and how it was employed in this grammar.)[13] The analyses and discussions presented below are often quite different from theirs, but I believe as a whole this grammar furthers the goals of the significant work they accomplished.

The data in this grammar comes from these field notes and—through my own linguistic fieldwork, records, and analyses—from the last speakers of the various Xinkan varieties. In this regard, this grammar is as much a historical reflection of the Xinkan community and their languages as are the linguistic developments described below. However, readers should keep in mind that I have not attempted to distinguish between the heritage data collected in the 1970s and my own data collected in 2007–2010 in the analyses in subsequent chapters. Because the few remaining speakers have great difficulty remembering their languages, it was only after weeks of helping them work with the heritage data that they regained some semblance of communicative competence. I imagine that the current speakers would have experienced much more difficulty recalling their languages without the recorded information. In all cases, they felt most comfortable commenting on, repeating, translating, or discussing the old audio recordings.[14] Consequently, the line between the two sources of data became indistinguishable.

In 2004 one of the governing bodies in the Xinkan community, Consejo del Pueblo Xinkan de Guatemala (COPXIG, see below), published a grammatical sketch of Xinkan, which was based largely on the speech of one of the speakers of Guazacapán Xinka.[15] The community members involved with that publication remark that the similarities between the Xinkan languages are more important than the differences in vocabulary and pronunciation. In fact, the similarities are important aspects of the necessary projects to build community and foment unity in the Xinkan towns.[16] In writing this present reference grammar, I hope to provide evidence that while the differences in the four varieties of Xinkan are linguistically significant, they are perhaps not politically significant. Speakers of the languages comment on how important these differences are for their appreciation of the Xinkan varieties as identity markers.[17] While the COPXIG grammatical sketch makes mention of some of the more important features of the Xinkan languages, its treatment of two of the languages as a single language has caused problems for many members of the community by complicating the achievement of their revitalization goals.[18]

Aside from the somewhat lengthier works described above, relatively few academic articles have been published about the Xinkan languages and culture.[19] The articles that have appeared provide initial explanations of the typological characteristics of the languages or offer vignettes into Xinkan cultural life.

These past linguistic descriptions and articles add relevance to this reference work. This grammar corrects misunderstandings about Xinkan grammatical characteristics, fills in the gaps, and offers the most comprehensive linguistic coverage of Xinkan as a whole and of each language individually.

1.3 The Xinkan social and cultural contexts

Just as a reference grammar is affected and shaped by previous ideas about and descriptions of the language, the social and cultural contexts of the language community also affect its value. In this case, the known cultural history and social organization of the Xinkan community provide an important framework. By fostering understanding of the cultural developments, politics, motivations, and goals that exist in the community, this grammar can have a significant cultural impact. On a cultural level, this work is significant because it contributes to the unification of the entire community. It underscores the solution to a number of social and interpersonal issues, and it points to the future of the Xinkan community as a whole and to the shared history of its ancestors.

The Xinkan people first came into contact with Europeans with the invasion of Guatemala by Pedro de Alvarado circa 1524.[20] Present-day members of Xinkan communities still occupy the same territory on the Pacific coast of Guatemala, in the departments of Santa Rosa, Jutiapa, and Jalapa, as their ancestors did at the time of the Spanish invasion. However, research on place names indicates that speakers of the language most likely occupied a larger territory before these encounters.[21]

While exact figures of the number of Xinkan speakers at the time of the invasion—or of the number of current ethnic Xinkan individuals—are difficult to pinpoint with any degree of certainty, there have been attempts with this end in mind. Guatemalan census numbers indicate that there are currently between 200 and 20,000 speakers of 'Xinka' alive.[22] In light of the current situation in the community, this numerical range probably refers only to people who self-identify as having 'Xinka' heritage—in other words, those for whom a Xinka language is the heritage language of their community. The reported number of Xinkas and speakers of Xinkan languages has varied from tens of thousands to a mere handful. The following paragraphs are included to explain the discrepancies in these census numbers.

Otto Schumann claimed in 1967 that there were 19,505 inhabitants of the towns where Xinkan was spoken, though he does not mention the number of fluent speakers.[23] Harry McArthur indicated that the number of speakers in 1966, one year earlier, was fewer than two hundred, and these were confined to the older generation: Spanish was preferred over Xinkan as the means of communication.[24] In 1918 Marshall Saville reported in his survey of the language that there were only five thousand speakers of Xinkan.[25] Calderón said that there were seventy-five hundred speakers in 1890 scattered around the department of Santa Rosa.[26] Maldonado, the author of the earliest record of a Xinka language, provides no information on the number of speakers in that era. What these numbers do show, despite the discrepancies, is that over the last one hundred years there has been a sharp decline in the number of native speakers of Xinkan languages. I can now safely state that as of 2015 there are fewer than six individuals who speak the languages. Nevertheless, a large number of people in Santa Rosa, Jutiapa, and Jalapa (most likely in the hundreds of thousands) identify as Xinkas, for whom the languages serve as a cultural heritage.[27]

In relation to the demographic numbers of speakers and community members, some unsubstantiated hypotheses also claim that the Xinkan culture predates the Mayan and Aztec cultures that flourished in this area of Mesoamerica. For example, Daniel Brinton remarks that "an investigation of [the Xinkan's] language might throw a new light on the migrations of the ancient inhabitants of that region," and also comments, "There are some reasons for believing that previous to the arrival of the Kiches and Kaqchikels on the plains of Guatemala that region was occupied by this [Xinkan] nation," though he does not say what those reasons are.[28] Similarly, Calderón considers the Xinkan people to be the original inhabitants of Guatemala and postulates that they predated the Maya-Quiché and Aztec invasions.[29] While these claims remain unproven, there is evidence that these hypotheses might be accurate. The wide distribution of Xinkan place names and the evidence of contact with various linguistic groups support the idea. The extent to which the Xinkas occupied this part of Mesoamerica and the time frame during which they predominated can only be based on careful examination of the linguistic evidence. There are few physical remains of their culture. To be accurate, the examination of this linguistic evidence can only be made after a complete description of the properties of Xinkan grammar. This reference grammar lays that foundation. It provides the necessary descriptive work so that the linguistic prehistory of the Xinkas can be evaluated.

Though the investigation of the extent of and time frame for the Xinkan occupation of Guatemala is only in its infancy, a few particulars about this area indicate the importance of the Xinkan territory to the Mesoamerican cultural area. The area occupied currently and historically by the Xinkas is a prime area for agriculture and trade, and it is considered one of the first regions of Native American settlement in Mesoamerica.[30] A number of different ethnic groups have occupied this region, and the Xinkas represent only one of them.[31] Providing relative dates for their occupations has proven challenging. Interestingly, however, this is one of the least studied areas of Guatemala (and of Mesoamerica in general) both ethnographically and archaeologically.[32]

Regarding social organization, the Xinkan community currently does not form a unified and autonomous entity. This is true historically as well. Since the time when the Xinkas became known to the Spanish invaders there has never been geographical or political unity among the communities. In fact, it is only a consequence of empirical scholarly research that these languages are grouped together. Consequently, there is no single centralized government (other than the national Guatemalan government) interested in the affairs of the Xinkas.

However, members of the various Xinkan communities recently have organized themselves for the purpose of revalorizing the Xinkan languages and culture. A number of competing grassroots efforts have emerged, and there are often disagreements about the best course of action in rebuilding the Xinkan community.[33] In one organized effort, about two dozen young adults who are Xinkan descendants but who know very little about their heritage, meet regularly with the few remaining speakers and rememberers, attempting to learn as much from them as possible. These activists have mobilized to meet once a week to discuss the language and set goals that will help them reach their revitalization objectives.

These men and women travel from numerous towns scattered across the region, including Chiquimulilla, Guazacapán, Jumaytepeque, and Yupiltepeque. They have access to some of the information that scholars have gathered in the past, but they have encountered a number of difficulties in organizing their efforts. For example, until recently these young people did not know that there were four Xinkan languages and assumed that all the information they possessed represented a single language. The often contradictory bits of information about grammatical patterns in each of the languages has proved daunting to them, to say the least.

Additionally, Xinkan has a number of sounds, structures, and patterns that are foreign to Spanish speakers (for example, glottalized consonants, the high central vowel, and verb classes), and while these linguistic elements can be learned, the Xinkan youth are intimidated by them and avoid producing them because they have not been trained or taught to use them.

In order to gain national and local political attention, the Xinkan community formed a local body of governance. As a result, two governing organizations have emerged. The Council of the Xinkan People of Guatemala (COPXIG) was formed first and set out to organize Xinkan peoples. Officers were named and a skeleton structure was put into place that was to unite the Xinkan area and the heirs of the Xinkan culture. Unfortunately, internal divisions within COPXIG caused a schism. The schism was based on governance policy and political power. The organization of COPXIG called for representatives from each of four Xinkan towns, each of whom would have a voice in decisions of the council. The first chairperson of this council, however, was thought to have abused his power; accusations that he was trying to involve COPXIG more with national politics than with local concerns were common. This led to a call by some of the officers to reorganize the council. When they were unable to do so, those opposed to COPXIG formed their own organization: the Parliament of the Xinkan People of Guatemala (PAPXIG). Both organizations are interested in cultural preservation, though for different reasons.

The Xinkan community has made one of their central objectives the revitalization of Xinkan languages. For them, this means that they are interested in reviving interest in the culture and the use of the language, and they seek to understand its historical roots. They have achieved national recognition in Guatemala. The community and the young adults are anxious to succeed, but they lack adequate direction. In weekly classes, one of the council members teaches some of the linguistic structures of Xinkan based on the community grammar. The usefulness and limitations of this grammar are indicated above. While this is encouraging to the learners, they are learning only a small portion of the Xinkan language(s). The phonetic description of the language makes no mention of the glottalized consonants, and the morphological description seems foreign and impractical. In order to sort out these problems, the community needs access to all of the available data and training on how to use it. This training would necessarily mean that they learn how to understand the data and how to use it to teach others.[34]

While none of the people actively involved in COPXIG or PAPXIG are native speakers of any Xinkan language, they are all descendants of people who were. The effort of the community to revitalize and learn about their language(s) and culture is hampered by the extreme state of endangerment of the Xinkan languages. Only two of the four languages still have any speakers (Guazacapán and Jumaytepeque). These men learned the language fluently over forty years ago, but they have had little opportunity to practice the language within the last four decades. The speaker in Jumaytepeque, in fact, is much less fluent in Xinkan than the speakers in Guazacapán, and all are elderly and infirm. This means they lack the stamina needed for prolonged work on the language in the form of interviews, fieldwork, or simple conversations.

1.4   Organization of the grammar

This grammar is organized into nine chapters (separated into two general parts), and includes an appendix and two indices. The goal of the entire work is to survey the complete synchronic and diachronic descriptions of the Xinkan languages, as far as the information is available. Part 1 focuses on the synchronic patterns of the Xinkan languages. Chapter 2 surveys the phonology of Xinkan; both the phonological inventory and segment distribution are discussed. Chapter 3 describes at length the morphology of the Xinkan languages. Chapter 4 details the syntactic patterns. Chapter 5 contains one of the texts, glossed and translated, showing how all of the synchronic patterns function in context.

Part 2 focuses on the diachronic development of the four Xinkan languages. Chapter 6 gives the sound correspondences of the languages and reconstructs a possible Proto-Xinkan phonological inventory. Chapter 7 provides a reconstruction of the functions of the morphological system in Proto-Xinkan. Chapter 8 uses the synchronic syntactic patterns to reconstruct the surface syntactic patterns in Proto-Xinkan. Chapter 9 provides a look forward to what might be accomplished as a consequence of this grammar. The appendix contains complete verb conjugations for regular and irregular verbs for all verb classes. The first index is a general topical index for the entire grammar. The second index offers a quick reference to the typologically salient characteristics of Xinkan.

1.4.1   Description of data sources

As mentioned above, all of the information recorded in the 1970s by Terrence Kaufman and Lyle Campbell has been compiled into a database. This database has been augmented by my own research and fieldwork with the Xinkan languages and the Xinkan community. The database, consequently, is a conglomeration of sources that have not been systematically differentiated in this grammar. The reason for this approach, as mentioned above, is that the last speakers of the languages were most successful in remembering and using their respective languages in conjunction with the information recorded in the 1970s. They retold stories, explained sentences, and discussed the speakers they heard in the audio recordings. This resulted in much of the same information being documented in my own fieldwork as was recorded in the 1970s. All of the words, morphemes, sentences, or texts used throughout this grammar are taken from this combined database.

A major portion of the database contains lexical information for each of the Xinkan languages. The information comes from documented word lists, example sentences, and the texts (see below). There are 3,000 lexical items in Jumaytepeque, Chiquimulilla, and Guazacapán, and 852 for Yupiltepeque (all analyzed from the sources listed above). These lexical items include words, parts of speech, and inflected and derived forms. There are two versions of this part of the database: first, the lexical information for each language is reported independently and organized alphabetically by lexical item; and second, it is organized by meaning, with cognate lexical items listed across all four Xinkan languages (where available). Since the lexical information is presented in this grammar according to the specific language to which it belongs, no tags or citations have been provided for these items.

Another portion of this database contains example sentences, with translations, in the four Xinkan languages. These context-free example sentences have been analyzed and glossed by morphemes following standard interlinear glossing conventions. The database is organized so that example sentences in each language are separated from each other. There are 2,500 example sentences in Guazacapán Xinka, 300 in Chiquimulilla Xinka, 170 in Jumaytepeque Xinka, and 200 in Yupiltepeque Xinka. Data used in this grammar that comes from this part of the database is tagged with the abbreviation EX followed by its number in the database. For example EX:300 is the 300th example sentence.

Finally, the database contains some 'texts'. These stretches of discourse are longer than an example sentence and tell a story or relate a major life event. These texts were all originally recorded in the 1970s by Kaufman and Campbell and then analyzed and glossed with the help of the lexical database and the last speakers of the Xinkan languages. Some texts have various versions recorded in different years; these versions have been systematically separated in the database and have been treated as such in my own fieldwork. All of the texts were analyzed and glossed in 2008 and 2009. As mentioned above, there are currently speakers of both Guazacapán Xinka and Jumaytepeque Xinka, and they collaborated with me in glossing and analyzing these texts: Carlos Méndez, Juan Santos Benito, and Nicolás Vásquez Hernández worked in Guazacapán Xinka; and Ignacio Pérez Realejo glossed Jumaytepeque Xinka. Both Lyle Campbell and Terrence Kaufman have told me that they also recorded texts in Chiquimulilla; however when I started working with the language, these texts could not be located.

In this grammar, examples that come from these texts are tagged and cited by the abbreviated form of the title, the year it was originally recorded, and the line within the text from which the example is taken. For example, BT:1972, 24 means the 24th line of the text 'Birth of Tuuru' from the version recorded in 1972. Tables 1.1 and 1.2 show a complete list of the texts in the database.

Table 1.1 List of Guazacapán Xinka texts

Abbreviation	Full title	Speaker
DF	'Don Federico'	Cipriano Gómez Yermo
CK	'Chuxaya Kela'	Cipriano Gómez Yermo
SP	'The Spirit Became a Pig'	Francisco Marroquín
LM	'Lord of the Mountain'	Alberto de López Vásquez
JW	'Jesus and the Wealthy Man'	Cipriano Gómez Yermo
WV	'War of the Volcanoes'	Cipriano Gómez Yermo
IW	'I Don't Want to Work'	Francisco Marroquín
HM	'History of Montezuma'	Cipriano Gómez Yermo
HL	'History of the Laborer'	Cipriano Gómez Yermo
FW	'Flooding of the World'	Cipriano Gómez Yermo
Con	'The Conquest'	Cipriano Gómez Yermo
MA	'Maize'	Cipriano Gómez Yermo
HK	'The History of Kela'	Cipriano Gómez Yermo
Sih	'Sihuanahua'	Cipriano Gómez Yermo
CoM	'The Two Compadres'	Francisco Marroquín
SH	'Sending a Son to Work'	Alberto de López Vásquez
EW	'I Enjoy Working'	Francisco Marroquín
LD	'A Lazy Man and the Devil Make a Pact'	Francisco Marroquín
SS	'Sam'u seema'	Francisco Marroquín
Sie	'Sierpa'	Cipriano Gómez Yermo
Sip	'Sipani'	Cipriano Gómez Yermo
TYA	'Tuuru' Youthful Adventures'	Cipriano Gómez Yermo
TG	'Tuuru' and Gringos'	Cipriano Gómez Yermo
TM	'Tuuru' and Maize'	Cipriano Gómez Yermo
BT	'Birth of Tuuru'	Cipriano Gómez Yermo
TK	'Tuuru' the King'	Cipriano Gómez Yermo
TT	'Trip to Taxisco'	Alberto de López Vásquez

Table 1.2 List of Jumaytepeque Xinka texts

Abbreviation	Full title	Speaker
WD	'The Women's Duties'	Unknown
MF	'The Man Speaks with His Father'	Unknown
FN	'The Flood and Noah'	Unknown
LF	'Life'	Unknown
AB	'Ability'	Unknown
GB	'Good-bye'	Unknown
WH	'Winter Harvest'	Guillermo
SH	'Summer Harvest'	Guillermo

Part 1

The use of the Xinkan languages

Synchronic grammar

TWO

Phonology

The aim of this chapter is to describe the articulatory and distributional properties of the vowels and consonants of the Xinkan languages—their phonology. For many people the sounds of an unknown language can seem difficult and extremely foreign. For others the sounds can be the most salient feature of a language. My goal is to make the sound systems accessible to the Xinkan community members and to reflect for the wider audience the implications they have for scientific linguistics. To accomplish this, I survey a number of the properties of Xinkan sounds, including an inventory of the sounds and their distributions, an analysis of syllable structure, an examination of stress assignment, and a review of alternations in pronunciation that are essential to the grammar. I end the chapter with an explanation and description of the practical orthography I use for the Xinkan languages.

The Xinkan languages do not have a long written tradition, yet community members have begun to develop an orthography. This has not yet been standardized, but the inheritors of the languages do prefer an orthographic representation of the sounds over one based on a phonetic alphabet. In keeping with this preference, I restrict the use of the phonetic alphabet to this chapter and to chapter 6 (both of which deal with sounds). I expect that this will make the discussion in subsequent chapters less daunting to those community members who do not have experience with a phonetic alphabet, while still being beneficial to researchers outside the community.

2.1   Vowels

There are twelve vowels in each of the Xinkan languages. The major properties of the vowels in the different languages are the same. To reduce repetition, I discuss the languages' vowels collectively rather than individually as is done with the consonants in section 2.2. Table 2.1 shows the vowel inventory of all four Xinkan languages.

The descriptive labels used for the vowels in table 2.1 are common and follow closely the traditional framework for phonetic descriptions of vowels.[1] The descriptive terms in the first column and the top row indicate the general position of the vowels in relation to each other. Table 2.1 also shows that there is no vowel in the central mid space, indicating that there is no contrastive /ə/, a fact that is expected and common

Table 2.1 Xinkan vowel inventory

		Front	Central	Back
High	Short	i	ɨ	u
	Long	ii	ɨɨ	uu
Mid	Short	e		o
	Long	ee		oo
Low	Short		a	
	Long		aa	

cross-linguistically with vowel inventories of six vowels. This fact may seem uninteresting on the surface, but the language is sensitive to this gap and accounts for it in the processes of vowel harmony discussed in section 2.1.2.[2]

2.1.1 Vowel length

Vowel length is phonemically contrastive in the Xinkan languages for all vowels (as seen in table 2.1). Long vowels can be lexically specified (underlying—part of the vocabulary) or they can be the result of phonological and morphological processes. (Vowels are lengthened in intransitive affective verb forms, when the agent noun suffix is added to the verb stem, and in the plural formation of noun roots ending with a vowel. In Jumaytepeque, vowel length is also the result of a phonological process that affects vowels in the verbal noun derived from a causative verb.)

Underlying long vowels are exhibited in any position within the word except word finally. Derived vowel length is restricted to specific locations within the word—the second-to-last syllable of the root in all situations except the Jumaytepeque verbal noun derivation that affects the final vowel in the root. In this section, each of these vowel-length alternations and patterns is surveyed. The phonotactic constraints on vowel length are treated in detail in section 2.4, while the verb morphology is surveyed in section 3.6 in the next chapter. As discussed in chapter 1, little linguistic information on Yupiltepeque is available; thus vowel length in Yupiltepeque is not indicated below.

2.1.1.1 *Lexical specification*

Lexically specified (underlying) vowel length means that the vowel length in a word is not a result of a phonological process but is rather a phonemically contrastive segment in the underlying word root. Underlying long vowels specified in the lexicon are found in both native Xinkan words and many words borrowed from Spanish. However, one of the important ways in which the Xinkan languages differ most noticeably from one another is in their vocabularies, and consequently not all of the words in each of the languages have the same underlying vowel-length specifications. Examples of words with lexically specified vowel length are given in 1–3; the etymological source is given to the right of a word if it is a loan word. Some of the words in these examples are similar in form to intransitive affective verb constructions (see section 4.3.1), though there is no evidence showing that this is their correct morpho-syntactic analysis. It may be that these forms are frozen and no longer have the intransitive affective semantic meanings.

(1)   Examples of Guazacapán words with lexically specified long vowels.

aaʔu	'corn'	*aara*	'worm'
ay'aała	'woman'	*č'iipi*	'last child'
eełe	'large pot'	*woona*	'hill'
haama ki'	'guilt'	*haamaʔ*	'ripe'
haaniʔ	'like, as'	*haar'un*	'tick'
huurak	'man'	*huuri*	'buttocks'
huuši	'head'	*huutak*	'anus'
huuts'uk	'center, middle'	*huutuk*	'soot'
iihuukah	'right here'	*iimaakah*	'over there (far)'
iimookah	'over there (close)'	*iipan*	'small, younger'
iipemaakuh	'there it comes'	*iiti*	'tomato'
išaapi	'remove'	*iiłik*	'jug, container'
iin'a	'defecate'	*k'iir'a*	'scratch, score'
k'iira	'cricket'	*k'iišu*	'exchange'
k'oočoʔ	'dirty clothes'	*k'oomo*	'elbow'
k'oosek	'big, enormous'	*k'ooso*	'small pox'
k'oošo	'penis'	*k'ooto*	'molars'
k'oots'ay	'type of ant'	*k'oroor'o*	'reed'
k'uunuʔ	'cloudy'	*k'uuyu*	'Castillian rabbit'
k'weets'a	'partridge'	*kaašik*	'mud'
kaayi	'sell'	*kiiw'i*	'patio'
kiiša	'half, part'	*kiiw'i*	'shin'
koolah	'(animal) tail' (<Sp. '*cola*')	*kookoʔ*	'crawdad'
kooraʔ	'where ever'	*kuukuʔ*	'pigeon, dove'
maałek	'fire wood'	*maali*	'ash'
maama	'ear'	*meeme*	'crazy'
miiči	'cat'	*miiku*	'small'
miimi	'sing'	*muur'a*	'ear of corn'
muuti-	'hair'	*naałik*	'they'
naana	'adult female'	*naatiikah*	'there (far)'
naay'ah	'there (close)'	*natiikah*	'that (far)'
natiiy'ah	'that (close)'	*neeła*	'for'
neełek	'us'	*nooya*	'grandma'
nuunuʔ	'mute'	*nuuru*	'pus'
oor'o	'only' (<Sp. '*solo*')	*oošo*	'heart, insides'
seema	'fish'	*šaaru*	'sea'
taata-	'father'	*ts'iin'an'a*	'scorpion'
tiim'al	'louse'	*weeša*	'iguana'
wiira	'pigeon, dove'	*yuu*	'you.VOC'

(2) Examples of Chiquimulilla words with lexically specified long vowels.

aaʔu	'corn'	aabuh	'hurry!'
aaluʔ	'guacamaya'	aara	'worm'
ačiimi	'business man'	akuuša	'needle' (<Sp. 'aguja')
boohoo	'light'	čʼiipi	'pregnant woman'
čʼɨɨrʼɨk	'gizzard'	čiiriʔ	'short'
duusi	'sweet' (<Sp. 'dulce')	goona	'hill, volcano'
goošał	'fence'	haalak	'axe'
haarʼu	'tick'	haari	'run (something) off'
haaru	'scratch, score'	hɨɨmʼa	'make fun of'
hoorʼo	'take care of'	huuri	'buttocks'
huuša	'blow'	huušiʔ	'head'
iipan	'small'	iiru	'monkey'
uśuł	'small flea'	ɨɨkɨ	'stomach'
ɨɨlʼɨ	'back'	ɨɨna	'defecate'
kʼaamiʔ	'good-bye'	kʼɨɨrʼa	'turn on light, light fire'
kʼiira	'cricket'	kʼiiša	'roast'
kʼiišu	'change'	kʼoomo	'ankle'
kʼoošo	'pain'	kooto-	'molar'
kʼooye	'visit'	kʼuuyu	'guinea pig'
kʼweetsʼa	'partridge'	kʼiiwʼi	'patio'
kɨɨši	'half'	kookał	'skeleton'
kuukuʔ	'pigeon, dove'	łuuri	'rabbit'
maama	'ear'	mačiiti	'machete'
małiiła	'rice tamale'	meeme	'crazy'
pʼuupu	'timbuco'	yaałaʔ	'thick, a lot'

(3) Examples of Jumaytepeque words with lexically specified long vowels.

aaru	'roof'	aara	'worm'
aayuʔ	'have'	čʼiipi	'last child'
čiibu	'goat'	eela	'tongue'
haalak	'hatchet'	haanʼah	'here'
haarʼu	'tick'	haari	'herd, hurry'
huhuuya	'jujuya'	huuma	'make fun of'
huuši	'head'	huutsʼi	'nixtamal'
ʔiiru	'monkey'	iišul	'chigoe'
iiwa	'toast'	ɨɨkɨ	'stomach'
ɨɨna	'defecate'	ɨɨtʼɨ	'behind'
kʼeetan	'large worn'	kʼiišu	'change'
kʼoočo	'dirty'	kʼoomo	'knee'
kʼuutu	'small ranch'	kaayi	'sell'
kiira	'cricket'	kiiwʼi	'outside'
kɨɨwɨ	'calf'	kuuku	'stake'
kuumʼi	'last child'	laamʼa	'tamale'
laayuʔ	'there is not'	leelan	'for'
luuuri	'rabbit'	maalɨ	'firewood'

maašin	'hairy worm'	*maayi*	'grandmother'
mee?	'green'	*meen'e*	'tender'
miiša	'heart'	*paaha*	'wing, arm'
paaši	'sharpen'	*tɨɨm'al*	'head lice'
wiik'i	'winter'	*woono*	'hill'

As seen above, words borrowed from Spanish that are pronounced with long vowels in Xinkan have a predictable pattern. The long vowel occurs on the vowel that is natively stressed in Spanish. This is a common adaptation strategy in the languages of the Americas.

2.1.1.2   *Vowel-length alternation*

Vowel length can also be the result of phonological processes determined by morphological context. That is, vowels can be lengthened in the environment of certain morphological affixes. (See chapter 3 for a discussion of Xinkan morphology.) In this situation, either the first vowel or the last vowel in the root may undergo lengthening. The determination between these options depends on the morphological context and on the affix involved. In this section the four vowel-length alternations are discussed and exemplified. First discussed is the lengthening of root vowels in the penultimate syllable, connected with a change in the transitivity of a verb. Next, I survey the lengthening of vowels in the final syllable of the root in conjunction with the agent noun of a derived causative verb in Jumaytepeque. Third, vowel lengthening due to the presence of the agent noun suffix is described. In the latter situation the first vowel in the root is lengthened in Guazacapán, and in both Chiquimulilla and Jumaytepeque the last vowel in the root is lengthened. Finally, I examine the lengthening of the last vowel in noun roots when the plural suffix is attached.

2.1.1.2.1   *Vowel length and verb transitivity.*   One phonological change resulting in vowel-length alternations is found in the derivation of the intransitive affective verb form from its corresponding transitive verb root (see section 3.6.1). However, vowel length is only exhibited in the intransitive affective verbs that contain two or more syllables and that have no word-medial consonant clusters. In this type of lengthening, the underlying canonical syllabic shape of the affected word is CV_1CV (Consonant-Vowel-Consonant-Vowel) and its surface realization is $CV_1V_1CV?$. While not all underlying intransitive affective verb roots take this shape, it is the most common shape for this class of words, making this type of vowel lengthening extremely common. Intransitive affective verbs with other underlying phonological shapes (i.e., CVVCV and VCCV), are discussed in chapter 4 (also see section 3.6.1).

Similarly, in order to derive an intransitive affective verb from a transitive verb root, the suffix *-?* 'IV.AFF' is attached to the end of the stem. When the transitive verb stem is of the phonological shape CVCV, the first vowel is lengthened in addition to the use of this suffix. That is, the stem is modified from underlying CV_1CV to $CV_1V_1CV-?$.[3] The lengthened vowel in the intransitive form is represented in the orthography and in the analysis below as two adjacent identical vowels. In the examples in 4–6 the basic (i.e., underlying) transitive verb is on the left and the derived intransitive (i.e., surface) form is on the right.

(4) Intransitive affective verbs derived from transitive verbs: Guazacapán.
   a. *ʔima-y* → *Ø-iima-ʔ*
      say.COMP-3SG.SETA 3SG.SETC-say.COMP-IV.AFF
      'He said it.' 'He was told.'
   b. *ts'imi-ka* → *Ø-ts'iimi-ʔ*
      water.COMP-2SG.SETA 3SG.SETC-water.COMP-IV.AFF
      'You watered it.' 'It was watered.'

(5) Intransitive affective verbs derived from transitive verbs: Chiquimulilla.
   a. *huša* → *Ø-huuša-ʔ*
      blow.TV.COMP 3SG.SETC-blow.COMP-IV.AFF
      'to blow it' 'It was blown.'
   b. *ts'aya* → *Ø-ts'aaya-ʔ*
      scale.TV.COMP (a fish) 3SG.SETC-scale.COMP-IV.AFF
      'to scale it' 'It was descaled.'

(6) Intransitive affective verbs derived from transitive verbs: Jumaytepeque.
   a. *kišu* → *Ø-kiišu-ʔ*
      change.TV.COMP 3SG.SETC-change.COMP-IV.AFF
      'to change it' 'It changed.'
   b. *hama* → *Ø-haama-ʔ*
      ripen.TV.COMP 3SG.SETC-ripe.COMP-IV.AFF
      'to ripen it' 'It ripened.'

2.1.1.2.2 *Vowel length in Jumaytepeque verbal nouns.* In Jumaytepeque, it is possible to form a verbal noun from a derived causative verb. When this verbal noun is formed, the vowel in the root that immediately precedes the causative suffix is lengthened. This is true only for Jumaytepeque; the other languages do not have the same vowel lengthening process, although they do have verbal nouns created with cognate affixes. Examples are given in 7.

(7) Jumaytepeque verbal nouns derived from causative verbs.
   a. *iy'awa* *iya-ha* *iyaa-ha*
      laugh.at.it.PERF laugh.at.it.PERF-CAUS laugh.at.it.VN-CAUS
      'to laugh at it' 'to make someone laugh at it' 'making someone laugh at it'
   b. *muč'u* *muč'u-ha* *muč'uu-ha*
      encoger.PERF encoger.PERF-CAUS encoger.VN-CAUS
      'to shrink it' 'to make shrink it' 'making shrink'

2.1.1.2.3 *Vowel length with deverbalizing suffixes.* In addition to the changes in vowel length due to verbal inflection, vowels are also lengthened when an agent noun is derived from a transitive verb. This agent noun suffix causes the last vowel in a verb stem to lengthen in Guazacapán, but in both Chiquimulilla and Jumaytepeque it causes the first vowel in the verb stem to lengthen. The agent noun suffix is *-ła* (Guazacapán), *-ł* (Chiquimulilla), or *-l* (Jumaytepeque).

This suffix lengthens the indicated vowel of the verb stem with two exceptions: first, when there is already a lexically specified long vowel in this position in the stem, where the process could be said to apply vacuously; or second, when there is an intervening suffix between the agent noun suffix and the verb stem. As with the other phonological processes involving vowel length, the lengthening of the vowel in conjunction with the agent nouns suffix is also restricted to verb roots without word-medial consonant clusters. This suffix is discussed in section 4.3.2.2.2 and derives a noun with the meaning 'one who [or thing which] Xs', where X is the placeholder for the action of the altered verb. Examples of the vowel-length alternations corresponding to the use of the agent noun suffix are given in 8–10.

(8) Guazacapán vowel lengthening with the agent noun suffix.
   a. *mɨka*   *mɨkaa-ła*
      work.PERF   work-AGT
      'worked'   'worker'
   b. *kits'i*   *kits'ii-ła*
      roast.PERF roast-AGT
      'roasted'   'roaster'

(9) Chiquimulilla vowel lengthening with the agent noun suffix.
   a. *k'ɨtɨ*   *k'ɨɨtɨ-ł*
      measure.PERF   measure-AGT
      'measured'   'measurer' (i.e., scales or a ruler)
   b. *kawi*   *kaawi-ł*
      cry.PERF   cry-AGT
      'to cry, shout' 'crier, one who cries'

(10) Jumaytepeque vowel lengthening with the agent noun suffix.
   a. *yawi*   *yaawi-l*
      make.firewoord.PERF   make.firewood-AGT
      'to make firewood'   'firewood chopper'
   b. *tutu*   *tuutu-l*
      suck.PERF   suck-AGT
      'sucked'   'sucker'

2.1.1.2.4 *Vowel length in plural noun formation.*   The last case where vowels are lengthened is in the plural formation. In all of the Xinkan languages, the last vowel in the nominal root is lengthened when the plural suffix is added, as shown in 11–13. This suffix is *-łi* (Guazacapán and Chiquimulilla) or *-li* (Jumaytepeque). The plural inflection is discussed in more detail in section 3.1.2.

(11) Guazacapán plural noun formation.
   miya   →   *miyaa-łi*
   hen   hen-PL
   'hen'   'hens'

(12) Chiquimulilla plural noun formation.

ʔiiru → ʔiiruu-łi
monkey monkey-PL
'monkey' 'monkeys'

(13) Jumaytepeque plural noun formation.

šima → šimaa-li
rat rat-PL
'rat' 'rats'

2.1.2 Vowel harmony

Vowel harmony is a phonological process that is exhibited, cross-linguistically, in one of two ways: (1) through the long-distance assimilation of vowel features; or (2) through underlying vowel co-occurrence restrictions (i.e., not involving assimilation). In general, these vowel co-occurrence restrictions and feature assimilations are confined to a specific linguistic context, such as the lexical word or the morphological word, depending on the specific language. In Xinkan languages, vowels are restricted in two different contexts. In the lexical word (i.e., the lexeme), vowels are restricted as to when and where they can occur. Across morphemes (i.e., the morphological word) vowels exhibit limited long-distance assimilation. The lexical co-occurrence restrictions create the primary and most general pattern for vowels and are discussed first. Vowel harmony assimilation is discussed second.

In lexical words (i.e., the underlying forms of the roots of Xinkan words) vowels can only co-occur with other vowels of similar relative height and centrality features. The specification of each vowel in terms of the parameters, [HIGH] and [CENTRAL], is indicated in table 2.1. For the [HIGH] feature, vowels belong to one of three groups: high, mid, or low. For the [CENTRAL] feature, vowels belong to one of two groups: central and non-central. Any individual vowel can be defined in contrast to all other vowels using these features. In Table 2.1, /i/, /u/, and /ɨ/ are high, /e/ and /o/ are mid, and /a/ is low; furthermore /ɨ/ and /a/ are central, and /i/, /u/, /e/, and /o/ are non-central. The length distinctions indicated in the vowel inventory do not affect the restrictions on vowel distribution. Consequently, for the purposes of discussing vowel harmony, long and short vowels may be conflated into six descriptive symbols: the high front vowel *i*, the mid front vowel *e*, the high back vowel *u*, the mid back vowel *o*, the high central vowel *ɨ*, and the low central vowel *a*.

Based on this phonological division of the vowels' space, vowels form groups and all vowels within a word must belong the same group. Vowels from one set cannot co-occur with vowels of another set in the same word. The low central vowel {a} is an exception as it can occur with any vowel in the inventory in any position. (It is neutral to vowel co-occurrence restrictions.) The three sets are {i, u, a}, {e, o, a}, and {ɨ, a}. The behavior and characteristics of each of these sets are exemplified below, starting first with the distribution of the non-central high vowels *i* and *u*. Examples are given in the lists in 14–16.

(14) Distribution of /i/ and /u/ in Guazacapán.

hiiru	'monkey'	*tułtu*	'stab/poke'	*ts'il'i*	'make smooth'
čiiriʔ	'short'	*ts'uułi*	'ladino'	*miya*	'hen'
tum'ay'	'tail'	*ts'am'u*	'close your eyes'	*pari*	'day'

(15) Distribution of /i/ and /u/ in Chiquimulilla.

k'isku	'remove'	*k'usu*	'armadillo'	*hiri*	'sharpen'
kiiwiʔ	'patio'	*huuri*	'buttocks'	*piya*	'leaf'
hun'a	'empty out'	*karumu*	'widower'	*aši*	'burn'

(16) Distribution of /i/ and /u/ in Jumaytepeque.

k'iišu	'change'	*huhul*	'beehive'	*hiši*	'stone'
siipi	'lips'	*k'uusi*	'elbow, joint'	*hiwa*	'to slice, to carve?'
hum'a	'fill mouth'	*amu*	'spider'	*k'an'i*	'to rope'

Three facts can be observed from these examples. First, the high vowels *i* and *u* are members of a subset of vowels that occur together, while all other non-low vowels are excluded from this subset. To reflect this property the descriptive label 'high non-central' is sufficient to separate them from all other vowels in the inventory and to define the group. Second, this subset of high vowels can co-occur with the low vowel *a*. Third, in relation to the other two observations, the linear order of these vowels within words is unrestricted. The vowels *i*, *u*, and *a* can appear in any order in relation to each other with a word.

The second vowel set, {e, o}, exhibits similar but not identical properties. Examples are given in 17–19.

(17) Distribution of /e/ and /o/ in Guazacapán.

| *šeek'e* | 'chest' | *ter'o* | 'want/die' | *ts'oko* | 'grackle' |
| *k'oosek* | 'large' | *seema* | 'fish' | *goona* | 'hill' |

(18) Distribution of /e/ and /o/ in Chiquimulilla.

| *meeme* | 'crazy' | *hero* | 'scrape pot' | *hok'o* | 'to mend?' |
| *k'ooye* | 'visit' | *weetan* | 'dangerous worm' | *nooya* | 'grandmother' |

(19) Distribution of /e/ and /o/ in Jumaytepeque.

| *meen'e* | 'tender' | *p'en'o* | 'peel' | *hon'o* | 'make another drunk' |
| *wooče* | 'snake' | *p'eesa* | 'hit' | *k'ooyaaya* | 'coral snake' |

While mid vowels occur with less frequency in Xinkan vocabulary than other vowel types, similar restrictions are evident. The data suggests three generalizations for this vowel subset. First, the mid vowels *e* and *o* form a subset that excludes all other non-low vowels. The descriptive label 'mid' for this subset best captures this separation. Second, the members of this mid vowel set {e, o} can co-occur with the low vowel *a*. The low-central vowel *a* belongs to neither the mid vowel subset nor the high non-central set, but has properties that allow it to co-occur with members of both of these sets. Third, and somewhat different than the high non-central set, the linear order of segments is marginally restricted. The members of this mid vowel set are unrestricted by linear order in regards to each other but are restricted to only occurring before the low vowel {a}. In the examples in 17–19, {a} never precedes the members of the mid vowel set. This restriction on the linear order of segments is neutralized in words borrowed from other languages, especially Spanish. The example in 20 gives an instance of this neutralization.

(20) /e/, /o/, and /a/ in loan words.
    adoobe 'adobe' (<Sp. *'adobe'*)   *paale'* 'priest' (<Sp. *'padre'*)

The examples in 14–19 show that vowels *i, u, e,* and *o* belong to either the set {i, u} or the set {e, o} with respect to their distributional patterns. These sets can be defined generally in terms of their relative heights with respect to each other. The central vowels also play a role in vowel distribution but in a completely different way. These vowels are not restricted according to their relative heights but according to their relative centrality or lowness in relation to all other vowels in the inventory. The distributional properties of the high central vowel {i} are shown in 21–23.

(21) Examples of the distribution of /i/ in Guazacapán.
pik'i	'liver'	*ts'iiriiri'*	'hummingbird'	*ts'iim'ał*	'flea'
waw'iya	'run' (water)	*ahi*	'yes'	*hil'a*	'to empty'
hini	'learn'	*hiyi*	'gopher'	*t'ini*	'complain'

(22) Examples of the distribution of /i/ in Chiquimulilla.
č'ingi?	'big eared'	*piiši*	'gourd (guacal)'	*k'iy'a*	'gather'
šangi	'stomach'	*ipi*	'close, cover'	*iina*	'defecate'
im'iłi	'write, read'	*indi*	'spy'	*k'in'a*	'to counsel'

(23) Examples of the distribution of /i/ in Jumaytepeque.
ahmi	'hide'	*siim'a*	'night'	*šihi*	'gravel'
hin'i	'hunt'	*iiki*	'stomach'	*irsi*	'bite'
lisk'iw'a	'waist'	*p'in'a*	'eat fast'	*piša*	'stinky'

Similar restrictions as those discussed above are evident in these examples. The high central vowel {i} can co-occur in words with *a*, just like the high central and the mid vowel subsets. However, what is unique about the distribution of {i} is that in all the words in 21–23, the only possible co-occurring vowels are /i/ and /a/. This distinction between the high central vowel and all other non-low vowels cannot be based on a restriction to similar height specification characteristics, as in 17–19 above, because the high central vowel does not pattern with other vowels with identical height specifications. The best descriptive label that captures the isolation of this vowel with regard to is distributional properties is 'central'. In terms of theoretical phonology, it is evident that a feature [CENTRAL] is necessary to capture the relevant behaviors of the vowels. Specifically, [-CENTRAL] vowels *i, u, e,* and *o* are restricted according to their relative heights, while the [+CENTRAL] vowel *i* is restricted only according to its relative centrality.

Finally, in light of the properties and descriptions of the other vowels, the characteristic of the low vowel *a* is made clearer. In all of the foregoing examples we see that *a* is unrestricted in terms of height or of centrality. It can co-occur with vowels belonging to all of the subsets discussed. In vowel harmony systems, vowels unrestricted in this manner are descriptively referred to as neutral vowels.

Xinkan vowels are specified underlyingly in stems and vowel harmony as a consequence of the underlying vowel co-occurrence restrictions discussed above. This is a salient typological feature of Xinkan, as the described patterns of vowel harmony are unusual and are not the result of assimilation. However, there is a related assimilatory phenomenon that alters the co-occurrence strategies just discussed. Across morpheme boundaries, vowels in suffixes are required to assimilate to the height specification of the last vowel of the root. Since this vowel assimilation process is about height, across morpheme boundaries the distinction between the high non-central vowels and the high central vowel is neutralized—they cause the same result in the suffix vowel. Consider the examples in 24–26.

(24)   Vowel harmony across morpheme boundaries in Guazacapán.
   a. *hiiruu-ɬi*   *ts'okoo-ɬe*   *pɨk'ɨɨ-ɬi*
       monkey-PL   grackle-PL   liver-PL
       'monkeys'   'grackles'   'livers'
   b. *ts'iriri-ki*   *oško-k'e*   *piɬɨɬɨ-k'ɨ*
       colored-INCH   rotted-INCH   smooth-INCH
       'become colored'   'become rotted'   'become smooth'

(25)   Vowel harmony across morpheme boundaries in Chiquimulilla.
   a. *nuun'uu-ɬi*   *onee-ɬe*   *iyɨɨ-ɬi*
       mute-PL   baby-PL   gopher-PL
       'mutes'   'babies'   'gophers'
   b. *wili-k'i*   *moro-k'e*   *iskɨ-k'ɨ*
       naked-INCH   wet-INCH   untied-INCH
       'become naked'   'become wet'   'become untied'

(26)   Vowel harmony across morpheme boundaries in Jumaytepeque.
   a. *mul'ɨɨ-li*   *k'otoroo-le*   *yik'ɨɨ-li*
       squirrel-PL   parrot-PL   dog-PL
       'squirrels'   'parrots'   'dogs'
   b. *šuwi-k'i*   *holo-k'e*   *k'ɨɨti-k'ɨ*
       swept-INCH   pretty-INCH   cold-INCH
       'become swept'   'become pretty'   'become cold'

A suffix containing a high front vowel /i/ is required to partially assimilate to the vowels within the word it attaches to. This process is completely productive, but due to the conditioning factors it is limited to three suffixes: the plural *-ɬi* (Guazacapán and Chiquimulilla), *-li* (Jumaytepeque), the 'INCHOATIVE/ANTIPASSIVE' *-k'i* (all languages), and the third-person agreement marker on transitive verbs in Jumaytepeque *-yi'*. The plural formation is described in section 3.12, the use of the inchoative/antipassive suffix is detailed in section 3.12.3, and Jumaytepeque verbal conjugation is detailed in section 3.6. As can be seen in the examples in 24–26, the suffix vowel /i/ is realized as [e] when preceded by members of the mid vowel set, and is realized as [i] when occurring after any other vowel in the inventory regardless of what subset it belongs to.

Since the high vowel /i/ is the underlying segment for these suffixes, assimilation only occurs by changing this high vowel to a mid vowel. There is no change when the vowel preceding the suffix is also high. This is a common occurrence in languages exhibiting vowel harmony (especially nonassimilatory vowel harmony, as in Xinkan). In Xinkan the vowels of roots are primarily distributed according to co-occurrence restrictions, but there is a secondary assimilatory process that is triggered only by mid vowels. This secondary process can be generalized as /i/ → [e] / {e, o}+C__.

In 24–26 above we see that within a word *i* can only occur with other instances of the same vowel or with the low vowel *a*. We might ask why the high central vowel behaves individually in this way and why it is not restricted to co-occurrences based on height as with the other vowels. Cross-linguistic evidence of the characteristics of vowel inventories similar to that of Xinkan provides an answer.

Central vowels tend to have a larger vowel space cross-linguistically than other vowels in a given inventory. That is, the precise perception of and articulation of these high central vowels in a six-vowel inventory are not as strict as for non-central vowels—the range of variation permitted is greater than that for other vowels.[4] This means that the high central vowel in a six-vowel inventory can be produced with greater subphonemic variation without losing its contrastive properties (in other words, without making it difficult to perceive or requiring increased effort to distinguish it from neighboring vowels). This is important for Xinkan vowel harmony. If languages tend to allow bigger vowel spaces for high central vowels, it appears that the Xinkan vowel harmony system is making use of this tendency. That is, the Xinkan vowel harmony system is based on the limitations of vowel height co-occurrence, while the idiosyncratic height specifications of the high central vowel tend to be less restricted subphonemically.

These generalizations lend credence to a more elegant phonological explanation of Xinkan vowel harmony. It is more elegant in the sense that fewer theoretical arguments need to be made in order to capture the relevant patterns. This explanation is simply that there is an important phonological distinction in Xinkan between peripheral and nonperipheral (i.e., internal to the vowel space) vowels.[5] Peripheral vowels are those on the edges of the vowel articulatory space, for example /i, u, e, o/. The nonperipheral (internal) vowels are those in the interior of the vowel articulatory space, for example /i, a/. With this label, the Xinkan vowel harmony system turns out to be merely a restriction on these two types of vowels. Xinkan peripheral vowels are restricted by limitations on vowel height co-occurrence, while interior vowels are not restricted by vowel height specifications. Moreover, the phonological requirement that vowels are restricted (possibly for perceptual and articulatory reasons) is still applicable to the high central vowel but not to the low central vowel. Since the high central vowel *i, ii* does not participate in height restrictions but still must be phonologically separated from the other high vowels, it is placed in a vowel set all by itself.

The low central vowel *a, aa* does not need to be distinguished (articulatorily or perceptually) from other low vowels, as it is the only low vowel in the inventory and so stands completely outside the vowel harmony restrictions.

2.2 Consonants

The consonant inventories of each of the Xinkan languages are slightly different. Since one of my goals is to provide evidence for the differences between the four languages, each inventory is discussed separately. Similarities do exist, of course, but the chosen presentation will underscore the independence of each variety. Just as with the vowels above, the consonants are organized according to their relevant descriptive labels. Sounds shown within parentheses are very rare in the lexicon of the particular Xinkan language involved or are found only in loan words. Chapter 6 compares the four inventories and explains how each developed from Proto-Xinkan.

2.2.1 Guazacapán

The Guazacapán consonant inventory in table 2.2 represents those sounds that are phonemes. Each of the sounds has the potential of affecting a change in meaning when used in a word. Most of the phonemes form phonetically similar pairs consisting of a glottalized segment and a nonglottalized (plain) segment. The members of these phonetic pairs are identical in all the other articulatory and acoustic characteristics labeled in the table.

For the phonetic pairs, the glottalized member is realized as an ejective consonant for obstruents and as a glottalized resonant for the sonorants. The phonemes /s/, /š/, /ts'/, /ł/, /h/, and /ʔ/ are unique in that these are not members of a glottalized-nonglottalized phonetic pair where all other phonetic properties are in common. The gaps that consequently exist in the phonemic inventory are a consequence of the phonetic properties of each of these aberrant sounds.

The sounds /ʔ/ and /h/ (both glottal) are produced in a part of the vocal tract that is outside of the articulatory sphere of glottalized consonants in specific ejectives. That is, since both of the glottal sounds require the use of the glottis as a primary articulator in their production, it is not possible for these to create the supraglottal pressure required for ejectives. Ejectives, on the other hand, involve articulations above the glottis (i.e., in the oral cavity) while the glottis itself is closed—the raising of the glottis creates the necessary air pressure for an ejective articulation. The gap in the manner of production for the glottal consonants is, therefore, not surprising.

The asymmetry in glottalization involving the four sounds /s/, /š/, /ts'/, and /ł/ is related to a prohibition of glottalized fricatives in Xinkan. This is most likely related to the general cross-linguistic difficulty in producing glottalized fricatives. Whatever the cause, Xinkan languages do not have glottalized fricatives. However, in certain morphological environments all consonants must undergo glottalization. When the consonants /s/, /š/, and /ł/ are glottalized in this morphological context they are

Table 2.2 Guazacapán consonants

			Labial	Alveolar	Alveo-palatal	Retro-Flex	Palatal	Velar	Glottal
Stops		Voiced	(b)	(d)				(g)	
		Voiceless	p	t				k	
		Ejective	p'	t'				k'	ʔ
Fricatives		Voiceless		s		ṣ			h
Affricates		Voiceless			č				
		Ejective		ts'	č'				
Nasal		Plain	m	n					
		Glottalized	m'	n'					
Liquid	Lateral	Plain		l					
		Glottalized		l'					
		Voiceless		ɬ					
	Rhotic	Plain		r					
		Glottalized		r'					
	Glides	Plain	w				y		
		Glottalized	w'				y'		

realized allophonically as either an affricate /ts'/ in the case of /š/ and /s/, or as the corresponding glottalized sonorant /l'/ in the case of /ɬ/. (See section 2.3.1 for details.)

The phonetic versus phonological characteristics of this last sound /ɬ/ are extremely important for the correct pronunciation of the sound and for its implications for phonological theory. This consonant is phonetically a voiceless lateral approximant rather than a lateral fricative as is suggested by the International Phonetic Alphabet. The phonetic production of voiceless laterals as approximants rather than fricatives is a common characteristic of many languages of the Americas. However, phonologically in Xinkan (in both Guazacapán and Chiquimulilla) /ɬ/ behaves like a fricative in terms of glottalization. The voiceless lateral is produced with a turbulent airflow that is difficult to maintain with the simultaneous glottal closure required for glottalization. It seems there is a general prohibition in Xinkan against ejective sounds that require this continual egression of air, and consequently the voiceless lateral approximant is allophonically realized without this continual airflow. The same is true for /s/ and /š/, where the continual airflow is omitted in glottalizing situations. Consequently, they are considered to pattern together in their manners of articulation phonologically, but not phonetically.

Lastly, the gap with the ejective alveolar affricate /ts'/, where there is only a glottalized member of the glottalized-nonglottalized pair (i.e., /ts'/ but not /*ts/), is peculiar.

It is not clear what motivates this gap, but it goes against typological generalizations that suggest an ejective consonant can only be produced at the same place as its plain counterpart.[6] I have no definitive phonetic or phonological explanations for this gap. Yet, language external facts suggest a possible areal trait. This same gap exists in some neighboring languages of Maya origin: Poqomam, Poqomchi', Q'eqchi', and varieties of Ch'orti'. In some varieties of these languages the plain alveolar affricate is being lost while the ejective counterpart is being retained. In other varieties the contrast is being maintained.[7] This gap in the Xinkan languages might exist as a consequence of the contact with these languages, or vice versa.

2.2.2 Chiquimulilla

The general characteristics of the consonant inventory of Chiquimulilla are practically identical with Guazacapán and Jumaytepeque, and they will not be repeated here. The phonetic gaps in the glottalized-nonglottalized pairs are the same for all the Xinkan languages. Section 2.3.1 discusses glottalization in detail. The most striking difference between Chiquimulilla and Guazacapán, however, is that the voiced bilabial stop /b/ has become a regular phoneme in the former but not in the latter.[8]

In addition, there has been a recent alternation in the pronunciation of /h/ in Chiquimulilla. In one word, a sporadic change of *h to /ɸ/ (voiceless bilabial fricative) is common, /ɸrak/ 'man' ← *huurak.[9] This sound is not used in any phonological processes and it is not considered part of the phonological inventory, but it is noteworthy in that only Chiquimulilla exhibits this alternation. Table 2.3 shows the consonant phonemes of Chiquimulilla.

2.2.3 Jumaytepeque

The consonant inventory in Jumaytepeque is very similar to the other Xinkan languages. Two differences are important. First, as with Chiquimulilla, recent sound change has resulted in the addition of some pertinent phonetic contrasts. Just as Chiquimulilla has recently added /b/ as a phoneme, so has Jumaytepeque added /b/ and /d/. These new sounds are used rarely, mostly in words borrowed from Spanish, although a few etymologically native words have them. Second, unlike the other languages, there is no voiceless lateral approximant /ɬ/ in Jumaytepeque. The consonant inventory of Jumaytepeque is shown in table 2.4.

2.2.4 Yupiltepeque

The consonant inventory of Yupiltepeque, of course, is a philological question. The phonemes are determined solely on the basis of published premodern materials. The description of Yupiltepeque consonants depends on the descriptions used in these resources and the contemporary analysis of the materials. The inventory represented in table 2.5, while assuredly not definitive, is an approximation of the phonetic de-

**Table 2.3
Chiquimulilla consonants**

		Labial	Alveolar	Alveo-palatal	Retro-Flex	Palatal	Velar	Glottal
Stops	Voiced	b	(d)				(g)	
	Voiceless	p	t				k	
	Ejective	p'	t'				k'	ʔ
Fricatives	Voiceless		s		ṣ			h
Affricates	Voiceless			č				
	Ejective		ts'	č'				
Nasal	Plain	m	n					
	Glottalized	m'	n'					
Liquid **Lateral**	Plain		l					
	Glottalized		l'					
	Voiceless		ł					
Rhotic	Plain		r					
	Glottalized		r'					
Glides	Plain	w				y		
	Glottalized	w'				y'		

**Table 2.4
Jumaytepeque consonants**

		Labial	Alveolar	Alveo-palatal	Retro-Flex	Palatal	Velar	Glottal
Stops	Voiced	b	d				(g)	
	Voiceless	p	t				k	
	Ejective	p'	t'				k'	ʔ
Fricatives	Voiceless		s		ṣ			h
Affricates	Voiceless			č				
	Ejective		ts'	č'				
Nasal	Plain	m	n					
	Glottalized	m'	n'					
Liquid **Lateral**	Plain		l					
	Glottalized		l'					
	Voiceless		ł					
Rhotic	Plain		r					
	Glottalized		r'					
Glides	Plain	w				y		
	Glottalized	w'				y'		

Table 2.5
Yupiltepeque consonants

		Labial	Alveolar	Alveo-palatal	Palatal	Velar	Glottal
Stops	Voiceless	p	t			k	
Fricatives	Voiceless		s	š			h
Affricates	Voiceless			č			
	Ejective		ts'				
Nasal	Plain	m	n				
	Glottalized		n'				
Liquid / Lateral	Plain		l				
	Voiceless		ł				
Liquid / Rhotic			r				
Glides		w			y		

scriptions of the consonants used in the descriptions found in Calderón's grammatical sketch (1908).

Overall, the phonetic pairing of glottalized and nonglottalized consonants is not evident in the available data for this language. The absence of these systematic phonetic pairs might either be a consequence of transcription (for example, if Calderón did not hear the difference between plain and glottalized consonants), or it might represent a general historical change (e.g., Yupiltepeque lost most of the glottalized consonants that occurred in Proto-Xinkan). However, two sounds definitely are described as being glottalized: /n'/ and /ts'/. Nevertheless, the behavior of these two glottalized segments is more restricted in Yupiltepeque than the other Xinkan languages. The cross-linguistic differences in these sounds and the development of the Yupiltepeque sound system are major themes of discussion throughout chapter 6.

2.2.5   Consonant distribution

Xinkan consonants have interesting distributional restrictions within a word. Subsets of the consonants in each language are prohibited in word-initial, word-medial, or word-final position.

2.2.5.1   *Word-initial consonants*

Glottalized sonorants and /r/ are prohibited from occurring word initially in all Xinkan languages. Guazacapán, Chiquimulilla, and Yupiltepeque also prohibit /l/ word initially, while Jumaytepeque does not.[10] Moreover, in words borrowed from Spanish both /r/ and /l/ can occur word initially in all four Xinkan languages. The terms in 27–29 give examples of words containing each of the possible word-initial consonants.

(27) Guazacapán words with word-initial consonants.

piya	'leaf'	*p'ahni*	'to dig'	*tol'o*	'yellow'
t'aru	'offer'	*kaɬi*	'smoke'	*k'iiw'i*	'patio'
wot'e	'break'	*ʔuy*	'water'	*seema*	'fish'
šaha	'mouth'	*hutu*	'tree'	*čawi*	'hard'
č'irwi	'tall and skinny'	*ts'oko*	type of bird	*miya*	'chicken'
naka	'you'	*looko*	'crazy' (<Sp. *'loco'*)	*ɬap'a*	'grandson'
waɬ	'three'	*yɨp'ɨ*	'to vomit'		

(28) Chiquimulilla words with word-initial consonants.

piyʔ	'two'	*p'eko*	'turn around'	*tawu*	'wind, air'
t'uuri	'child'	*kara*	'heavy'	*k'ots'o*	'to dry something'
bar	'already'	*dimi*	'how'	*gooša ɬ*	'fence'
frak	'man'	*seema*	'fish'	*šir'i*	'turn around in circles'
hiri	'sharpen'	*čikwit*	'basket'	*č'iw'i*	'skinny'
ts'ama	'good'	*mere*	'drag'	*naw'u*	'child'
ɬakma	'count'	*wiya*	'yellow'	*yɨw'a*	'to lose'
lweego	'later' (<Sp. *'luego'*)				

(29) Jumaytepeque words with word-initial consonants.

pipil	'butterfly'	*p'en'o*	'roll'	*taata*	'father'
t'ay'a	'kick'	*kama*	'blood'	*k'uusi*	'elbow, joint'
bar	'already'	*sap'u*	'grab'	*šaha*	'mouth'
hiši	'stone'	*čumu*	'old man'	*č'oy'e*	'fold'
ts'aama	'chew'	*mɨimɨ*	'sing'	*naru*	'earth, ground'
lam'u	'taste'	*weeša*	'iguana'	*yut'u*	'fry'
duusi	'brown sugar loaf' (<Sp. *'dulce'*)				

2.2.5.2 *Word-medial consonants*

The fewest restrictions occur on the consonants that can be used word medially. In general the sounds /b/, /d/, /g/, and /ɸ/ are never used in this position, except in words borrowed from Spanish. In three of the languages /ʔ/ is also prohibited for the word-medial position, but in Guazacapán it occurs in contextual variations of three words: *paɬ* 'epistemic mood marker', *naɬ* 'past tense marker', and *tiʔ* 'direct object marker'. Clause finally, these words are lengthened by epenthesizing a word-medial glottal stop [paʔaɬ] or [naʔaɬ], or by epenthesizing an echo vowel word finally [tiʔi].

In addition, the phoneme [ts'] can occur word medially, but it is the surface representation of three underlying sounds: /s'/, /š'/, and /ts'/. The first two of these sounds are not part of the phonetic inventory of these languages, and there is a general prohibition against glottalized fricatives in Xinkan pronunciation (see above). These sounds are always pronounced as [ts']. Nevertheless, underlyingly, some words make a distinction between these sounds. Deglottalization indicates why this analysis is accurate. Deglottalization is a process whereby a consonant phoneme loses its glottalized characteristic. It is a regular occurrence and happens when an intransitive affective verb is derived from a transitive verb. Deglottalization ensues because of the glottal stop suffix attached to the derived intransitive verb. The example in 30 shows this process for a single word in Jumaytepeque.

(30) Deglottalization.
      CVC'V → CVVCV-ʔ
      hupʼi → *huupi-ʔ*
      'fondle'   'fondled'

The consonant in bold in the left column loses its glottalization and becomes the consonant in bold on the right. When [ts'] is deglottalized it is pronounced either as [s] or [ṣ]: for example, /masʼa/ 'to stick together', [matsʼa hutu] 'stick two trees together', [maasaʔ] 'it was stuck together' (Guazacapán); /kʼoṣʼo/ 'to dry', [kʼotsʼo waṣiɬin] 'dry my clothes', [kʼoošoʔ] 'it was dried' (Chiquimulilla). Which of the two fricatives, [s] or [ṣ], will be the result of the deglottalization of [ts'] can be predicted based only on a set of underlying glottalized fricatives. In other words, due to these languages' constraints on consonant phonemes, all glottalized fricatives are pronounced as glottalized affricates. Glottalized fricatives are never pronounced and are only 'real' on a deeper lexical level. Glottalization and deglottalization are surveyed in detail in section 2.3.1 and 2.3.1.1.

The examples in 31–33 show the permitted word-medial consonants. In words with /tsʼ/ the appropriate underlying glottalized fricatives is given in slashes / / immediately following the word.

(31) Guazacapán word-medial consonants.

ɬapi	'to carry'	*hapʼa*	'to wait'	*hutu*	'tree'
tsʼotʼo	'to tire'	*ɬiki*	'to reach'	*nikʼi*	'to press'
naʔu-	'son'	*pʼeese*	'lizard'	*išakʼa*	'a drink'
hahi	'avocado'	*pačin*	'cockroach'	*ɬačʼa*	'talker'
etsʼe /esʼe/	'to open'	*iwitsʼi* /iwšʼi/	'hearing'	*kitsʼi*	'add'
tsʼuma	'kiss/suck'	*tsʼamʼu*	'close your eyes'	*hini*	'stomach'
čenʼo	'throw fire'	*ipalʼa*	'bath'	*hila*	'to empty'
eɬa	'new'	*pari*	'day'	*erʼeɬaʔ*	'to scare'
iwi	'to drown'	*uwʼaɬ*	'ant'	*hayu*	'to clean'
tšʼoyʼe	'to fold'				

(32) Chiquimulilla word-medial consonants.

ayapaʔ	'year, time'	*išapʼa*	'leaving'	*taata*	'father'
utʼa	'mother'	*naki*	'chile'	*pikʼi*	'bird'
meʔe	'green'	*eeseʔ*	'opened'	*huuṣa*	'blow'
čehe	'woodpecker'	*kʼači*	'rascar'	*učʼu*	'dirty'
atsʼi /ašʼi/	'burning'	*kʼotsʼo*	'to dry'	*nama*	'pain'
homʼa	'rinse'	*pʼene*	'despise'	*šinʼak*	'beans'
yulʼu	'atol'	*walapʼu*	'turtle'	*muɬa*	'storm'
saara	'cold'	*ṣurʼu*	'collecting'	*taawu*	'turtle'
ṣawʼa	'sheet, blanket'	*ṣayʼa*	'acidic'		
payi	'daughter-in-law'	*paatsʼa* /paasʼa/	'to stuff in a basket'		

(33) Jumaytepeque word-medial consonants.

šipi	'cut metal'	hup'i	'fondle'	k'uutu	'small ranch'
šit'ɨ	'to weed'	lakuw'a	'son-in-law'	šak'a	'carry'
k'usi	'remote/yerbas?'	ašu	'pig'	pahu	'wax'
ačih	'native person'	moč'o	'to wet'	amu	'spider'
šam'a	'inside'	kunu	'buy'	hɨn'ɨ	'hunt'
epel'e	'fear'	eela	'tongue'	hura	'armadillo'
hur'u	'turkey'	iwi	'winnow'	k'ɨw'ɨ	'close'
aya	'female'	č'oy'e	'fold, bend'		
ets'e	'to mash down'	šawats'a /šawaš'a/	'planting'		
luuts'u	'bite' (insect) cf. /luus'u/				

2.2.5.3 *Word-final consonants*

The greatest number of restrictions on the use of consonants is found word finally. Some of these word-final restrictions are true for all of the languages, while others are unique to only one or two of them. The general set of word-final consonants in all languages is /k, ʔ, h, n, n', y, y'/. The phoneme /ɬ/ is also possible word finally in Guazacapán and Chiquimulilla; Jumaytepeque uses /l/ instead due to sound change.

The phonemes /t/, /š/, and /r/ can be used word finally also, but these are found in only a very few words or in loans from other languages. For example, word-final /r/ occurs in only one word in Guazacapán, three words in Chiquimulilla, and seven words in Jumaytepeque. Jumaytepeque is the only language that has the phoneme /s/ word finally. Examples of all the possible word-final consonants in each language are shown in 34–36.

(34) Guazacapán word-final consonants.

asɨk	'when'	haamaʔ	'ripened'	nah	's/he'
šan	'in, on'	iišin'	'I woke up'	ur'uɬ	'egg'
pɨy	'two'	nukay'	's/he gave it'		
mušwap	'toes'	čikwit	'basket'	aɬtepet	'town'
muš	'appendage'	teneš	'lime'	wir'iš	'crying child'
waakaš	'cow'	hur	'straight'		

(35) Chiquimulilla word-final consonants.

aɬawak	'tomorrow'	haapaʔ	'past'	anuh	'my niece'
han	'how'	hirin'	'I sharpened'	maɬ	'firewood'
uy	'water'	ašiy'	's/he burned it'		
čikwit	'basket'	ep'ɬeš	'afraid'	emur'uš	'flower bud'
bar	'already'	gar	'still'		

(36) Jumaytepeque word-final consonants.

hɨlak	'spoon'	haarɨʔ	'scraped'	ačih	'native person'
kaš	'where'	leelan	'for'	aplan'	'I bathed'
koy	'horse'	it'ul	'flea, tick'		
wap	'foot'	k'ap/k'ar	'tight'	k'ɨt	'frozen'
mur'us	'flower bud'	p'ot'os	'lung'	t'ulis	'a nude'

bar	'already'	*gar*	'still'	*wašar*	'how many?'
piy'ar	'two'	*wahl'ar*	'three'	*ɨndar*	'go!'

The words with the uncommon, or rare, word-final consonants /p/, /t/, /š/, /s/, /r/, and /l/ can be attributed to either borrowing from another language or recent sound change in one of the Xinkan languages. These consonants were not permitted word finally in Proto-Xinkan.

2.2.5.4 *Consonant clusters*

Consonant clusters consist of only two members in Xinkan and occur as the result of inflection paradigms (such as possession) or as part of the lexical root word. Cluster patterns, such as the most common cluster type in each language, are interesting but are irrelevant to the grammatical properties of the languages. They have been discussed elsewhere.[11] As with individual segments, there are four general restrictions on the properties of a cluster in Xinkan.

1. Only one obstruent stop can be used in a cluster.
2. Consonant clusters are always divided by a syllable boundary (see section 2.4).
3. Members of a cluster can never be phonetically identical.
4. A glottalized consonant can never be part of a cluster.

This last restriction has begun to be relaxed in the utterances of all of the speakers of the Xinkan languages. So while CC' clusters are rare, processes of language change, and possibly attrition, mean the languages now exhibit some instances of CC' clusters—although an active phonological process in all of the Xinkan languages is sensitive to this restriction (see section 2.3.1 below).[12] Occasionally because of word conjugation or other morphological phenomena, words might end up with clusters violating one or all these four constraints. In this scenario an epenthetic vowel is inserted to break up the cluster (see section 2.3.1). Other phonological alternations sensitive to the makeup of consonant clusters are discussed in section 2.3, such as stop-voicing (2.3.2), nasal assimilation (2.3.3), lenition to /h/ (2.3.4), and consonant deletion (2.3.8.2).

Examples of all permitted consonant clusters for each Xinkan language are given in 37–39. Some clusters not native to Xinkan are allowed in loans from Spanish and are pronounced as they are in the donor language. If the translation is unknown, there is a ʔ in its stead.

(37) Guazacapán consonant clusters.

apla	'open'	*pipri*	'to weed'	*mutku*	'to hustle'
čitnaʔ	'to make oily'	*mutru*	'pull out hair'	*piktak*	'arrow'
šakša	'steal'	*k'okmaʔ*	'kneeled'	*ɬikni*	'obey, believe'
kukru	'wrinkle'	*čikwit*	'basket'	*iskɨ*	'untie'
weskoy	'pixcoy' (bird)	*p'osna*	'jump, leap'	*išpa*	'leave'
pašpa	'divide, share'	*wašta*	'enter'	*wiški*	'spill'
ošk'o	'rotten'	*ušmu*	'smell'	*hešna*	'sneeze'

mušwap	'toes'	*pɨhta*	'shoot arrow'	*ehka*	'cover'
łuhsu	'peck'	*šahši*	'strain'	*nuhts'u*	'smoke'
č'ehče	'missing a piece'	*p'ehč'e*	'short'	*łahma*	'count, tell'
pahni	'dig'	*łahla*	'poke'	*p'uhru*	'make holes'
k'ahwa	'pass over'	*yahyik*	'grinding stone'		
p'ump'un	'owl'	*lɨnp'ene*	'disgust'	*č'onko*	'pot'
t'unk'u	'short'	*sɨnsɨn*	'tight'	*pɨnts'ɨ*	'wild dog'
manča	'many'	*punyu*	'measure'	*pułpu*	'dust'
p'ɨłp'ɨł	'butterfly'	*ałtepet*	'town'	*hałt'a*	'crooked'
hułku	'stick in'	*yɨłk'ɨ*	'accuse'	*ełma*	'loan, borrow'
č'ełna	'wreck'	*ełwa*	'cover with clay'	*hurpi*	'rub'
hurta	'loosen'	*ɨrt'ay*	'miserable'	*urku*	'swallow'
wirk'i	'speak'	*erse*	'old'	*merše*	'break'
hurhur	'straight'	*kařč'ɨ*	'tashy'	*surmu*	'knit/wrinkle'
yarmi	'scrape'	*ts'orna*	'drip'	*urlu*	'entire'
yɨrłɨ	'heels?'	*harwi*	'dig'	*hawka*	'empty'
iwša	'to thread'	*k'ewče*	'toothless'	*wowłak*	'grave'
lawruła?	'dance'	*haypu*	'receive'	*taytak*	'ladder'
iykɨ	'pull, drag'	*ayma*	'corn'	*koyna*	'break'

(38) Chiquimulilla consonant clusters.

hupni	'insert'	*ipła*	'bathe'	*opro*	'break'
netka	'push'	*p'ɨtna?*	'jump'	*k'atra*	'drag'
toktok	'mockingbird'	*šakša*	'steal, rob'	*č'ikč'ik*	'kind of bird'
k'okma	'swell'	*łɨkmɨ?*	'believe, obey'	*'kakra*	'to duck, bend, squat'
čikwit	'basket'	*łɨski*	'tighten'	*p'osko*	'to string, thread'
k'osme?	'to thunder'	*p'osna*	'burst'	*musru*	'furrow'
p'usyu?	'wrinkle'	*išpa?*	'leave'	*p'ošp'oš*	'flabby'
ištu	'rash'	*uški*	'smoke'	*tišk'ɨ*	'far away'
hišma	'sneeze'	*kušnu*	'wrinkle'	*ošwe*	'scrape'
p'ehse	'turn upside down'	*awhšaya*	'wife'	*łuhts'u*	'sting, bite'
p'ehč'e	'flat-nosed'	*č'ahma*	'chew'	*pahni*	'dig'
łahła	'sew'	*muhra*	'white hair'	*kahwa*	'pass over'
mihya	'chicken'	*p'ump'un łiw'a*	'owl'	*łonk'o*	'tall'
šanhuri	'canjura'	*p'olp'ol*	?	*tult'u?*	'pullar'
p'ɨłp'ɨł	'butterfly'	*pałta*	'pay'	*k'ełke*	'hang wet rags'
hołmo	'rinse mouth'	*p'ełnaka?*	'slip'	*ełwa*	'sweep'
harpu	'to claw'	*hurta*	'loosen'	*ɨrt'ay*	'miserable'
mɨrkɨ	'rip cloth'	*erse*	'old'	*kɨrša*	'comb'
hurhur	'straight'	*murča*	'white-haired'	*yarmi*	'scratch'
morna	'bite'	*arła*	'open'	*karwa*	'be alone'
hawtuma	'leather'	*hawka*	'empty'	*k'awk'aw*	'crunching sound'
uwšɨ	'hear'	*awhšaya*	'wife'	*k'ewče*	'peck'
awłak	'tortilla griddle'	*wrik'ih*	'language'	*haypu*	'receive'
č'uytiiti	?	*iykɨ*	'drag'	*hayhay*	'barking'
eyma	'corn'	*k'oyna*	'decompose'	*piyłɨ*	'round'
ɸrak	'man'				

(39)   Jumaytepeque consonant clusters.

ɨpts'ɨʔ	'was grown'	hupni	'bend, fold'	apla	'bathe'
eple	'be afraid'	šapri	'thresh'	etka	'to harvest corn'
p'ɨtn'alaʔ	'jump'	mutru	'beard'	k'atr'aʔ	'squat, duck'
suksin	'jar made of mud'	šakša?	'steal'	č'ikč'ik	'kind of bird'
kukma	'kneel'	k'okro	'spine'	kraw'a	'the wild'
čikwiti	'basket'	mɨkyay	'let's do it'	pispil	'burl'
mistun	'cat'	iska	'open'	ut'usma	'join'
mɨsna	'burst'	nislik'ɨ	'blow nose'	musru	'go under a fence'
p'usy'uʔ	'wrinkled'	išpa	'leave'	k'ušta	'poke'
iška	'drink'	kɨšma	'to gift'	kušnu	'to curl up'
tišl'ɨlaʔ	'withdraw'	ošwe	'scrape'	pahta	'pay'
tahku	'half'	sahsi	'to strain'	šahšɨ	'sprinkle water'
ahmɨ	'hide'	tihnik'ɨ	'to lie'	wahlar	'three'
uhru	'swallow'	kahwa	?	pahyi	'hollow'
ampuki	'snake'	tamšɨ	'twist'	tamts'ɨʔ	'twisted'
pɨmrɨʔ	'thick'	hanta	'foolish'	šɨnkɨ	'chew, mash'
sinsin	'kind of bird'	hunhun'alaʔ	'be dark'	ts'ents'erek	'kind of bird'
honw'ala	'a drunk'	hulpi	'stick hand in food'	alte	'penis'
kolko	'empty'	k'ulmi	'wash mouth'	t'elnaha	'push over'
elwa	'embarrar'	harpɨ	?	hurta	'loosen'
hirki	'stir'	ɨrsɨ	'bite'	kɨrša	'to comb'
ormo	'raise'	k'orno	'bring close'	erleke	'fright'
harwi	'dig'	šan lɨɨryɨ	'heel'	hawki	'skin'
šašwa	'to plant'	uwlak	'comal'	haypu	'receive, answer'
taytak	'ladder'	ɨyki	'pull'	hayhay	'dog's bark'
uyču	'wrinkle'	uymu	'wound, hurt'	ɨylɨw'a	'honey'
haywi	'call'				

Also, with the addition of the inherent possessive suffixes and the transitive verb completive suffixes, there is the possibility that other clusters may occur. However, these types of clusters are extremely rare, as most inherently possessed nouns have vowel-final roots. In fact, in the entire database only two such roots have been found: *taɬ-* (Guazacapán and Chiquimulilla), *tal-* (Jumaytepeque) 'neck' (Sp. 'pescuezo'); and *wap-* 'foot'. Importantly, both of these are given in two forms: the first as just listed and the second as *taɬi-* (*tali-* in Jumaytepeque) and *wapa-*, respectively. Both are used without a change in meaning. Example 40 shows instances of the two possible conjugations for each word. An epenthetic vowel is inserted between the final consonant and the personal possessive suffix, if the latter is a sonorant, in the case of the consonant-final root.

(40)   Consonant clusters with inherent possessive suffixes.

  a. /taɬ-n'/ → [taɬan'] 'my neck'
  b. /taɬi-n'/ → [taɬin'] 'my neck'
  c. /taɬ-ka/ → [taɬka] 'your neck'
  d. /taɬi-ka/ → [taɬika] 'your neck'
  e. /wap-n'/ → [wapan'] 'my foot'

  f. /wapa-nʼ/ → [wapanʼ] 'my foot'
  g. /wap-ka/ → [wahka] 'your foot'
  h. /wapaka/ → [wapaka] 'your foot'

Root-final consonants are even more uncommon for verb roots. Unfortunately, there is no data on consonant-final verb roots in the incompletive aspect. Note that most of the word-final consonants above are themselves morphemes added to the verb root. The few cases where the final consonant is part of the root all occur in noninherently possessed nouns and therefore are not expected to form clusters with the possessive suffixes.

 Finally, while still word internal, the addition of some pronominal prefixes creates consonant clusters across morpheme boundaries at the beginning of the root. For example, the suffix *in-* '1SG' in Guazacapán creates clusters composed of the alveolar nasal and any of the permitted word-initial consonants discussed above. Examples are given in 41.

(41) Guazacapán consonant clusters across morpheme boundaries.
  a. /ɨn-tʼumʼay/ [ɨn-dʼumʼay] 'my tail (bone)'
  b. /ɨn-tiya/ [ɨn-diya] 'my uncle'
  c. /ɨn-waakaʼ/ [ɨŋ-waakaʼ] 'I left'
  d. /ɨn-pikʼi/ [ɨm-bikʼi] 'my bird'

2.3 Phonological alternations

The phonemes in every language in the world are not a static set of sounds. Variation in pronunciation occurs when consonants and vowels are used in certain environments or under specific conditions. This is true for Xinkan as well. The vowels and consonants have allophonic variations that alter their pronunciations. Consonants have allophones as result of glottalization, voicing, nasal assimilation, stop-lenition to /h/, and dissimilation. Vowels have allophonic variations in conjunction with vowel harmony (discussed above in section 2.1.2) and with vowel raising.

2.3.1 Glottalization

In Xinkan languages the phonetic pairing of glottalized and nonglottalized consonants is phonologically important. These differences signal changes in meaning in minimal pairs. In general they also have similar distributional patterns; both are used word initially and word medially. However, there are three areas of interest where this phonological distinction is neutralized. First, in the speech patterns of some individuals glottalized and nonglottalized pairs are used randomly. Second, a nonglottalized consonant is pronounced as its glottalized counterpart in some morphological environments. Third, a glottalized consonant loses its glottalization when followed by a glottal stop in the next syllable.

2.3.1.1   *Individual speaker variation of glottalized consonants*
Individual speaker variation in the production of glottalized consonants is common in the speech of the few current remaining speakers of the languages. This variation results in an ordinarily plain consonant being pronounced as its glottalized counterpart, or vice versa. This variation occurs with no apparent motivating contextual factors. This is not surprising considering the lack of a speaking community and the absence of fully native speakers of any of the Xinkan languages. This variation is a type of phonetic deterioration caused by language loss and is not a native part of Xinkan grammar or a historical part of the grammar of Proto-Xinkan.

One plausible explanation for these alternations is that the phonological contrasts between plain and ejective consonants are being lost through contact with more 'prestigious' languages where these contrasts do not exist, such as Spanish. Related to this case of free variation is an interesting case of hypercorrection and social-linguistic distancing. Speakers know that ejective consonants exist in Xinkan, though at times they are unsure of where they should pronounce them according to Xinkan grammar. This results in many instances of overgeneralization, and glottalized consonants are included in every possible location within a word (i.e., hypercorrection). In other cases speakers attempt to distinguish themselves from other surrounding languages and communities by sounding more 'Xinkalike'. This results in a higher number of glottalized consonants in the speakers' use of both Xinkan and Spanish.

This type of speaker-specific variation does not create a problem in determining the phonological patterns of Xinkan because generalized patterns clearly emerge when looking at the data across speakers and speaking times. However, it is of interest in documenting the ongoing changes in the languages. An example of the free variation between glottalized and nonglottalized consonants is shown in 42. The speaker variation is on the left between square brackets and the target pronunciation is given between slashes. The gloss is given on the right.

(42)   Free variation in glottalized consonants: Guazacapán.
        [maku] ~ [mak'u]   /mak'u/   'house'

Speakers have been documented producing this type of variation for only a small portion of Xinkan words.[13] It is interesting to note that in all the previous work on Xinkan languages, none of the previous grammars or dictionaries indicates the use of ejective or glottalized consonants by their consultants (although Calderón was at least aware of them in Chiquimulilla and Yupiltepeque; see my discussion of his 'letras heridas' [wounded letters] in section 6.3.1.2).

2.3.1.2   *Morphological contexts of glottalization*
While the idiolectal variation mentioned above is important to the understanding of language obsolescence, it does not form part of the native Xinkan grammar. In contrast, there is a phonological process of glottalization that is essential to the description of Xinkan phonology and morphology. In this process, and in specific morphological situations (see below), nonglottalized consonants are regularly pronounced as their glottalized counterparts.

Specifically, the rightmost consonant of a verb is glottalized (pronounced as a glottalized consonant) when the stem is inflected for the incompletive aspect or derived into the verbal noun.[14] This process of glottalization is shown in 43–45, with the underlying verb on the left and the verbal noun on the right.

(43) Guazacapán glottalization with verb aspect.

    a. *hini*   *hin'i*
       learn.PERF   learn.IPERF
       'learn, know' '(the) learning'

    b. *k'ani*   *k'an'i*
       trap.PERF   trap.IPERF
       'trap'   '(the) trapping'

    c. *miimi*   *miim'i*
       sing.PERF   sing.IPERF
       'sing'   'song'

    d. *tałi*   *tal'i*
       burn.PERF   burn.IPERF
       'burn'   '(the) burning'

    e. *waki*   *wak'i*
       play.PERF   play.IPERF
       'play'   '(the) game'

(44) Chiquimulilla glottalization with verb aspect.

    a. *ts'uru*   *ts'ur'u*
       wet.PERF   wet.IPERF
       'wet'   'wetting'

    b. *uwi*   *uw'i*
       call.PERF   call.IPERF
       'call'   '(the) call'

    c. *wiiša*   *wiits'a*
       shake.out.PERF   shake.out.IPERF
       'shake out'   '(the) shaking out'

    d. *šuka*   *šuk'a*
       bite.PERF   bite.IPERF
       'bite'   '(the) biting'

(45) Jumaytepeque glottalization with verb aspect.

    a. *ima*   *im'a*
       say.PERF   say.IPERF
       'say'   '(the) saying'

    b. *kiri*   *kir'i*
       pull.PERF   pull.IPERF
       'pull'   '(the) pulling'

    c. *niwa*   *niw'a*
       ask.PERF   ask.IPERF
       'ask'   '(the) asking'

While this process is completely productive for all verb and verbal noun pairs, there are additional characteristics of this change that play a role in the grammar of Xinkan. The first trait is that glottalization applies vacuously in verbs that already have an underlying glottalized consonant as their rightmost consonant. This is shown in 46–48. Only one example is given from each language because verbal aspect is treated in more detail in section 3.6.3 and because it is the same process as that detailed in 43–45 above.

(46)   Guazacapán glottalization opacity.
    hilʼa   *hilʼa*
    empty.PERF empty.IPERF
    'empty'   '(the) emptying'

(47)   Chiquimulilla glottalization opacity.
    hikʼa   *hikʼa*
    sew.PERF sew.IPERF
    'sew'   '(the) sewing'

(48)   Jumaytepeque glottalization opacity.
    hitʼa   *hitʼa*
    empty.PERF empty.IPERF
    'empty'   '(the) emptying'

The second important characteristic of this glottalization process is exhibited in verbs with word-medial consonant clusters. The glottalization of the rightmost consonant affects the last member of the cluster, often creating a prohibited consonant CCʼ cluster (see section 2.2.4.4 above). In this situation an epenthetic vowel is inserted between the two consonants in the cluster, thereby making the sound string acceptable. The epenthetic vowel is [a] if the vowels on either side of the consonant cluster differ from one another; or the epenthetic vowel mirrors the vowels on either side of the cluster if these two vowels are identical to one another. In general, phonological notation the epenthetic vowel follows the rule in 49.

(49)   Epenthetic vowel rule.
$$\emptyset \to \begin{cases} [a] & / & V_1C\_\_C'V_2 \\ V_1 & / & V_1C\_\_C'V_1 \end{cases}$$

However, in Jumaytepeque the epenthetic vowel has a further limitation. If the vowel immediately preceding the consonant cluster is the mid vowel [o] and the vowel following the consonant cluster is [e], then the epenthetic vowel is [e]. This only happens in a very few words, but it is predictable. Consequently the phonological rule in 50—an additional modification of 49—applies only in Jumaytepeque.

(50)   Jumaytepeque epenthetic vowel rule.
$$\emptyset \to [e] \ / \ oC\_\_C'e$$

Examples of vowel insertion are given in 51–53.

(51) Guazacapán vowel epenthesis.

    a. *apla*   *apal'a*
       open.PERF   open.IPERF
       'open'   '(the) opening'

    b. *p'ahni*   *p'ahan'i*
       dig.PERF   dig.IPERF
       'dig'   '(the) digging'

    c. *p'uhru*   *p'uhur'u*
       make.holes.PERF   make.holes.IPERF
       'make holes'   '(the) hole-making'

    d. *k'eɬke*   *k'eɬek'e*
       extend.PERF   extend.IPERF
       'extend'   '(the) extending'

    e. *hurpi*   *hurap'i*
       rub.PERF   rub.IPERF
       'rub'   '(the) rubbing'

(52) Chiquimulilla vowel epenthesis.

    a. *eɬwa*   *eɬaw'a*
       sweep.house.PERF   sweep.house.IPERF
       'sweep house'   '(the) house-sweeping'

    b. *č'arka*   *č'arak'a*
       open.mouth.PERF   open.mouth.IPERF
       'open one's mouth'   '(the) opening of one's mouth'

    c. *tintu*   *tinat'u*
       play.music.PERF   play.music.IPERF
       'play music'   '(the) music-playing'

    d. *hirki*   *hirik'i*
       wag.PERF   wag.IPERF
       'wag'   '(the) wagging'

    e. *ohro*   *ohor'o*
       singe.PERF   singe.IPERF
       'singe'   '(the) singeing'

(53) Jumaytepeque vowel epenthesis.

    a. *hulku*   *huluk'u*
       poke.PERF   poke.IPERF
       'to poke'   '(the) poking, prodding'

    b. *hupni*   *hupan'i*
       bend.PERF   bend.IPERF
       'bend, fold'   (the) bending, folding'

    c. *ɨrsɨ*   *ɨrits'ɨ*
       bite.PERF   bite.IPERF
       'bite'   '(the) biting'

    d. *kolko*   *kolok'o*
       vacate.PERF   vacate.IPERF
       'to vacate'   '(the) moving out'

e. *eple*   *epel'e*
   be.afraid.PERF   be.afraid.IPERF
   'be afraid of'   'fear'

f. *k'orwe*   *k'orew'e*
   dig.PERF   dig.IPERF
   'dig'   '(the) digging'

g. *ošwe*   *ošew'e*
   scrape.pot.PERF   scrape.pot.IPERF
   'scrape pot'   '(the) scraping of a pot' (by washing)

An epenthetic vowel is also inserted between a word-final [n] and a suffix-initial [ɬ] as in the plural morpheme. The same rules as discussed immediately above apply, but see sections 3.1.2 and 2.1.1.2.4 for examples.

2.3.1.3   *Glottalization processes*

Beside the glottalization of consonants, a few other related changes also take place. Specifically, not all the plain consonants in the inventory have glottalized counterparts (fricatives in particular), meaning that when these sounds occur in the glottalizing context, an additional phonological alteration occurs. For example, the consonants /s/ and /š/ become [ts'] in the glottalized processes, and /ɬ/ when glottalized becomes [l'] in Guazacapán and Chiquimulilla but [t'] in Jumaytepeque. The process in 54 indicates this in a more visually depictive way.

(54)   Consonant alternation under glottalization in Xinkan.

$$\left.\begin{array}{c} /s/ \\ /š/ \end{array}\right\} \;\rightarrow\; [\text{ts'}] \quad \text{All Xinkan languages}$$

    $/ɬ/^{15} \;\rightarrow\; [\text{l'}] \quad$ Guazacapán, Chiquimulilla only

    $/ɬ/ \;\rightarrow\; [\text{t'}] \quad$ Jumaytepeque only

Examples of these generalizations are given in 55–57.

(55)   Guazacapán glottalized consonant alternations.

  a. *ɨrsɨ*   *irits'i*
     bite.PERF   bite.IPERF
     'bite'   '(the) biting'

  b. *kiši*   *kits'i*
     roast.PERF   roast.IPERF
     'roast'   '(the) roasting'

  c. *k'oɬo*   *k'ol'o*
     peel.PERF   peel.IPERF
     'peel'   '(the) peeling'

(56)   Chiquimulilla glottalized consonant alternations.

  a. *paasa*   *paats'a*
     store.in.a.tanate.PERF   store.in.a.tanate.IPERF (tanate = a kind of basket)
     'to store in a basket'   '(the) storage in a basket'

b. *aši*   *ats'i*
   burn.PERF   burn.IPERF
   'burn'   '(the) burning'
c. *t'oło*   *t'ol'o*
   wrap.up.PERF   wrap.up.IPERF
   'wrap up'   '(the) wrapping up'

(57)   Jumaytepeque glottalized consonant alternations.
     a. *p'eesa*   *p'eets'a*
        knead.dough.PERF   knead.dough.IPERF
        'knead dough'   '(the) kneading of dough'
     b. *šawša*   *šawats'a*
        SOW.PERF   SOW.IPERF
        'sow'   '(the) planting'

2.3.1.4 *Deglottalization processes*

A related process occurs in the formation of an intransitive affective verb from a transitive verb (see section 3.12.3.2). When the IV.AFF suffix *-ʔ* is added to a transitive verb, any underlying glottalized consonant in the immediately preceding syllable is deglottalized—the inverse of the process of glottalization just discussed. It is theoretically significant that this deglottalization process can happen to any consonant manner: stops, affricates, fricatives, or sonorants, as shown below. Examples are given in 58–60. In these examples, the transitive verb is given on the left. In the middle column the derived intransitive verb form is given. The rightmost column indicates the underlying form of the verb.

(58)   Guazacapán deglottalization in the intransitive affective derivation.
     a. *her'o*   *heero-ʔ*   /her'o/
        smooth.TV   smooth-IV.AFF
        'smooth'   'it smoothed'
     b. *p'el'o*   *p'eeło-ʔ*   /p'eľo/
        peel.TV   peel-IV.AFF
        'peel'   'it peeled'
     c. *paats'i*   *paaši-ʔ*   /paaš'i/
        grind.TV   grind-IV.AFF
        'grind'   'it ground'
     d. *poč'o*   *poočo-ʔ*   /poč'o/
        rot.TV   rot-IV.AFF
        'rot'   'it rotted, spoiled'

(59)   Chiquimulilla deglottalization in the intransitive affective derivation.
     a. *hap'a*   *haapa-ʔ*   /hap'a/
        pass.TV   pass-IV.AFF
        'pass'   'it passed'

    b. *mats'i*   *maaši-ʔ*   /maš'i/
        fry.TV   fry-IV.AFF
        'fry'   'it fried'

    c. *ɬuhts'u*   *ɬuhts'u-ʔ*   /luhts'u/
        sting.TV   sting-IV.AFF
        'sting'   'it stung' (insect)

    d. *mɨy'a*   *mɨɨya-ʔ*   /miy'a/
        help.TV   help-IV.AFF
        'help'   'it helped'

(60)   Jumaytepeque deglottalization in the intransitive affective derivation.

    a. *ets'e*   *eese-ʔ*   /es'e/
        flatten.TV   flatten-IV.AFF
        'to flatten'   'it flattened'

    b. *ir'i*   *iiri-ʔ*   /ir'i/
        see.TV   see-IV.AFF
        'see'   'it saw'

    c. *hiɬ'a*   *hiɨla-ʔ*   /hiɬ'a/ < *hiɬ'a
        empty.TV   empty-IV.AFF
        'empty'   'it emptied'

    d. *lit'a*   *liita-ʔ*   /lit'a/
        press.against.TV   press.against-IV.AFF
        'press against (wall)'   'it pressed against (a wall)'

    e. *t'ol'o*   *t'oolo-ʔ*   /t'ol'o/ < *t'oɬ'o
        wrap.up.TV   wrap.up-IV.AFF
        'wrap up'   'it wrapped up'

The historical significance of deglottalization is treated in section 6.5.

2.3.2   Voicing of stop following a nasal

As with many languages in the world, and specifically in several other Mesoamerican languages, plain (nonglottalized) voiceless stops become voiced stops when they are immediately preceded by a nasal consonant.[16] This voicing process is exhibited both within words and across morpheme boundaries. A rule representing this phonological process is offered in 61.

(61)   Voicing of plain voiceless stop.
       {p, t, k} → / [+nasal] _____
       {b, d, g}

This is true for all words that exhibit the phonetic environment, except for one word in Jumaytepeque Xinka. The word 'snake' [ampuki] does not undergo voicing assimilation in Jumaytepeque, but it does in both Guazacapán and Chiquimulilla, [ambuki]. There do not seem to be any apparent linguistic reasons that this isolated word does not require stop-voicing after the nasal. The examples in 62–64 provide words illustrating this alternation. In these examples the citation form is given as the underlying form in slashes, and the surface phonetic pronunciation is given in square brackets.

(62) Guazacapán voiceless stop-voicing.

/ampuki/	[ambuki]	'snake'
/tumpiya/	[tumbiya]	'basket'
/tulumpuʔ/	[tulumbuʔ]	'longnose'
/hanta/	[handa]	'why?'
/ɨnta/	[ɨnda]	'let's ...'
/ɨntɨ/	[ɨndɨ]	'spy'
/manta/	[manda]	'how about ... ?'
/tunti/	[tundi]	'play music'
/tonton/	[tondoŋ]	'sea turtle'
/činkɨʔ/	[čiŋgɨʔ]	'skinny, thin'
/nankun/	[naŋguŋ]	'late'
/ɬunku/	[ɬuŋgu]	'stub, stump, cut off'
/šinkɨʔ/	[šiŋgɨʔ]	'scarred'
/t'inka/	[t'iŋga]	'hit'
/šan pari/	[šam bari]	'in day, during day, in the daytime'
/ɨn-taata/	[ɨn-daata]	'my father'
/ɨn-kawayu/	[ɨŋ-gawayu]	'my horse' (<Sp. *'caballo'*)

(63) Chiquimulilla voiceless stop-voicing.

/hampaʔ/	[hambaʔ]	'gall'
/ampuki/	[ambuki]	'snake'
/ɬantiʔ/	[ɬandiʔ]	'no'
/tintu/	[tindu]	'play music'
/intiʔ aɬi/	[indiʔ aɬi]	'why?'
/intɨ/	[indɨ]	'spy'
/šanki/	[šaŋgi]	'stomach'
/sonkoʔ/	[soŋgoʔ]	'tall'
/šan pu-h/	[šam buh]	'in his hand'
/ɨn-tal'a/	[ɨn-dal'a]	'I burned it.'
/ɨn-kɨɨši/	[ɨŋ-gɨɨši]	'my half'

(64) Jumaytepeque voiceless stop-voicing.

/ampuki/	[ampuki]	'snake'
/hanta/	[handa]	'foolish'
/ɨntar/	[ɨndar]	'go!'
/šinkɨ/	[šiŋgɨ]	'chew'
/tɨnkɨ/	[tɨŋgɨ]	'push backwards'
/n-paaši/	[əm-paaši]	'I sharpened it.'
/n-tamši/	[ən-damši]	'I twisted it.'
/n-kunu/	[əŋ-gunu]	'I bought it.'

2.3.3   Nasal assimilation

In conjunction with the voicing of stops preceding a nasal consonant, there is also alternation in the place of articulation for the nasal consonants. Specifically, the place of articulation of a nasal consonant assimilates to the place of articulation of an adjacent consonant. The phonological rule in 65 indicates how nasal assimilation works in all of the Xinkan languages.

(65)   Nasal assimilation rule.

$$[+\text{nasal}][\text{alveolar}] \rightarrow \left\{ \begin{array}{l} [\alpha \text{ place}] \\ \eta \end{array} \right\} \quad \begin{array}{l} /\_\_\_ \\ /\_\_\_ \\ /\_\_\_ \end{array} \left\{ \begin{array}{l} [+\text{consonantal}][\alpha \text{ place}] \\ \{\#\} \\ [\text{m}] \end{array} \right\}$$

Examples of nasal assimilation are presented for each of the Xinkan languages in 66–68.

(66)   Guazacapán nasal assimilation.
   a. /šan pari/   [šam bari]   'during day, in the daytime'
   b. /ɨn-taata/   [ɨn-daata]   'my father'
   c. /ɨn-kawayu/   [ɨŋ-gawayu]   'my horse' (<Sp. '*caballo*')
   d. /ɨn-maku/   [ɨŋ-maku]   'my house'

(67)   Chiquimulilla nasal assimilation.
   a. /šan pu-h/   [šam buh]   'in his hand'
   b. /ɨn-tal'a/   [ɨn-dal'a]   'I burned it.'
   c. /ɨn-kɨ̈ši/   [ɨŋ-gɨ̈ši]   'my half'
   d. /ɨn-mačiti/   [ɨŋ-mačiti]   'my machete' (<Sp. '*machete*')

(68)   Jumaytepeque nasal assimilation.
   a. /n-paaši/   [əm-paaši]   'I sharpened it.'
   b. /n-tamši/   [ən-damši]   'I twisted it.'
   c. /n-kunu/   [əŋ-gunu]   'I bought it.'
   d. /n-mɨɨmɨ/   [əŋ-mɨɨmɨ]   'I sing.'

2.3.4   Lenition to [h]

Three consonants, /t/, /k/, and /ɬ/, are reduced to [h] when they occur as the first member of a consonant cluster. In general this allophonic change occurs both word internally in consonant clusters and across morpheme boundaries (i.e., when the sound undergoing the change is word final before another word or before a bound morpheme beginning with a consonant). The rule in 69 shows how this change occurs.[17]

(69)   Lenition to [h].
   {/t/, /ɬ/, /k/} → [h]/V___{(##)/(+)}C

The three consonants targeted in this process of change are always affected across morpheme boundaries. However, when it is part of a word-internal consonant cluster this change is less strict. Speakers consistently offer an alternate pronunciation with the unreduced stop for these words. Note that similar processes are exhibited in Mayan languages within the linguistic area. For example, in Yucatec Mayan a velar stop is reduced to [h] when it occurs before another consonant: /k/ → [h]/__C.[18] This change, furthermore, is common cross-linguistically. The Yucatec example is relevant only to show that this process is not isolated to Xinkan languages within the linguistic area. The examples in 70–72 show how these changes occur.

(70) Guazacapán.
    a. /netka/   [nehka] or [netka]   'push'
    b. /toktok/   [tohtok] or [toktok]   'mockingbird'
    c. /pełteme/   [pehteme]   'return something'
    d. /ełma/   [ehwa]   'loan, borrow'
    e. /huurak-łi/   [huurahłi]   'the men'
    f. /hoorol-łi/   [hoorohłi]   'guardians'

(71) Chiquimulilla.
    a. /etka/   [ehka] or [etka]   'cover'
    b. /pałta/   [pahta]   'pay'
    c. /čikwit-łi/   [čikwihłi]   'baskets'
    d. /harnał-łi/   [harnahłi]   'sick people'

(72) Jumaytepeque.
    a. /netka/   [nehka] or [netka]   'push'
    b. /etka/   [ehka] or [etka]   'cover'
    c. /šakša/   [šahša] or [šakša]   'steal'
    d. /nɨm'a-k-li/   [nɨm'ahli]   'napkins'
    e. /ay'al-li/   [ay'ahli]   'women'

2.3.5   Vowel raising

There are only two allophonic processes that affect vowels. The first is the vowel assimilation discussed in conjunction with vowel harmony. Nothing more will be said about that here. The second is limited in scope but entirely productive in Xinkan; I refer to this process as vowel raising.

As a result of this process, a low vowel /a/ is pronounced as the mid vowel [e] before the palatal glide [y] or [y']. Moreover, a distributional restriction on this variation is observed: vowel raising only happens across morpheme boundaries and never stem-internally. The palatal glide pairing that acts as trigger for this process is the first segment in certain grammatical suffixes, and it is with these suffixes that the process is observed. Vowel raising is indicated in standard phonological rule format in 73.

(73) Vowel raising.
    /a/ → [e]/__{+/##}{y', y}

Examples are given in 74–76. The underlying form is given on the left and the surface form, after vowel raising, is shown on the right.

(74) Guazacapán.
  a. /ima-y'/   [imey']
    say.PERF-3SG
    'S/he said it.'
  b. /hɨya-y'/   [hɨyey']
    chop.PERF-3SG
    'S/he chopped it.'
  c. /hut'a-y'/   [hut'ey']
    blow.PERF-3SG
    'S/he blew (on) it.'

(75) Chiquimulilla.
  a. /šuka-y/   [šukey]
    bite.PERF-2SG.INFORM
    'You bit it.'
  b. /yɨw'a-y'/   [yɨw'ey']
    lose.PERF-3SG
    'S/he lost it.'
  c. /niwa-y/   [niwey]
    ask.PERF-2SG.INFORM
    'You ask someone.'

(76) Jumaytepeque.
  a. /eela-y/   [eeley]
    tongue-2SG.INFORM
    'your tongue'
  b. /k'ušta-yi/   [k'ušteyi]
    poke.PERF-3SG
    'S/he poked it.'
  c. /hɨka-y/   [hɨkey]
    weave.PERF-2SG.INFORM
    'You weave it.'

This would appear to clash with the vowel harmony rules given above in section 2.1.2, since as a result of this process [e] can occur with non-mid vowels. However, the vowel harmony patterns apply to a word before this phonological operation affects the surface vowel—before these *y* or *y'* initial suffixes trigger vowel raising. Vowel harmony is a process constraining underlying co-occurrence of vowels while vowel raising targets the surface (phonetic) representation of /a/ before [y] or [y'].

2.3.6 Glottal-stop epenthesis

There is one phonetic context where consonant epenthesis occurs. Specifically, a phonetic glottal stop is added to all words that begin with a vowel—especially when the word that immediately precedes a vowel-initial word ends with a vowel. This process is presented in rule 77, and examples are provided in 78–80.

77) Word-initial consonant epenthesis.

Ø → [ʔ]/#__V

(78) Guazacapán word-initial glottal-stop epenthesis.
   a. /aara/ → [ʔaara] 'worm'
   b. /em'a/ → [ʔem'a] 'sew'
   c. /ima/ → [ʔima] 'say'
   d. /ɨra/ → [ʔɨra] 'big'

(79) Chiquimulilla word-initial glottal-stop epenthesis.
   a. /apla/ → [ʔapla] 'open'
   b. /em'a/ → [ʔem'a] 'handkerchief'
   c. /iw'aɬ/ → [ʔiw'aɬ] 'ant'
   d. /ɨyɨ/ → [ʔɨyɨ] 'gopher'

(80) Jumaytepeque word-initial glottal-stop epenthesis.
   a. /al/ → [ʔal] 'on, in'
   b. /eple/ → [ʔeple] 'be afraid of'
   c. /ir'i/ → [ʔir'i] 'look'
   d. /in'ɨ/ → [ʔin'ɨ] 'stretch'

2.3.7 Consonant dissimilation

There is a marginal process of consonant dissimilation in Xinkan. Two glottalized consonants in adjacent syllables are prohibited, and (usually) the second consonant is deglottalized. This is represented in 81; Co in the equation means any number (including zero) and type of consonants, glottalized or plain.

(81) Glottalized consonant dissimilation.

C' → C / C'V(V)(Co)+__

There are idiosyncratic patterns for the pronunciation of glottalized consonants (see section 2.3.1). However, in general consonant dissimilation is true for all Xinkan languages. Examples with the INCHOATIVE/ANTIPASSIVE suffix -*k'i* are provided in 82–84; the suffix -*k'i* is discussed in sections 3.12.3.1 and 3.12.3.5.

(82) Guazacapán dissimilation.
   a. /em'a-k'i/ → [em'aki] 'sew'
   b. /ets'e-k'i/ → [ets'eke] 'break open'
   c. /hɨl'a-k'i/ → [hɨl'aki] 'empty'
   d. /k'iir'a-k'i/ → [k'iir'aki] 'scratch'
   e. /k'et'o-k'i/ → [k'et'oke] 'hang'
   f. /ur'ulh/ → [ur'ulhki] 'lay eggs'
   g. /tz'orna+k'i/ → [tz'ornaki] 'drip'

(83) Chiquimulilla dissimilation.
    a. /hišm'a-k'i/ → [hišm'aki] 'sneeze'
    b. /moor'o-k'i/ → [moor'oke] 'become spotted'
    c. /č'oy'e-k'i/ → [č'oy'eke] 'fold, bend'
    d. /pałt'a-k'i/ → [pałt'aki] 'pay'
    e. /sɨm'a-k'i/ → [sɨm'aki] 'to dirty'
    f. /hur'uł-k'i/ → [hur'ulhki] 'to straighten'
    g. /k'osna-k'i/ → [k'osnaki] 'to whip'

(84) Jumaytepeque dissimilation.
    a. /saar'a-k'i/ → [saar'aki] 'become cold'
    b. /t'ɨk'ɨ-k'i/ → [t'ɨk'iki] 'become miserable'
    c. /yoč'o-k'i/ → [yoč'oke] 'wash'
    d. /łɨk'ɨ-k'i/ → [łɨk'iki] 'find'
    e. /uyč'u-k'i/ → [uyč'uki] 'to wrinkle'
    f. /ɨp'iš-k'i/ → [ɨp'iški] 'to breed, bring up'
    g. /k'ašna-k'i/ → [k'ašnaki] 'to measure, weigh'

2.3.8 Guazacapán consonant deletion

Guazacapán has a minor allophonic change that is restricted to only two words. They are important to the grammar of this language but are not a part of general Xinkan grammar. In this variation, a word-medial glottal stop is deleted when the words *paʔał* and *naʔał* are used anywhere but clause finally. The rule for the variation is given in 85. Examples are presented in 86 with the clause-final variants on the left and the variants corresponding to other clause positions on the right.

(85) Word-internal *[ʔ]* deletion.
    [ʔ] → Ø / CV₁___V₁C (non–clause final)

(85) Word-internal *[ʔ]* deletion.
    [ʔ] → Ø / CV_1___V_1C (non–clause final)

(86) Guazacapán word-internal glottal-stop deletion.
    [paʔał] clause final [pał] non–clause final 'epistemic mood particle'
    [naʔał] clause final [nał] non–clause final 'past tense particle'

It is possible to view this process as the reverse, as epenthesizing a glottal stop rather than deleting it. In this view, the glottal stop would be added clause finally in these two words. There seems to be little evidence that the correct analysis favors one way or the other—either as a deletion or as epenthesis.

2.3.8.1 *Other consonant deletion*

In one other marginal case, both Guazacapán and Chiquimulilla exhibit consonant deletion. When the plural suffix -*łi* is used with a noun that ends in the lateral approximant segment [ł], this word-final consonant is deleted. The example in 87 below is taken from the data on Guazacapán; for the plural formation in general see section 3.1.2.

(87) Consonant deletion with the plural suffix.

/ts'iimał/	/ts'iim'ał-i/	/tz'iimalhi-lhi/
'person from Guaz.'	'people from Guazacapán'	
'Guazacapaneco'	'Guazapenecos'	

2.4 Syllable structure

Xinkan syllable structure is uncontroversial. Each syllable consists of three abstract elements: a required nucleus, a required onset, and an optional coda. Vowels are the only segments that are permitted to serve as the nucleus. Only one consonant is permitted in either the onset or the coda-position syllables. This means that the basic syllable in Xinkan can be illustrated as CV. Phonotactic constraints on segment occurrence are discussed in sections 2.2.5 and 2.1.2.

Beyond the basic syllable structure, Xinkan does have constraints on what can make up a legal string of syllables. First, in general, bisyllabic roots predominate for Xinkan words: CVCV. However, a few lexical roots and words with inflectional and derivational morphology have one, two, three, or four syllables. Second, long vowels are restricted to specific types of syllables. Long vowels cannot be the nucleus of a closed syllable and cannot be the nuclei of two adjacent syllables: neither **.CVVC. nor **.CVVCVV. is permitted as a syllable type.[19] Third, all syllables must phonetically have an onset. If there is not an underlying consonant in the onset position, a glottal stop is epenthesized. Onsets and codas are never complex.[20] Consider the words in 88, taken from the Guazacapán lexicon, that show relevant examples of the possible syllable structures. In all of these examples a period represents a syllable boundary, or margin.

(88) Guazacapán syllables.

[na]	'the'	CV.	
[ʔuy]	'water'	CVC.	
[na.ka]	'you'	CV.CV	
[hɨ.yak]	'hatchet'	CV.CVC	
[ʔa.ku.k'i]	'walk'	CV.CV.CV	
[ʔa.ra.t'ak]	'century plant'	CV.CV.CVC	
[ʔi.pa.ła.k'i]	'bathe'	CV.CV.CV.CV	← /ipła-k'i/
[mɨ.ka.ki.łaʔ]	'employ'	CV.CV.CV.CVC	← /mɨka-k'i-łaʔ/
[ʔii.pe.maa.kuh]	'There he comes.'	CVV.CV.CVV.CVC	← /iipemaaku-h/
[peh.te.me]	'return'	CVC.CV.CV	← /pełteme/
[haypu]	'receive'	CVC.CV	
[ʔɨy.kɨk]	'dragging tool'	CVC.CVC	

These observations suggest, consequently, that the basic syllable structure in Xinkan is '#CV(V/C)' word initially (i.e., V, VV, VC, CV, CVV, or CVC), but 'CV(V/C)' word internally (i.e., CV, CVV, CVC).

As discussed in section 2.2.5.4, consonant clusters are allowed word internally in

Xinkan but only following specific phonotactic constraints and only when they belong to separate syllables.

2.5   Stress

Alternations in acoustic pitch in Mesoamerican languages result in lexical tonal contrasts (i.e, tones), or lexical stress (i.e., accent). Xinkan languages do not have tonal contrasts. However, Xinkan lexical stress, similar to other languages in the linguistic area, is predictable and regular. Stress assignment in Xinkan languages is straightforward: the stressed syllable, or more accurately the stress-bearing vowel, is always the last vowel before the rightmost consonant. This is represented in 89.

(89)   Xinkan stress placement.
$$V \rightarrow \acute{V} \, / \, \_C(V)\#$$

Because stress is highly predictable in Xinkan languages, it is normally not indicated in the practical orthography (see section 2.6), but is marked in 90 as a means of illustration: stress is marked with the acute accent. The words in 90 are taken from the Chiquimulilla lexicon, though the stress patterns are applicable to all of the Xinkan languages.

(90)   Chiquimulilla word stress.
    a. *t'um'á-y*   'his/her tail'
    b. *áɬi*   'on, over'
    c. *párni*   'break'
    d. *t'uúri*   'child'
    e. *t'uurí-n'*   'my child'
    f. *saɬtáma*   'ant'

As a note of clarification, in most words (i.e., those that end in a vowel), stress is placed on the penultimate syllable. However, if a grammatical morpheme of the shape /-C(V)/ is added to a word, the stress shifts to immediately before this suffix, as in *t'uúri* 'child' and *t'uurí-n'* 'my child' in 90. To the point: stress is not specified in a lexical component of Xinkan grammar but is sensitive to the morphophonological level of word formation.

2.6   Orthography

In this section, the orthographic equivalent of each of the Xinkan phonemes given above is presented. The orthography is that provided in Guatemala, sanctioned by the Guatemalan government as the standardized spelling of native languages in that country, and it has been accepted by Xinkan communities.[21]
All Xinkan examples in subsequent chapters, except for chapter 6, which deals with the historical reconstruction of Xinkan sounds, are presented using this orthographic system.

Sound/IPA	Letter	Sound/IPA	Letter
i	i	ʔ	'
ɨ	ü	h	h
u	u	s	s
e	e	š	x
o	o	f	f
a	a	l	l
p	p	l'	l'
p'	p'	ɬ	lh
b	b	r	r
t	t	r'	r'
t'	t'	m	m
d	d	m'	m'
k	k	n	n
k'	k'	n'	n'
g	g	w	w
ts'	tz'	w'	w'
č	ch	y	y
č'	ch'	y'	y'

THREE

Morphology

This chapter explains the morphology of the Xinkan languages. I focus on describing the four major grammatical categories (parts of speech) and the six minor grammatical categories observed in Xinkan grammar. The distributional restrictions and inflectional and derivational processes that define each category are outlined in detail. The four major grammatical categories are NOUNS, ADJECTIVES, PRONOUNS, and VERBS. The six minor grammatical categories are DETERMINERS, RELATIONAL NOUNS, VERBAL PARTICLES, NOMINAL PARTICLES, QUESTION WORDS, and CONJUNCTIONS. All of the major grammatical categories are characterized by content morphemes, while the minor grammatical categories are composed of function morphemes.

Each of these ten grammatical categories are defined based on various morphological patterns and distributional characteristics, including

- meaning
- number
- person
- possession
- use of the diminutive suffix
- predicate arguments
- use of the intransitiver suffix -k'i
- grade
- predication
- tense-aspect-mood.

3.1   Nouns

Xinkan nouns semantically denote a physical object, abstract concept, or entity.[1] In addition to this broad semantic definition, nouns are defined based on five morphosyntactic properties: (1) they can be inflected for number; (2) they can be inflected for possession; (3) they can be inflected with the diminutive suffix; (4) they can be the base of a derived inchoative verb using the suffix -k'i; and (5) they can function as the dependents, or arguments, of verbs and prepositions.[2]

Each of these morphological properties organizes nouns into definable subgroups, or subtypes. For example, some nouns can be inflected for number while others cannot be, leaving two broad noun types. Similarly, some nouns may be possessed while others may not, isolating two broad types that crosscut the other noun groups. Based on this morphological grouping of nouns, three broad noun classes are evident: COMMON NOUNS, PROPER NOUNS, and MASS NOUNS. There is no morphological marking of these noun classes (such as nominal classifiers), but understanding the lexically specified class of each noun is necessary for creating acceptable utterances in Xinkan.

Common nouns can be inflected for possession without a change in the semantics, can be marked for number, can host the diminutive clitic, and can be the base of a derived inchoative verb. In comparison, proper nouns are never possessed, are not inflected for number, may be inflected with the diminutive, and never function as the base of a derived inchoative verb. Finally, mass nouns are never inflected for number; when possessed they imply a change in the semantics;[3] they are not inflected with the diminutive clitic; and they may be the base of an inchoative verb. These differences are summarized in table 3.1.

Table 3.1 Comparison of the morphological properties of Xinkan noun classes

	Possession	Number	Diminutive clitic	Inchoative verb
Common noun	Yes	Yes	Yes	Yes
Proper noun	No	No	Yes	No
Mass noun	Yes, with a change in semantics	No	No	Yes

The majority of nouns in Xinkan are common nouns. There are not many mass nouns (attested), and when possessed they always pattern like alienable nouns (see section 3.1.1.1). Proper nouns have a single referent that is part of the shared experience of all participants in a conversation—these include the names of people and places. Examples from Guazacapán Xinka of the three Xinkan nouns types are given in 91–93, but the general pattern holds for all the Xinkan languages.

(91) Examples of proper nouns.
   a. *hwan* 'John'
   b. *tuuru'* name of the cultural hero of the Xinkan myths
   c. *tz'üümalh* 'the town of Guazacapán'

(92) Examples of mass nouns.
   a. *uy* 'water'
   b. *wati* 'mud'
   c. *nuuru* 'pus'

(93) Examples of common nouns.
   a. *pak'i* 'wall'
   b. *huurak* 'man'
   c. *peelo'* 'dog'

Each of the properties of nouns specified in table 3.1 is detailed in the rest of this section. The one exception is the derived inchoative verbs using the suffix *-k'i*; this characteristic of nouns is discussed in connection with derivation morphology in section 3.12.1.

3.1.1 Possession

As discussed above, and summarized in table 3.1, possession is a property of common nouns (see below, this section). Possession can also be a property of mass nouns, but this indicates a shift in the meaning of the noun (see section 3.1.1.1.4).

There are three strategies for marking common nouns for possession: using prefixes, using suffixes, or using both. Determining which strategy is appropriate for each noun is based on the general meaning of the noun and is lexically specified. This results in three common-noun subclasses: ALIENABLE, INALIENABLE, and VARIABLE.

Semantically, an alienable noun (the majority of all nouns) is not inherently a part of or intimately connected with the possessor. An inalienable noun is an inherent part of or is intimately connected with the possessor (including body parts, kinship terms, and some other cases of intimate possession: see section 3.1.1.1). A variable noun can be used as either an alienable or inalienable noun. Furthermore, this three-way distinction is marked in the morphology: alienable nouns are inflected for possession by prefixes, inalienable nouns are inflected for possession by suffixes, and variable nouns can be inflected for possession by using either prefixes or suffixes.

As with most noun class systems based on alienability, the strict semantic basis for this three-way division has exceptions. There are some kinship terms, for example, that pattern as alienable nouns, others that pattern as inalienable nouns, and still others that pattern as variable nouns. Due to these exceptions, the determination of class membership is more accurately established from morphological inflections. All nouns in any of the three classes always pattern morphologically like the others in the group.[4] The properties of each of these types of common nouns are surveyed and exemplified in the following sections.

3.1.1.1 *Alienable nouns*

Alienable nouns are the largest group of common nouns in Xinkan. These nouns can only be inflected for possession with **pronominal prefixes**. This possessive inflection indicates that the noun is not an inherent part of the possessor—the possessive relationship can be dissolved or voided. This type of relationship is often established through the work, or effort, of the possessor. Examples are given for each language in 94–96.

(94)　Guazacapán alienable possession.
　　a.　*ün-miya*
　　　　1SG.POSS-chicken
　　　　'my chicken'
　　b.　*mu-peelo'*
　　　　3SG.POSS-dog
　　　　'his dog'
　　c.　*ka-xuxi*
　　　　2SG.POSS-beard
　　　　'your beard' (not recorded in Jumaytepeque)
　　d.　*ün-kiüixa*
　　　　1SG.POSS-half
　　　　'my half'

(95)　Chiquimulilla alienable possession.
　　a.　*ün-seema*
　　　　1SG.POSS-fish
　　　　'my fish'
　　b.　*müy-ur'ulh*
　　　　2SG.INFORM.POSS-egg
　　　　'your egg'
　　c.　*mülhik-tumin*
　　　　2PL.FORM.POSS-money
　　　　'your (pl.) money'

(96)　Jumaytepeque alienable possession.
　　a.　*n-hur'u*
　　　　1SG.POSS-turkey
　　　　'my turkey'
　　b.　*lki-misaka*
　　　　1PL.POSS-seashell
　　　　'our seashell'
　　c.　*h-sipaani*
　　　　3SG.POSS-corpse
　　　　'his corpse'
　　d.　*y-miixa*
　　　　2SG.INFORM.POSS-heart
　　　　'your heart'

3.1.1.2　*Inalienable nouns*

Inalienable nouns form the second largest group of common nouns in Xinkan and mostly connote body parts and kinship terms. When possessed these are inflected with **possessive suffixes**. These nouns form an inherent, insoluble part of the possessor when so inflected. There are, however, language-specific irregularities and exceptions—not all Xinkan languages classify nouns with identical meanings as inalienable. Irregularities and representatives of the inalienable class membership for each language are given in 97–99. See section 3.5 for a comparison table of the alienable and inalienable affixes.

(97)   Guazacapán inalienable possession.
    a.   *paama-n'*
        arm/wing-1SG.POSS
        'my arm'
    b.   *uxti-ka'*
        spouse's.parents-2SG.POSS
        'your spouse's parents'
    c.   *nawak'u-h*
        woman's.skirt-3SG.POSS
        'her skirt' (alienable in Chiquimulilla)
    d.   *lak'uwa-k*
        daughter's.husband-1PL.POSS
        'our daughter's husband'
    e.   *ay'a-ka 'ay*
        wife-2PL.POSS PL.
        'your (pl.) wife(s)' (literally your companion)
    f.   *naru-h 'ay*
        land-3SG.POSS PL.
        'their land'

(98)   Chiquimulilla inalienable possession.
    a.   *k'oomo-h*
        knee-3SG.POSS
        'his knee'
    b.   *xa-k*
        name-2SG.FORM.POSS
        'your name'
    c.   *ɬap'a-n*
        grandchild-1SG.POSS
        'my grandchild' (unknown in Guazacapán)
    d.   *uma-lhik*
        grandfather-2PL.FORM.POSS
        'your (pl.) grandfather(s)'
    e.   *aya-lhki'*
        sibling-1PL.POSS
        'our sibling'

(99)   Jumaytepeque inalienable possession.
    a.   *nari-h*
        nose-3SG.POSS
        'his nose'

b. *tahaawa-lki'*
relative-1PL.POSS
'our relative'

c. *map'ü-y*
tortilla-2SG.INFORM.POSS
'your tortilla, food'

d. *yak'i-hri*
rope-3PL.POSS
'their rope'

e. *tahku-y*
half-2SG.INFORM.POSS
'your half, part' (alienable in Guazacapán and Chiquimulilla)

3.1.1.3 *Variable nouns*

The third class of nouns I have chosen to label 'variable nouns'. This is the smallest group of common nouns. They can be inflected with either **pronominal prefixes** or **suffixes** when possessed. Speakers have the option of indicating whether or not the relationship between these nouns and the possessor is inherent and insoluble. In each case, the meaning of the possessed noun changes with the choice of inflectional strategy. For variable nouns that refer to parts of the body, the change is in the meaning of the noun root (see 100 a, b, e, and f below). Variable nouns that do not signify parts of the body indicate that the possessive relationship was earned through self-effort and that the noun is the property of the possessor and cannot be reallocated. For example, as shown in 100c and 100d, the possessor of the house has paid for the house after working for many years to earn the money, and this house can no longer be owned by anyone else. The examples in 100 are given with Guazacapán possessive affixes, although the classification of each of these words as variable inalienable or alienable nouns is true for all three languages.

(100) Inalienable/alienable noun possession.
a. *mün'a-h*
fruit-3SG.POSS
'his semen' (lit. his fruit)

b. *mu-mün'a*
3SG.POSS-fruit
'his fruit' (i.e., his apples and oranges)

c. *mak'u-ka'*
house-2SG.POSS
'your house' (you earned it from personal effort and not as an inherent property)

d. *ka-maku*
2SG.POSS-house
'your house'

e. *wirik'i-h*
tongue-3SG.POSS
'his tongue'

f. *mu-wirik'i*
3SG.POSS-tongue
'his language'

Though members of the sets of alienable, inalienable, and variable nouns are easily determined based on possessive strategies, none of these nouns must be morphologically possessed. When unmarked for possession, every common noun indicates an unspecific, indefinite instantiation of the referent. For example, *pu* 'hand' is an inalienable noun, and it inflects with pronominal suffixes in all of the Xinkan languages (e.g., *pu-n* 'my hand'). However, this noun can also be used without a possessive affix to refer to hands in general or to a nonspecific hand (e.g., *süüma pu* 'the hand is/hands are black'). The class membership of common nouns cannot be determined in these situations in which possession is unmarked.

3.1.1.4 *Mass nouns*

Mass nouns, called noncount nouns in the descriptions of other languages, are nouns that cannot be counted or divided into quantifiable units. However, mass nouns are similar to common nouns in that they can be marked for possession. When they are marked this way the possessor must be indicated via the alienable **possessive prefixes**. However, thus marked, mass nouns have a slight change in semantics—there is an implied quantity. Examples are given in 101.

(101) Possession of mass nouns.

a. *ün-uy*
1SG.POSS-water
'my UNIT of water' (lit. 'my water')

b. *ka-wati*
2SG.POSS-mud
'your UNIT of mud' (lit. 'your mud')

c. *mu-lhüwü*
3SG.POSS-honey
'his UNIT of honey' (lit. 'his/her honey')

3.1.1.5 *Genitive construction*

The genitive construction is discussed here because it also deals with noun possession. This construction differs from alienable/inalienable possession, however, because it indicates that a noun is possessed by another noun, not just a pronominal possessor. The genitive construction is consistent across the Xinkan languages in that the possessed always precedes the possessor. More specifically, the genitive construction takes the form $N_1 N_2$ with the meaning N_1 of N_2 (N_2's N_1). The variable 'N' in this formula represents any noun. Additionally, alienable/inalienable affixal possession may optionally be indicated on the possessed noun (N_1) in the genitive construction. Examples of the genitive construction in each language are given in 102–104.

(102) Genitive construction in Guazacapán.

   a. *xuk'a-lh seema*
      eat-AGT. fish
      'Martin pescador' (lit. 'eater of fish')

   b. *uw'i(-h) kaxkax*   (EX:741)
      flesh(-SG.POSS) gopher
      'gopher's meat', 'meat from a gopher'

   c. *(mu-)müüm'ü toktok*   (EX:231)
      (3SG.POSS-)song mocking.bird
      'song of the mockingbird'

   d. *(mu-)uytut'uk na waakax*   (EX:2272)
      (3SG.POSS-) water.breast the cow
      'cow's milk'

   e. *ulululu' puumu(-h) pik'i*   (EX:1040)
      white wing(-3SG.POSS) bird
      'The bird's wing is white.'

   f. *hawi(-h) ur'ulh*   (EX:1388)
      skin(-3SG.POSS) egg
      'egg shell' (lit. 'skin of egg')

(103) Genitive construction in Chiquimulilla.

   a. *ülü-(h) na maku*   (EX:9)
      side(-3SG.POSS) the house
      'side of the house'

   b. *ur'ulh mihya*   (EX:196)
      egg chicken
      'chicken egg'

   c. *na hur'a-(h) kolhmena* (<Sp. 'colmena')   (EX:77)
      the queen(-3SG.POSS) beehive
      'the queen of the beehive'

   d. *anu-(h) ay'alh*   (EX:112)
      niece(-3SG.POSS) woman
      'the niece of a woman'

   e. *nah na man ut'a-(h) tum'u lhik ki'*   (EX:78)
      she the that mother(-3SG.POSS) all them REFL
      'That one is the mother of them all.'

   f. *huuxi-(h) na waakax*   (EX:122)
      head(-3SG.POSS) the cow
      'cow's head', also 'head of cattle'

(104) Genitive construction in Jumaytepeque.

   a. *maku huhul*   (EX:158)
      house bee
      'beehive' (lit. house of bee)

   b. *xan xaha maku*   (EX:28)
      LOC mouth house
      'in front of the house' (lit. 'in mouth of house')

    c. *espuma-(h) a t'ut'u*   (EX:24)
        foam(-3SG.POSS) the soap
        'foam of the soap'
    d. *oriya(-h) a talma*   (EX:149)
        side(-3SG.POSS) the road
        'side/edge of the road'
    e. *naa sombra(-h) a utu*   (EX:100)
        the shadow(-3SG.POSS) the tree
        'the shadow of the tree'

3.1.2   Number

As shown in table 3.1 above, inflection for number is a property of common nouns in Xinkan languages, but it is not used for either proper nouns or mass nouns. Unmarked common nouns are understood as referring to singular entities, while those marked with the plural suffix are understood as referring to multiple entities (two or more). The plural suffix is *-lhi* in Guazacapán and Chiquimulilla, or *-li* in Jumaytepeque. The phonological shape of the noun root interacts with this suffix in a number of ways in each language. The phonetic outcomes of these interactions are described in sections 2.1.1.2.4, 2.1.2, and 2.3 and are summarized here for convenience.

1. Word-final vowels are lengthened before the plural suffix.
2. The rightmost consonant of the noun root may be optionally glottalized in conjunction with vowel lengthening.
3. In Guazacapán, a word-final [ɬ] coalesces with the first consonant of the plural suffix.
4. In Jumaytepeque, a word-final [l] coalesces with the first consonant of the plural suffix.
5. In Chiquimulilla, an epenthetic vowel [a] is inserted between a word-final [ɬ] in the noun root and the first consonant of the plural suffix.
6. In all of the Xinkan languages, an epenthetic vowel is inserted between a word-final [n] and the first consonant of the plural suffix.
7. In all of the Xinkan languages, the first consonant of the plural suffix is deleted after a noun root-final [y].
8. In all of the Xinkan languages, a noun root-final /k/ or /t/ is lenited to [h] when immediately preceding the plural suffix

Examples of plural nouns are given in 105–107, with the singular, base form on the left and the plural form in the middle. The actual pronunciation of these nouns, after various phonological processes, is given on the right in square brackets.

(105) Guazacapán plural nouns.
    a. *tz'oko*   *tz'ok'oo-lhe*   [ts'ok'ooɬe]
        'grackle'   'grackles'

b. *toktok*   *toktok-lhe*   [tohtohłe]
'mockingbird' 'mockingbirds'

c. *tz'iim'alh*   *tz'iimalh-lhi*   [ts'iimałi]
'person from G.' 'people from Guazacapán'
'Guazacapaneco' 'Guazacapenecos'

(106) Chiquimulilla plural nouns.

    a. *iiru*   *iir'uu-lhi*   [iir'uułi]
       'monkey' 'monkeys'

    b. *iw'alh*   *iw'alh-aalhi*   [iw'ałaałi]
       'ant'   'ants'

    c. *frak*   *frak-lhi*   [frahłi]
       'man'   'men'

(107) Jumaytepeque plural nouns.

    a. *xüma*   *xüm'aa-li*   [šïm'aałi]
       'rat'   'rats'

    b. *üyü*   *üyüü-li*   [ïyïïli]
       'gopher' 'gophers'

    c. *animal*   *animal-i*   [animal+li] (<Sp. '*animal*')
       'animal' 'animals'

Number is marked morphologically on the noun only if the noun is definite and specific (i.e., either marked by the determiner or a possessed noun). In all other contexts, plurality is unmarked morphologically, although it is indicated through the presence of quantifiers or other modifiers of nouns. The Guazacapán words in 108 show all possible markings of plurality—the other languages behave identically.

(108) Guazacapán plural formation complete paradigm.

    a. *ay'aalha*
       'woman'

    b. *na ay'aalha-lhi*
       the woman-PL
       'the women'

    c. *walh lhap'a-lhi-n'*
       three grandchild-PL-1SG.POSS
       'my three grandchildren'

    d. *ay'aalha-lhi hü'*
       woman-PL this
       'these women'

    e. *ay'aalha-lhi man*
       woman-PL that
       'those women'

    f. *piy' ay'aalha*
       two woman
       'two women'

g. *teena' ay'aalha*
many woman
'many women'

3.1.3   Diminutive constructions

As seen in table 3.1 above, inflection with diminutives is a property of common nouns and proper nouns. The diminutive clitic used in this construction is *chu-* in Guazacapán and Chiquimulilla and *nuu-* in Jumaytepeque.[5] As in the grammars of many other languages, the diminutive does not always mark the actual size of the modified noun. For example, a Xinkan noun inflected with the diminutive clitic has a similar meaning to the *-ito/-ita* suffixes of Spanish (e.g., *casa* 'house' → *casita* 'little house'). The size of the modified noun may be part of the intended meaning, but in both Spanish and Xinkan it can also express a positive emotional, or endearing, relationship.

While this suffix appears to be a regular part of Xinkan grammar and is included in field notes, past grammatical descriptions, and in the speech of the few remaining speakers, very few linguistic examples are recorded that use it.[6] Thus, while it is clear that there was a diminutive in Chiquimulilla, and we know how it was pronounced, no data beyond this has been collected—nor can it be now, due to the state of the language. The same is true for Jumaytepeque, with the exception of one example recorded that used this clitic. This example is given below in 110. Many examples were recorded in Guazacapán as shown in 109.

(109) Guazacapán diminutive nouns.
   a. *chu-mak'u*
      DIM-house
      'the little house'
   b. *chu-pikii-lhi*
      DIM-bird-pl
      'the little birds'
   c. *chu-t'uuri*
      DIM-child
      'the small child'
   d. *chu-xaya*
      DIM-old.woman
      'the little old woman'
   e. *chu-hura'i-h*
      DIM-eye-3sg.poss
      'his little eye'
   f. *chu-hutu hina' machiiti*
      DIM-tree with machete
      'the little tree with a machete'
   g. *chu pu-n*
      DIM-hand-1sg.poss
      'my little hand'

(110) Jumaytepeque diminutive nouns.
    a h-nuu-one
    the 3sg.poss-DIM-baby
    'her small baby'

3.2   Adjectives

Adjectives are linguistically defined in three ways: meaning, function, and inflection. For each of these properties, adjectives pattern differently than nouns and consequently are considered a separate grammatical category in Xinkan. The specific ways that adjectives differ from nouns are summarized below.

1. Adjectives in Xinkan principally refer to properties of color and size, though other properties such as taste or smell can also be adjectives.
2. An adjective can be used to modify nouns, verbal nouns, and other adjectives.
3. Adjectives can function as the sole verbal argument (e.g., subject or direct object).
4. Adjectives are not inflected for number (singular or plural).
5. Adjectives can be used in comparative and superlative constructions, while nouns cannot be.

As mentioned in note 1, there are striking similarities between adjectives and nouns. Both can function as a verbal argument (see number 3 in the list above), and both can be used as the base in deriving an inchoative verb. This is done by adding the suffix *-k'i* to the noun or adjective, as discussed in section 3.12.2. However, the differences between nouns and adjectives present sufficient grounds for distinguishing them from each other in a grammatical description.

3.2.1   Adjectives as modifiers of nouns

Adjectives can either precede or follow the noun they modify, though adjectives preceding the noun form the most common scenario (i.e., head final). However, structural ambiguity results in those cases where the adjective precedes the noun. Specifically, an adjective preceding a noun can be the predicate of a copular construction, with the noun as its sole argument; alternately, the adjective is understood as part of the noun phrase. (Copula verbs are discussed in section 4.2.2.) When there is a full verb (i.e., not a copula), the adjective preceding the noun phrase is always part of the noun phrase. Examples of noun phrases containing adjectives are given in 111–113. The syntax of full noun phrases is discussed in section 3.4. (See table 1.1 for full text titles.)

(111) Guazacapán noun phrases with adjectives.   (BT:1972, 4)
    a. *tenuwa hawa*
        sapodilla unripe
        'unripe sapodilla'

b. *üran haxu*   (SP:1979, 17)
   big pig
   'big pig' 'The pig is big.'

c. *pari naru*   (EX:1649)
   hot land
   'desert', 'The land is hot.'

d. *pari uy*   (DF:1979, 87)
   hot water
   'hot water', 'The water is hot.'

(112) Chiquimulilla adjectives.
   a. *pu' derecho*[7]   (EX:108)
      hand right
      'right hand'

   b. *pari wok'o*   (EX:119)
      hot tascal
      'hot tortilla', 'The tascal is hot.'

   c. *ololo' na paama-h*   (EX:212)
      white the wing-3SG
      'the white wings', 'The wings are white.'

   d. *piy' bes*   (EX:171)
      two time
      'two times'

(113) Jumaytepeque adjectives.
   a. *piy'ar k-baaka*   (EX:163)
      two 2SG-cow
      'your two cows', 'two cows of yours', 'Your cows are two.'

   b. *ür'an hurak*   (EX:146)
      big man
      'big man', 'The man is big.'

   c. *tz'ih aa mak'u-h*   (EX:108)
      quiet the house-3SG
      'his quiet house', 'His house is quiet.'

   d. *na h-nuu one*   (EX:145)
      the small child
      'the small child', 'The child is small.'

While most of the phrases in 111, 112, and 113 are ambiguous, in that they can be interpreted semantically as either a noun phrase or a nominal predicate, note that they do not require any other added morphology to make the meaning clear.

As mentioned above, adjectives can also occur as the sole argument of a verb. This is similar to Spanish where the adjective can modify a seemingly empty noun head. In this regard adjectives are similar to nouns. For example, in 114 below the adjective *üran* 'big' is the argument of the verb *tik'ilha'* 'slept'.

(114) Adjectives as verbal arguments in Guazacapán.
    Ø-tik'i-lha' na üran   (EX:1388)
    3SG.SETC-sleep.COMP-IV.AGT the big
    'The big [one] slept.'

3.2.2 Adjectives modified by *ki* 'very'

Adjectives can be modified by the adverb *ki* 'very', emphasizing the property of the adjectives. This adverb has a phonological variant *kü* which often surfaces as the result of vowel harmony, although it does so inconsistently.[8] When this adverb is used, the adjective always bears the third-person singular possessive suffix *-h*. The adverb always precedes the adjective that it modifies. Examples 115–117 illustrate adverb order in Guazacapán, Chiquimulilla, and Jumaytepeque.

(115) Guazacapán adverb order.
    a. *ki til'a-h*   (EX:850)
        very salt-3SG.POSS
        'very salty', 'It is very salty.'
    b. *ki tz'am'a-h*   (EX:793)
        very good-3SG.POSS
        'very good', 'It is very good.'
    c. *ki xuka-k'i-h*   (EX:838)
        very bite-NOM-3SG.POSS
        'It (my head) is hurting a lot.' (lit. 'it is very biting')
    d. *kü üra' maku man*   (EX:765)
        very big house that
        'that very big house', 'That house is very big.'

(116) Chiquimulilla adverb order.
    a. *ki nam'a-h na huuxi*   (EX:23)
        very painful-3SG the head
        'My head hurts a lot.' Or 'My head is very painful.'
    b. *ki/kü mür'a-h na yelh*   (EX:26)
        very bitter-3SG the bile
        'The bile is very bitter.'
    c. *ki lhak'a-h na tz'uutz'u pari*   (EX:200)
        very itchy the rash hot
        'Heat rash is very itchy.'
    d. *ki pütz'a-h tixtak*   (EX:123)
        very smelly anus
        'The anus is very smelly.'
    e. *ki t'ünk'ü-h na naak'uh*   (EX:20)
        very short-3SG the skirt
        'The skirt is very short.'

(117) Jumaytepeque adverb order.
    a. *ki üla-h na dyos*   (EX:18)
       very big-3SG.POSS the god
       'God is great.' (lit. 'God is very big.')
    b. *ki nama t'i-n*   (EX:93)
       very painful DIR-1SG
       'It is very painful to me.'
    c. *ki nu holok yuuka*   (EX:307)
       very DIM pretty you
       'You are very pretty.'

3.2.3 Comparative and superlative constructions

The Xinkan languages employ adjectives in comparative and superlative constructions. This formation, however, is borrowed directly from Spanish. There is no data
in any of the published descriptions of Xinkan explaining how these constructions
might be organized natively—and the last speakers only use the constructions borrowed from Spanish. The comparative construction uses *mas . . . ke* (<Sp. *'más . . .
que'*) and the superlative construction is made using *la mas . . .* (<Sp. *'la más . . .'*)—the
ellipses indicate the location of the adjective. Note that this construction borrowed
from Spanish never used *el más . . .* despite the possible gender differences in Spanish
grammar.

    The data contains a number of instances of these two constructions in Guazacapán
and only one in Jumaytepeque. The information on Chiquimulilla in the database does
not indicate how comparative and superlatives were formed. Note that many languages do not have an overt way of making superlative constructions, so it is possible
that there might not have been a native way of forming these constructions prior to
Spanish contact. In fact, Calderón (1908: 12) asserts that while no such construction
existed for Yupiltepeque, "comparative and superlative constructions do not exist in
all of the languages in question" (translation mine).[9] Also note that Pipil, a neighboring Uto-Aztecan language, borrowed this construction from Spanish as well.[10] The
examples in 118 and 119 illustrate the use of comparatives and superlatives in Guazacapán and Jumaytepeque.

(118) Guazacapán comparatives and superlatives.
    a. *Hwan mas iipan ke nen'*   (EX:1295)
       Juan more young than I
       'Juan is younger than I.'
    b. *la mas ün-iipan nen'*   (EX:1066)
       more 1SG-young.child I
       'I am the youngest.'
    c. *na haya sumaya mas üra mu-faaha*   (EX:1179)
       the female crab more big 3SG-strip
       'The female crab has the biggest strip.'

    d. *hin, nuk'a nen' mas chürükü ke Hwan*   (EX:533)
       no give me more little than Juan
       'No, give me less than Juan.'

    e. *mas üra mu-maku ke ün-maku*   (EX:1077)
       more big 3SG-house than 1SG-house
       'His house is bigger than my house.'

(119) Jumaytepeque comparatives and superlatives.
    a. *yak'a-kan mas roosa*   (EX:45)
       make.PERF-2SG.TV more red
       'You make it redder.'

3.3   Determiners

Articles, demonstratives, quantifiers, and numerals are loosely grouped together in Xinkan, based on distributional and morphological properties. The label DETERMINER is used here as a representation of this linguistic group. The properties of determiners, including what makes them different from each other, are detailed in this section.

    All determiners function within a noun phrase and can occur either before or after the head noun (but not both). Articles and numerals must precede the noun, while demonstratives, quantifiers, and relative pronouns must follow the noun. Noun phrases are discussed in section 3.4.

3.3.1   Articles

There are two articles in Xinkan languages: a definite article and an indefinite article. The indefinite article is the same as the number one: *ik'alh* (Guazacapán), *k'alh* (Chiquimulilla), and *k'al* (Jumaytepeque).[11] The definite article is *na* (Guazacapán, Chiquimulilla) and *naa, aa* (Jumaytepeque). The choice between the various definite articles in Jumaytepeque is based on syntactic factors: if a definite Jumaytepeque noun phrase is used in isolation, *naa* is preferred (e.g., *naa one* 'the child'); but if the definite noun is used in a larger clause, *aa* is prefered (e.g., *ut'uyi' a ur'ul a miya*, lay the egg the hen, 'The hen laid the egg').

    In addition, all bare (morphosyntactically unmarked) nouns have a definite connotation, and the overt definite article is usually only preferred in focus constructions or other pragmatic and discourse functions.

(120) Guazacapán definite article.
    a. *na naki*   (EX:1278)
       'the chile'
    b. *na maku*   (EX:1248)
       'the house'
    c. *na miya*   (EX:1262)
       'the chicken'

(121)   Chiquimulilla definite article.
   a.   *na iiru*   (EX:167)
         'the monkey'
   b.   *na chuchuu-lhi*   (EX:168)
         the dog-PL
         'the dogs'
   c.   *na hur'a-h kolhmeena*   (EX:77)
         the queen-3SG beehive
         'queen's beehive'

(122)   Jumaytepeque definite article.
   a.   *naa hurak*   (EX:114)
         'the man'
   b.   *naa wap'ik*   (EX:154)
         'the shoe'
   c.   *la h-iri a talma*   (EX:358)
         no 3SG.TV-see.IPERF the road
         'He isn't watching the road.'

The definite article either is, or is homophonous with, the relative marker of subordinate clauses (see section 4.6.3).

3.3.2   Demonstratives

Demonstratives are words with deictic connotations. In Xinkan there are only two demonstratives: one for referring to objects close to the speaker, *hü'* 'this' (Guazacapán), *nan'ah* 'this' (Chiquimulilla), and *nahan'ah* 'this' (Jumaytepeque); and a second for referring to objects not close to the speaker, *man* 'that' (Guazacapán and Jumaytepeque) and *ma'* 'that' (Chiquimulilla).

   While demonstratives are used most commonly as deictic modifiers of nouns, they can also be used as heads of noun phrases (called fused-heads in some grammar books) that will act independently as the arguments of verbs. When used to modify nouns, they always follow the head they modify—the opposite of articles.

(123)   Guazacapán demonstratives.
   a.   *hiiru man*   (EX:1084)
         monkey that
         'that monkey'
   b.   *miya hü'*   (EX:955)
         chicken this
         'this chicken'

(124)   Chiquimulilla demonstratives.
   a.   *t'um'ay ma'*   (EX:278)
         tail that
         'that tail'

    b. *mak'u nan'ah*   (EX:140)
       house this
       'this house'

(125) Jumaytepeque demonstratives.
    a. *uta man*   (EX:55)
       mother that
       'that mother'
    b. *hur'u nahan'ah*   (EX:327)
       turkey this
       'this turkey'

In each Xinkan language a noun can be modified by both a demonstrative pronoun and the definite article. The indefinite article does not co-occur with the demonstrative pronouns in this way due to a clash in specificity.

(126) Guazacapán demonstratives with definite articles.
    a. *na maku man*   (EX:1247)
       the house that
       'that house' (a specific one)
    b. *na tay'uk hii'*   (EX:1351)
       the hat this
       'this hat' (a specific one)

(127) Chiquimulilla demonstratives with definite articles.
    a. *na aara ma'*   (EX:60)
       the worm that
       'that worm' (a specific one)
    b. *na lhuuri nan'ah*   (EX:45)
       the rabbit this
       'this rabbit' (a specific one)

(128) Jumaytepeque demonstratives with definite articles.
    a. *naa chumu man*   (EX:36)
       the old.man that
       'that old man' (a specific one)
    b. *naa k'otete nahan'ah*   (EX:139)
       the frog this
       'this frog' (a specific one)

This so-called 'flanking' demonstrative construction is the only way to make these constructions. That is, in Jumaytepeque a sentence corresponding to 128b with the order **naa nahan'ah k'otete* would not be a grammatical construction in Xinkan.

Finally, demonstratives can be used in conjunction with the definite article as demonstrative pronoun constructions, one of which indicates something in proximity to the speaker, and another that indicates something at a distance. The demonstrative and the article in this construction do not modify an overt lexical head.

(129) Guazacapán demonstrative pronouns.
    a. *na man*
       the that
       'that one'
    b. *na hü'*
       the this
       'this one'

(130) Chiquimulilla demonstrative pronouns.
    a. *na ma'*
       the that
       'that one'
    b. *na nan'ah*
       the this
       'this one'

(131) Jumaytepeque demonstrative pronouns.
    a. *naa man*
       the that
       'that one'
    b. *naa nahan'ah*
       the this
       'this one'

3.3.3   Quantifiers

Quantifiers belong to a class of words that indicate the quantity of a noun, and as such they are understood to be nominal modifiers. There are two types of quantifiers in Xinkan languages: abstract quantifiers and numerals.

Numerals indicate a specific number of instances of a given noun: for example, *piy' miya* 'two chickens' (Guazacapán). Abstract quantifiers indicate the quantities of referent nouns in a more abstract sense: for example, *teena miya* 'many chickens' (Guazacapán). The difference between the two types of quantifiers lies in the specificity of the number denoted.

3.3.3.1 *Numerals*
Xinkan languages have a vigesimal number system, but a lack of information means the native number system in the languages is largely unknown. Xinkan languages, as analyzed here, use Spanish numbers for all but the lower numbers.[12] In fact, native numbers above six are only known in Chiquimulilla.[13] Table 3.2 compares the numbers across Xinkan languages. In all the languages where there are parallel numbers, they are clearly cognates. This has led to the conclusion that all Xinkan languages had numbers above six and that these numbers were most likely similar to those found in Chiquimulilla. However, reconstruction of these higher numbers is unwarranted, as we have evidence of them in only one of the four languages.

Table 3.2 Xinkan numerals

	Guazacapán	Chiquimulilla	Jumaytepeque	Yupiltepeque	Chiquimulilla (North)
1	*ik'alh*	*ik'alh ~ k'alh*	*k'alh*	⟨ical⟩	⟨ical⟩
2	*piy'*	*piy'*	*pi'/piy'ar*	⟨piar⟩	⟨piar⟩
3	*walh*	*walh*	*wahla*	⟨hualar⟩	⟨hualar⟩
4	*hirya*	*hirya*	*irya*	⟨iriar⟩	⟨iriar⟩
5	*pühü*	*pühü*	*püh 'ar*	⟨püj⟩	⟨püj⟩
6	*tak'alh*	*tak'alh*	*tak'al 'ar*	⟨tacá⟩	⟨tacá⟩
7	—	*p'ulhwa*	—	—	⟨puljna⟩
8	—	*ünya*	—	—	⟨jüörte⟩
9	—	*ünya*	—	—	?
10	—	*pak'ilh*	—	—	⟨pakil⟩
11	—	—	—	—	⟨pakincal⟩
12	—	—	—	—	⟨pakinpi⟩
13	—	—	—	—	⟨pakinhuajl⟩
14	—	—	—	—	⟨pakiniriar⟩
15	—	—	—	—	⟨pakinpüj⟩
16	—	—	—	—	⟨pakintacá⟩
17	—	—	—	—	⟨pakinpuljna⟩
18	—	—	—	—	⟨pakinjüörte⟩
20+	—	—	—	—	etc.

Note that I have taken the last two columns in table 3.2 from Calderón (1908: 15–16) without any attempt to analyze the phonetic makeup of the sounds involved. The Chiquimulilla North variant that he recorded was one of two mutually unintelligible languages spoken in Chiquimulilla during his stay; this variant he gives as that spoken in the north part of the city.[14] In addition, the number *ünya* in Chiquimulilla (second column) is either 8 or 9 but not both. It is unclear from the data how this number should be interpreted or what the other number in the pair would be. Instances of the use of numerals are given in examples 132–134.

(132) Guazacapán numeral modifiers.
    a. *hirya maku*   (EX:1794)
       four house
       'four houses'
    b. *tak'alh map'u*   (EX:1826)
       six tortilla
       'six tortillas'

(133) Chiquimulilla numeral modifiers.
    a. *ünya iw'alh*   (EX:95)
       8/9 ant
       'eight ants' or 'nine ants'
    b. *pak'ilh xurumu*   (EX:149)
       ten young.man
       'ten young men'

(134)   Jumaytepeque numeral modifiers.

    a.   *wahla kïïtïl*   (EX:126)

        three thief

        'three thieves'

    b.   *k'alh pari*   (EX:200)

        one day

        'one day'

3.3.3.2   *Abstract quantifiers*

Abstract quantifiers are different from numerals in that they do not indicate a specific quantity. These quantifiers are largely the same across all of the Xinkan languages. In most cases, the nouns modified by these quantifiers pattern like those modified by numerals—they are not inflected with the plural morphology. However, one abstract quantifier *yaalha'* 'many, a lot', which only occurs in Guazacapán, requires the plural morpheme on the noun it modifies. In addition, the quantifier *puulha'* 'much, a lot' is the only modifier that can be used in conjunction with mass nouns, although it also is found only in Guazacapán.

(135)   Guazacapán abstract quantifiers

    a.   *ik'alh mulhi*   (EX:26)

        one squirrel

        'some squirrels', 'one squirrel'

    b.   *tumuki' ay'aalha*   (EX:116)

        all woman

        'all the women'

    c.   *teena' ay'aalha*   (EX:73)

        many woman

        'many women'

    d.   *kït'ïk pulhpu* (<Sp. *'polvo'*)   (EX:1974)

        too.much dust

        'too much dust'

    e.   *yaalha' huurak-lhi*   (EX:2545)

        many man-PL

        'a lot of men'

    f.   *puulha' hente uuka'*   (EX:685)

        large.quantity people there.is

        'there are a lot of people'

    g.   *puy pari*   (EX:826)

        half day

        'middle of the day' (only used with nouns referring to time)

    h.   *hin 'ik'alh ay'aalha*   (EX:399)

        not one woman

        'no woman'

    i.   *k'alh ay'aalha-lhi hï'*   (EX:245)

        one woman-PL this

        'each of these women'

    j. *ik'alh lhik ki' ay'aalha*   (EX:350)
       one PL only woman
       'only some women'

(136) Chiquimulilla abstract quantifiers.
    a. *tum'iki' mihya*   (EX:148)
       all hen
       'all the hens'
    b. *(i)k'alh pukuyu*   (EX:49)
       one bird
       'some birds', 'one bird'
    c. *lha (i)k'alh mihya*   (EX:68)
       no one hen
       'not one hen'
    d. *taha' ampuki*   (EX:111)
       many snake
       'a lot of snakes'
    e. *(i)k'alh mihyaa-lhi nan'ah*   (EX:72)
       one hen-PL this
       'each of these hens'

There is no data in any of the field notes or recorded texts for quantifiers in Jumayte-peque except for *k'al*, which can mean the number one, the indefinite article, or 'some'.

(137) Jumaytepeque abstract quantifiers.
    a. *k'al pipil*   (EX:126)
       one butterfly
       'some butterflies', 'one butterfly', 'a butterfly'

3.4   Noun phrases

This short section has the goal of illustrating how nouns phrases are constructed. The only obligatory portion of a noun phrase is the head, which can be either a full lexical noun or an adjective. The head can be modified with an adjective, quantifier, article, demonstrative, or relative pronoun. With parentheses indicating an option and braces indicating a choice, the formula for the construction of a noun phrase is as follows:

(article)(quantifier){(adjective)head/head(adjective)}(demonstrative)(relative pronoun)

    Pronouns can replace the entire noun phrase or a portion of it (see section 3.2). It is important to note that adjectives can occur on only one side of a given head noun in any given noun phrase. That is, a noun phrase cannot contain an adjective both before and after the head noun; it can only have one either preceding the head noun or following it. The last element of a noun phrase, the relative pronoun, is discussed in section 4.6.3.

3.5 Pronouns ▾ 81

3.5   Pronouns

Pronouns refer anaphorically to an independent noun or a noun phrase and are said to substitute for the noun or noun phrase in discourse. There are both dependent and independent pronouns in Xinkan languages, defined by their distributional properties. The independent pronouns, if used, always function as subjects or objects and are free morphemes. Dependent pronouns are either suffixes or prefixes and always attach to other grammatical categories (but not to verbal auxiliaries and prepositions). The dependent pronouns are not a distinct grammatical category themselves; rather, they are part of the grammatical category of the words they attach to, and these are discussed below in connection with these head categories.

3.5.1   Independent personal pronouns

Independent personal pronouns are lexical items that share distributional properties with lexical nouns. Syntactically, they can function as the grammatical arguments of a verb, as a subject, and as an object. In terms of the noun phrase construction mentioned in section 3.4, pronouns can occur with the definite article and can be relativized via the relative pronoun.

There is no morphological case in Xinkan marking the grammatical function of nouns, so there is a single form for each independent pronoun. Similarly, these pronouns take no inflectional or derivational morphology.[15] Table 3.3 shows all of the pronouns given in Guazacapán in all of the published works and field research. The ellipsis marks in this table are intended to indicate a discontinuous construction. That is, the forms listed for the first-person plural exclusive and the second-person plural allow a word, or phrase, to intervene between the pronoun itself and the plural marker *ay*.

Table 3.3 Guazacapán pronouns

1SG	*nen'*	1PL.INCL	*neelhek*
		1PL.EXCL	*neelhek … ay*
2SG	*naka*	2PL	*naka … ay*
3SG	*nah*	3PL	*naalhik*

However, not all of these pronouns are attested in texts and example sentences. This makes the exact behavior of some of these forms uncertain. For example, Guazacapán is the only Xinkan language with an inclusive/exclusive distinction in the first-person plural. However, these forms do not occur in examples outside of the paradigm just given and copied from the attested information; this is specifically the case of the 1PL.EXCL pronoun *neelhek … ay*.

Furthermore, in the majority of cases the singular and plural for non–first-person pronouns are conflated when they are used in long-discourse chunks, such as stories, where both numbers are represented by the singular pronoun. This does not create a serious comprehension issue because required subject-agreement markers on the verb disambiguate the intended meaning.

Lastly, the pluralizing particle *ay*, seen in table 3.3 in conjunction with the first-person plural exclusive pronoun and the second-person plural pronoun, is most likely a recent addition to the morphology in Guazacapán (see chapter 7 on historical morphology). Only the most recent descriptions of the language mention it, and it is unattested in each of the other languages.

Chiquimulilla pronouns are unique compared to those in Guazacapán in that there is a distinction between INFORMAL and FORMAL in the second-person singular. Additionally, the third-person plural pronouns can optionally end in an [h]. The optionality of this segment must be indicated because it is unknown if there were any linguistic (or pragmatic) motivating factors involved in the variation. Table 3.4 illustrates the pronouns in Chiquimulilla.

Table 3.4 Chiquimulilla pronouns

1SG	*ni'*	1PL	*nalhik*
2SG.FORM	*nak*	2PL	*naylhik*
2SG.INFORM	*nay*		
3SG	*nah*	3PL	*nalhi(h)*

Jumaytepeque has a very similar pronoun system to that just discussed for Chiquimulilla. The only exception is an extension of the formal/informal distinction to plural pronouns as well. Table 3.5 lists the pronouns in Jumaytepeque. It exhibits the same optional final [h] in the third-person plural pronoun as in Chiquimulilla.

Table 3.5 Jumaytepeque pronouns

1SG	*ni'*	1PL	*nalki*
2SG.FORM	*nak*	2PL.FORM	*nalka/naalik*
2SG.INFORM	*nay*	2PL.INFORM	*nayliy*
3SG	*nah*	3PL	*naali(h)*

Finally, table 3.6 provides the pronominal system of Yupiltepeque as remembered by speakers of other Xinkan languages during the 1970s, and table 3.7 gives the Yupiltepeque pronouns as given by Calderón (1908: 12).

Table 3.6 Yupiltepeque pronouns

1SG	*nen/nin*	1PL	*nelek*
2SG	*nay*	2PL	*nalika*
3SG	*nah*	3PL	*nah*

Table 3.7 Yupiltepeque pronouns as given in Calderón (1908)

1SG	⟨nen⟩	1PL	⟨nec⟩
2SG	⟨nay⟩	2PL	⟨nalica⟩
3SG	⟨naj man⟩	3PL	⟨naj man aya⟩

In Yupiltepeque, pronouns lack an exclusive/inclusive or formal/informal distinction—or rather, if such distinctions existed, they were not recorded in the extant data.

Since Calderón's treatment of Chiquimulilla also lacks the formal/informal contrast in second-person singular pronouns that is represented in later documentation, it is possible that Yupiltepeque had additional contrasts among the pronouns not recorded in the data available to us. The absence of these pronominal categories in the written and recorded data does not indicate their absence in the language.

The pronominal systems of all four languages indicate the possible categorization of the abstract pronominal system of Proto-Xinkan. However, in practice, as mentioned above, often the singular forms are used for the plural persons, especially when there is not additional morphology. This is not an unusual attribute of pronominal systems cross-linguistically. The pronouns are compared more closely in section 7.1.1, with relevant reconstructions for Proto-Xinkan.

3.5.2 Dependent pronouns

Dependent pronouns, like independent pronouns, are used in place of a noun or noun phrase; that is, they refer anaphorically to a noun or noun phrase within the discourse. The two types of pronouns differ in that while independent pronouns are free morphemes, dependent pronouns are bound morphemes and must be attached to some word representing some other grammatical category. There are two types of dependent pronouns: prefixes and suffixes. When used with verbs, dependent pronouns always refer to the subject of the verb and never to its object. When used with nouns they represent possession of the noun.

3.5.2.1 *Pronominal prefixes*
Pronominal prefixes are attached to alienably possessed nouns (see section 3.1.1.1) and to verbs that indicate incompletive aspect (see section 3.6.3). Table 3.8 shows the pronominal prefixes in Guazacapán for nouns and transitive verbs. Throughout this grammatical description, this is referred to as pronominal SET B.

Table 3.8 Guazacapán pronominal SET B prefixes
for nouns and transitive verbs

1SG	*ün-*	1PL	*muk-*
2SG	*kaʔ-*	2PL	*ka-…ay*
3SG	*mu-*	3PL	*mu-…ay (lhik)*

The first-person plural prefix *muk-* is pronounced [muh-] when it is used with a consonant-initial root. This is a common process in the Xinkan phonology called lenition to [h] (see section 2.3.4). Similar to independent pronouns, the particle *ay* 'many, a lot' allows for an intervening word in certain word orders. The particle *lhik*, used with the third-person plural prefix, is a plural marker and is only used in very careful speech.

Intransitive verbs use two sets of personal pronominal prefixes that can be distinguished from SET B based on the third-person singular forms. One of these two intransitive prefix sets is used for the completive aspect (called SET C), while the other is used for the incompletive aspect (called SET D). These two pronominal prefix sets are shown in tables 3.9 and 3.10, respectively. Grammatical aspect and verb conjugation are discussed in sections 3.6.2 and 3.6.3.

Table 3.9 Guazacapán pronominal SET C prefixes for completive intransitive verbs

1SG	*ün-*	1PL	*muk-*
2SG	*ka?-*	2PL	*ka-. . . ay*
3SG	Ø- PERF	3PL	*Ø-. . . ay(lhik)*

Table 3.10 Guazacapán pronominal SET D prefixes for incompletive intransitive verbs

1SG	*ün-*	1PL	*muk-*
2SG	*ka?-*	2PL	*ka-. . . ay*
3SG	*a-* IPERF	3PL	*a-. . . ay(lhik)*

In Chiquimulilla, the pronominal prefixes are organized in a way quite distinct from that of Guazacapán. Specifically, as with the independent pronouns for this language, there is a formal/informal distinction. Table 3.11 shows the Chiquimulilla SET B prefixes for nouns and transitive verbs.

Table 3.11 Chiquimulilla SET B prefixes for nouns and transitive verbs

1SG	*ün-*	1PL	*mülhki-*
2SG.FORM	*mük-*	2PL.FORM	*mülhik-*
2SG.INFORM	*müy-*	2PL.INFORM	*mülhay-*
3SG	*mü-*	3PL	*mülhi(h)-*

In Chiquimulilla (and in Jumaytepeque, below) there is a distinction between formal and informal prefixes for the second-person singular and plural. Furthermore, due to lenition (see section 2.3.4) the second-personal singular formal prefix *mük-* is pronounced [müh-] before a consonant. Two things should be noted about the phonological shape of these prefixes. First, the 3PL prefix occurs with an optional word-final coda [h] which occurs in free variation in the data. Second, the 1PL and the 3PL prefixes are the only instances in Xinkan that do not obey the vowel harmony restrictions (see section 2.1.2). This might indicate that a recent morphological development or sound change has occurred in Chiquimulilla.

Like all the other Xinkan languages, Chiquimulilla has a separate set of personal pronominal prefixes that are used with intransitive verbs. Chiquimulilla personal pronominal prefixes SET C and SET D are given in tables 3.12 and 3.13, respectively.

The organization of Jumaytepeque SET B prefixes is identical to that of Chiquimulilla. However, the phonological shape of each of the prefixes is different. These are given in table 3.14.

Table 3.12 Chiquimulilla SET C prefixes for intransitive verbs

1SG	*ün-*	1PL	*mülhki-*
2SG.FORM	*mük-*	2PL.FORM	*mülhik-*
2SG.INFORM	*müy-*	2PL.INFORM	*mülhay-*
3SG	Ø-	3PL	*Ø-...lhik*

Table 3.13 Chiquimulilla SET D prefixes for intransitive verbs

1SG	*ün-*	1PL	*mülhki-*
2SG.FORM	*mük-*	2PL.FORM	*mülhik-*
2SG.INFORM	*müy-*	2PL.INFORM	*mülhay-*
3SG	*a-*	3PL	*a-...lhik*

Table 3.14 Jumaytepeque SET B prefixes for nouns and transitive verbs

1SG	*n-*	1PL	*lki-*
2SG.FORM	*k-*	2PL.FORM	*lka-/lik-*
2SG.INFORM	*y-*	2PL.INFORM	*liy-*
3SG-	*h-*	3PL	*lih-*

The pronunciation of the singular prefixes that consist of a single consonant requires [ə] to be epenthesized [ən-], [ək-], [əy-], and [əh-], respectively. This vowel is not phonemically contrastive, but it is phonetically predictable and is pronounced as a mid-central vowel. The reason for the variation between *lka-* and *lik-* is not clear, and both are given in the data.

Finally, Jumaytepeque SET C and SET D pronominal prefixes are slightly different than the ones for Chiquimulilla or Guazacapán. These prefixes are provided in tables 3.15 and 3.16, respectively.

Table 3.15 Jumaytepeque SET C prefixes for intransitive verbs

1SG	*n-*	1PL	*lki-*
2SG.FORM	*k-*	2PL.FORM	*lka-/lik-*
2SG.INFORM	*y-*	2PL.INFORM	*liy-*
3SG	Ø- PERF	3PL	*Ø-...lik* PERF

Table 3.16 Jumaytepeque SET D prefixes for intransitive verbs

1SG	*n-*	1PL	*lki-*
2SG.FORM	*k-*	2PL.FORM	*lka-/lik-*
2SG.INFORM	*y-*	2PL.INFORM	*liy-*
3SG	*a-*	3PL	*a-...lik*

The precise pronunciations of the Yupiltepeque prefixes are not known, but the system is organized similarly to the other Xinkan languages. A difference between the various sets of prefixes, as in the other Xinkan languages, is suggested through incomplete evidence: only Yupiltepeque SET B prefixes are attested. These are given in table 3.17.

Table 3.17 Yupiltepeque SET B pronominal prefixes

1SG	n-	1PL	muh-
2SG	y-	2PL	lika-
3SG	—	3PL	-...ay

The 3SG and 3PL prefixes are null—they have no phonetic content—although as can be seen, they contrast with the forms in the rest of the system. Furthermore, the 3PL makes use of the particle *ay* and is placed directly after the word to which the 3PL applies. This particle is not listed as having any independent meaning in the data available.

3.5.2.2 *Pronominal suffixes*

Each of the Xinkan languages possesses two sets of pronominal suffixes: one set for nouns (called SET E) and one for transitive verbs (called SET A). With nouns the suffixes indicate inalienable possession (see section 3.1.1.2), while with verbs they indicate the completive aspect (see sections 3.6.2 and 3.6.3). Table 3.18 shows the SET E noun suffixes for Guazacapán.

Table 3.18 Guazacapán SET E noun suffixes

1SG	-n'	1PL	-k
2SG	-ka(ʔ)	2PL	-ka ay
3SG	-h	3PL	-h lhik

The optional glottal stop [ʔ] at the end of the 2SG suffix is used only when the noun being possessed is clause final or sentence final. The particles *ay* and *lhik*, in the plural form of the second and third persons, respectively, are placed directly after the noun. Table 3.19 shows SET A suffixes used for transitive verbs in Guazacapán.

Table 3.19 Guazacapán SET A verbal suffixes

1SG	-n'	1PL	-k
2SG	-kaʔ/-kan	2PL	-ka ay
3SG	-y'	3PL	-y' ay

The only aspect of the suffixal system that requires note is the variation indicated for the 2SG suffix between *-kaʔ* and *-kan*. The difference is based on the position of the verb within the sentence. If the verb is in the main clause, *-kaʔ* is used; if the verb is in a subordinate or other dependent clause, *-kan* is used.

In Chiquimulilla, nouns can be inalienably possessed using the SET E suffixes given in table 3.20 (see section 3.1.1.2). The 1SG suffix is a glottal stop [ʔ]. (See section 2.6 for the orthography.) The distinction made between formal and informal second-person independent pronouns is also found with the dependent pronouns. The Chiquimulilla

SET A transitive verb suffixes are provided in table 3.21. These verbal suffixes are used to indicate the subject/agent of a verb in the incompletive aspect (see section 3.6.3).

Table 3.20 Chiquimulilla SET E nominal suffixes

1SG	-'	1PL	-lhki'
2SG.FORM	-k	2PL.FORM	-lhik
2SG.INFORM	-ay	2PL.INFORM	-y lhik
3SG	-h	3PL	-lhi(h)

Table 3.21 Chiquimulilla SET A verbal suffixes

1SG	-n'	1PL	-lhik'
2SG.FORM	-kan	2PL.FORM	-lhik
2SG.INFORM	-y	2PL.INFORM	-y lhik
3SG	-y'	3PL	-lhi(h)

Jumaytepeque SET E nominal suffixes are given in table 3.22. As in all other Xinkan languages, these suffixes are used to inalienably possess a noun. Furthermore, like Chiquimulilla (but different from Guazacapán), there is an important distinction between formal and informal second person dependent pronouns. Table 3.23 indicates the SET A transitive verb suffixes in Jumaytepeque.

Table 3.22 Jumaytepeque SET E nominal suffixes

1SG	-n	1PL	-lki'
2SG.FORM	-ka'	2PL.FORM	-lik
2SG.INFORM	-y	2PL.INFORM	-liy
3SG	-h	3PL	-hri

Table 3.23 Jumaytepeque SET A verbal suffixes

1SG	-n'/-n	1PL	-lki'
2SG.FORM	-ka'/(-ili)	2PL.FORM	-lik
2SG.INFORM	-y	2PL.INFORM	-liy
3SG	-yi'	3PL	-hri

The data on Yupiltepeque is taken from my philological analysis of Calderón (1908: 17–20) described in chapter 1. As one major characteristic of my analysis, I have given all of the forms in the original source their approximate phonetic values in order to provide a more straightforward comparison between the four languages. Table 3.24 provides the SET E nominal suffixes and table 3.25 provides the SET A verbal suffixes.

Table 3.24 Yupiltepeque SET E nominal suffixes

1SG	-n	1PL	-k
2SG	-y	2PL	-lika
3SG	-h	3PL	-h

Table 3.25 Yupiltepeque SET A verbal suffixes

1SG	-n	1PL	-k
2SG	-y	2PL	-lika
3SG	-i	3PL	-i

There are other verbal suffixes, such as the imperative suffixes, for all of the Xinkan languages. These are described in the next section. The dependent pronouns are discussed at length in section 7.1.2, and reconstructions for Proto-Xinkan are hypothesized there as well.

3.6 Verbs

In Xinkan languages verbs can denote a variety of meanings, including events, actions, states, and achievements, as the most obvious examples. Verbs are clearly defined based on four morphosyntactic properties: (1) they can be inflected for subject agreement (the only grammatical category that exhibits any kind of agreement); (2) they are inflected for changes in grammatical aspect; (3) they can be used as the predicates of a sentence; and (4) they act as the base for a number of verbal and nominal derivations. These broad characteristics are discussed in this section.

The form of verbs varies with differences in meaning. For example, verbs can be used in an infinitive form or a finite form. For transitive verbs, the infinitive form is the bare verb root, while for intransitive verbs the infinitive form is the root marked for the completive aspect. Along with being the infinite forms of the verb bases, these also serve as the dictionary headwords for entries involving verbs. All finite forms of the verb are produced from these infinitive bases. When used in the infinitive form, a verb is understood as being uninflected for grammatical aspect and is typically used on serial verb constructions (see section 4.6.2) or in citation forms. Nonfinite forms of the verbs can be inflected for subject agreement and for one of two grammatical aspects: either the completive or the incompletive.

Verbs marked for the completive aspect indicate a completed action; verbs marked for the incompletive aspect indicate an uncompleted action, such as imperative, durative (progressive), future, and habitual actions. Each of the inflectional processes related to verbs is discussed in this section. Derivational operations including causative verbs, passive verbs, antipassive verbs, and nouns which can be derived from verb roots are discussed in section 3.12.

3.6.1   Verb classes and transitivity

Xinkan verbs are lexically and morphologically divided into four classes or categories: TRANSITIVE VERBS, INTRANSITIVE AGENTIVE VERBS, INTRANSITIVE AFFECTIVE VERBS, and FLUID INTRANSITIVE VERBS. Fundamental to this categorization are differences in transitivity and the relationship between the verb root and the grammatical subject. Other grammatical systems are highly correlated to transitivity and verb categorization, including subject-verb agreement (section 3.6.2), grammatical aspect (section 3.6.3), grammatical voice (section 3.6.7), and syntactic alignment (section 4.1). The verb class system is discussed below, and where necessary these specific correlations are discussed in the other respective sections of the grammar.

Transitive verbs in Xinkan have two or three core nominal arguments. These arguments can be nouns, pronouns, determiners, or adjectives and are required by the verb root. Grammatically these arguments function as the subject, direct object, or indirect object. Semantically they function as either the agent or patient in the case of verbs with two nominal arguments; or as the agent, patient, or beneficiary/recipient in the case of verbs with three nominal arguments. Morphologically there is no overt distinction in the marking of two-argument transitive verbs or three-argument transitive verbs (called ditransitive verbs in traditional grammatical descriptions).

Intransitive verbs in Xinkan have a single core nominal argument. Like transitive verbs, arguments of intransitive verbs can be nouns, pronouns, determiners, or adjectives, as required by the verb root. This sole nominal argument always functions grammatically as the subject. The core argument—the subject—of intransitive agentive verbs semantically functions as the agent, controller, or performer of the verb. The core nominal argument of intransitive affective verbs semantically functions as the undergoer or experiencer of the verb.

Grammatical functions, such as subject and direct object, are not marked through nominal case but are indicated on the verb (via subject agreement marking) and by linear word order in cases of ambiguity (see section 4.1.1). Semantic functions of core nominal arguments, such as agent or undergoer, are unmarked on transitive verbs but are marked on the verb root for both types of intransitive verbs.

Verb transitivity is a property of lexical organization in Xinkan as all the inflectional and derivational processes are dependent on the underlying (i.e., lexically specified) value of transitivity for any given verb root. Similarly, the division of verb roots into the four verb categories is also a property of the lexical organization and is language-specific. That is, while the general pattern and organizational scheme is the same for all of the Xinkan languages, each of the languages divides their verbs into these classes differently; what is an intransitive agentive verb in Guazacapán, for example, may be an intransitive affective verb in Chiquimulilla, Jumaytepeque, or Yupiltepeque.

What is cross-linguistically quite interesting about the collective Xinkan languages is that the verb categorization system is based on the underlying lexical and semantic relationships and that these are marked overtly in the morphology. This is similar, though not identical, to verb class systems in other languages and to what has been called semantic alignment—though the Xinkan system does not mark grammatical function.[16]

Transitive verbs in Xinkan are not marked overtly for class membership, though they are the only verb roots that have more than one core argument. They contrast with both types of intransitive verbs, which are overtly marked for class membership and which have only one core argument. Intransitive agentive verbs are marked by the presence of the suffix *-lha'* [-ɬaʔ] (Guazacapán and Chiquimulilla), *-la'* [-laʔ] (Jumaytepeque), and ⟨-lá⟩ in Yupiltepeque. Intransitive affective verbs are marked by the presence of the suffix *-'* [-ʔ] in all Xinkan languages. (There is no data that indicates this is or is not the case in Yupiltepeque.) The class of intransitive agentive verbs is much smaller than the class of intransitive affective verbs. Fluid intransitive verbs constitute a minor group of verbs that can be marked for either the agentive class or the affective class. Since these are not morphologically different from the intransitive affective or intransitive agentive verbs, the fluid verbs are not discussed independently here but are discussed further below in this section (see examples 147–149).

Class membership markers are required on all intransitive verbs whether they are derived from transitive verbs or are lexically specified as being intransitive (i.e., non-derived intransitive verb roots). Note that the translations of the Xinkan intransitive verbs do not clearly correspond to English verb forms. This means that the translations do not always represent the exact semantics in the Xinkan languages.

Examples of verbs in each of the three classes from each language are given in 138–140. The letters in boldface mark the suffix.

(138) Guazacapán verbs.

IV.AFF:	*kïïrï'*	'pulled out'	*ormo'*	'gathered'	*palhka'*	'nailed'
IV.AGT:	*tik'ilha'*	'sleep'	*eplelha'*	'be afraid'	*poch'olha'*	'rot'
TV:	*hük'a*	'sew'	*kixi*	'roast'	*paaxi*	'chew'

(139) Chiquimulilla verbs.

IV.AFF:	*kïïwï'*	'dried up'	*parni'*	'broken'	*xarni'*	'strain'
IV.AGT:	*ch'aw'ikilha'*	'agonize'	*ïïn'alha'*	'get dirty'	*lharw'ulha'*	'dance'
TV:	*chuyku*	'smash'	*etz'e*	'open'	*hawka*	'empty'

(140) Jumaytepeque verbs.

IV.AFF:	*ahm'ï'*	'hidden'	*hayp'u'*	'received'	*hïïiya'*	'chopped'
IV.AGT:	*ïy'ala'*	'laugh'	*mïïm'üla'*	'sing'	*xür'ürüla'*	'shake'
TV:	*hükayi'*	'weave'	*uuxayi'*	'blow'	*uxtuyi'*	'gather'

The data from Yupiltepeque does indicate that these classes most likely existed for this language, but much of the information needed to support the claim is not available. Calderón (1908: 19) does list one verb that may show the intransitive agentive class marker: ⟨ne saparikilá⟩ 'I threshed the corn' ('*desgrané la mazorca*'). However, I have listed it as a transitive verb. Similarly, throughout the glossary accompanying Calderón's grammatical descriptions, an accent is often placed on the final syllable of some intransitive verbs, for example ⟨ixí⟩ 'wake up' (cf. [iišiʔ] in the other three languages). If stress assignment in Yupiltepeque is consistent with the other languages, the word-final accent in Yupiltepeque indicates the presence of a word-final consonant, probably a glottal stop. This would be a marker of the intransitive affective verb class, as in the other languages.

Intransitive verbs that denote an action that is always performed by an 'agent' in control of the action itself, such as 'work' *müka*, always belong to the agentive class and denote an action that is an event or temporary state. That is, the core semantic relationship between the verb and the subject is one of control; the subject of an intransitive agentive verb has control over the action and the resultant state caused by the action. This is understood to mean that the subject can avoid doing the action if desired or undo the action once done. The agentive class marker serves to indicate that the grammatical subject is also the logical agent of the action (i.e., is equivalent semantically to the subject/agent of a transitive verb). This agentivity of the subject does not imply that the nominal argument is animate and/or volitional; the subject must merely be the *performer* of the action denoted—what Klaiman (1991: 112–137) refers to as being able to have the 'exercise of outcome control'.

In contrast, intransitive verbs that belong to the affective class are those whose subjects are not in control of the action or ensuing state. The subject of an intransitive affective verb cannot undo or avoid the action but rather undergoes the action. The core semantic relationship between the verb and the grammatical subject is one of affectedness; the subject is the logical patient of the action. These subjects are understood as lacking the properties of performance and control present in intransitive agentive verbs.

The lists of intransitive verbs in 141–146 provide examples of each intransitive verb class and are not an exhaustive catalog of all the intransitive verbs in each language. As mentioned above, intransitive agentive verbs are always marked with the suffix -*lha'* (Guazacapán and Chiquimulilla), or -*la'* (Jumaytepeque), while intransitive affective verbs always end with the suffix -*'* [-ʔ] (in all languages).

(141) Guazacapán intransitive agentive verbs.

mük'alha'	'work'	*tik'ilha'*	'sleep'
ohoomelha'	'cough'	*hüyük'ülha'*	'nod from sleepiness'
hat'ixmalha'	'sneeze'	*uxk'ilha'*	'smoke (a cigarette)'
yürnalha'	'fall'	*t'uhmilha'*	'spit'
püpr'ülha'	'burp'	*lhawrulha'*	'dance'
tüxk'ülha'	'retreat'	*iplalha'*	'bathe'
harnalha'	'be sick'	*yanalha'*	'be ashamed'
nümalha'	'eat'	*purilha'*	'answer'
xiin'alha'	'defecate'	*müümülha'*	'sing'
k'ün'ülha'	'complain, gossip'	*kawilha'*	'cry'
p'elelelha'	'drool'	*polholholha'*	'pass liquidlike gas'
xay'ay'alha'	'be nauseous'	*wayalha'*	'work the corn field'

(142) Guazacapán intransitive affective verbs.

iixi'	'be alive, awake'	*saaka'*	'get up, be lifted'
meete'	'take heart, be encouraged'	*muuchu'*	'be tired'
paata'	'be able'	*uupu'*	'stand up'
k'aata'	'lie down'	*lhiik'a'*	'descend'
wereke'	'be angry'	*pelhteme'*	'turn around, return'
porna'	'burst'	*uuchu'*	'dirty one's face'
waxta'	'enter'	*tahna'*	'sprout'
p'uski'	'burst'	*p'ühna'*	'leap, jump'
mutku'	'to hustle, swindle'	*murki'*	'break'
k'okma'	'kneel'	*ixpa'*	'leave'
p'arna'	'rip, tear'	*siiru'*	'hurry'
lhaara'	'ascend, climb'	*uulhu'*	'be fallen'
toone'	'be quiet'	*iiwi'*	'drown'
kakra'	'bend over/down, squat, duck'		

(143) Chiquimulilla intransitive agentive verbs.

tuk'ulha'	'be able'	*sik'ulha'*	'hiccup'
werek'elha'	'have a tantrum, be angry'	*lhotor'olha'*	'snore'
k'üsük'ülha'	'fight'	*ohomelha'*	'cough'
hüyük'ülha'	'nod (from being sleepy)'	*hor'orolha'*	'snore loudly'
haw'axmalha'	'yawn'	*wrik'ilha'*	'speak'
t'ixt'alha'	'pass gas'	*püp'rülha'*	'burp'
larw'ulha'	'dance'	*iplalha'*	'bathe'
harn'alha'	'be sick'	*eplhelha'*	'be afraid'
lhot'elha'	'be buggary'	*yan'alha'*	'be ashamed, shy'
müüm'ülha'	'sing'	*pur'ilha'*	'burn'

k'ün'ülha'	'think'	*wayalha'*	'work in the cornfield'
wech'elha'	'drool, slobber'		

(144) Chiquimulilla intransitive affective verbs.

iixi'	'be alive, awake'	*maasa'*	'be stuck (with glue)'
meete'	'take heart, be encouraged'	*uupu'*	'stand up'
k'aata'	'lie down'	*haapa'*	'cross, occur, appear'
lhiik'a'	'descend'	*'tiik'i'*	'sleep'
p'elhteme'	'turn around, return'	*silhik'alhu'*	'confess'
p'orna'	'explode fireworks'	*k'osme'*	'to thunder'
yahyi'	'go by water, float away'	*p'ütna'*	'jump, leap'
k'uxku'	'be cloudy'	*k'okma'*	'kneel'
k'atra	'be dragged'	*kakra'*	'squat, duck, bend'
üptz'ü'	'be old'	*tüxk'ü'*	'be far away'
t'uulhu'	'for eyes to get rheum'	*ixpa'*	'leave'
hopna'	'burst, explode'	*erlheke'*	'be scared'
lhaara'	'climb' (<Sp. *'subirse'*)	*p'eeno'*	'be to one side'
p'oocho'	'for a boil/pimple to develop/come out'		

(145) Jumaytepeque intransitive agentive verbs.

mük'ala'	'work'	*sik'ula'*	'hiccup'
tik'ila'	'sleep'	*hurn'ala'*	'be very hot (weather)'
hür'ür'ula'	'spark (fire)'	*werek'ela'*	'cry, make a frog's sound'
tur'ur'ula'	'to thunder'	*ten'en'ela'*	'be asleep'
sur'ur'ula'	'for there to be a whirlwind'	*müür'üla'*	'complain'
luukuk'ala'	'be crazy from being drunk'	*k'or'oxela'*	'drag'
kühühüla'	'laugh'	*hunhun'ala'*	'be dark'
ohomela'	'cough'	*hawaxmala'*	'yawn'
wixt'ala'	'whistle'	*worn'ola'*	'boil'
tixt'ala'	'pass gas'	*püpr'üla'*	'burp'
p'ütn'ala'	'leap, jump, skip'	*larw'üla'*	'dance'
t'ür'ür'üla'	'shake, tremble'	*tüxk'üla'*	'be far away'
apl'ala'	'bathe'	*küm'üm'üla'*	'smell'
hür'ünün'üla'	'arrive starving and eat everything'		

(146) Jumaytepeque intransitive affective verbs.

ch'iichi'	'defecate'	*iixi'*	'wake up, remember'
k'ooxo'	'be dried up'	*meete'*	'get better'
k'aata'	'lie down'	*haapa'*	'pass, get ahead'
liiha'	'descend'	*yuxtuha'*	'slip out, overflow'
puur'iki'	'be married'	*pelteme'*	'turn around, turn to one side'
hürlami'	'return'	*charaha'*	'fall doing the splits'
p'ornoha'	'burst'	*waxt'a'*	'arrive, enter, come close'
utr'u'	'to curl up, not able to walk'	*tahna'*	'grow, achieve'
telna'	'slip'	*p'usn'u'*	'to curl up'

salk'a'	'be face up'	*lüsk'ü'*	'be thin'
kukm'a'	'kneel'	*k'atr'a'*	'crawl, be dragged' (<Sp. *'agacharse'*)
kakr'a'	'be hunched over'	*üptz'ü'*	'grow' (<Sp. *'sazonarse'?*)
yahy'i'	'drown, be carried away by the river'		

There are some intransitive verbs that can belong to either the agentive class or the affective class. That is, some verbs can take as their only nominal argument either undergoers (logical patients) of the action (intransitive affective) or doers (logical agents) of the action. Because of the unique membership status of these verbs, they are called FLUID INTRANSITIVE VERBS. There are only a handful of these verbs in each language; the complete list of fluid intransitive verbs for each language is given in 147–149.

(147) Guazacapán intransitive fluid verbs.
    a. *purik'ilha'/puriki'*   'marry, be married'
    b. *p'ihnaykilha'/p'ihnayki'* 'thunder'
    c. *tixtala'/tixta'*   'pass gas'
    d. *üyalha'/üya'*   'laugh'
    e. *kup'anilha'/kup'ahni'* 'trip'

(148) Chiquimulilla intransitive fluid verbs.
    a. *p'ilhnaykilha'/p'ilhnayki'* 'thunder'
    b. *müt'alhkila'/müt'alhki'* 'dream'
    c. *sir'ula'/siiru'*   'hurry'
    d. *melhelha'/melhe'*   'drool, slobber'
    e. *müür'ükilha'/müür'üki'* 'complain a lot'

(149) Jumaytepeque intransitive fluid verbs.
    a. *hat'ismala'/hat'isma'* 'sneeze'
    b. *üy'ala'/üya'*   'laugh'

I must emphasize that the distinction between an agentive and an affective intransitive verb is an inherent part of the verb's semantics and that class membership determines the argument structure a verb root permits. That is, the division into two verb classes is a characteristic of the verbs themselves, based on their meaning and made within the lexicon; it is not the consequence of specific (postlexical) grammatical processes.

In addition, while intransitive verbs are inherently members of one or the other classes depending on their meaning, the membership of both intransitive verb classes can be augmented through derivation from transitive verbs. In this case, the newly derived intransitive verb is assigned to one of the two classes. Most commonly, a transitive verb can derive either an affective *or* an agentive verb, the choice being determined in the lexicon. However, certain transitive verbs can derive an affective verb *and* an agentive verb, the choice being dependent on the intended meaning of the speaker's utterance. Verb derivation is discussed in section 3.12.3.

3.6.2 Subject agreement

The grammatical subjects of all verbs are indicated through agreement affixes on the verb. Transitive verbs use SET A and SET B affixes, and all intransitive verbs use SET C and SET D affixes—these sets of affixes are defined and described in section 3.5.2. These affixes mark agreement of the verb with the subject in terms of the latter's person and number characteristics. When the grammatical subject is a pronoun, the affix may be omitted since the agreement information is encoded in the pronominal affix. This omission usually happens in continuous speech rather than in elicited or isolated speech. The choice between the two pronominal agreement sets for each verb indicates a change in the grammatical aspect of the verb (see section 3.6.3). In the example sentences in 150–152, subject-verb agreement is first shown for transitive verbs (the a and b examples) and then for intransitive verbs (the c examples). The agreement-marking affix is in boldface; parentheses around the grammatical subject indicate its optionality in the clause.

(150) Guazacapán subject-verb concord.
    a. *im'a-y nen' (nah)*   (SS:1979, 7)
       tell.COMP-3SG.SETA I (he)
       'He told me.'
    b. *lhek'e-n na tumin (nen')*   (COM:1979, 47)
       find.COM-1SG.SETA the money (I)
       'I found the money.'
    c. *ün-mük'a-lha' (nen')*   (EX:1089)
       1SG.SETC-work.COMP-IV.AGT (I)
       'I worked.'

(151) Chiquimulilla subject-verb concord.
    a. *tuura-k na ma' (nak)*   (EX:138)
       bring.COMP-2SG.SETA the that (you.FORM)
       'You bring that one.'
    b. *kuy xuk'a-y nak na wilhay*   (EX:122)
       FUT eat.COMP-3SG.SETA you.FORM the tiger
       'The tiger will eat you.'
    c. *müy-harn'a-lha' (nay)*   (EX:2)
       2SG.FORM.SETC-be.sick-IV.AGT (you.INFORM)
       'You were sick.'

(152) Jumaytepeque subject-verb concord.
    a. *müya-ka' nin (nak)*   (EX:144)
       help.COMP-2SG.SETA I (you.FORM)
       'You helped me.'
    b. *ut'u-yi' a ur'ul a miya*   (EX:319)
       lay.egg.COMP-3SG.SETA the egg the chicken
       'The chicken laid the egg.'

c. ***Iki-k'aama-' (nalki)***   (EX:421)
   1PL.SETC-hug-stat (We)
   'We hugged.'

The agreement marker indicates a relationship between the verb and one grammatical function, the subject. In this it is independent from the verb class system that
marks semantic role relationships. That is, for transitive verbs and intransitive agentive
verbs the subject and the agent of the verb coincide—are one and the same thing—
while subjects of intransitive affective verbs coincide with the logical (i.e., semantic)
patient (undergoer), and there is no agent argument. In both cases, agreement refers
to the grammatical subject of the verb.

3.6.3   Grammatical aspect

Xinkan verbs can also be inflected for one of two grammatical aspects: COMPLETIVE or
INCOMPLETIVE. In the case of the completive aspect, the action is seen as completed,
over, or unchangeable. Often this coincides with the past tense in other languages. The
incompletive aspect indicates an incomplete or ongoing action and can coincide with
the past, present, or future tenses in other languages. Grammatical aspect is indicated
in two ways on the verb: through the choice of pronominal agreement affixes, and by
alternations in the pronunciation of the rightmost consonant of the verb root as either
a plain or glottalized consonant.

Each verb root can be marked with one of two agreement strategies: SET A or SET B
for transitive verbs, and SET C or SET D for both types of intransitive verbs. The choice
between these two options is correlated with changes in grammatical aspect. For transitive verbs, the completive aspect is marked by SET A *suffixes,* while the incompletive aspect is marked by SET B *prefixes.* For intransitive verbs, the completive aspect is
marked by SET C *prefixes,* while the incompletive aspect is marked by SET D *prefixes.*
Examples 153–156 showing changes in grammatical aspect are from Guazacapán, but
the same pattern holds true for the other Xinkan languages.

(153) Guazacapán completive transitive verb.
       *piri-**n'** Hwan nen'*   (EX:2263)
       see.COMP-1SG.SETA Juan I
       'I saw Juan.'

(154) Guazacapán incompletive transitive verb.
       ***ün-**pir'i Hwan nen'*   (EX:2262)
       1SG.SETB-see.ICOMP Juan I
       'I see Juan.'

(155) Guazacapán completive intransitive verb.
       Ø-tik'i-lha' nah   (TYA:1979, 23)
       3SG.SETC-sleep.COMP-IV.AGT he
       'He slept.'[17]

(156) Guazacapán incompletive intransitive verb.
    a-tik'i nah   (TYA:1979, 6)
    3SG.SETD-sleep.ICOMP he
    'He sleeps.'

As a second marker of grammatical aspect, the rightmost consonant of the verb stem shows variation between its underlying pronunciation (the completive aspect) and its glottalized counterpart (the incompletive aspect). This process of glottalization is discussed in section 2.3.1. Often the rightmost consonant of the verb stem is a glottalized consonant underlyingly (i.e., by lexical specification); in these cases there are no discernible changes in pronunciation from one grammatical aspect to the other. (In other words, the glottalizing process applies vacuously.) Furthermore, if the outcome of the glottalization process creates an unacceptable string of segments (i.e., a consonant cluster with a glottalized consonant, CC') then a vowel is epenthesized to break this cluster (see section 2.3.1). Examples 157–160 show the changes due to glottalization in boldface and are taken from Chiquimulilla.

(157) Chiquimulilla completive transitive verb.
    hüya-n' utu   (EX:25)
    chop.COMP-1SETA tree
    'I chopped the tree.' (i.e., cut wood)

(158) Chiquimulilla incompletive transitive verb.
    ün-hüy'a utu   (EX:26)
    1SETB-chop.ICOMP tree
    'I chop the tree.' 'I am chopping the tree.'

(159) Chiquimulilla completive intransitive verb.
    müy-ohome-lha'   (EX:144)
    2SETC-cough.COMP-IV.AGT
    'You coughed.'

(160) Chiquimulilla incompletive intransitive verb.
    müy-ohom'e-Ø   (EX:145)
    2SG.SETD-cough.ICOMP-IV.AGT
    'You cough.'

In terms of lexical organization, the verb in the completive form without prefixes can be seen as the basic form on which all other verb inflections and derivations are based—this is phonologically identical to the infinitive verb form in Guazacapán and Chiquimulilla. In Jumaytepeque, however, all verb forms are bound morphemes. Consequently, in this language the infinitive forms are homophonous with the completive form of the verb with the 3SG.SETA suffix *-yi'* (with an allomorph *-ye'* based on vowel harmony rules: see section 2.1.2). For example, *luusu-yi'* bite.COMP-3SG.SETA 'it bit' is the infinitive form of the verb—not **luusu 'to bite'. The appendix contains a complete paradigm of verbal conjugations in each language, along with listings of some irregular verbs.

As seen and discussed in detail throughout this chapter, intransitive verb conjugation patterns are distinct from those of transitive verbs. The two intransitive verb agreement sets contain only prefixes (in contrast to the prefixes and suffixes in the transitive verb sets), and intransitive verbs must be marked for class membership. However, intransitive agentive verbs do not mark class membership on incompletive verb forms. This is highlighted, in boldfacing, in the example phrases in 161.

(161) Guazacapán intransitive agentive verb aspects.
    a. *ka-tik'i-**lha'** naka*
       2SETC-sleep.COMP-IV.AGT you
       'You slept.'
    b. *ka-tik'i-**Ø** naka*
       2SETD-sleep.ICOMP-IV.AGT you
       'You sleep.'

Lastly, intransitive affective verbs exhibit a variation in vowel length in the two aspectual forms: a long vowel is required in the completive form and a short vowel is required in the incompletive form. This lengthening variation is dependent on the phonotactic constraints in Xinkan and is only observable in bisyllabic verb roots that lack consonant clusters (i.e., CVCV). The phonotactic constraints are discussed in section 2.1.1.2.

(162) Chiquimulilla intransitive affective verb in both aspects.
    a. *Ø-paawa-'*
       3SG.SETC-light.on.fire.COMP-IV.AFF
       'It was lit on fire.'
    b. *a-pawa-'*
       3SG.SETD-light.on.fire.ICOMP-IV.AFF
       'It is lit on fire.'

Each of these three requirements on intransitive verbs is applicable to all Xinkan languages. (It is unclear if this is true also for Yupiltepeque, but see the appendix for the data on Yupiltepeque verb conjugations.)

3.6.4   Imperative form

All verb types (transitive, intransitive agentive, intransitive affective, and fluid intransitive) can be used in an imperative form. This form of the verb stem is not marked for aspect, tense, or mood and is often used as a command from the speaker to the hearer. Each of the Xinkan languages has a different set of constructions that create the imperative form, although suffixation is used in all of the languages to create the imperative.

In Guazacapán, there are two ways to form the imperative of transitive verbs: through the use of the infinitive form, or by adding the suffix *-ki'* to the verb base. In contrast, in this language there is only a single construction to form the imperative of intransitive verbs: attaching the suffix *-y'a* to the incompletive verb base. This suffix becomes an allomorph [-ya] without the glottalized consonant when it occurs after a verb stem with another glottalized consonant in the final syllable. (This process of deglottalization is discussed in section 2.3.1.4.) In the following examples all options for constructing the imperative form of a verb are given. For transitive verbs, in 163, the form on the left is the imperative form created by suffixation, while the form on the right is the imperative form that is homophonous with the infinitive form of the verb. For intransitive verbs, in 164a and 164b, the lexical verb class is also indicated (on the right) because the class membership suffixes are omitted in this form of the verb.[18]

(163) Guazacapán transitive verb imperatives.

    a. *wïïïxa-ki'*   or   *wïïïxa*
       shake.it.out-IMPV.TV   shake.it.out
       'Shake it out!'

(164) Guazacapán intransitive verb imperatives.

    a. *itz'i-ya*   intransitive affective verb
       wake.up-IMPV.IV
       'Wake up!'

    b. *müka-y'a*   intransitive agentive verb
       work-IMPV.IV
       'Work!'

In Chiquimulilla, the imperative form of a transitive verb is most commonly formed by lengthening the last vowel in the stem and adding in the suffix *-k* 2SG.SETE. However, due to the phonotactic constraints of the language (see sections 2.1 and 2.2), if the first syllable of the verb base has a long vowel in the nucleus, the lengthening of the vowel of the last syllable in the imperative is blocked. (There is no evidence attested that a second imperative construction for transitive verbs is possible, unlike Guazacapán, described above, in which the infinitive form can also function as the imperative meaning.) In contrast, the imperative of all intransitive verbs in Chiquimulilla is formed by adding the suffix *-y'* to the verb root. Transitive verb imperative forms are given in 165 and intransitive verb imperative forms are given in 166; the verb class is indicated to the right.

(165) Chiquimulilla transitive verb imperatives.

    a. *huuxa-k*
       blow-IMPV.TV
       'Blow it!'

    b. *k'üt'üü-k*
       weigh-IMPV.TV
       'Weigh it!'

(166) Chiquimulilla intransitive verb imperatives.

    a. *upu-y'*   intransitive affective verb
       stand.up-IMPV.IV
       'Stand up!'

    b. *ipla-y'*   intransitive agentive verb
       bathe-IMPV.IV
       'Bathe!'

In Jumaytepeque the imperative verbs forms are constructed in the same way as in Chiquimulilla: for transitive verbs, the last vowel of the root is lengthened and the suffix *-k* is attached; for intransitive verbs the suffix *-y'* is attached. Similarly, there is variation in the intransitive verb suffix based on phonotactic constraints (see section 2.1 and 2.2). Additionally, like Chiquimulilla, there is no evidence attested that the infinitive form of the verb can also be used as an imperative, as it can be in Guazacapán. The examples in 167 give the imperative forms of transitive verbs and those in 168 give intransitive verbs with verb class indicated.

(167) Jumaytepeque transitive verb imperatives.
    a. *k'uhmii-k*
       fold-IMPV.TV
       'Fold it!'
    b. *mütz'aa-k*
       bury-IMPV.TV
       'Bury it!'

(168) Jumaytepeque intransitive imperatives.
    a. *mete-y'*   intransitive affective verb
       feel.better-IMPV.IV
       'Get well!'
    b. *tik'i-y'*   intransitive agentive verb
       sleep-IMPV.IV
       'Sleep!'

3.6.5   Contrastive construction in Guazacapán

There is one other inflectional suffix that is used with transitive verbs in Guazacapán but not in the other Xinkan languages: *-lhan* CONTRASTIVE. When a verb carries this suffix, it signifies that the speaker is contrasting the actual agent of an action with an assumed agent of that action. The label contrastive reflects this meaning. This suffix cannot be used in isolated sentences (such as elicited example sentences) as the contrast is made with an assumption from earlier on in a discourse situation. For example, if in a conversation (the discourse situation) a particular individual was assumed to have performed an action, this suffix can be used to correct this assumption by indicating who or what actually performed it; examples are in 169. This suffix provides contrastive emphasis on the performer (agent) of an action and it requires subject agreement affixes. The examples in 169 are based on the transitive verbs *kaayi* 'to sell' and *kawi* 'to yell' or 'to call'. In 169a and 169c, these two verbs are shown without the contrastive suffix; in 169b and 169d, they are shown with the contrastive suffix. Unfortunately, there is no data which attests this construction for any of the intransitive verb classes.

(169) Guazacapán contrastive emphasis.

    a. *kaayi-n map'u*   (EX:1779)
        sell.COMP-1SG tortilla
        'I sold tortillas.'

    b. *ün-kaayi-lhan map'u*   (EX:666)
        1SG-sell.COMP-CONTR tortilla
        'It is I who sold the tortillas, and not someone else.'

    c. *kawi-n naka*   (EX:2340)
        call.COMP-1SG.SETA you
        'I called (to) you.'

    d. *ün-kawi-lhan naka*   (EX:700)
        1sg-call.COMP-CONTR you
        'It is I who called (to) you.'

3.6.6   Tense

The aspectual system described in section 3.6.3 is the most prominent property of Xinkan verbs—it is an obligatory inflection on all verbs, and it is marked on the verb head itself. However, the grammatical marking of time, or tense, can optionally be made through one of two verbal particles. These particles indicate if the verbal action occurred before the moment of utterance (i.e., past tense), or if the verbal action will occur after the moment of utterance (i.e., future tense).

3.6.6.1   *Past tense*

Past tense is indicated by the particle *na'alh* (Guazacapán), *kiwi'* (Chiquimulilla), or *k'i'* (Jumaytepeque). The past-tense particle is optional and can be used with verbs in the completive or incompletive aspects, or with the participles that have been derived from verbs (see section 3.12.3.5). The past tense in Xinkan means that the beginning of the event or state denoted in the verb was performed sometime previous to the time of speaking. Past tense does not indicate an endpoint for this verbal action; it may be unknown or unimportant in reference to the speaking time. Consequently, when modifying verbs, the past-tense particle is often translated as the past perfective or the past progressive since these tenses in English, Spanish, and many other languages indicate uncertainty in the endpoint of a past action. Finally, past tense may be relative. That is, the past-tense particle can be used within a string of discourse to indicate that a verbal action was initiated previously in the discourse world.

While the overall pattern of past-tense marking is accurate for all Xinkan languages, the individual past-tense particles in each language are not cognates and may have developed independently.[19] In addition, in Guazacapán the past-tense marker can be pronounced in one of two ways: before the verb, it is pronounced [naɬ]; anywhere in the clause following the verb, this particle is pronounced [naʔaɬ]. The choice between these options does not seem to be motivated by any linguistic facts, but see section 4.2 for a discussion of sentence formation that might indicate some reasons. In the examples below the past-tense particles are given in boldface.

(170) Guazacapán past tense.
    a. *Watemaala **nalh** uk'a-n anik*   (EX:674)
       Guatemala.city PST be-1SG today
       'I was in Guatemala City (earlier) today.'
    b. *haran'a **nalh** hi'*   (EX:1309)
       sick PST DUR
       'I was sick.'

(171) Chiquimulilla past tense.
    a. *pul'a ya-kan **kiwi'***   (EX: 38)
       do DUR-2SG PST
       'You were doing it.'
    b. *nüm'a ay' **kiwi'***   (EX:37)
       eat DUR.3SG PST
       'He was eating it.'

(172) Jumaytepeque past tense.
    a. *a-yi' **k'i'** pero tuumu-'*   (EX:182)
       DUR-3SG PST but 3SG-finish-IV.AFF
       'There was some but it was finished.'

3.6.6.2 *Future tense*

Future tense is indicated by the particle *ku-y* go-3SG.SETA (Guazacapán), *kway* (Chiquimulilla), or *ku* (Jumaytepeque). Like the past-tense particle, the future-tense particle is optional for all verbs and can be used with the completive form, the incompletive form, or a derived participle form of the verb stem (see section 3.12.3.5). The future-tense verbal particle means that the action of the verb will be performed subsequent to speaking time and that the future action is understood as a whole (perfective aspect). Verbs modified by this particle are often translated with the future perfect in English or Spanish, since this is the closest meaning equivalent (e.g., the action will have been performed). Despite the aspectual meanings of this particle, it refers to an action that will be performed subsequent to the time of speaking; it is predominantly understood as a tense marker.

Future tense is quite common in Guazacapán, is less commonly attested in Chiquimulilla, and is almost nonexistent in any of the Jumaytepeque data. The etymology of this particle is quite apparent: for example, in Guazacapán *ku* literally means 'go' and is an intransitive agentive verb indicating movement; *-y* is the 3SG.SETA suffix used for transitive verbs. Most likely, the future markers being discussed here are grammaticalizations of *ku* 'go' in all three Xinkan languages that exhibit it—a cross-linguistically common source for future markers. Examples 173–175 show the use and meaning of the future-tense particles, which are in bold.

(173) Guazacapán future-perfect tense.
    a. ***kuy** üra-k'i hutu man*   (EX:974)
       FUT big-INCH tree that
       'The tree will become big.'

    b. *anik **kuy** tum'u-n xawatz'a*   (EX: 2135)
       today FUT finish.COMP-1SG.SETA planting
       'Today I will finish planting.'

(174) Chiquimulilla future-perfect tense.
    a. ***kway** xuka-n na seema*   (EX:10)
       FUT eat.COMP-1SG.SETA the fish
       'I will eat the fish.'
    b. ***kway** palht'a-n nak*   (EX:79)
       FUT pay.COMP-1SG.SETA you
       'I will pay you.'

(175) Jumayetepeque future-perfect tense.
    ***ku** n-yak'a xa a-ku-k'I*   (EX:53)
    FUT 1SG.SETB-do.ICOMP in 3SG.SETD-go.ICOMP-ANTIP
    'I will go on a walk.'

In addition to the two tense particles being used with verbs marked for either grammatical aspect (completive or incompletive), they can also be used in conjunction with the epistemic mood marker (see section. 3.6.8).

3.6.7   Grammatical voice

M. H. Klaiman (1991: 261) defines grammatical voice as a verbal morphosyntactic category 'encoding alternations in the configurations of nominal statuses with which verbs are in a particular relationship'. This definition is useful in that it coincides with the definition of grammatical voice traditionally adhered to in language descriptions. Grammatical voice indicates a specific relationship between the nominal grammatical arguments of a verb and the action or state that the verb expresses.

This characterization of grammatical voice is clearly correlated with notions of verbal valency and syntactic case marking. (See section 3.12.3 for a discussion of valency.) Case marking and grammatical voice can morphosyntactically signal similar grammatical functions; the difference is that grammatical voice is a property of verbs, and case marking is a property of nouns. It is relevant that Xinkan languages do not mark these grammatical functions through nominal case morphology. However, grammatical voice is central to the acceptability of Xinkan clauses and to the understanding of Xinkan morphosyntactic organization, because it marks the relationships between verbs and their nominal arguments. In other words, grammatical voice in Xinkan languages is a morphological property of verbs that indicates how the nominal arguments associated with them (e.g., the subject and object, etc.) are organized—what relationships the nominals have to the predicate.

As an important cross-linguistic comparison it is relevant to note that the verbal morphology described in this section is very different from neighboring Mayan languages. It has been argued that Mayan languages exhibit grammatical voice in order to highlight nominals that are salient in the information structure of a clause.[20] Each of the Mayan voices involves an underlying verb with affixes that indicate the particular voice: for example, in K'ichean (Mayan) languages, voices include active, two passives, and two antipassives. In these Mayan languages different voice morphology has the potential to alter the valency, and thereby the transitivity, of the underlying verb.[21]

In contrast, Xinkan languages exhibit a voice system that is characterized by classes of verbs (based on the meaning of their roots). Classes are determined based on the argument(s) that is/are core to the predicate (see section 3.6.1). The difference, when compared to Mayan languages, lies in the fact that the Xinkan languages are not dependent on morphological processes for changes in verbal voice, although that is an option. The result of the Xinkan system is a semantically split intransitive system (not to be confused with active-stative alignment or other split-S systems) that is based on clear semantic criteria for determining which class each intransitive verb belongs to.[22]

In the Xinkan languages one of the functions of grammatical voice is to determine which *logical* nominal argument of a predicate is the grammatical subject of the clause. That is, verbs logically have arguments that are part of their underlying predicate structure. For example, the verb *eat* in English has a logical agent (the entity doing the eating) and a logical undergoer, or patient (the entity being eaten). Languages differ in the ways these logical arguments are marked overtly in the grammatical system.

In Xinkan, verbal voice and verb classes have the function of specifying which of the logical arguments is the overt subject of the verb (grammatically controlling person and number agreement) in contrast to the entity controlling the action. A discussion on the importance of subjects in Xinkan syntax is provided in section 4.1.

3.6.8   Mood and modality

Cross-linguistically, when mood is a grammatical function, mood differences are typically signaled by different forms of the verb. These differing verb forms indicate the speaker's attitude toward the truth and/or likelihood of the action or state expressed by the verb. This means that cross-linguistically grammatical mood is closely related to both grammatical aspect and grammatical tense.

In Xinkan languages grammatical mood is indicated through a single (optional) word, *pa'alh* (Guazacapán) and *bar* (Chiquimulilla and Jumaytepeque). This particle is used in conjunction with verbs and expresses confidence on the part of the speaker in the action being discussed. This confidence can come from the speaker's past personal experience or from personal knowledge. In discourse situations, it is used to imply a level of belief about and trust towards what is being related. Because this particle represents the logical possibility of necessity of an utterance, the particle is referred to as the epistemic modal marker.

In Guazacapán, this particle is pronounced differently when it used in different positions within the clause: if it is placed before the verb it is pronounced [paɬ]; if it is placed anywhere in the clause after the verb it is pronounced [paʔaɬ]. The epistemic modal marker in the other two languages is always pronounced [bar], independent of the position it occupies in a clause. Xinkan sentences that use the mood particles are not easily translated into English because of the lack of exact meaning equivalents. Consequently, the gloss 'indeed' (or 'really') is used to indicate the presence of the modal particle but not necessarily its exact semantic interpretation. In examples 176–178, the epistemic mood particle is given in bold.

(176) Guazacapán mood particle.
    a. *erse **palh** maku man*   (EX:2221)
       old EPIST house that
       'That house is old now, indeed.'
    b. *uulhu' **pa'alh** hutu*   (EX:2430)
       fall.IV.AFF EPIST tree
       'The tree has fallen already.'

(177) Chiquimulilla mood particle.
    a. *waak'a' **bar** na winak*   (EX:6)
       go.IV.AFF EPIST the witch
       'The witch left already.'
    b. *wašta' **bar** na süüm'a*   (EX:7)
       enter.IV.AFF EPIST the night
       'The night has fallen, indeed.'

(178) Jumaytepeque mood particle.
    a. *n-narila **bar** aa xurum'uu-li*   (EX:51)
       1SG.SETB-teach.ICOMP EPIST the young.man-PL
       I taught the young men, indeed.'
    b. *ki **bar** ter'o-n nüma*   (EX:348)
       a.lot EPIST want.PERF-1SG.SETA to.eat
       'I am really hungry, I know it.'

3.7   Relational nouns

As in many other Mesoamerican languages, all the Xinkan languages have relational nouns. These words are used to describe the spatial relationship, situation, or organization of nouns and are usually translated into Spanish or English as prepositions. They are called relational nouns because in structure they are typically possessed nouns (see section 3.1.1). Furthermore, cross-linguistically, and in Xinkan languages specifically, they are often derived from terms for body parts and serve functions similar to the prepositions, postpositions, or locative case endings in other languages. In Xinkan languages, relational nouns use the possessive pronominal suffixes (SET E, see section 3.5.2) to indicate these spatial relationships. However, in Xinkan, in contrast to other languages spoken within Mesoamerica, marking relational nouns with possessive affixes is optional. While all relational nouns in Xinkan can occur with the possessive affixes, they do not have to. When they are used without suffixes, relational nouns function more like prepositions.

An observation here about language contact is relevant. The prepositional uses of relational nouns in Xinkan (when they are not marked with SET E suffixes) might be due to influence from the national language, Spanish. Spanish has prepositions but not relational nouns, and Xinkan is/was spoken in a context of high contact and multilingualism. It is unclear if the words in Xinkan functioned as prepositions or relational nouns before Spanish contact, though some of the past documentation does mention prepositions. Nevertheless, since these documents were mostly produced in a time of extreme Spanish contact, it is not surprising that Xinkan was assumed to have prepositions. In fact, Sachse (2010: 403–434) shows evidence that Maldonado (1770) called them case markers—many of these examples are considered relational nouns here. For example ⟨anneła⟩ 'mine' (Sachse 2010: 417) could be analyzed as 'anneła', 1SG.SETA-BEN, my-for, 'for me' (an analysis Sachse also suggests). In terms of cross-linguistic comparisons, however, the term 'relational noun' is not used outside of Mesoamerica. The same elements are called 'person-marked adpositions' (prepositions and postpositions) more commonly.[23] Despite the difference in nomenclature, the earliest colonial documents clearly show evidence of what are called relational nouns.[24] All that can be surmised is that, since the first documentation, Xinkan has exhibited relational nouns that double as unmarked prepositions. Table 3.26 compares relational nouns across Xinkan languages.

The relational noun meaning 'with'—*hina*' (Guazacapán), *lhi*' (Chiquimulilla), or *li*' (Jumaytepeque)—loses its word-final glottal stop when marked with the pronominal suffixes. Additionally the relational noun glossed as 'for, for that'—*neelha* (Guazacapán), *nelha* (Chiquimulilla), or *leelan* (Jumaytepeque)—has a unique function depending on its syntactic position. When used before a noun it means 'for', *neelha-n maku* 'the house for me' [lit. '(the) for-my house']. When used before a verb, it means 'for that, or in order to', *uy neelha ün-ixak'a* 'water for me to drink' [water in.order.

Table 3.26 Xinkan relational nouns

	Guazacapán	Chiquimulilla	Jumaytepeque	Yupiltepeque
'on, over, on top of'	*alh-*	*alhi-*	*al-*	⟨ajli⟩, ⟨ata⟩[a]
'in, on'	*xa-(~xan)*	*xa-(~xan)*	*xa(a)-(~ xan)*	⟨san⟩
'for, for that'	*neelha-*	*nelha-*	*leelan-*	—
'with'	*hina'-*	*lhi'-*	*li'-*	⟨ti⟩
'inside'	*xam'a-*	*xam'a-*	*xam'a-*	—
'below'	*par'a-*	*par'a-*	*par'a-*	⟨alata⟩
'behind' (lit. 'back')	*üül'ü-*	*üül'ü-*	*üüt'ü-*	⟨(s)utu⟩
'in front of' (lit. 'head, face')	*huuxi-*	*huuxi-*	*huuxi-*	—
'on the side of, beside'	—	*haw'ah xa-*	*haw'akxa-*	—
'with-me, [with-my]'	—	—	*niina-n*	—

[a] In the Yupiltepeque data of Calderón (1908), the first of these forms is given as meaning 'on' and the second is given as meaning 'on top of'. Also note that Calderón gives the following forms for Chiquimulilla: ⟨ala⟩ or ⟨ajla⟩ 'on', ⟨ti⟩ 'with', and ⟨ulu⟩ 'behind'.

for I-drink]. In the verbal environment this relational noun bears no possessive pronominal suffixes.

3.8 Verbal particles

Particles are independent words (i.e., free morphemes) that are used in conjunction with one of the four major grammatical categories discussed at the top of this chapter. There are two broad types of particles in Xinkan: those occurring with verbs and those occurring with nouns and adjectives. In this section verbal particles are discussed; nominal particles are discussed in section 3.9.

There are four verbal particles in Xinkan: the directional particle, the optative particle, the negative imperative particle, and a particle that is used when borrowing verbs from another language. The negative imperative particle, however, is part of the grammar of Guazacapán only. These particles alter the denotation of the verb in specific ways and are essential to a complete understanding of clause construction in Xinkan. The following four sections focus on these verbal particles.

3.8.1 *p'e/p'eh* directional particle

The particle *p'e* (Guazacapán) or *p'eh* (Chiquimulilla and Jumaytepeque) indicates the direction of the action in relation to the speaker. Specifically, it means that the verbal action is performed 'in the direction toward the speaker'. Consequently, it is called a directional particle. Obviously, this particle cannot occur with all verbs, as it requires physical movement. In all cases this particle is optional and is collocated directly after the verb it is modifying. Examples are given in 179–181 below for Guazacapán, Chiquimulilla, and Jumaytepeque; there is no data on this particle existing in Yupiltepeque.

(179) Guazacapán 'hither'.
- a. *müy'a pe' nen'*　　　　　　　　　(EX:164)
  help **hither** me
  'Come here and help me.' 'Come help me.'
- b. *tura-n pe' maalhük*　　　　　　　(EX:60)
  bring.COMP-1SG.SETA **hither** firewood
  'I brought the firewood here.'

(180) Chiquimulilla 'hither'.
- a. *tuura-k p'eh na hiüük'a*　　　　　(EX:130)
  bring-IMPV.TV **hither** the weaving
  'Bring the weaving here.'
- b. *tuura-k p'eh na ukxumu*　　　　　(EX:69)
  bring-IMPV.TV **hither** the old.man
  'Bring the old man here.'

(181) Jumaytepeque 'hither'.
    a. *maara-y' **p'eh***   (EX:191)
       rest-IMPV.IV **hither**
       'Come here and rest.'
    b. *aku-y' **p'eh***   (EX:151)
       walk-IMPV.IV **hither**
       'Come here.'

In the grammar of Guazacapán only, the directional particle has been semantically extended so that it can be used in conjunction with nouns that show inherent time, such as year, week, day, and so on. When used in conjunction with this type of noun, this particle indicates a future time.

(182) Guazacapán directional particle with nouns.
    a. *ayapa **pe'***   (EX:2179)
       year **hither**
       'It will have been a year.' 'next year'

In example 182 the time reference of the noun *ayapa* 'year' describes about a full year's temporal cycle. Used in this way the directional particle in 182 indicates that the *completion* of the cycle is in the future, not the cycle itself.

Importantly, however, the noun that is used as the temporal reference can itself be in the future or past time as indicated by verbal tense. The following examples are also taken from Guazacapán.

(183) Guazacapán directional particles on nouns in clauses.
    a. *ayapa **pe'** alhk'alht'iilhi nalh Hwan*   (EX:2183)
       year **hither** mayor PST Juan
       'Juan was mayor last year.'
       'It will have been a year since Juan was appointed mayor.'
    b. *ayapa **pe'** kuy pul'a-y' huurak na naw'u-n'*   (EX:2181)
       year **hither** FUT do.COMP-3SG.SETA man the son-1SG.SETE
       'Next year my son will be a man.'
       'The year will end and my son will be a man.'
    c. *minak'i **pe'** aku-n alhape'*   (EX:1097)
       early **hither** leave.VN-1SG.SETE tomorrow
       'Tomorrow I will leave early.'
       'Tomorrow, it will be early when I leave.'

In the examples in 183, the directional particle indicates the verbal action is performed at some future time in relation to the modified noun. Furthermore, when used with these temporal nominals (e.g., year, day, week, etc.), the action is seen as more irrealis than an action with only a future-tense marker as discussed above (see section 3.6.6.2). For example, the directional particle used in conjunction with nouns indicates that the speaker expects that a nominal state will exist following general assumptions of the human experience. This particle is not used by the speaker in order to make a judgment about when the action will be performed, started, or completed, as is done with the future-tense marker.

3.8.2   *wa* optative particle

The grammars of both Guazacapán and Jumaytepeque use an optative particle in conjunction with verbs: *wa'* and *wa*, respectively. There are not many examples of this particle in the data available, so by and large its meaning and use are unknown. However, what can be ascertained is that this particle optionally precedes a verb and that it can denote a hypothetical situation or a conditional statement.

(184)   Guazacapán optative particle.

    a.   *si a-tero-' a-ku-', **wa'** ku-kin*   (EX:1747)
        if 3SG.SETD-want.ICOMP-IV.AFF 3SG.SETS-go.ICOMP-IV.AFF, OPT go-?
        'If he wants to leave, let him go.'

    b.   *ima-y nah ke **wa'** ulhu-y'a-y nalh hi' k'alh*   (BT:1972, 3)
        say.COMP-3SG.SETA him that **opt** fall-CAUS COND.STATE-3SG.SETA PST DUR.3SG one
        'She said to him that perhaps he was dropping one.' (fruit out of a tree)

    c.   *nuk'a nah chu kür'ü-n **wa'** tunt'i-y' ka-marimba*   (TYA: 1979, 38)
        give him DIM younger.brother-1SG.SETE OPT play.COMP-3SG.SETA 2SG.SETB-marimba
        'Give it to him, my dear younger brother, he might play your marimba.'

(185)   Jumaytepeque optative particle.

    a.   ***wa** bar wa-hri li-h*   (FN:1979, 26)
        opt EPIST go-3PL.SETA with-3SG.SETE
        'They might have left with him already.'

3.8.3   Negative imperative particle in Guazacapán

A negative second-person imperative particle, *wan*, exists only in the grammar of Guazacapán. It is most likely a recent addition to the Guazacapán lexicon through the combination of *wa* 'optative' + *hin* 'negation'.

(186)   Guazacapán negative imperative particle.

    a.   ***wan** nuka-ka waxat'a-h*   (FW:1974, 29)
        NEG.IMPV give.COMP-2SG.SETA entrance-3SG.SETE
        'Don't let him in.'

    b.   ***wan** yüw'a-ka*   (EX:1004)
        NEG.IMPV lose.COMP-2SG.SETA
        'Don't get lost.'

3.8.4   Verbs borrowed from Spanish

A special construction is used in connection with verbs borrowed from other languages, and the data comes specifically from words borrowed from Spanish. Spanish verbs can be incorporated into the languages quite easily as long as they are introduced by the word *uuka'* 'be added' immediately before the verb. (This word is an intransitive affective verb derived from the transitive verb *uka* 'add, throw on'.)[25] Since it can be conjugated like regular verbs this word is not strictly speaking a verbal particle, but the construction to which it belongs is special: it can only take a Spanish infinitive verb as its complement. Due to the vitality of the language, this special verb construction—and the word *uuka'*—is found often in the more recently collected data. This most likely occurred because speakers were unable to remember native verb roots and needed to borrow Spanish verbs into the Xinkan languages. Example 187 shows this construction as used in all of the more recent research on Xinkan languages.

(187) Borrowed verbs from Spanish into Xinkan.
    a. *uuka' enseñar*   'to teach' (<Sp. *'enseñar'*)
    b. *uuka' madrugar*   'to get up early, to stay up late' (<Sp. *'madrugar'*)

3.9   Nominal particles

Nominal particles are independent words that affect the meaning of nouns. There are five nominal particles in the Xinkan languages: (1) *kumu* 'as'; (2) *ti'i/t'i-* 'direct object'; (3) *i* 'reflexive'; (4) *ki'* 'and no more'; and (5) *kiki-/kih* 'pronominal intensifier'. Each of these is discussed in turn.

3.9.1   *kumu* 'as'

The nominal particle *kumu* 'role of' refers to the social role of the referent of the nominal within the discourse—which is usually longer than a single sentence.[26] For example, when used this particle is often translated as the word 'as': 'as a child' or 'as president'. Similarly it can be used to highlight which nominal is functioning as the lead protagonist in a story. Cross-linguistically this might be compared to languages that have an essive nominal case. This nominal particle occurs only in the grammar of Guazacapán.

(188) Guazacapán *kumu*.
    a. *na **kumu** rey tuuru'*   (TK:1972, 1)
       the **as** king tuuru'
       'as the king tuuru'
    b. *k'alh **kumu** üran haxu*   (SP:1979, 17)
       one **as** big pig
       'as the one which is the big pig'

The *kumu* particle might be a Spanish loanword (i.e., Spanish *como* 'like, as'). However, it has a unique grammatical function when compared to Spanish. The Spanish word is used in comparative constructions when two entities are being equated such as *el hombre es como el rey* 'The man is like the king'. In the Xinkan languages this word cannot be used in this construction (see section 4.2.2.5) and can only mean a specific noun is functioning in a certain role within the discourse situation. Because of these differences, I have chosen to treat this word as native element of Xinkan grammar, but its source is unclear.

3.9.2　*ti'i-/t'i-* direct object

The nominal particle *ti'i-* (Guazacapán) or *t'i-* (Chiquimulilla and Jumaytepeque) has pronominal meanings and is used in conjunction with a verb to indicate an oblique argument or a reflexive direct object. Importantly, this functions similarly to a relational noun. However, there is a key difference between the two: a relational noun is used to indicate temporal-spatial relationships between two nominals (cross-linguistically having a function similar to adpositions), while the direct-object particle is used to indicate a specific relationship between a verbal action and a nominal. In both Chiquimulilla and Jumaytepeque this particle is indicated in the unpublished field notes from the 1970s as occurring after the verb and having one of four meanings: (1) indirect object (to, for . . .); (2) reflexive pronoun (the agent and the patient are coreferential); (3) 'on, against' (actually just an additional nuance of the indirect object meaning); and (4) as the possessor, with the existential auxiliary *ay* (Chiquimulilla), *aayu'* (Jumaytepeque) 'there is'.[27] Unfortunately, some of these uses are only mentioned but not exemplified. I have shown only those functions that are exhibited in sentences from examples and the recorded texts.

(189)　Chiquimulilla indirect object particle.

    a.　*ay **ti-'** p'ek'o tuma*　　　　　　　　　(EX:198)
       there.is **to**-1SG.SETE cramp
       'I have a cramp.'

    b.　*iima-k **ti-'** kwando kway t'a-k*　　　　　(EX:244)
       tell.COMP-2SG.SETA **to**-1SG.SETE when FUT come.COMP-2SG.SETA
       'Tell me when you will come.'

    c.　*wixu-kan **t'i-h** na na'u-k neeła müh-hün'ü*　　(EX:95)
       beat.COMP-2SG.SETA **to**-3SG.SETE the son-2SG.SETE so 3SG.SETB-learn.ICOMP
       'Beat your son so that he will learn.'

(190)　Jumaytepeque indirect object particle.

    a.　***t'i-h** maku*　　　　　　　　　　　　(EX:70)
       against-3SG.SETE house
       'It is against the house.'

    b.　*muk-waxat'a süüim'a **t'i-k***　　　　　　(EX:165)
       1PL.SETB-enter.ICOMP night **to**-1PL.SETE
       'We enter night to ourselves.' 'We are staying out late.'

In Guazacapán, on the other hand, this particle is given as having only two meanings: as an indirect object, or as 'on, against'.

(191)　Guazacapán indirect object particle.

    a.　*syempre mu-niw'a map'u **t'i-n***　　　　(EX:1472)
       always 3SG.SETB-ask.ICOMP tortilla **to**-1SG.SETE
       'She always asks tortillas of me.' 'She always asks me for tortillas.'

    b.　*Ø-tz'üütü-' ün-machiiti **ti'** hixi*　　　　(EX:74)
       3SG.SETC-dent.COMP-IV.AFF 1SG.SETB-machete **against** rock
       'My machete was dented against a rock.'

In all three languages the third-person form of this particle is irregular; it is not inflected with affixes. In Guazacapán this form is *ti'*, and in both Chiquimulilla and Jumaytepeque it is *t'i*. Some analyses might treat it as a restricted relational noun (see section 3.7), although it is not clear that this should be the case.

3.9.3 *'i-* reflexive in Guazacapán

The reflexive particle *'i-* is known only in the grammar of Guazacapán. This is inflected with pronominal possessive suffixes SET E and indicates that the referent of the agent of a verbal action is the same as the reference of the patient of that action. In example 192, the agent and patient of the verb *sün'ülhki* 'to become fat' is the pig.

(192) Guazacapán reflexive particle.
    humu haxu ixapi-ki-' na mu-ur'ulh neelha a-sün'ü-lh-ki 'i-h   (EX:595)
    male pig take.out-ANTIP-IV.AFF the 3SG.SETB-testes for 3SG.SETD-fat.ICOMP-
        CAUS.CONTR-ANTIP REFL-3SG.SETE
    'The testicles of the (male) pig were removed for him to make himself fat.'

In Guazacapán, this word can also be used as a marker of indirect possession. For example, when used to indicate a genitive construction this particle has a generic noun referent with no semantic information (i.e., 'it' in English) and is used when the element being possessed is not a lexical noun. This restricts this particle to constructions with adjectives. Importantly, however, the indirect possession indicates the property being possessed is an inalienable quality of the possessor.

(193) Guazacapán indirect possession.
    na pipilh ki ulhk'a 'i-h na paama-h   (EX:1318)
    the butterfly very pretty REFL-3SG.SETE the wing-3SG.SETE
    'The butterfly's wing is very pretty.'

3.9.4 *ki'*

There is a particle *ki'* in the grammar of Guazacapán that is difficult to translate but roughly means 'and no more', 'alone', or 'only'. It is used to indicate that a given declaration is limited to the facts of the utterance and should not be construed as having a broader application. There is no data on this particle in any of the other Xinkan languages.

(194) Guazacapán *ki'*.
    oor'o kastiya ki' mu-wirik'i Hwan   (EX:2339)
    only Spanish and.no.more 3SG.SETB-speak.ICOMP Juan
    'Juan speaks only Spanish and nothing else.'

3.9.5 *kiki-/kih*

Finally, the pronominal intensifier *kiki-* (Guazacapán) or *kih* (Chiquimulilla and Jumaytepeque) is used in conjunction with verbs and has an intensifier and reflexive meaning (see the discussion of *t'i-* and *'i-* above).[28] This *kiki/kih* particle has an anaphoric relationship with a noun phrase elsewhere in the clause, but its primary function is not reflexivity. Rather this particle intensifies the prominence of a noun phrase within the clause. Look at example 192 (section 3.9.3 above), where the pig does something to himself, or rather does something that will affect himself, and it seems that this particle is consequently best understood as a reflexive pronoun. In contrast, the pronominal intensifier particle being discussed here indicates the salience and prominence of the anaphoric noun in a given clause. In Guazacapán this particle agrees in person and number with the coreferential noun by using the possessive SET E suffixes. In Chiquimulilla and Jumaytepeque this particle is morphologically constant and is not inflected to agree with the coreferential noun in any way. Examples are given in 195–197.

(195) Guazacapán reflexive pronoun.
    *ün'ü-y' **kiki-h** huurak man*   (EX:562)
    stretch.COMP-3SG.SETA INTS-3SG.SETE man that
    'That man himself stretched [out].'

(196) Chiquimulilla reflexive pronoun.
    *one ay **kih** na mool'a*   (EX:27)
    young be INTS the moon
    'The moon itself is young.' (i.e., not full; lit. 'The moon is itself young.')

(197) Jumaytepeque reflexive pronoun.
    *nuka-yi' **kih** a koy*   (EX:50)
    give.COMP-3SG.SETA INTS the horse
    'The horse itself was tired out.' (lit. 'the horse itself gave')

3.10   Question words

Question words are independent words (i.e., free morphemes) used in question clauses (see section 4.3). There are seven question words in each of the Xinkan languages. Syntactically these are always used clause initially. A comparison of the question words in all of the Xinkan languages is provided in table 3.27; a dash indicates that

Table 3.27 Xinkan question words

	Guazacapán	Chiquimulilla	Jumaytepeque	Yupiltepeque
'where'	*ka(a) (ta)*	*ka'*	*kax*	⟨na ca⟩
'who'	*weena*	*wanin*	*w(an)ix*	⟨huenin⟩
'what'	*handa'*	*ndi'*	*dix*	⟨xin⟩, ⟨xanijan⟩
'how'	*han*	*ndi' mi'*	*dimi lki*	—
'why'	*han alhi*	*ndi' alhi*	*dix pati'*	⟨xintí⟩
'when'	*lhükü*	*lhik wak*	—	⟨lüöcan⟩
'how many'	*iwał*	*ıwał, waš*	*wax('ar)*	⟨ihualar⟩

no data exists in this language for this particular meaning. The use of the words is exemplified in section 4.3.

3.11   Conjunctions

Xinkan languages have no native lexical conjunctions to indicate coordination in
noun phrases (such as 'Bill **and** Mary'). To signal noun phrase coordination, Xinkan
languages permit a pattern of simple juxtaposition of the conjoined elements to one
another.

Other types of native conjunctions are also unknown in the grammar of the Xinkan
languages (such as 'but' or 'or'). However, *i* 'and' (<Sp. '*y*'), *pero* 'but' (<Sp. '*pero*'), and *o*
'or' (<Sp. '*o*') have been borrowed from Spanish and now function as conjunctions in
Xinkan languages. Examples of conjoined phrases and clauses are given in section 4.6;
the purpose here is only to show that they are a part of the Xinkan grammar.

3.12   Derivational morphology

The final section of this chapter is devoted to the DERIVATIONAL morphology used in
conjunction with each of the foregoing grammatical categories. Derivational is identified here as a change in meaning or grammatical class that consequently affects the
use of a word in an utterance. Derivational morphology is a central characteristic of
Xinkan grammar. First, derivations affecting noun roots (section 3.12.1) are discussed.
Second, adjectival derivational morphology (section 3.12.2) is discussed. Third, verbal
derivational morphology (3.12.3) is described.

3.12.1   Noun derivations

Only one morphological derivation uses nouns as the base. Intransitive verbs can be
derived when the INTRANSITIVIZER suffix *-k'i* is used with a noun. This suffix can be
used with nouns (discussed here), adjectives (discussed in section 3.12.2), and transitive
verbs (discussed in section 3.12.3.1), though the resultant meaning is slightly different
in each case.

When attached to a noun root, the suffix *-k'i* creates an intransitive verb stem with
the derived meaning of 'to noun' or 'to become nounlike'. Consequently, it can be
considered a kind of inchoative verb. In some descriptions of Xinkan (Kaufman and
Campbell, unpublished field notes) the term 'inchoative' is strategically avoided to
reduce confusion with the label inchoative in the grammatical descriptions of other
languages. Often cross-linguistic descriptions of the inchoative refer to both inceptive
actions 'begin to become X' and inchoative 'become X'. While few languages actually
distinguish between the two meanings, the confusion is difficult to avoid. These derived verbs in Xinkan have the inchoative meaning without the inceptive semantics.
Since Xinkan languages have a very unique system of intransitive verb classification,
it is important to understand how these derived intransitive verbs fit into that system.

Intransitive verbs derived from nouns mostly require a nominal argument that semantically functions like the performer of the action (rather than the undergoer). This
is similar to the intransitive agentive verbs discussed in section 3.6.1. However, a very
small subset of noun roots (and all adjective roots) require a nominal argument that
semantically functions like the undergoer of the action when used as the base for this
derivation. However, the requirements on the nominal argument are not indicated
through morphological marking. For example, these derived intransitive verbs do not
require the class membership morphemes required for all lexical intransitive verbs. In
all cases of nouns deriving an intransitive verb with an undergoer nominal argument,
the root is understood to refer to an adjective that is closely related to the noun. For
example, *ukxumu* 'old man' (in 198j) is understood to mean 'old' after the derivation.
Hence the output of the derivation means 'to become old' (i.e., to age), rather than 'to
become an old man', and refers to both males and females. These affective meanings
of these derived intransitive verbs are exceptionally rare, and these roots might be
more adjectivelike than nounlike.

While few concrete examples of this derivation exist, it is clear that the derived intransitive verbs are affected by phonological constraints such as vowel harmony and
consonant dissimilation (see sections 2.1.2 and 2.3.7, respectively). All of the extant
data is given below in 198–200.

(198) Guazacapán noun derivation.
    a. *pari-k'i*
       day-INCH
       'to become day, to dawn' also 'summer' (i.e., 'become hot')
    b. *kama-k'i*
       blood-INCH
       'bleed' (lit. 'to blood')
    c. *charnalhte-k'i*
       bum-INCH
       'to bum (around), be useless'
    d. *muhra-k'i* (irregular: affective verb)
       gray.hair-INCH
       'become gray-haired'
    e. *oxto-k'i*
       sore-INCH
       'to become sore, rot'
    f. *pulhpu-k'i* (<Sp. *'polvo'*)
       dust-INCH
       'to become dust'
    g. *taahu-k'i*
       piece-INCH
       'to become a piece', 'break into pieces'
    h. *til'a-ki*
       salt-INCH
       'to beomce salty'

    i. *tuuru-k'i*
      mythical.person.(baby)-INCH
      'to cry aloud'
    j. *ukxumu-k'i* (irregular: affective reading)
      old.man-INCH
      'to age'

(199) Chiquimulilla noun derivation.
    a. *aara-k'i*
      worm-INCH
      'to be wormlike'
    b. *ch'arnalhte-k'e*
      bum'-INCH
      'to bum, be lazy, useless'
    c. *lhot'e-ke*
      booger-INCH
      'to be boogery'
    d. *p'ochocho-k'e*
      drunk-INCH
      'to be drunk'
    e. *parii-k'i*
      day-INCH
      'summer' (lit. 'to become hot')
    f. *püümü-k'i*
      foam-INCH
      'to foam'
    g. *taahu-k'i*
      piece-INCH
      'break in pieces'
    h. *til'a-k'i*
      salt-INCH
      'to salt'

(200) Jumaytepeque noun derivation.
    a. *humu-ki*
      male-INCH
      'to be strong, have strength'
    b. *p'ooch'o-ke'* (irregular: /p'oč'o-ke'/)
      foam-INCH
      'to foam'
    c. *parii-k'i* (irregular: /pari-k'i/)
      day-INCH
      'summer' (lit. 'to heat')
    d. *ur'ul-k'i*
      egg-INCH
      'to lay an egg'

e. *werwe-k'e*
   scar-INCH
   'to scar'

f. *t'iixi-k'i*
   bum-INCH
   'to bum, be lazy, useless'

g. *uwxumu-ki*
   old.man-INCH
   'to age'

3.12.2 Adjective derivations

Like nouns (see section 3.12.1), intransitive verbs can be derived from adjective roots by the suffix *-k'i* intransitivizer. When used with adjective roots, the result is a derived inchoative verb whose specific meaning is 'to become X', where X refers to semantic properties of the adjective. As mentioned above in section 3.12.1, the large majority of intransitive verbs derived from noun roots require the sole nominal argument to function as the semantic agent. In contrast, when adjectives serve as the root of this derivation, the nominal argument always functions as the semantic undergoer/patient (similar to intransitive affective verbs). These verbs are conjugated as intransitive affective verbs. (See the appendix for examples of verb conjugations.)

(201) Guazacapán inchoative verbs.
   a. *üra-ki*
      big-INCH
      'to become big'

   b. *tol'o-ke*
      yellow-INCH
      'to become yellow'

   c. *tul'u-ki*
      rheumy-INCH
      'to become rheumy'

   d. *püxa-k'i*
      stinky-INCH
      'to become stinky'

   e. *pilhilhi-k'i*
      smooth-INCH
      'to become smooth'

   f. *penene-k'e*
      sweet-INCH
      'to become sweet'

   g. *pari-k'i, par'iki*
      hot-INCH
      'to become hot'

h. *sününü-k'i*
stretched.tight-INCH
'to become stretched tight'

i. *süm'a-ki*
dark/black-INCH
'to become dark', 'nightfall'

j. *sarara-k'i*
cold-INCH
'to become cold'

(202) Chiquimulilla inchoative verbs.

a. *orop'o-ke*
rough-INCH
'to become rough' (i.e., not smooth)

b. *mulh-k'i*
white-INCH
'to become white'

c. *moor'o-ke*
motley-INCH
'to become motley in color' (i.e., black, white, and yellow)

d. *me'e-ke*
green-INCH
'to become green'

e. *lhawawa-k'i*
shiny-INCH
'to become shiny'

f. *k'ütütü-k'i*
sick.to.the.stomach-INCH
'to become sick to the stomach' (i.e., nauseous)

g. *kara-k'i*, kar'aki
heavy-INCH
'to become heavy'

h. *üxüxü-k'i*
tasty-INCH
'to become tasty'

i. *erse-k'e*
old-INCH
'to become old'

j. *elha-k'i*
new-INCH
'to become new', 'renew'

(203) Jumaytepeque inchoative verbs.

a. *k'oocho-k'e*
dirty-INCH
'to become dirty'

b. *ch'aar'a-k'i*
snotty-INCH
'to become snotty'

c. *awa-k'i*
raw/unripe-INCH
'to become raw', 'to become unripened'

d. *braabu-k'i* (<Sp. '*bravo*')
angry-INCH
'to become angry'

e. *warü-k'i, war'üki*
stinky-INCH
'to become stinky'

f. *uchu-k'i*
hunched.back-INCH
'to become hunched over'

g. *sonk'o-ke* (referring to clothing)
short-INCH
'to become short'

h. *muhra-ki'*
white.haired-INCH
'to become white-haired'

i. *lünk'ü-ki*
lame-INCH
'to become lame'

j. *t'ük'ü-ki*
poor-INCH
'to become poor' (i.e., not functioning well)

In Guazacapán and Jumaytepeque there is a causative inchoative which is derived from adjectives using the suffix *-ka* or *-k'a*, respectively. Historically, this suffix is most likely derived from the combination of the intransitivizer suffix *-k'i* plus the causative suffix *-ha*. This suffix may have also existed in Chiquimulilla, but there is no evidence to support that it did. Section 3.12.3.3 provides a complete treatment of these suffixes and their derived verbs.

3.12.3 Verbal derivation

Verbs can act as the base for a number of derivations. Some of these affect the required/core number of arguments the verb may have (called valency), while others change verbs into nouns and participles. Each of the possible derivations is exemplified in this section.

Valency-changing derivations in Xinkan alter the number of core arguments a verb stem requires for an acceptable utterance. For example, a prototypical transitive verb has at least two arguments, agent and patient (or subject and object), thus having a valency of two. Intransitive verbs by definition have only one argument, the subject, thus having a valency of one. Valency changes refer to a derivational process whereby the number of arguments of a verb is increased or decreased.

In Xinkan languages there are derivations that decrease the valency of a verb (for instance, the antipassive construction and changes in grammatical voice), and a number of derivations that increase the valency of the verb (causatives). Valency-decreasing derivations are discussed first, followed by valency-increasing derivations.

3.12.3.1 *Antipassive construction*

The antipassive form of a verb stem suppresses the object of a transitive verb and consequently affects the relationship between the underlying transitive verb and its nominal arguments. In the antipassive, the subject of the derived intransitive verb always corresponds to the agent of the underlying transitive verb, while the underlying object may be implied but never specified overtly. The antipassive is formed by adding the intransitivizer suffix *-k'i* to the verb stem. As a point of emphasis, verbs derived in this way always have an active meaning; the subject of the antipassive verb formation always refers to the person doing the action, similar to intransitive agentive verbs.

This construction is similar to the antipassive constructions found in neighboring Mayan languages and is referred to by Mayanists as the 'absolute antipassive'.[29] However, because antipassive verb derivations prototypically exist in ergative languages (and not generally in nominative-accusative languages like Xinkan), this verb form is highlighted as probably being a historically recent development, possibly with its etymological source in the reflexive (see section 3.9.3 and section 3.9.4) or the inchoative (see section 3.12.1).

In terms of pronunciation, if the transitive verb that serves as the base of the derivation has a glottalized consonant in the last syllable of the stem, the suffix is realized as [-ki]. (See section 2.3.1.4 for a discussion of glottalization processes.) This suffix is also affected by vowel harmony (see section 2.1.2). In examples 204–206, the transitive verb base is shown on the left and the derived antipassive verb form is on the right.

(204) Guazacapán antipassive derivation.
    a. *wüüxa*   →   *wüüxa-k'i*
       shake.out   shake.out-ANTIP
       'shake (it) out'   'shake out'   (omitted object)
    b. *hük'a*   →   *hük'a-ki*
       weave   weave-ANTIP
       'weave (it)'   'weave'   (omitted object)

(205) Chiquimulilla antipassive derivation.
    a. *mütz'a*   →   *mütz'a-ki*
       bury   bury-ANTIP
       'bury (it)'   'bury'   (omitted object)
    b. *moch'o*   →   *moch'o-ke*
       wet   wet-ANTIP
       'wet (it)'   'wet'   (omitted object)

(206) Jumaytepeque antipassive derivation.
    a. *wilwiyi'*   →   *wilwi-k'i*
       sew   sew-ANTIP
       'sew, mend (it)'   'sew, mend'   (omitted object)
    b. *k'aniyi'*   →   *k'ani-k'i*
       tie.up   tie.up-ANTIP
       'tie (it) up'   'tie up'   (omitted object)

Often the antipassive verb form is marked with the intransitive agentive verb class marker. In this case the suffix *-k'i* intransitivizer always precedes the suffix *-lha'/la'* intransitive agentive. When used in conjunction with this verb class suffix, the antipassive suffix is always realized as *-ki*.

(207) Guazacapán.
   ïn-mutalh-kï-lha'
   1SG.SETC-dream.COMP-ANTIP-IV.AGT
   'I dreamed.'   (omitted object and emphasized agent)

(208) Chiquimulilla.
   Ø-müür'ï-ki-lha'
   3SG.SETC-complain.COMP-ANTIP-IV.AGT
   'S/he complained.'   (omitted object and emphasized agent)

(209) Jumaytepeque.
   Ø-uutu-ki-la'
   3SG.SETC-enlarge.COMP-ANTIP-IV.AGT
   'S/he enlarged.'   (omitted object and emphasized agent)

Lastly, the antipassive formation should not be confused with the homophonous present participle derivation discussed in section 3.12.3.5. A clear distinction between the two word classes can be made if we consider the other types of morphology that can be added to the derived stem. Specifically, a derived present participle uses nominal possession strategies (SET B and SET E), while the antipassive verb form uses verbal subject agreement markers (SET C and SET D). Similarly, the agentive noun suffix (discussed in section 3.12.3.4.2) can only be added to verb stems; derived antipassive verb forms permit this suffix while derived present participles do not. Examples 210–212 show the agent noun suffix attached to the antipassive verb form.

(210) Guazacapán.
    a. *k'its'i-ki-lha*
       roast-ANTIP-AGT
       'roaster', 'one who roasts things'
    b. *pooxa-ki-lha*
       wash.clothes-ANTIP-AGT
       'clothes washer'

(211) Chiquimulilla.
    a. *tonoha-k'i-ɬ*
        decieve-ANTIP-AGT
        'one who decieves'
    b. *ümülü-k'i-ɬ*
        write-ANTIP-AGT
        'writer'

(212) Jumaytepeque.
    a. *laraha-k'i-l*
        cure-ANTIP-AGT
        'one who cures'
    b. *tami-k'i-l*
        speak-ANTIP-AGT
        'speaker'

3.12.3.2 *Voice changes*

A second type of valency-decreasing derivation involves changes in the grammatical voice of transitive verb roots. The result of this derivation is that a transitive verb is used as the base to derive one, or both, of the intransitive verb types. Most transitive verbs can be used to derive *either* an intransitive agentive verb *or* an intransitive affective verb, but not both. Very few transitive verbs can be used to derive both intransitive verb types.

In all cases of intransitive verbs derived from transitive verb bases, there is a restructuring of the semantic roles of the verbal arguments. In these terms a derived intransitive affective verb is structurally equivalent to the passive voice in other languages: the logical agent is either omitted or demoted and does not function as the grammatical subject, while the logical patient is promoted to function as the grammatical subject. This derivation is marked on verb stems in one of two ways. First, if the phonological shape of the transitive verb base is CVCV, then the first vowel is lengthened and the intransitive affective verb class marker suffix -' is added to the verb. (This has the consequence of shifting stress as well.) Second, if the transitive verb base has the phonological shape CVVCV or CVCCV, then no change is made and a verb class suffix is added to the verb base. The resulting phonological shapes are identical to the allowable shapes for basic (nonderived) intransitive affective verbs.

Lastly, the derived intransitive affective verb form can function as a participle when it is not inflected with any grammatical affixes, and it can be used in a noun phrase as an adjective (see section 3.2). The glosses of some of the examples in 213–214 have a passive reading in English, but the derived verbs should be thought of as having an undergoer subject.

(213) Guazacapán transitive → intransitive affective derivation.
    a. *apla*   →   *apla-'*
        open   open-IV.AFF
        'open (it)'   '(it) opened'

    b.　*poch'o*　　→　*poocho-'*
       rot　　　　　rot-IV.AFF
       'rot, spoil (it)'　　'(it) rotted'
    c.　*müümü*　　→　*müümü-'*
       sing　　　　　sing-IV.AFF
       'sing (it)'　　'(it) sang'

(214)　Chiquimulilla transitive → intransitive affective derivation.
    a.　*huutz'i*　　→　*huuxi-'*
       blow　　　　　blow-IV.AFF
       'blow (it)'　　'(it) blew'
    b.　*axi*　　→　*aaxi-'*
       burn　　　　　burn-IV.AFF
       'burn (it)'　　'(it) burned'
    c.　*wilhwi*　　→　*wilhwi-'*
       sew　　　　　sew-IV.AFF
       'sew, mend (it)'　　'(it) be sewn, mended'

    This derivational process is identical in Jumaytepeque with one minor change. If the transitive verb root is of the shape CVCCV, then the rightmost consonant is glottalized in the intransitive affective verb derivation. This change is consistent for all transitive verbs of the appropriate phonological shape and must be reported as part of the language at the time of description. However, the speakers in Jumaytepeque consistently were confused about the glottalization process. This means that the glottalization of the last consonant in a cluster in this derivation might be due to language obsolescence more than to a genetic change in the language. The transitive verb stems in Jumaytepeque are given in their surface forms as infinitives (see section 3.6).

(215)　Jumaytepeque transitive → intransitive affective derivation.
    a.　*k'itz'yi'*　　→　*k'iisi-'*
       roast　　　　　roast-IV.AFF
       'roast (it)'　　'it be roasted'
    b.　*paaxiyi'*　　→　*paaxi-'*
       sharpen　　　　sharpen-IV.AFF
       'sharpen (it)'　　'it be sharpened'
    c.　*pornoye'*　　→　*porn'o-'*
       explode　　　　explode-IV.AFF
       'explode (it)'　　'it be exploded'

    In a similar derivation, a transitive verb derives an intransitive affective verb that only permits the nominal pronominal affixes. This derivation might be called a passive-voice derivation. In this derived intransitive verb, the nominal argument is the grammatical subject and always functions semantically as the undergoer (i.e., patient) of the action denoted. That is, the logical subject of the transitive verb, the agent, is optional, and the direct object, the patient, becomes the new grammatical subject. With transitive verbs this voice alternation decreases valency, as the new subject (the logical object) is now the only core argument of the passive verb form. Note that the required verb-subject agreement in the following example agrees in person and number with the patient and not the agent. Demoted agents are not signaled overtly as being non-core. The verb form in 216 is marked for agreement using a transitive verb SET B prefix.

(216) Guazacapán passive verb construction.
    mu-kiixi-' wakax (nen')   (EX:1964)
    3SG.SETB-roast.COMP-IV.AFF meat (I)
    'The meat was roasted (by me).'

In some cases, the grammatical subject of the derived intransitive verb is seen as the undergoer of the action as well as the performer of the action. In this case, the verb in the passive voice (intransitive affective in form) has a reflexive-type meaning. (See section 3.9.3 for use of a real reflexive.) The following is from Guazacapán.

(217) Guazacapán intransitive verbs as reflexives.
    ün-wiixu-' nen'   (EX:1474)
    1SG.SETC-hit.COMP-IV.AFF I
    'I hit myself.' (lit. 'I was hit by me.')

In addition, the nominal argument can be omitted entirely, resulting in a meaning similar to the impersonal passive (i.e., 'that which was hit'). In summary, derived intransitive affective verbs either result in a decrease in the valency (impersonal passive) or the valency is unaffected but the nominal configuration structure is altered. (This is the most common result.)

(218) Guazacapán derived passive and intransitive affective verb semantics.
    a. *mu-uupu-' Hwan*   (EX:434)
       3SG.SETB-stood.up-IV.AFF John
       'John stood (himself) up.'
    b. *a-xuka-'*
       3SG.SETD-eat-IV.AFF
       'that which is eaten', 'food'

(219) Chiquimulilla derived passive and intransitive affective verb semantics.
    a. *mü-siiru-'*
       3SG.SETB-hurry-IV.AFF
       '(for it to) be hurried'
    b. *a-tero-'*
       3SG.SETD-want-IV.AFF
       'that which is wanted'

(220) Jumaytepeque derived passive and intransitive affective verb semantics.
    a. *h-üyalha-'*
       3SG.SETB-laugh-IV.AFF
       'It laughs.'
    b. *a-müka-'*
       3SG.SETD-work-IV.AFF
       'that which is worked', 'job'

The second way that grammatical voice can be altered in Xinkan verbs is through the addition of the intransitive agentive suffix *-lha'* (Guazacapán and Chiquimulilla) or *-la'* (Jumaytepeque) to the transitive verb stem. This results in deriving an intransitive agentive verb. As mentioned above, most transitive verbs can derive either an affective or an agentive intransitive verb, but not both. Those transitive verbs that can derive an agentive intransitive verb do so by the addition of the suffix *-lha'/la'*. Functionally, this derivation requires the demotion or omission of the grammatical object of transitive verbs, similar to the antipassive (see section 3.12.3.1). However, there is one important difference: a derived intransitive agentive verb can function like all other intransitive verbs by taking pronominal agreement affixes SET C and SET D, while derived antipassive verbs are not marked with agreement affixes (see section 3.6.2). From this fact, it is clear that Xinkan grammar treats the results of these two derivations differently, and I have chosen to separate them here on the basis of this difference.

A derived intransitive agentive verb is structurally equivalent to the antipassive in other languages: the logical patient is omitted, leaving only the logical agent to act as the grammatical subject. The resultant action of the verb is always an event and never a state (in contrast to derived intransitive affective verbs and the passive voice discussed above).

(221) Guazacapán transitive → intransitive agentive derivation.
    a. *kaayi*   →   *kaay'i-lha'*
       sell   sell-IV.AGT
       'sell (it)'   'sell', 'do selling'
    b. *wixta*   →   *wixta-lha'*
       play   play-IV.AGT
       'play (it)' (music)   'whistle'
    c. *waki*   →   *waki-lha'*
       play   play-IV.AGT
       'play (it)' (game)   'play'

(222) Chiquimulilla transitive → intransitive agentive derivation.
    a. *yüp'ü*   →   *yüp'ü-lha'*
       throw.up   throw.up-IV.AGT
       'throw (it) up'   'throw up'
    b. *lhokn'a*   →   *lhokn'a-lha'*
       boil   boil-IV.AGT
       'boil (it)'   'boil'
    c. *üüna*   →   *üüna-lha'*
       defecate   defecate-IV.AGT
       'defecate (it)'   'defecate'

(223) Jumaytepeque transitive → intransitive agentive derivation.
    a. *tut'uyi'*   →   *tut'u-la'*
       suck   suck-IV.AGT
       'suck (it)'   'suck'

b. *kürxayi'*   →   *kürtz'a-la'*
    comb   comb-IV.AGT
    'comb (it)'   'comb'

c. *uut'uki*   →   *uutuki-la'*
    enlarge   enlarge-IV.AGT
    'enlarge (it)'   'enlarge'

Intransitive verbs derived from transitive verbs can be conjugated just like any of the nonderived basic intransitive verbs. (See the appendix for examples.)

3.12.3.3 *Causative constructions*

There is one general valency-increasing operation in Xinkan languages: the causative. However, there are a number of causative derivations in each language. That is, there are multiple suffixes in each language that derive a causative verb form. The use of each causative suffix depends on the type of stem it is attached to and the specific semantic denotations of the agent in the action of causation. In some ways, all of the Xinkan languages are similar in their use of the causative suffixes, but in others they are quite distinct. Consequently, each of the causative derivations is discussed individually for each language. In general terms, each of the causative suffixes derives a multivalent verb having the meaning 'to cause/make to V', where V is a variable standing for the verbal action of the base.

In Guazacapán there are four causative morphemes, and as in the other languages each is attached through suffixation. The four suffixes in this language can be divided into those that denote control by the causee (the one being caused to perform the action of the verb) and those that denote that the causee does not have control. There are two suffixes in each category. In the first category, the suffix *-lha* is used to emphasize the event or process of causation, while the suffix *-y'a* is used to emphasize the resulting state of causation. The first suffix *-lha* is used primarily with adjectives, though it can be used with a few intransitive verbs and is phonologically identical to the agent noun suffix discussed in section 3.12.3.4.2. The second suffix *-y'a* is used primarily with intransitive verbs, and it should be noted that it is phonologically identical to the imperative forms of intransitive verbs (see section 3.6.4). The reason the imperative suffix and the agent noun suffix are treated differently from the causative morphemes being discussed here is because in the other Xinkan languages these suffixes are not phonologically identical (i.e., they are not homophonous) and there are two distinct morphological functions: the imperative, or the agent noun, on the one hand, and the causative constructions on the other. This alone is seen as sufficient evidence to suggest that they should be treated distinctly in the grammatical description of Xinkan.

(224) Guazacapán causatives denoting control.

a. *sara-lha*
    cold-CAUS.CONTROL.EVENT
    'make cold', 'to refrigerate'

b. *kara-lha*
heavy-CAUS.CONTROL.EVENT
'make heavy', 'to weigh down'

c. *uch'u-lha*
dirty.face-CAUS.CONTROL.EVENT
'make one's face dirty'

d. *k'ata-y'a*
lay.down-CAUS.CONTROL.STATE
'make to be laying down'

e. *lhona-y'a*
boiling-CAUS.CONTROL.STATE
'make boil'

f. *k'okma-y'a*
kneel.down-CAUS.CONTROL.STATE
'make to kneel'

In the category of causative morphemes that do not denote control by the causee, the first is the suffix *-ha* which is used to denote a process that the causee does not control (i.e., nonvolitional) and is not a natural process (i.e., does not happen naturally to the body, like vomiting). Unlike in the other Xinkan languages, this suffix is rarely used in Guazacapán. The second suffix in this category is *-ka* (derived from *-k'i* intransitivizer + *-ha* causative), which denotes that a causee is not in control but is undergoing a natural process (e.g., coughing). The latter can also be called the causative inchoative and is almost always attached to adjective stems.

(225) Guazacapán causative not denoting control.

a. *elha-ha*
new-CAUS
'make new'

b. *xawi-ha*
hard-CAUS
'make hard'

c. *siru-ha*
hurry-CAUS
'make hurry'

d. *til'a-ka*
salt-CAUS.INCH
'make become salty', 'make salty'

e. *k'ocho-ka*
dirty.clothes-CAUS.INCH
'make one's clothes become dirty', 'make one's clothes dirty'

f. *me'e-ka*
green-CAUS.INCH
'make become green', 'make green'

g. *üra-ka*
big-CAUS.INCH
'make become big', 'make big'

In Chiquimulilla there are three ways to form causative verbs, with slightly different meanings in each form. All three causative formations are made by suffixation
and all add a nominal argument to the verb as the person causing the action to occur.
The first option is the suffix *-ha*, which is used to form the causative of transitive verbs
and adjectives. The second option is the suffix *-lha*, which is used to make causative
verbs derived from intransitive verbs and, rarely, transitive verbs. The semantics of this
second suffix emphasize the process or event of causing. The third option is the suffix
-y'a, which is used with intransitive verbs to emphasize a resultant state affected by
the causative verb.

(226) Chiquimulilla causatives.
    a. *püxa-ha*
       stink-CAUS
       'make stink'
    b. *k'üpü-ha*
       fill-CAUS
       'make full'
    c. *yolhna-lha*
       slip-CAUS
       'make slip/fall'
    d. *hono-lha*
       drunk-CAUS
       'make (someone) drunk'
    e. *up'u-ya*
       stand.up-CAUS
       'make stand up'
    f. *lhara-y'a*
       climb-CAUS
       'make be elevated'

In Jumaytepeque there are four causative morphemes and each is used through
suffixation: (1) the suffix *-ha* is used with most transitive verbs and adjectives; (2) the
suffix *-yi* is used with intransitive affective verbs and emphasizes a resultant state;
(3) the suffix *-la* is use with adjectives and some intransitive verbs and emphasizes
the process or event denoted through causation; and (4) the suffix *-k'a*, which is rare
and found in conjunction with only two words: in both cases the derived meaning is
'cause to become' and as such can be considered a causative inchoative. (Guazacapán
has a similar suffix in abundance. It probably stems from *-k'i* plus *-ha*; in other words
the inchoative plus the causative suffix. The causative inchoative is usually achieved
through the use of the regular causative suffix *-ha*.

(227) Jumaytepeque causative derivations.
    a. *itz'i-ha*
       be.awake-CAUS
       'make be awake', 'to wake up'
    b. *puuri-k'a*
       marry-CAUS
       'make be married', 'marry (someone to someone else)'

c. *maar'a-yi*
rest-caus
'make rest'

d. *punu-la*
steam.iv-caus
'make steamed', 'make steam'

3.12.3.4 *Verb → nominals*

This section is devoted to the description of the derivation of nouns from verb roots. Specifically, there are four ways of deriving nominals from verbs in the Xinkan languages: the verbal noun, the agent noun, the patient noun, and the instrumental noun. These are discussed in turn in this section. In addition, some of the inflections and derivations discussed above can also have nominal characteristics. For example, both the antipassive formation and the intransitive affective derivation can be used as participles. These are discussed below in section 3.12.3.5. In each of the nominalizations discussed in this section, the resulting meaning is closely related to the verb root.

3.12.3.4.1 *Abstract verbal nouns.*   These nominal derivations are productive in all of the Xinkan languages. Verbal nouns can be derived from either transitive or intransitive verbs. For transitive verbs, the rightmost consonant of a verbal base is glottalized. In cases where the newly glottalized consonant is the last member of a cluster, an epenthetic vowel is inserted (see section 2.3.1). This form is identical to the incompletive form of verbs, except that the personal pronominal prefixes are not attached. If the verbal prefixes are used, then the verb in the incompletive aspect is denoted. Consequently, verbal nouns cannot be possessed. Another possible analysis is that the incompletive aspect form of a verb is actually a possessed verbal noun (possessed through prefixes) or that the verbal noun denotes an action that is not inflected for person or number agreement. No matter which analysis is preferred, it is clear that the verbal noun exhibits a close relationship between nominal semantics and verbal semantics.

(228) Guazacapán transitive verb verbal nouns.

a. *ipla*   →   *ipal'a*
'bathe'   'bath'

b. *nuk'a*   →   *nuk'a*
'give'   '(the) giving, gift'

c. *wisu*   →   *witz'u*
'hit'   '(the) beating, fight'

(229) Chiquimulilla transitive verb verbal nouns.

a. *k'üt'ü*   →   *k'üt'ü*
'weigh'   '(the) weighing, weight'

b. *hüka*   →   *hük'a*
'weave'   '(the) weaving'

    c. *alpa*   →   *apal'a*
       'open'   '(the) opening'

(230) Jumaytepeque transitive verb verbal nouns.
    a. *nani*   →   *nan'i*
       'loosen'   '(the) loosening'
    b. *k'itz'i*   →   *k'itz'i*
       'roast'   '(the) roasting'
    c. *netka*   →   *netak'a*
       'push'   '(the) pushing'

For intransitive verbs, the verbal noun is identical with the third-person singular inflected form of the verb in the incomplete aspect. That is, verbal nouns derived from intransitive verbs always begin with the prefix *a-* 3SG (see section 3.4.2). Furthermore, they can be possessed using the personal pronominal prefixes.

(231) Guazacapán intransitive verb verbal nouns.
    a. *müka-lha'*   →   *a-müka*
       work-IV.AGT   3SG.SETD-work
       'work'   'the working, job'
    b. *iixi-'*   →   *a-ixi'*
       be.awake-IV.AFF   3SG.SETD-be.awake
       'be awake'   'the being awake, life'

(232) Chiquimulilla intransitive verb verbal nouns.
    a. *werek'e-lha'*   →   *a-werek'e*
       cry-IV.AGT   3SG.SETD-cry
       'cry'   'the crying, tantrum'
    b. *uupu-'*   →   *a-uup'u*
       be.standing-IV.AFF   3SG.SETD-be.standing
       'stand'   'the standing'

(233) Jumaytepeque intransitive verb verbal nouns.
    a. *tik'i-la'*   →   *a-tik'i*
       sleep-IV.AGT   3SG.SETD-sleep
       'sleep'   'the sleeping'
    b. *k'ooxo-'*   →   *a-k'oxo*
       'be.dried.up-IV.AFF   3SG.SETD-be.dried.up
       'be dried up'   'the drying up'

3.12.3.4.2 *Agent nouns.*   The agent noun is also derived from a verb. The agent noun has the meaning of 'one who Xes' where X is a placeholder for the action of the verb being used (like the suffix *-er* of English, e.g., 'runner'). Like abstract verbal nouns, agent nouns are never possessed. They are derived by adding the suffix *-lha* (Guazacapán), *-lh* (Chiquimulilla), and *-l* (Jumaytepeque) to the end of the verb and by lengthening the last vowel of the stem.

This suffix is remarkably similar to the suffix used to indicate an intransitive agentive verb (see section 3.6.1). Importantly, in both instances (the agent noun derivation and the intransitive agentive verb), there is a meaning of agentivity. Consequently, it might be argued that there is a single suffix *-lha* 'agentive' that is used in two different ways and a suffix *-'* [-ʔ] that is used to derive an intransitive verb. This last suffix is always used on intransitive verbs. However, there is no evidence that this is the case, although it might point to a likely source of diachronic development. In Section 4.1 verbal alignment and the significance of these suffixes are discussed.

Lastly, often the final vowel of the suffix is deleted in Jumaytepeque; this sometimes occurs in Chiquimulilla but never in Guazacapán.

(234) Guazacapán agent nouns.

    a. *xawxa*   →   *xawxaa lha*
       plant   plant-AN
       'plant'   'planter'

    b. *hoor'o*   →   *hoor'oo-lha*
       take.care.of   take.care.of-AN
       'take care of'   'caretaker'

    c. *ündü*   →   *ündüü-lha*
       spy   spy-AN
       '(to) spy'   '(the) spy'

(235) Chiquimulilla agent nouns.

    a. *tiik'i'*   →   *tiik'i-lh*
       sleep   sleep-AN
       'sleep'   'sleeper'

    b. *p'ooxa*   →   *p'ooxa-lh*
       wash   wash-AN
       'wash'   'washer'

    c. *tz'uum'a* →   *tz'uum'a-lh*
       kiss   kiss.AN
       'kiss'   'kisser', 'one who kisses'

(236) Jumaytepeque agent nouns.

    a. *k'er'o*   →   *k'eer'o-l*
       write   write-AN
       'write'   'writer'

    b. *wak'i*   →   *waaki-l*
       play   play-AN
       'play'   'player', 'one who is habitually playing'

    c. *xakxa*   →   *xakxa-l*
       steal   steal-AN
       'steal'   'thief'

3.12.3.4.3 *Patient noun.* In Guazacapán and Chiquimulilla, there is a suffix *-wa*, with a variant *-w'a*, that can be attached to verb stems. This results in the derivation of a patient noun with the meaning 'something (that was) Xed', where X denotes the action of the verb root. Patient nouns in Xinkan are always possessed by the possessive pronominal suffixes SET B. Evidence for this type of verb nominalization is not found in any other Xinkan language.

(237) Guazacapán patient nouns.
    a. *xipi-wa-h*
       cut-PN-3SG.SETB
       'his wound' (lit. 'his thing that was cut', 'his cut')
    b. *ixpa-wa-h*
       leave-PN-3SG.SETB
       'his birthplace'
    c. *ta-w'a-h*
       come-PN-3SG.SETB
       'his thing that was come', 'his place from which he came'

While this suffix can derive a noun from a verb base in Guazacapán, this derived noun retains many verblike characteristics. For example, verb pronominal affixes can be used in conjunction with this derived noun, resulting in a word that focuses on a state in consequence of the verbal action. The meaning template for this construction when used with these verb suffixes is 'X is (made to have been) verbed'; X is the placeholder for the semantic patient of the underlying verbal action. This construction is obviously similar to the passive or antipassive constructions, since it involves changes in valency (see sections 3.12.3.1 and 3.12.3.2). The difference between those constructions and the one with *-wa* is that the latter emphasizes the state of the verbal action rather than the nominal functions as either agent or patient. The suffix can be used this way in both Guazacapán and Chiquimulilla.

(238) Guazacapán patient verbs.
    a. *tup'a-wa-y'*   (TM:1978, 32)
       leave-PN-3SG.SETA
       'She left it.' 'It was left by her.'
    b. *na tondon xa xaaru a-lhükü-wa*   (EX:1355)
       the turtle in ocean 3SG.SETD-be.found-PN
       'The turtle is found in the ocean.'
    c. *a-kayi-wa koko*   (EX:1700)
       3SG-SETD-sell-PN coconut
       'Coconuts are sold.'

(239) Chiquimulilla patient verbs.
    a. *akümi' pul'a-w'a-n*   (EX:29)
       like.that do.COMP-PN-1SG.SETA
       'I did it like that.'
    b. *mük'a-wa-kan na waya'*   (EX:115)
       work-PN-2SG.FORM.SETA the corn.field
       'You worked in the cornfield.'

3.12.3.4.4 *Instrumental noun.*   All verb roots can be used to derive an instrumental noun. These derived nouns result in the general meaning of 'something used to do X', where X denotes the action of the verb. This noun is derived by adding the suffix *-k* to the verb stem in Guazacapán, Chiquimulilla, and Jumaytepeque. (This derivation is unattested for Yupiltepeque.) Instrument nouns can be marked with the SET B pronominal prefixes (see section 3.5.2.1); this groups them with the lexically specified alienable nouns.

In relation to the pronunciation, often the rightmost consonant of the verb stem is glottalized in conjunction with this suffix. However, speakers do not consistently apply glottalization for any individual verb stem—sometimes the same derived instrumental noun will be pronounced with glottalization of the rightmost consonant and sometimes without. Due to the state of vitality for the languages, it is unclear if this is due to speaker error or if it has some other linguistic significance.

(240) Guazacapán instrumental nouns.
    a. *atz'i-k*   cf. *axi* 'burn'
       burn-INSTR
       'match'
    b. *etk'a-k*   cf. *etka* 'cover'
       cover-INSTR
       'lid'
    c. *ixka-k*   cf. *ixka* 'drink'
       drink-INSTR
       'cup'

(241) Chiquimulilla instrumental nouns.
    a. *hapu-k*   cf. *hapu* 'receive'
       receive-INSTR
       'container'
    b. *harwi-k*   cf. *harwi* 'dig'
       dig-INSTR
       'shovel'
    c. *hut'a-k*   cf. *hut'a* 'blow'
       blow-INSTR
       'bellows'

(242) Jumaytepeque instrumental nouns.
    a. *xiina-k*   cf. *xiina* 'urinate'
       urinate-INSTR
       'toilet'
    b. *oxwe-k*   cf. *oxwe* 'scour'
       scour-INSTR
       'cleaner' (for pots)
    c. *xuw'i-k*   cf. *xuwi* 'sweep'
       sweep-INSTR
       'broom'

3.12.3.5 *Participles*

Participles are words that are derived from verb roots and that retain verbal semantics, but they function differently than lexical verbs. In English, for example, the verb 'hire' can be used in the following ways: 'John is hiring' and 'John was hired', among others. In the first sentence, the verb is in the present participle form, while in the second it is in past participle form. This is similar to what occurs in the Xinkan languages.

Xinkan participles are verb forms that have verblike meanings but are morphologically marked like nouns and verbs (often simultaneously). Two participle forms can be derived: the present participle and the past (passive) participle. The present participle is formed just as in the antipassive derivation, using the suffix *-k'i* (see section 3.12.3.1); the past passive participle is formed as in the intransitive affective derivation, except that the word-final glottal stop indicating verb class membership is omitted (see section 3.6.1).

Both participle forms can be, but do not need to be, inflected for possession by using pronominal affix SET B or SET E (use of SET E is most common, which means participles can be grouped with inalienable nouns). In contrast to lexical noun roots, participles never occur with the definite article.

(243) Guazacapán participles.

a.	*kixi*	→ *-kiixi*	'roasted'
	'roast'	*-kitz'i-ki*	'roasting'
b.	*weske*	→ *-weske*	'thrown'
	'throw'	*-weske-k'e*	'throwing'

(244) Chiquimulilla participles.

a.	*wilhwi*	→ *-wilhwi*	'sown'
	'sew'	*-wilhwi-k'i*	'sewing'
b.	*k'olhko*	→ *-k'olhko*	'peeled'
	'peel'	*-k'olhko-k'i*	'peeling'

(245) Jumaytepeque participles.

a.	*k'iixu-yi'*	→ *-k'iixu*	'changed'
	change-3SG	*-k'iixu-k'i*	'changing'
b.	*uuxa-yi'*	→ *-uuxa*	'blown'
	blow-3SG	*-uuxa-k'i*	'blowing'

Present participle forms and antipassive forms (section 3.12.3.1) appear to be homophonous. However, morphologically they behave differently: the antipassive can host the agent noun suffix *-lha/-lh/-l* (section 3.12.3.4.2), while the present participle form cannot; the present participle can be inflected with noun *and* verb affixes, while the antipassive form can only be inflected with verb affixes. The following Guazacapán example shows the present participle form with nominal possession.[30]

(246) Marking of the present participle in Guazacapán.

a. *oor'o xandiwina ki' a-ku-**k'i-h** na kuxkux*   (EX:2344)
  only sky and.no.more 3SG.SETD-walk-PRES.PART-3SG.SETE the hawk
  'The hawk only flies [lit. 'walks'] in the sky.'

FOUR

Syntax

This chapter discusses the structure of the Xinkan languages at the level of the sentence or clause, including word-order changes in different clause types. However, the differences in the syntax of each Xinkan languages are not significant. There has been little historical change from Proto-Xinkan into the daughter languages, and each language has nearly identical syntactic structures. Thus, a separate discussion of syntax for each Xinkan language would be unnecessarily cumbersome. The discussion in this chapter is more general (i.e., referring to Xinkan) rather than language-specific (Guazacapán Xinka, Chiquimulilla Xinka, Jumaytepeque Xinka, or Yupiltepeque Xinka). Where there is significant variation in the syntactic patterns, separate discussions are provided for each language.[1]

Xinkan is a morphologically rich language, meaning that syntactic relationships and categories are primarily signaled through morphological changes. As a note of comparison only, this means that where other languages (Spanish and English, for example) rely on syntactic constructions to encode linguistic or grammatical characteristics, Xinkan usually relies on morphological characteristics (see chapter 3). There are, of course, some important syntactic constructions in Xinkan, such as the use of the negative imperative *wan* in Guazacapán or using subtle changes in word order to add emphasis, but in general the morphological characteristics are grammatically more predominant. This, of course, is not unusual in languages with complex morphological derivations and inflections.

Sentences and clauses in Xinkan can be divided into those with verbs and those without. This fundamental division is relevant in determining the formation of sentences and their functions within long discourses. Sentences with verbs can contain a transitive or intransitive verb along with the appropriate number of nominal arguments. (Transitive verbs require two or more arguments; intransitive verbs require a single argument: see section 3.6.1.) Sentences without verbs can be existential predicates or stative predicates and are typically considered to be copular sentences. Copular sentences can be formed around an overt copula verb or a covert zero-copula verb. This chapter surveys both types of sentences and discusses word order in each sentence type. Additionally, there are sections on question formation and complex sentences.

4.1 Syntactic alignment

There are two general elements in Xinkan sentences: verbs and nominal arguments. The elements are grouped into constituents—sentence elements relevant to syntactic patterns. Verbs are the most important element in a Xinkan sentence and can be transitive or intransitive (see section 3.6.1). A transitive verb forms a constituent with one or more required nominal argument complements, while an intransitive verb forms a constituent without a nominal complement. Both verb types can require grammatical subjects that are nominal arguments that do not act as complements. The nominal arguments of a verb can be the heads of noun phrases or the entire noun phrase (see sections 3.1 and 3.4). For sentences without overt verbs, nominal arguments (as just defined) can additionally function as predicate complements. In most cases, the predicate complement is a noun phrase that attributes one or more characteristics to the grammatical subject.

In addition to defining the constituent parts of a sentence, we can show how these parts are related grammatically and semantically. These relationships indicate the syntactic alignment of Xinkan sentences.

4.1.1 Grammatical relations

As indicated above, nominal arguments can function in a sentence in a number of ways, including as subject, direct object, indirect object, or complement (among others), which are called the grammatical relations of a verb. In Xinkan languages, only the grammatical function of the subject is indicated by formal marking on the verb, and it is consequently the only grammatical function, or grammatical relation, essential to Xinkan grammar.

Semantically in the Xinkan languages the subject can be defined as the nominal argument most closely resembling the doer/agent of a transitive verb or the sole nominal argument of an intransitive verb. Morphologically, this function is indicated through subject-verb agreement affixes attached to the verb (see section 3.5.2). These affixes agree with the person and number of the grammatical subject. In other words, the grammatical subject of a clause is the nominal argument that controls the grammatical inflection of person and number on the verb, although it may or may not control (semantically) the actual verbal action. While the grammatical subject is the only function indicated morphologically in Xinkan grammar, the linear order of constituents can also play a role in indicating the function of other nominal arguments in a clause or sentence (see section 4.2.1).

Morphologically, then, in the grammar of Xinkan all nominal arguments that are not indicated through agreement are best classified as nonsubjects.[2] In general, nonsubject nominal arguments are the patients/objects of transitive verbs, indirect objects, or obliques such as relational noun phrases indicating instrumentality or location.[3]

The label 'nonsubject nominal argument' should not be understood as indicating equity in grammatical function. The functions of this type of nominal argument can be distinguished from each other based on the linear order of the syntactic constituents: for example, the direct object of a transitive verb immediately follows the verb in unmarked contexts; and the indirect object and other oblique nominals, if there are any, follow the grammatical object of transitive verbs. In relation to grammatical subjects, speakers vary when placing these nominals. For some speakers the indirect object and oblique nominals follow the subject (i.e., Verb-Object-Subject-Indirect Object-Oblique), and for others indirect objects can precede the subject (i.e., Verb-Object-Indirect Object-Subject-Oblique). No clear pragmatic criteria in the data indicate a linguistically motivated explanation for this variation. However, the grammatical object always precedes the other nonsubject nominals. Obliques can be independently identified because they are always preceded by a relational noun.

While the linear order of nonsubject nominal arguments is important to the grammar of the Xinkan languages, the linear order of subjects in relation to the grammatical object is relevant only to a limited extent. When the grammatical subject and the grammatical direct object logically refer to an entity with same grammatical person and number (e.g., third-person singular), linear order is the only way to disambiguate meaning. This type of sentence can potentially be ambiguous in that it is not necessarily clear which is the actor and which is the patient, since either can have the same kind of subject-verb agreement. For example, in the Guazacapán example in 247a, the grammatical subject *nah* and the grammatical direct object *nah* are both morphologically identical and are both third-person singular.

(247)   Linear order of constituents.
    a. *ima-y' nah nah*   (EX:60)
        tell.PERF-3SG.PERF.TV 3SG 3SG
        'He told him.'
    b. *ima-y' nah Hwan*   (EX:25)
        tell.PERF-3SG.PERF.TV 3SG Juan
        'Juan told him.'

In each of the examples in 247 both the subject and the object denote third-person singular referents. Furthermore, the verb is marked for agreement with the subject by the third-person suffix SET A. Sentences such as these are potential sources of ambiguity due to the absence of overt morphological marking of the relevant grammatical relations. However, this ambiguity is resolved when the order of the nominal arguments is considered. (Of course, the referent of the pronominal argument must be understood by the speech-act participants.) In situations where there is variation from the basic VOS (Verb-Object-Subject) word order, pragmatic knowledge is sufficient to indicate which argument is the subject and which is the direct object. However, in most cases of word-order changes, when the subject does not follow the direct object (e.g., when it is preposed in front of the verb), it is always modified by the definite article *na* (see section 4.4).

The fact that Xinkan languages lack overt case marking but show similar behaviors among subjects of transitive verbs and subjects of intransitive verbs (i.e., they both are marked by subject-verb agreement and must be the last core argument in the clause structure) leads to the conclusion that the Xinkan languages are of the NOMINATIVE-ACCUSATIVE type and are head marking in this pattern.

(248) Verb agreement and alignment: Guazacapán.
    a. *ixka-y' uy **Hwana***   (EX:879)
       drink.COMP-3SG.SETA water Juana
       'Juana drank water.'
    B. *a-uupu-' **Hwan***   (EX:1324)
       3SG.SETD-stand-IV.AFF Juan
       'Juan is standing.'

In the example sentences in 248, the subject and the verb agreement are given in boldface. Note that the subject of a transitive verb and of an intransitive verb both trigger verb agreement, while the object of a transitive verb does not. This is consistent with nominative-accusative alignment, which is a label used to indicate that the subjects of transitive and intransitive verbs pattern the same but act differently than the direct object of a transitive verb. Furthermore, word order can help indicate these relationships. In a basic sentence, the object immediately follows the verb while the subject does not. The subject is the last core argument in both examples in 248.

However, recall that subjects of intransitive verbs can be semantically different than those of transitive verbs. Specifically, transitive verb subjects are always semantically the agent of the clause (the doer of the action), while intransitive verb subjects can be either agents or patients of the verbal action. This was discussed in section 3.6.1 in conjunction with the verb class system in Xinkan. This difference in semantics does not affect the alignment patterns.

Lastly, as mentioned above, there is a lack of verb agreement with the participle formations (see section 3.12.3.5). For example, the subject of the present participle verb does not require verbal agreement marking. This is similar to the behavior of the objects of transitive verbs, which require no agreement marking either. In some of the examples in the database, these verbs are occasionally inflected using the possession pronominal suffixes (using SET E suffixes). The sentences in 249 show the contrast between agreement marking. In 249a the verb *wixu* 'to beat' is marked with an subject-agreement suffix SET A and is not a participle. In 248b the same verb is derived as a present participle using the suffix *-k'i* and is not marked with any subject agreement affixes.

(249) Subject agreement with present participle in Jumaytepeque.
    a. *wixu-ka' ma(a) naw'ü-k*   (EX:102)
       beat.COMP-2SG.SETA OPT SON-2SG.SETE
       'You should have beaten your son.'
    b. *wixu-k'i nak*   (EX:181)
       beat-PRES.PART you.FORM
       'You beat (it).'

Since this marking is the strongest indication of syntactic alignment in Xinkan languages, it is significant that it is absent here.

4.1.2   Semantic relations

In addition to specifying the grammatical relations between a verb and its nominal arguments, it is also appropriate to describe the verb-argument relationships in terms of semantic relations or roles. For example, nominal arguments can be either doers of an action (i.e., AGENTS) or nondoers (i.e., NONAGENTS) of an action. Nondoers can further be classified into two types: undergoers of the verbal action (i.e., PATIENT or recipient) and obliques (for example, INSTRUMENTS, GOALS [not undergoers], or BENEFICIARIES). From the perspective of semantic roles, the subject-nominal argument of a *transitive verb* always functions as the doer/agent/experiencer of the action, while the core nonsubject-nominal argument (typically the direct object) is always the undergoer/patient of the action. Similarly, the subject-nominal argument of an *intransitive verb* can function as either the doer/agent or the undergoer/patient of the action depending on whether the given verb is semantically intransitive agentive or intransitive affective.

The distinction between semantic (logical) roles and grammatical function will not be upheld in most cases in the remainder of this chapter. That is, the grammatical role of a nominal argument and its semantic (logical) role within a clause will not be greatly distinguished and they will be used interchangeably. The difference is largely unimportant to the description of Xinkan grammar. However, for both types of intransitive verbs the semantic role of the grammatical subject is one of the defining characteristics of verb class membership, and it will be indicated appropriately.

4.1.3   Antipassive and verb agreement

One final note about syntactic alignment is in order. Verbs in the antipassive form (see section 3.12.3.1) do not require subject-verb agreement. This means that the subject of a derived antipassive verb (which is a type of intransitive verb) is marked in the same way as the object of an nonderived transitive verb. When applied to verbs in general, and not just to antipassive verbs in Xinkan, this is the canonical description of ergative-absolutive alignment. The subject of an intransitive verb is marked/indicated in the same way as the object of a transitive verb. In the examples that follow, the grammatical subject of the derived antipassive intransitive verbs are not marked using pronominal affixes, just like the objects of transitive verbs. The general pattern for these derived antipassive verbs is ergative-absolutive; however, this is a minor pattern in the grammar and should not be considered to be an indication of primary alignment patterns. These patterns are shown in the examples in 250–252.

(250) Guazacapán antipassive subject-verb concord.
    kunu-k'i hi' taata-n' xa merkado   (EX:906)
    buy-ANTIP DUR.3SG father-1SG.SETE in market
    'My father is shopping in the market.'

(251) Chiquimulilla antipassive subject-verb concord.
    suka-k'i ay' na chuchu   (EX:218)
    bite-ANTIP DUR.3SG the dog
    'The dog is barking.' (lit. 'The dog is biting.')

(252) Jumaytepeque antipassive subject-verb concord.
    niwa-k'i ay' Hwan   (EX:164)
    ask-ANTIP DUR.3SG Juan
    'Juan is asking.'

4.2   Simple sentence formation

This section discusses in detail the order of sentence constituents and includes two subsections: one for sentences with verbs and one for sentences without. Sentences with verbs are considered first in their most basic form: the declarative sentence. Variations on the basic word order will also be surveyed. (The word order in complex sentences is discussed in section 4.6.) Sentences without verbs are discussed second and are divided into five types: those that denote temporal duration; two types of copular; those that show existence; and equational constructions.

4.2.1   Sentences with verbs

Declarative sentences assert information and, as such, can be understood as a simple statement. Additionally, declarative sentences are considered the most simple and basic examples of sentence structure because all other sentence types and functions are derived from them. Consequently, the word order of declarative sentences is considered to be the basic, unmarked, or canonical word order in Xinkan clauses. Word order in complex sentences (section 4.6) is understood only in comparison to the word order in declarative clauses.

Verbs in declarative sentences are almost always clause initial, though there are a few isolated examples of non–verb-initial clauses. This conforms to the characterization of the Mesoamerican Linguistic Area in general, where all the languages included in the sample show a preference for non–verb-final clauses.[4] Core nonsubject nominal arguments of a transitive verb, the undergoers (patients), are most likely to be placed directly after the verb head. However, in a few instances the nonsubject nominal can precede the verb. Subject-nominal arguments of a given verb exhibit the most variation in where they can occur within a clause. In the most basic situation, the subject nominals are clause final, though they can appear clause initially and clause medially. Examples are in 253–255.

(253) Guazacapán declarative sentences.
    a. *mu-im'a Hwan Maria*   (EX:455)
       3SG.SETB -say.ICOMP Juan Maria
       'Maria tells Juan.'

b. *kuy tz'iriri-k'i naki man* (EX:924)
FUT red-INC chile that
'That chili will become red.'

c. *Ø-waak'a-' Hwan* (EX:15)
3SG.SETC-go.COMP-IV.AGT Juan
'Juan left.' 'Juan has left.'

(254) Chiquimulilla declarative sentences.
a. *kuy xuk'a-y nak na wilhay* (EX:144)
FUT eat.COMP-3SG.SETA you the jaguar
'The tiger will eat you.'

b. *Ø-waxta-' bar na süüm'a* (EX:7)
3SG.SETC-enter.COMP-IV.AFF EPIST the night
'The night has entered.' 'The night has fallen.'

(255) Jumaytepeque declarative sentences.
ut'u-yi' a ur'ul a miya (EX:320)
lay.COMP-3SG.SETA the egg the hen
'The hen laid the egg.'

The canonical word order, as seen in these examples, is VOS for sentences with transitive verbs and VS (Verb-Subject) for sentences with intransitive verbs. Variations in this order are discussed next.

This canonical word order can be altered for a number of different reasons. Perhaps the most important recognizes the fact that often grammatical subjects are not represented by an overt independent nominal argument. This is similar to Spanish—and other languages—and occurs because the subject agreement–marking verb encodes all the information necessary to understand a sentence. (This is called 'pro-drop' in some theoretical investigations of syntax.)

However, the subject-nominal argument can only be omitted if it is understood within the context of the discourse. For example, when talking about the things that a specific dog does (and once it is understood that the dog is the subject of the verbal actions), a speaker may omit reference to the dog, though verbal concord is still required. If the topic of the discourse changes (e.g., to something that is not the dog), then any new subject must be made independently overt. Consequently, sentences in which the subject has been omitted are typically translated as having an independent pronominal subject in English.

(256) Guazacapán pro-drop sentences.
waxku-y hixi ti' pak'i (EX:1998)
throw.COMP-3SG.SETA rock against wall
'**He** threw rocks against the wall.'
(third-person referent understood in discourse)

(257) Chiquimulilla pro-drop sentences.
a. *tupa-' na ün-wap'ik xa xaha-h na talhma* (EX:186)
leave.COMP-1SG.SETA 1SG.SETB-foot-INSTR in the side-3SG.SETE the road
'**I** left my shoes on the side of the road.'

b. *Ø-yüüwii-'* (EX: 282)
3SG.SETC-lose.COMP-IV.AFF
'It has been lost.'

(258) Jumaytepeque pro-drop sentences.
a. *la h-ir'i a talma* (EX: 359)
no 3SG.SETB-see.ICOMP the road
'He doesn't look at the road.' 'He isn't looking at the road.'
b. *n-narila bar naa xurum'uu-li* (EX: 51
1SG.SETB-teach.ICOMP MOD the young.man-PL
'I already taught the young men.'

While the canonical word order of declarative clauses is VOS, as mentioned above, other word orders are occasionally used. These alternative orders include SVO, VSO, SOV, and OVS. It is common for some languages to exhibit word-order changes such as these for pragmatic reasons. For example, topicalization of a certain constituent might require reordering of constituents, while it is also common in some languages to change the word order to correspond to a change of focus in the discourse. Similarly, there can be nonpragmatic factors that determine specific word orders in some languages. For example, the length (weight) of the constituent and where it lies on a language-specific animacy hierarchy can affect word order.[5] It is probable that the variations in word order in Xinkan are also based on these linguistic motivations.

However, an analysis of the factors that affect word order requires detailed information about the changes in meaning or structure in relation to changes in word order. This information is simply not available for two reasons: first, current speakers are unable to produce variations in word order; and second, while past documentations of Xinkan show word-order variations, none discusses the pragmatic differences between identical sentences with different word orders. Furthermore, with regard to nonpragmatic changes, the data often shows differing word orders used without consideration for animacy or constituent weight. For example, example sentences 259–261 were delivered by the same speaker of Guazacapán in the 1970s. They are included here in pairs or sets—though they did not necessarily occur that way in the data—in order to add to the clarity of the examples.

(259) Guazacapán word order changes: Set 1.
a. *hooro-y ut'um'a-h peel'oo-lhe*   VOS (EX: 1300)
have-3SG.SETA tail-3SG.SETE dog-PL
'The dogs have (their) tails.'
b. *na peel'oo-lhe hooro-y ut'um'a-h*   SVO (EX: 1301)
the dog-PL have-3SG.SETA tail-3SG.SETE
'The dogs have (their) tails.'

(260) Guazacapán word order changes: Set 2.
a. *hin hooro-y teena muuti-h Hwan*   VOS (EX: 473)
no have.COMP-3SG.SETA a.lot hair-3SG.SETE Juan
'Juan does not have a lot of hair.'

b. *hin hooro-y Hwan teena muuti-h*   VSO   (EX:470)
   no have.COMP-3SG.SETA Juan a.lot hair-3SG.SETE
   'Juan does not have a lot of hair.'

c. *na Hwan hin hooro-y teena muuti-h*   SVO   (EX:1218)
   the Juan no have.COMP-3SG.SETA hair-3SG.SETE
   'Juan does not have a lot of hair.'

(261) Guazacapán word order changes: Set 3.

a. *im'a-y nen Hwan ke ka-tonto*   VOS   (EX:2258)
   say.COMP-3SG.SETA I John that 2SG.SETB-fool
   'John called me a fool.' (lit. 'said to me John that "you [referring
   to the speaker, in direct reported speech] are a fool".')

b. *Hwan (na) im'a-y nen' ke ka-tonto*   SVO   (EX:2259)
   John (the) say.COMP-3SG.SETA I that 2SG.SETB-fool
   'John called me a fool.' (lit. 'John said to me that "you
   [referring to the speaker] are a fool".')

The sentences in each of the sets can be glossed identically, without a change in the apparent pragmatic or semantic meaning. The reasons for the variations in the word order are not completely understood, but four observations can be made. First, whenever the subject precedes the verb, it is always modified by the definite article.[6] Second, although OVS is possible, it does not occur in these pairs and is in fact rare in the entire database.[7] Third, although not completely indicated here, VSO order is also rare in the database (although more common than OVS) and is often accompanied by an alternate clause with VOS order (e.g., the same sentence from two elicitations in both orders). Consequently, VSO order must be considered either as a marked order used for a specific pragmatic function, a relic, or a product of imperfect learning of the speaker. Forth, Spanish has had a significant impact on Xinkan grammar as indicated through the morphology and the large number of borrowed lexical items (i.e., function words). In light of these many borrowings, it is quite feasible to suppose, though quite speculative as well, that SVO order in Xinkan may be due to Spanish influence. The hypothesis that SVO is a borrowed order is supported by the fact that it is not as common as VOS or VSO orders (and is typically given with these alternate word orders), and clauses exhibiting SVO order often have a greater number of Spanish loan words in them compared to clauses with other orders. However, lexical borrowings and syntactic change through contact seem to be different processes that occurred at different times.[8]

Variations in word order cannot be entirely discounted, however, as merely borrowings or errors. There is simply not enough evidence to support a strong claim one way or the other. However, given that most languages have alternative possible word orders at variance with their basic word orders, that these alternations are determined by pragmatic factors, and that those factors are often linguistically motivated (e.g., topicalization, focus, or emphasis), it may be legitimate to suppose that Xinkan languages did have variation in word order even before Spanish contact.

4.2.2 Copular sentences

In Xinkan, full lexical verbs are not required in all types of sentences. For sentences that (1) indicate temporal duration; (2) ascribe a characteristic to the subject noun; (3) express the existence of a noun; or (4) indicate that two nominals are equal or are the same thing, a copular verb is used instead. This type of sentence is traditionally referred to as a predicate nominal, and in Xinkan it can have either nouns or adjectives as complements. In these types of sentences, a copular verb is often used to equate a subject noun with an adjective, to specify existence, to detail the temporal duration of the complement, or as a locative phrase. Some languages in the world also indicate possession using these types of sentences, but in Xinkan this is usually signaled by a specific transitive verb of possession. These functions are exhibited in only three syntactic patterns. This section discusses the constituent parts and the order of each of these three types.

4.2.2.1 *Temporal duration*

The temporal duration marker is an irregular verb. It is conjugated using SET A suffixes (like a transitive verb), but it is highly irregular. The full conjugation of this verb is given in the appendix. It is considered a verb based on the use of the transitive verb suffixes, but it is not marked for changes in grammatical aspect, voice, or valency in any way; consequently, I have opted to offer it here with the verbless sentences. This temporal duration marker is *y'a* (Guazacapán), *ay'* (Chiquimulilla), or *ayaw'a* (Jumaytepeque) and is always placed between the nominal argument and the predicate complement. It results in a clause that reflects the durative quality, characteristic, or state of the modified nominal.

(262) Guazacapán temporal duration construction.
    haran'a y'a-n nen'   (EX:1113)
    sick TEMP.DUR.1SG I
    'I am sick.'

(263) Chiquimulilla temporal duration construction.
    wak'i ay' na iiru   (EX:2)
    playing TEMP.DUR.3SG the monkey
    'The monkey is playing.'

(264) Jumaytepeque temporal duration construction.
    xüük'ü ayaw-ka'   (EX:150)
    below TEMP.DUR.2SG.SETA
    'You are down below.'

As seen in the examples in 262–264, this auxiliary verb has a temporal (time) meaning. Temporally, it refers to an action or state that is ongoing at the time of speaking or that is attached to some other temporal anchor (e.g., tomorrow, yesterday, today, etc.). It has been glossed as 'to be', but in reality it has no semantic meaning beyond the grammatical function of temporal duration within a sentence. Examples 265–267 give further instances of this word's use and function.

(265) Guazacapán temporal duration.
    k'iitz'i y'a-n na waakax   (EX:962)
    roast TEMP.DUR-1SG.SETA the cow
    'I am roasting the meat.' (at the time of speaking)

(266) Chiquimulilla temporal duration.
    xa mak'u-n ya-'   (EX:259)
    in house-1SG.SETE TEMP.DUR-1SG.SETA
    'I am in my house.' (at the time of speaking)

(267) Jumaytepeque temporal duration.
    naa wapi-k xaa hixi ay-ili   (EX:155)
    the foot-INSTR in rock TEMP.DUR-3PL.SETA
    'The shoes are among the rocks.' (at the time of speaking)

As seen in the examples above, this verb is translated as a present progressive (with verbs) or as a stative (with nouns and adjectives), since this best represents the temporal scheme of the construction. However, the temporal duration marker can also be used in conjunction with the past-tense marker (see section 3.6.6.1). When used with the past-tense marker, the result is best translated as the past progressive (when speaking of events) or past (when speaking of states of being).

(268) Guazacapán temporal duration particle with past tense.
    a. *haran'a nalh y'a-n ahmukan*   (EX:312)
       sick PST TEMP.DUR-1SG.SETA yesterday
       'I was sick yesterday.'
    b. *koocho' nalh hi' suunik man*   (EX:873)
       dirty PST TEMP.DUR.3SG pot that
       'The pot was dirty.'

(269) Chiquimulilla temporal duration particle with past tense.
    pula ya-kan kiwi'   (EX:37)
    do TEMP.DUR-2SG.SETA PST
    'You were doing it.'

Lastly, the temporal duration marker can be used in conjunction with the future tense marker *ku* 'go' to indicate future progressive action (see section 3.6.6.2 for the future construction). The two sentences in 270 compare the use of the plain future (270b) with the future progressive (270a).

(270) Guazacapán temporal duration particle with future tense.
    a. *ku y'a-n xuk'a xin'ak*   (EX:1631)
       go DUR-1SG.SETA eat bean
       'I am going to eat beans.'
    b. *kuy xuk'a-n xin'ak*   (EX:1632)
       FUT eat.COMP-1SG.SETA bean
       'I will eat beans.'

The temporal continuation indicated by this auxiliary does not imply permanence. That is, at the time of speaking an action may be in progress, but there is no commitment or judgment about the future (i.e., time outside the temporal reference) completion or temporal continuation of the action.

(271) Guazacapán temporal duration particle.
    tüxk'ü hi' alhtepet   (EX:677)
    far.away TEMP.DUR.3SG village
    'The village is far away.' (i.e., right now; in the future it might be closer)

(272) Chiquimulilla temporal duration particle.
    ixap'a ay' na uy   (EX:161)
    leaving TEMP.DUR.3SG the water
    'The water is escaping.' (i.e., leaking right now, but it may stop)

(273) Jumaytepeque temporal duration particle.
    naa tumin xa kaaha ayi'   (EX:72)
    the money in drawer TEMP.DUR.3SG
    'The money is in the drawer.' (i.e., right now, but someone may take it out)

As seen in examples 271–273, the temporal duration marker can be used with both verbal and verbless sentences. In verbless clauses, the temporal marker is placed immediately following the predicate complement. In clauses with verbs, the temporal marker is placed after all constituents of the verb phrase except the object, if there is one.

(274) Guazacapán temporal duration.
    na naki tz'iriri-k'i palh hi'   (EX:1278)
    the chile red-INC EPIST TEMP.DUR.3SG
    'The chile is becoming red now.'

(275) Chiquimulilla temporal duration.
    ut'u-k'i ay' ur'ulh na mihya   (EX:196)
    lay-ANTIP TEMP.DUR.3SG egg the chicken
    'The chicken is laying eggs.'

(276) Jumaytepeque temporal duration.
    a. *xa wina ayi'*   (EX:258)
       in festival TEMP.DUR.3SG
       'He/She/It is in the festival.'
    b. *la a-ta-' ayi'*   (EX:85)
       no 3SG.ICOMP.SETD-come-IV.AFF TEMP.DUR.3SG
       'He is not coming.'

There is another temporal duration marker that, in contrast to the auxiliary verb just seen, has inherent incompletive aspectual meanings. That is, it denotes an action that occurs over a stretch of time and indicates that there is no endpoint to this time period. This particle has been attested in Guazacapán, Chiquimulilla, and Jumaytepeque, but is more common in Guazacapán. In all the languages, this particle is *k'e-*. In Jumaytepeque, it has a unique meaning and functions as an irrealis marker of an event that is hypothetical, and in this instance it is not inflected for agreement.

(277) Guazacapán imperfective temporal duration.
    a. *pul'a nalh k'e-y war'i*   (EX:2305)
       make PST IDUR-3SG.SETA bad.weather
       'It was storming.'
    b. *xiin'a k'e-y naka*   (EX:2377)
       lie IDUR-3SG.SETA you
       'He is lying to you.'
    c. *tik'i-ya k'e-y mu-t'uuri Mariya*   (EX:1063)
       sleep-CAUS IDUR-3SG.SETA 3SG.SETB-child Maria
       'Maria is putting her child to sleep.'

(278) Chiquimulilla imperfective temporal duration.
    ku-n k'e-y witz'u-n   (EX:13)
    go-1SG.SETA IDUR-3SG.SETA beat.COMP-1SG.SETA
    'I am going to beat (you).'

(279) Jumaytepeque imperfective irrealis marker.
    mas k'e müya-ka' ma nin, lan k'e n-pahat'a nak   (EX:294)
    but IRR help-2SG.SETA IRR I, no IRR 1SG.SETB-pay.ICOMP you
    'Even though you had helped me I would not have paid you.'

4.2.2.2 *The zero copula*

Utterances that function to ascribe a specific quality or characteristic to a noun or that indicate the equivalence between two noun phrases are formed using simple juxtaposition. In fact, most sentences described in this section show verbless clauses. For some syntactic functions, these utterances can be considered to have a null (empty) copular verb, here called the zero copula. While there is no need to suggest that this is an actual verb without phonetic form (it is just simple juxtaposition), for ease in cross-linguistic comparison and translation such utterances can be considered to have a null copula.

As with the sentences indicating temporal duration, null-copula sentences consist of a predicate and a nominal argument. Furthermore, the order of these two constituents is most often such that the predicate precedes the nominal argument (PREDICATE + NOMINAL). The opposite order, with the nominal preceding the predicate, is also given in the Xinkan data (NOMINAL + PREDICATE). However, this variation does not seem to be conditioned by linguistic factors. The most that can be claimed is that the predicate precedes the nominal argument in the preferred form, although the opposite order is available. However, when the nominal argument is the first element of the sentence, the definite article *na* must be used before the nominal argument. In all of the following examples, the predicate is underlined while the nominal argument is not.

In addition, the sentences are glossed with the verb 'to be' in English (and in Spanish with the verb *ser*). This is meant to highlight that this type of sentence indicates a natural characteristic of a nominal argument: a state that is likely to be more permanent.

(280) Guazacapán null-copula sentences.

    a. *na tz'ok'o* <u>pik'i</u>   (EX:88)
         the grackle bird
         'The grackle is a bird.'

    b. <u>maestro</u> *Hwan*   (EX:1056)
         teacher Juan
         'Juan is the teacher.'

    c. <u>erse palh</u> *maku man*   (EX:2221)
         old MOD house that
         'That house is old now.'

    d. <u>hin elha</u> *na maku hü'*, <u>erse pa'alh</u>   (EX:2222)
         no new the house this, old MOD
         'This house is not new; it is old now.'

    e. <u>pari k'alh</u> *na a-suka-'*   (EX:689)
         hot still the 3SG.SETD-eat.ICOMP-IV.AFF
         'The food is hot still.'

    f. *na naka* <u>ka-chirw'i</u>   (EX:1274)
         the you 2SG.SETB-skinny
         'You are skinny.'

    g. <u>ün-neelha</u> *chikwit man*   (EX:238)
         1SG.SETB-for basket that
         'That basket is mine.'

    h. *na naki man* <u>tz'iriri' pa'alh</u>   (EX:1279)
         the chile that red MOD
         'That chile is red (ripe) now.'

    i. <u>ki ür'a-h</u> *hutu man*   (EX:764)
         very big-3SG.SETE tree that
         'That tree is very big.'

    j. <u>üran</u> *hutu nalh pa'alh*   (EX:2210)
         big tree PST MOD
         'The tree was already big.'

(281) Chiquimulilla null-copula sentences.

    a. <u>ki mür'a-h</u> *na til'a*   (EX:98)
         very bitter-3SG.SETE the salt
         'The salt is very bitter.'

    b. <u>lhan tz'ama</u> *na wap'alh na'*   (EX:247)
         no good the stool this
         'This stool is not good.' (i.e., broken)

    c. *na hixi ma'* <u>ün-neelha</u>   (EX:141)
         the rock that 1SG.SETB-for
         'That rock is mine.'

    d. <u>tawalhki uy</u> *xa mak'u dyux*   (EX:68)
       holy water in house god
       'In the church is the holy water.'
    e. <u>ki t'ünk'ü-h</u> *na naakuh*   (EX:20)
       very bent.back-3SG.SETE the skirt
       'The skirt is very pushed back.' (i.e., as if one was walking bent over backwards)

(282) Jumaytepeque null-copula sentences.
    a. <u>ki ür'a-h</u> *na dyos*   (EX:18)
       very big-3SG.SETE the god
       'God is great.' (lit. 'God is very big.')
    b. <u>ahunhun'a ar</u>   (EX:188)
       dark still
       'It is dark still.'
    c. <u>ür'an</u> *hurak*   (EX:302)
       big man
       'The man is big.' (i.e., influential)
    d. <u>Ø-uupu-'</u> *xa eskiina*   (EX:100)
       3SG.SETC-stand-IV.AFF in corner
       'In the corner it is standing.'
    e. <u>tz'ih t'i</u> *aa mak'u-h*   (EX:408)
       quiet 3SG.DIRECT.OBJECT the house-3SETE
       'His house is quiet.'
    f. <u>ki hwerte</u> *aa hurak*   (EX:110)
       very strong the man
       'The man is very strong.'

4.2.2.3 *The copula uk'a*

In contrast to the zero-copula, or null-copula, constructions just described, Guaza-capán also has a sentence type that employs an overt copula verb. In fact, while this particle is used in the language of Guazacapán, the other two Xinkan languages make use of the temporal duration marker (see section 4.2.2.1). This copula verb is *uk'a*, and its use contrasts with the other types of verbless sentences seen above. Furthermore, this verb is irregular in that it takes pronominal suffixes.

    It means 'be' and can refer to a location or a noninherent characteristic of a nominal argument, much like Spanish *estar*. This verb is also used in conjunction with Spanish infinitives when Xinkan verbs are incorporated into that language. (This is common for many languages.)[9] Since it is not conjugated like any other verb in the language, sentences with this verb are considered in this section.[10]

(283) Guazacapán copula sentences.
    a. *limpyo palh uk'a-h xuun'ik*   (EX:1032)
       clean MOD be-3SG.SETE pot
       'The pot is clean now.'

b. *serka palh uk'a-h*   (EX:1745)
close MOD be-3SG.SETE
'It is close now.'

c. *chirw'i uka-ka*   (EX:170)
skinny be-2SG.SETE
'You are skinny.'

d. *naatüy'ah uk'a-h xa maku taata-n*   (EX:663)
there be-3SG.SETE in house father-1SG.SETE
'My father is always at home.'

e. *Watemaala nalh uk'a-n anik*   (EX:2007)
Guatemala.City PST be-1SG.SETE today
'I was in Guatemala City today.'

4.2.2.4 *Existence*

Utterances that are existential in meaning have only two essential constituents: the existential marker and the predicate. Consequently, they are grouped here with the verbless sentences. In Guazacapán the existential marker is formed by using the intransitive affective form of the copular verb *uk'a/uuka'*. In Chiquimulilla, the existential marker is the third-person singular conjugation of the temporal duration marker *ay* often followed by the word *k'i*. In Jumaytepeque, the existential marker is *ayuu'*, which appears to be the intransitive affective form of the temporal marker (see section 4.2.2.1). Negative existential sentences are irregular in Guazacapán.

(284) Guazacapán existential sentences.

a. *hin xan uy xa xuun'ik*   (EX:515)
no in water in pot
'There is no water in the pot.'

b. *xa xuun'ik man uuka-' xin'ak*   (EX:531)
in pot that 3SG.SETC-be-IV.AFF bean
'There are beans in that pot.'

c. *si uuka' tuma xa graw'a*   (EX:490)
if 3SG.SETC-be-IV.AFF deer in forest
'if there are deer in the forest'

d. *uuka' ik'alh ke hin kuy ta'*   (EX:246)
3SG.SETC-be-IV.AFF one that no FUT come
'There is one that will not come.'

(285) Chiquimulilla existential sentences.

a. *ay taha' goona*   (EX:112)
EXIST a.lot hill
'There are a lot of hills.'

b. *ay k'i pero tuumu-' bar*   (EX:142)
EXIST REFL but 3SG.SETC-finish-IV.AFF EPIST
'There was some, but now it has been finished.'

    c. *wina ay*   (EX:201)
       festival EXIST
       'There is a festival.'

(286) Jumaytepeque existential sentences.
    a. *Ø-ayuu' ar map'ü*   (EX:136)
       3SG.SETC-TEMP.DUR-IV.AFF still tortilla
       'There still are tortillas.'
    b. *l-Ø-aayu' wix yamu-yi'*   (EX:135)
       no-3SG.SETC-TEMP.DUR-IV.AFF who know.COMP-3SG.SETA
       'There is nobody that knows it.'
    c. *lan ti' Ø-ayuu'*[11]   (EX:171)
       no DIR 3SG.SETC-TEMP.DUR-IV.AFF
       'There is nothing.'

4.2.2.5 *Equational construction*

An equational construction indicates that two noun phrases are equal. That is, this construction shows that any two given noun phrases are one and the same thing. In Guazacapán this is accomplished through the use of the word *haani'* 'equal', and this word always immediately precedes the predicate of a verbless construction or the verb in a construction with a full verb. There is no information from my fieldwork, the unpublished field notes, or past historical sources that indicates how equational constructions were formed in the other Xinkan languages. It is probably a valid assumption that they were similar to Guazacapán, but undoubtedly Chiquimulilla, Jumaytepeque, and Yupiltepeque would have different lexical items for use here.

(287) Guazacapán equational constructions.
    a. *haani' tz'ok'o piki man*   (EX:244)
       EQUAL grackle bird that
       'That bird looks like a grackle.'
    b. *haani' hura'i-h mixt'un huurak man*   (EX:628)
       EQUAL eye-3SG.SETE cat man that
       'That man has cat eyes.'
    c. *na tay'uk hü' akani' piri-k'i-h haani' ka-neelha*   (EX:1352)
       the hat this like that see-ANTIP-3SG.SETE EQUAL 2SG.SETB-for
       'this hat like that is looks like yours.'
    d. *üra' haani' tz'ok'o*   (EX:392)
       big EQUAL grackle
       'It is big like a grackle.'
    e. *haani' nawu-ka lhonk'o' nen'*   (EX:557)
       EQUAL child-2SG.SETE tall I
       'I am as a tall as your son.'
    f. *harmu-y' haani' xüma*   (EX:318)
       gnaw.COMP-3SG.SETA EQUAL rat
       'He gnaws it like a rat.'

4.3 Question formation

Two types of utterances ask questions in Xinkan: yes/no questions and content questions (also referred to as wh-questions). Each type is organized differently, so they are discussed separately in this section.

4.3.1 Yes/no questions

Yes/no questions are those that only can be answered by either a 'yes' or 'no'. In all the Xinkan languages, verbal and nonverbal sentences can be formed into yes/no questions. However, different ways of forming these questions are exhibited in each sentence type. Specifically, verbal sentences use no overt question morphology to signal a statement or a question. The only change is in the sentential intonation, which, like Spanish and English (and many other languages), rises at the end of the clause to indicate a question.

Nonverbal sentences are treated differently in the three languages. In Guazacapán no overt morphology is used to indicate a question, and as with verbal sentences, intonation indicates whether a clause is a question or not. In Jumaytepeque a question particle *we'* is used in nonverbal sentences to indicate that it is a question. In Chiquimulilla there are only two examples of yes/no questions. In one the particle *we'* is employed, while in the other it is clearly not. In both cases, a verb is present in the clause; thus, from the limited amount of data available, the patterns seem to be different from either of the other two Xinkan languages.

For yes/no questions, word order is identical to declarative sentences (see section 4.2.1). The same variation in word order discussed in relation to declarative sentences is also exhibited for yes/no questions. However, the question particle in Jumaytepeque and Chiquimulilla is always located between the predicate and the (subject) nominal argument.

(288) Guazacapán yes/no questions.
    a. *ka-niw'a map'u*   (EX:716)
       2SG.SETB-ask.ICOMP tortilla
       'Do you want tortillas?'
    b. *xa-maku hi' taat'a-ka'*   (EX:1693)
       in-house TEMP.DUR father-2SG.SETE
       'Is your father home?'
    c. *naatüy'ah hi' taat'a-ka'*   (EX:1395)
       there TEMP.DUR father-2SG.SETE
       'Is your father there?'
    d. *teena' ka-niw'a*   (EX:1842)
       a.lot 2SG.SETB-ask.ICOMP
       'Do you want a lot?'
    e. *ka-niw'a k'alh libra til'a* (EX:715)
       2SG.SETB-ask.ICOMP one pound salt
       'Do you want a pound of salt?'

    f. *uuka' xin'ak xa xuun'ik*   EX:1337)
        EXIST bean in pot
        'Are there beans in the pot?'
    g. *na nah niwa-y naka map'u ti'i-ka'*   (EX:1271)
        the he ask.COMP-3SG.SETA you tortilla to-2SG.SETE
        'Did she ask you for tortillas?'

In Jumaytepeque, as mentioned above, yes/no questions are signaled by the use of a question particle *we'*. This particle always follows the verb in sentences with verbs and the predicate in sentences without verbs. This particle is given in one yes/no question in Chiquimulilla, but since the data is so restricted, it is not clear what part it plays in the Chiquimulilla grammar. It could be speculated that since these two languages show use of this particle it is either an innovation in the languages or a reflex of a Proto-Xinkan particle. In the first case, it would serve to group Chiquimulilla and Jumaytepeque within the family, while in in the latter case it would be appropriate to reconstruct it as part of Proto-Xinkan. However, these two options must be left unresolved due to the absence of information. In 289 two Chiquimulilla examples are given, one exhibiting the question particle (289a) and one that shows the normal pattern (289b).

(289) Chiquimulilla yes/no questions.
    a. *mük-tik'i-lha' we'*   (EX:49)
        2SG.FORM.SETC-sleep-IV.AGT QP
        'Did you sleep?'
    b. *mük-niw'a k'alh muur'a nak*   (EX:134)
        2SG.FORM.SETB-ask.ICOMP a corncob you
        'Do you want a corncob?'

(290) Jumaytepeque yes/no questions.
    a. *k-tik'i-la' we'*   (EX:291)
        2SG.SETC-sleep.COMP-IV.AGT QP
        'Did you sleep?'
    b. *nama we' t'i-k*   (EX:288)
        hurt QP to-2SG.SETE
        'Are you in pain?'
    c. *n-maar'a we'*   (EX:287)
        1SG.SETB-rest.ICOMP QP
        'I rested?'
    d. *n-titz'i we'*   (EX:289)
        1SG.SETB-stick.it.in.ICOMP QP
        'Did I stick it in?'
    e. *aayu' we' map'ü*   (EX:134)
        EXIST QP tortilla
        'Are there tortillas?

4.3.2   Content questions (wh-questions)

Content questions are used to ask for information about nominal arguments of a verb. Any of the nominal arguments of the verb (subject, nonsubject, or oblique) can be used in this type of question construction. The unknown questioned constituent is replaced with one of the question words (see section 3.10), and the question word is moved to the front of the clause. The rest of the sentence is given in the basic word order.

(291) Guazacapán content questions.

    a. *iwalh baara hooro-y' maku man*   (EX:2313)
        how.many bars have.COMP-3SG.SETA house that
        'How many bars does that house have?'

    b. *han hi' a-pulha-' map'u*   (EX:263)
        how TEMP.DUR 3SG.SETD-make-IV.AFF tortilla
        'How are tortillas made?'

    c. *handa' pul'a ka-kan*   (EX:1059)
        what make IDUR-2SG.SETA
        'What are you doing?'

    d. *kaa hi' Ø-xaawu-' t'uuri*   (EX:668)
        where TEMP.DUR 3SG.SETC-sit.ICOMP-IV.AFF child
        'Where is this child seated?'

    e. *lhük'ü ku ya-ka' ta*   (EX:1016)
        when go TEMP.DUR-2SG.SETA come
        'When are you going to come?'

    f. *weena ta' kaayi-wa-kan na miya ti'i-h*   (EX:1542
        who come buy-PNT-2SG.SETA the chicken to-3SG.SETE
        'Who is coming that you sold the chicken to?'

    g. *na peel'oo-lhe handa alhi hin hooro-y' ut'uyma-h*   (EX:1301)
        the dog-PL what for no have.COMP-3SG.SETA tail-3SG.SETE
        'The dogs, why don't they have their tails?'

(292) Chiquimulilla content questions.

    a. *han xa-k nak*   (EX:157)
        how name-2SG.SETE you
        'What is your name?'

    b. *ka' y'a-k nak*   (EX:169)
        where TEMP.DUR-2SG.SETA you
        'Where are you going?'

    c. *ndi' alhi pulha-ka' nak*   (EX:170)
        why made-2SG.SETA you
        'Why did you do it?'

    d. *ndi na nah*   (EX:173)
        what the it
        'What is this?'

    e. *wax 'ar ayapa' aara-ka'*   (EX:60)
        how many year have-2SG.SETA
        'How old are you?'

  f. *wanin na ma'*   (EX:92)
     who the that
     'Who is that?'
  g. *ndi' alhi maara-k ay kih nak*   (EX:136)
     what for mad-2SG.FORM.SETE TEMP.DUR REFL you.FORM
     'Why are you mad at me?'
  h. *ndi' mi' pul'a-wa-kan*   (EX:59)
     how make-PNT-2SG.SETA
     'How did you do it?'

(293) Jumaytepeque content questions.
  a. *wax 'ar tuwa-h*   (EX:22)
     how much value-3SG.SETE
     'How much is it worth?'
  b. *dix pati' wixu-ka'*   (EX:157)
     why beat-2SG.SETA
     'Why did you hit him?'
  c. *dix a nah*   (EX:39)
     what the it
     'What is that?'
  d. *kax tur'a-ka'*   (EX:223)
     where bring-2SG.SETA
     'Where are you taking it?'

4.4   Preposing

Preposing is the name of a syntactic construction in which one constituent is moved
out of its expected position in the basic word order to a position at the beginning of
an utterance. In Xinkan this occurs when one of the nominal arguments (subject or
object) of a verb is moved from its basic position after the verb (VOS) to a place before
the verb (SVO, OVS, SOV). While both of the nominal arguments can be preposed,
preposing occurs most commonly with the subject of a verb. The preference in preposing subjects over objects is related to the syntactic alignment indicated through
word order. The subject agrees with the verb and is not required to be in a specific
syntactic position for the meaning of a clause to be clear. However, the object is only
understood as such when it is immediately postverbal. This is especially the case when
both arguments refer to the same number and person (e.g., third-person singular); the
object immediately follows the verb to disambiguate meaning. (See section 4.1 for a
more complete discussion.)

   There are referential restrictions, however, on any nominal constituent that is preposed: it must be identifiable and referential within the discourse context. That is,
the preposed constituent must be old, specific information that can be identified and
clearly referred to in the discourse context. Consequently, the preposed nominal arguments are always modified by the definite article *na*. The one exception to this restric-

tion is question words, which are preposed but do not require the definite article as a modifier.

Preposing is quite common among Guazacapán speakers, while the other four languages have only one example (Chiquimulilla) or no examples (Jumaytepeque and Yupiltepeque). Preposing is an essential part of Xinkan grammar, but clear linguistic motivations (such as a pragmatic force) are unknown.

(294) Preposed constituents in Guazacapán.
   a. *na nen' tura-n pe' maalhük*   (EX:14)
      the I bring.COMP-1SG.SETA hither firewood
      'I brought the firewood here.'
   b. *na Hwan hooro-y' k'alh hixi xa mu-bolsa*   (EX:1222)
      the Juan have.COMP-3SG.SETA a rock in 3SG.SETB-pocket
      'Juan has a rock in his pocket.'
   c. *na huurak pir'i-n nen' ke xawatz'a nalh hi'*   (EX:1208)
      the man see.COMP-1SG.SETA that planting PST TEMP.DUR.3SG
      'I saw the man that was planting.'
   d. *na graw'a hü' tz'ama ki' neelha axuka'*   (EX:1176)
      the forest this good and.no.more for food
      'This forest is good for food.'
   e. *na hutu hü' kuy palh Ø-uulhu-'*   (EX:1192)
      the tree this FUT EPIST 3SG.SETC-fall-IV.AFF
      'This tree is going to fall now.'

(295) Preposed constituents in Chiquimulilla.
      na seema ay til'a t'i-h   (EX:10)
      the fish TEMP.DUR.3SG salt to-3SG.SETE
      'This fish is salted.'

4.5   Negation

Clauses with negation follow similar patterns to those discussed above for simple, declarative clauses except that the negative constituent must always occur before the verb or the predicate. This is because the negative element takes scope over the entire predicate.

(296) Guazacapán negative sentences.
   a. *hin elha na maku hü'*   (EX:739)
      no new the house this
      'This house is not new.'
   b. *hin hooro-y' til'a asuka' man*   (EX:478)
      no have.COMP-3SG.SETA salt food that
      'That food doesn't have salt.'
   c. *hin piri-ka' nen'*   (EX:330)
      no see.COMP-2SG.SETA I
      'You didn't see me.'

(297) Chiquimulilla negative sentences.
    a. *lhan tz'ama na huuxi-h*   (EX:253)
       no good the head-3SG.SETE
       'His head is not good.' 'He is stupid.'
    b. *lhan tüxk'ü ya-lhki'*   (EX:179)
       no far.away TEMP.DUR-1PL.SETE
       'We are not far away.'
    c. *lhan üin-ku' bar*   (EX:246)
       no 1SG.SETB-go EPIST
       'I don't go now.'

(298) Jumaytepeque negative sentences.
    a. *la h-ir'i a h-talma*   (EX:39)
       no 3SG.SETB-look.ICOMP the 3SG.SETB-road
       'He dosen't watch his way.'
    b. *lan ar k-wak'a'*   (EX:187)
       no still 2SG.FORM.SETB-left.ICOMP
       'Don't leave yet.'
    c. *la h-im'a*   (EX:299)
       no 3SG.SETB-tell.ICOMP
       'He doesn't say it.'

From the examples in 296–298, the general pattern or template NEG-VP/Predicate NP (Negative-Verb Phrase/Predicate Noun Phrase) can be seen for all utterances with a negative element. This is the basic order of constituents with a negative element. In more complex sentences, however, two additional syntactic patterns can be observed: first, a preposed noun phrase (see section 4.4) precedes the negative element; and second, question words must always be clause initial (see section 4.3). Each of these are shown in the following examples.

(299) Negative sentences with preposed constituents in Guazacapán.
    a. *na üin-kawayu man hin süm'a hin ololo'*   (EX:1144)
       the 1SG.SETB-horse that no black no white
       'My horse is not black or white.'
    b. *na taata-n hin narilha-y' nen'*   (EX:1342)
       the father-1SG.SETE no teach.COMP-3SG.SETA I
       'My father didn't teach me.'
    c. *handa alhi hin hooro-y' ut'uym'a-h*   (EX:607)
       why no have.COMP-3SG.SETA tail-3SG.SETE
       'Why don't they have their tails?'

(300) Negative sentence with preposed constituent in Chiquimulilla.
    na peelo' lhan xuk'u-y' ne nen'   (EX:247)
    the dog no bite.COMP-3SG.SETA the I
    'The dog didn't bite me.'

(301) Negative sentence with preposed constituent in Jumaytepeque.
a nin la n-k'u' (EX:298)
the I no 1SG.SETB-go.ICOMP
'I am not going.'

Lastly, in Guazacapán there is an interesting structure involving the negative existential and a transitive verb. In this construction the negative existential *hin xan* can be the object of a transitive verb. When this construction is used, the negative constituent is always preposed.

(302) Guazacapán negative objects.
    a. *hin xan hünü-n'* (EX:498)
       no LOC know.COMP-1SG.SETA
       'I don't know anything.'
    b. *hin xan im'a-y'* (EX:500)
       no LOC tell.COMP-3SG.SETA
       'He didn't say anything.'
    c. *hin xan ün-niw'a* (EX:497)
       no LOC 1SG.SETB-ask.ICOMP
       'I didn't ask for anything.'

All of the examples above show how negation is used at the clause level. There are no examples of negation used below the clause level in the database, such as the negation of noun phrases. It is unknown if this type of construction would be treated differently than those described above.

4.6 Complex sentence formation

This section considers sentences that have a more complicated syntactic structure or that exhibit variations on the basic constructions. In particular the syntactic patterns are given of conjoined clauses, serial verb constructions, relative clauses, complement clauses, adverbial clauses, and conditional clauses.

4.6.1 Conjoined clauses

In Xinkan utterances, constituents that are syntactically similar can be conjoined. For example, two noun phrases or two verb phrases may be conjoined. Conjunction is possible through the use of the coordinating conjunction construction or through the use of one of the disjunctive conjunctions. Only coordinating conjunctions are used in native Xinkan syntax; the disjunctive conjunctions have been borrowed from Spanish. Coordination is accomplished in the Xinkan languages through simple juxtaposition of elements. Prior to Spanish contact, this appears to have been the only possible way to form these constructions. However, it is more common for speakers to use the three Spanish conjunctions: *i* (<Sp. *'y'*) 'and'; *peero* (<Sp. *'pero'*) 'but'; and *o* (<Sp. *'o'*) 'or'. Example 303 shows juxtaposition, and 304–309 show the more common strategy of borrowed coordinating conjunctions, which appear in boldface.

(303) Guazacapán coordination through juxtaposition.
    a. *pwes Ø-waaka-' uwi-y' k'otoro uw'alh*   (EX:125)
        well 3SG.SETC-go.COMP-IV.AFF call.COMP-3SG.SETA leafcutter ant
        'Well they went [and] called the leafcutter ants.'
    b. *na tuuru' xawxa-y' mu-waya' tahna-'*   (EX:128)
        the tuuru plant.COMP.3SG.SETA 3SG.SETB.cornfield 3SG.SETC-grew.COMP-IV.AFF
        'Tuuru' planted his cornfield [and] it grew.'

(304) Guazacapán coordinating conjunction.
    a. *Ø-tik'i-lha' t'uuri xa kamioneeta i hin Ø-itz'i-lha'*   (EX:1898)
        3SG.SETC-sleep.COMP-IV.AGT child in truck **and** no 3SG.SETC-wake.up.COMP-IV.AGT
        'The child slept in the truck and didn't wake up.'
    b. *na tz'iiwi neelha uy a-ixap'a i a-xuka-'*   (EX:1151)
        the cat.fish for water 3SG.SETD-remove.ICOMP **and** 3SG.SETD-eat-IV.AFF
        'The catfish is caught and eaten.'

(305) Chiquimulilla coordinating conjunction.
    Ø-tay'a-lha' i Ø-hoono-'   (EX:186)
    3SG.SETC-come.COMP-IV.AGT **and** 3SG.SETC-drunk-IV.AFF
    'He came and got drunk.'

(306) Guazacapán disjunction: 'or'.
    a. *xawatz'a hutu o xuw'an a-müka-' neelha xum'uku maku*   (EX:1718)
        planting tree **or** laurel tree 3SG.SETD-work-IV.AFF for board house
        'The planted tree or laurel serves for house boards.'
    b. *han hi' mu-kolor nawak'u man? süm'a o ololo' o me'e*   (EX:700)
        what 3SG.SETB-color skirt that black **or** white **or** green
        'What color is that skirt? Is it black or white or green?'

(307) Guazacapán disjunction: 'but'.
    a. *hoor'o-n' nalh k'alh kawayu **peero** k'aay'i-n'*   (EX:1409)
        have.COMP-1SG.SETA PST one horse **but** sell.COMP-1SG.SETA
        'I had a horse but I sold it.'
    b. *hün'ü-n üm'ülha **pero** hin hoor'o-n lapis*   (EX:352)
        know.COMP-1SG.SETA write **but** no have.COMP-1SG.SETA pencil
        'I know how to write but I don't have a pencil.'

(308) Chiquimulilla disjunction: 'but'.
    a. *ay k'i' **pero** Ø-tuumu-' bar*   (EX:142)
        TEMP.DUR.3SG and.no.more **but** 3SETC-finish.COMP-IV.AFF EPIST
        'There was some but it is gone now.'
    b. *Ø-yüüwü-' **pero** Ø-lhükü-' bar*   (EX:282)
        3SG.SETC-lose.COMP-IV.AFF **but** 3SG.SETC-find.COMP-stat now
        'It was lost but now it is found.'

(309) Jumaytepeque disjunction: 'but'.
    a. *aw'al'an n-mük'a-la' **pero** lan bar n-mük'a*   (EX:297)
        yesterday 1SG.SETC-work.COMP-IV.AGT **but** no now 1SG.SETD-work.ICOMP
        'Yesterday I worked but now I am not working.'

b. *hünü-yi' **pero** la h-im'a*   (EX:299)
know.COMP-3SG.SETA **but** no 3SG.SETB-say.ICOMP
'He knows it but doesn't say it.'

4.6.2   Serial verb constructions

Serial verb constructions are those utterances that contain a sequence of verbs that structurally belong within the same clause. That is, while conjoined clauses (see section 4.6.1 above) and complement clauses (see section 4.6.4 below) contain a sequence of verbs, the individual verbs are structurally and syntactically members of different constituents (i.e., clauses). However, a serial verb construction contains a sequence of verbs within the same clause or constituent. In Xinkan languages, as in most languages, there are restrictions on which verbs are permitted to participate in a serial verb construction. In Xinkan languages, the first member of the series must be one of the following verbs: 'know,' 'finish,' 'want,' 'move', or 'teach'. The second member in the series can virtually be any verb in the lexicon.

In all serial verb constructions, the first member of the chain is inflected for grammatical aspect and the corresponding strategy for subject agreement. The second member in the verb chain (whether transitive or intransitive) is used in what might be called its bare or underlying form; in section 3.6 this was called the infinitive form of the verb. This is the primary diagnostic for differentiating serial verb constructions from complement clauses. If the second verb in the series is an intransitive verb, the root is given without subject agreement-marking or verb class suffixes despite the fact that these are usually necessary with such verbs (see section 3.6.1). Also recall that transitive verbs do not have class-marking suffixes. Examples 310–312 highlight serial verb construction.

(310) Serial verb constructions in Guazacapán.
    a. *ki tero-n' nüm'a*   (EX:540)
       very want.COMP-1SG.SETA eat
       'I am really hungry.'
    b. *kuy hün'ü-y iw'a k'alh ay'aalha*   (EX:168)
       FUT know.COMP-3SG.SETA toast one woman
       'A woman will know how to cook.'
    c. *na Hwan tumu-y' pul'a mu'u maku*   (EX:90)
       the Juan finish.COMP-3SG.SETA make white house
       'Juan finished making the house white.'
    d. *na ün-poocha narila-y nen' müüm'ü*   (EX:1425)
       the 1SG.SETB-grandmother teach.COMP-3SG.SETA I sing
       'My grandmother taught me to sing.'
    e. *pir'i-n han hapa xa maku man*   (EX:1541)
       see.COMP-1SG.SETA what occur.IV.AGT in house that
       'I saw what happened in that house.'

f. *ter'o pir'i k'a-y Hwan ke ün-tupa-' xa maku* (EX:265)
   want see IDUR-3SG.SETA Juan that 1SG.SETD-stay-IV.AFF in house
   'Juan wanted me to stay at his house.'

g. *hin hün'ü-n handa' kaay'i hi' Hwan* (EX:238)
   no know.COMP-1SG.SETA what sell TEMP.DUR.3SG Juan
   'I don't know what Juan is selling.'

h. *hün'ü-n üm'ülha pero hin hooro-n laapis* (EX:1291)
   know.COMP-1SG.SETA write but no have.COMP-1SG.SETA pencil
   'I know how to write but I don't have a pencil.'

(311) Serial verb constructions in Chiquimulilla.

   a. *Ø-waak'a-' tur'a uy* (EX:75)
      3SG.SETC-went.COMP-IV.AFF bring water
      'S/he went to bring water.'

   b. *lha a-tero-' mük'a* (EX:126)
      no 3SG.SETD-want.ICOMP-IV.AFF work
      'S/he doesn't want to work.'

(312) Serial verb constructions in Jumaytepeque.

   a. *yamu-hri' tamik'i xa xaha* (EX:22)
      know.COMP-3SG.SETA speak in tongue
      'S/he knows how to speak in Xinkan.'

   b. *la a-tuk'u-' k'er'e laapis nah* (EX:385)
      no 3SG.SETD-be.able.ICOMP-IV.AFF break pencil he
      'He can't break the pencil.'

Other than the differences from other syntactic constructions, the serial verb construction is also important in other ways. When speakers incorporate a word from Spanish, the serial verb construction is used. Specifically, the copular verb *uk'a* 'be, exist' is used before any borrowed Spanish infinitive. This verb is only used in a serial verb construction in conjunction with verbs borrowed from Spanish; it is never used in conjunction with verbs native to Xinkan grammar. Each of the Xinkan languages uses this verb to incorporate Spanish verbs into the Xinkan lexicon. This fact may indicate that this verb may once have had a different function in the Xinkan languages. In the data used for this grammatical description, it appears in the Spanish verb construction (see the examples in 313) and is an overt copula in Guazacapán only (see section 4.2.2.3). When used in conjunction with incorporated Spanish verbs, this verb is always marked with the SET E nominal possession suffixes.

(313) Spanish verb loan construction.

   a. *uk'a-h recomendar*
      be-3SG.SETE recommended
      'It was recommended.'

   b. *uk'a-n' rezar*
      be-1SG.SETE pray
      'I prayed.'

4.6.3   Relative clauses

Relative clauses always follow the pattern HEAD-RELATIVIZER-RELATIVE CLAUSE and can be exemplified in four very similar ways. All four options are simply variations on what word can be used as the relativizer. First, and most common, is the use of *ke*, the relative marker borrowed from Spanish 'que'.

(314)   Borrowed Spanish relative marker in relative clauses in Guazacapán.

     a.   *xa-maku hooro-n k'alh machiiti **ke** hin ün-neelha*   (EX:593)
        in-house have.COMP-1SG.SETA one machete **that** no 1SG.SETB-for
        'In the house is a machete that is not mine.'

     b.   *nah nahü' huurak **ke** pir'i-k **ke** xawatz'a nalh hi'*   (EX:1539)
        he here man that see.COMP-1PL.SETA that planting PST TEMP.DUR.3SG
        'the man here **that** we saw **that** was planting'

     c.   *kuy kun'u-n na miyaa-lhi man **ke** tumukɨ ololo'*   (EX:936)
        FUT buy.COMP-1SG.SETA the chicken-PL that **that** all white
        'I will buy those chickens **that are** all white.'

The second option for relative clauses just juxtaposes the relative clause with its head noun. This is the most nativelike manner of forming relative clauses as it is observed in most of the Xinkan languages. In this strategy the relativizer, which must be structurally present, is not phonetically spelled out.

(315)   Juxtaposition as relative clause in Guazacapán.

     a.   *na nen' hooro-n' machiiti küwa-ha-ka' nen'*   (EX:1297)
        the I have.COMP-1SG.SETA machete borrow.COMP-CAUS-2SG.SETA I
        'I have the machete that you lent me.'

     b.   *talhma hü' kuy tur'a-n'*   (EX:1835)
        road this FUT take.COMP-1SG.SETA
        'This is the road that I will take.' (i.e., follow)

     c.   *na huurak Ø- ixpa-' na nen' hünü-n'*   (EX:417)
        the man 3SG.SETC-leave.COMP-IV.AFF the I know.COMP-1SG.SETA
        'I am the man that left.'

(316)   Juxtaposition as relative clause in Chiquimulilla.

     a.   *kway xuka-n na seema ay til'a*   (EX:11)
        FUT eat.COMP-1SG.SETA the fish TEMP.DUR.3SG salt
        'I will eat the fish that is salted.'

     b.   *na puup'u kway hayp'u-y na paatz'i*   (EX:104)
        the mat FUT receive.COMP-3SG.SETA the dough
        'the mat that will be used with the dough'

The third option is acceptable in Guazacapán only. In this form of the construction, a relativizer that is phonologically identical to the definite article (which is probably its historical source) is used. This strategy for forming relative clauses is not exhibited in the other Xinkan languages, but it is common in neighboring Pipil, a Uto-Aztecan language, and in some Mayan languages.[12] The definite articles are in boldface.

(317) *Na* relativizer in Guazacapán.

    a. *hin hünü-n' huurak **na** ka-taayi-' hina'*   (EX:462)
        no know.COMP-1SG.SETA man **that** 2SG.SETC-came.COMP-IV.AFF with
        'I don't know the man that you came with.'

    b. *hooro-n' nen' k'alh machiiti **na** küxma-ka' nen'*   (EX:584)
        have.COMP-1SG.SETA I still machete **that** give.COMP-2SG.SETA I
        'I still have the machete **that** you gave me.'

    c. *nuk'a nen' kuchiyu **na** ka-tz'ür'ü waakax hina'*   (EX:1467)
        give.IMP I knife **that** 2SG.SETB-cut.ICOMP meat with
        'Give me the knife that you cut the meat with.'

In the last option, instead of *na* the word *weena* 'who' can be used as a relativizer when the head noun is a human being and is specifically identified within the discourse context. This may be due to Spanish influence. Spanish has a similar relative clause construction: for example, *veo al hombre, **quien** siempre canta* [see.I OBJ.the man **who** always sings] 'I see the man, who always sings'.

(318) 'Who' as relativizer in Guazacapán.

    a. *pir'i-n na huurak **weena** ta'*   (EX:1544)
        see.COMP-1SG.SETA the man **who** come
        'I saw the man who is coming.'

    b. *pir'i-n na huurak **weena** ta' kaayi-kan nah miya* (EX:1545)
        see.COMP-1SG.SETA the man **who** come sell.COMP-2SG.SETA he chicken
        'I saw the man who came and sold him the chicken.'

    c. *na taata-n hin **weena** xa-maku*   (EX:15)
         the father-1SG.SETE not **who** in-house
        'My father is not who is in the house.'

4.6.4   Complement clauses

Complement clauses act as one of the core arguments in a verb phrase by filling the role of either subject or object, for example.[13] They are different from serial verb constructions because in complement clauses each verb is structurally placed in a different clause and each can use the regular verbal morphology. This means that both the matrix verb and the subordinate verb are inflected for agreement with their respective subjects. For second-person singular agreement in Guazacapán, however, there is a unique suffix indicating that the subject is dependent on the matrix clause (see section 3.5.1).

In most cases one of the nominal arguments in the matrix clause is coreferential with one in the embedded clause. This coreferentiality can exist with subjects or objects in the matrix clause.

(319) Complement clauses in Guazacapán.

    a. *mu-poy'o nah ke maestro pa'ał*   (EX:1121)
         3SG.SETB-believe.ICOMP he that teacher now
        'He believes that he is the teacher now.'

b. *hin ün-niw'a ke pat'a-kan ki-ka ka-tupa-' naha'* (EX: 262)
    no 1SG.SETB-ask.ICOMP that be.able-2SG.DEP REFL-2SG.SETA 2SG.SETD-remain.
        ICOMP-IV.AFF here
    'I don't want you to stay here alone.' 'I don't want that you stay here alone.'

c. *uk'a-y prometer ke hin palh kuy Ø-hoono-'* (EX: 2382)
    be-3SG.SETA promise that no now FUT 3SG.SETC-drunk.COMP-IV.AFF
    'He promised that he will not get drunk.'

d. *im'a-y nen' Hwan ke ka-tonto* (EX: 2258)
    tell.COMP-3SG.SETA I Juan that 2SG.SETB-stupid
    'Juan told me that you are stupid.'

e. *im'a-y nen' Hwan ke ün-tonto* (EX: 624)
    tell.COMP-3SG.SETA I Juan that 1SG.SETB-stupid
    'Juan told me that I am stupid.'

f. *im'a y nen' ke ün kun'a k'ulh tuy'uk neelha taata-h* (EX: 2259)
    tell.COMP-3SG.SETA that 1SG.SETB-buy.ICOMP one hat for father-3SG.SETE
    'He told me to buy a hat for his father.'

g. *na pik'i man hin a-pata-' Ø-saaka-'* (EX: 1315)
    the bird that no 3SG.SETD-be.able.ICOMP-IV.AFF 3SG.SETC-lift.COMP-IV.AGT
    'That bird is not able to fly.'

(320) Complement clauses in Chiquimulilla.
    iima-k t'i-h ke lha müh-pul'a (EX: 187)
    tell.COMP-2SG.IMPV to-3SG.SETE that no 3SG.SETB-do.ICOMP
    'Tell him not to do it.'

(321) Complement clauses in Jumaytepeque.
    nin sí yam'u-n ke a-ta-' bar ayi' (EX: 303)
    I indeed know.COMP-1SG.SETA that 3SG.SETD-come.ICOMP-IV.AFF now TEMP.DUR.3SG
    'I indeed know that he is coming.'

It will be noted that the coreferences in the examples above all refer to nominal arguments that are more or less specific and identifiable. That is, there are no examples in the database that suggest that a nonspecific nominal argument can be the head of the relative clause or a complement clause. This is also true for some of the neighboring Mayan languages, but only for relative clauses. However, without evidence about the speakers' grammaticality judgments for complement clauses, this can only be hypothesized to hold for the grammar here but not confirmed conclusively.

4.6.5 Adverbial clauses

Adverbial clauses indicate the time of an action denoted in a separate verb phrase or clause. They are similar to complement clauses in that the adverbial clauses contain independently inflected verbs. These are always introduced by *asük* (Guazacapán and Chiquimulilla) or *sük* (Jumaytepeque).

(322) Adverbial clauses in Guazacapán.
  a. *üran hutu nalh pa'alh **asük** muk-taayi-' naha'*   (EX:2210)
     big tree PST now **when** 1PL.SETC-came.COMP-IV.AFF here
     'It was already a big tree when we came here.'
  b. *kuy a-pata-' wawü-n uy **asük** chürükü' hooro-y uy*   (EX:927)
     FUT 3SG.SETD-be.able.ICOMP-IV.AFF cross.COMP-1SG.SETA water **when** a.little have.
        COMP-3SG.SETA water
     'I will be able to cross the river when there is a little water.'

(323) Adverbial clauses in Chiquimulilla.
  a. *pul'a ya-kan kiwi' **asük** ün-waxta-' ni'*   (EX:42)
     do TEMP.DUR-2SG.DEP PST **when** 1SG.SETC-enter.COMP-IV.AFF I
     'You were doing it when I came in.'
  b. ***asük** ta-k kway müy'a-n nak*   (EX:244)
     when come.COMP-2SG.SETA FUT help.COMP-1SG.SETA you
     'When you come I will help you.'

(324) Adverbial clauses in Jumaytepeque.
  a. ***sük** pu ta-k n-pahat'a nak*   (EX:178)
     when PART come.COMP-2SG.SETA 1SG.SETB-pay.ICOMP you
     'When you come I will pay you.'
  b. ***sük** pu ir'i-n t'i-k ün-witz'u nak*   (EX:180)
     when PART see.COMP-1SG.SETA to-2SG.SETE 1SG.SETB-hit.ICOMP you
     'When I see you I will hit you.'
  c. *n-nüm'a-la' bar, **sük** Ø-uulu-' a mak'u-h*   (EX:134)
     1SG.SETC-eat.COMP-IV.AGT already **when** 3SG.SETC-fall.COMP-IV.AFF the house-3SG.SETE
     'I already ate when his house fell down.'

4.6.6   Conditional clauses

Conditional clauses in Xinkan indicate that the assertion in a verb phrase is unreal or hypothetical. There are two parts to a conditional clause: the condition (protasis) and the resulting action in case the condition holds (apodosis). In this regard conditional clauses can be seen as similar to adverbial clauses, since both types of clauses modify an action. However, conditional clauses differ from adverbial clauses in that the clause modifying the action in the former type refers to a hypothetical reality, while in the latter the adverb does not.[14] The speakers of Guazacapán and Chiquimulilla most often use the Spanish loanword *si* 'if' to introduce conditional clauses.

(325) Conditional clauses in Guazacapán.
  a. ***si** ka-suk'a weren ka-tero-'*   (EX:1751)
     if 2SG.SETB-eat.ICOMP frog 2SG.SETC-die.COMP-IV.AFF
     'If you eat frogs, then you die.'

b. **si** *ka-tero-' wirik'i hina' nah, kuri-y'a xa goona* (EX:1187)
if 2SG.SETC-want.COMP-IV.AFF speak with him run-IMPV in the hill
'If you want to talk with him go to the hill.'

(326) Conditional clauses in Chiquimulilla.
  a. **si** *lhan nah na Pegro lha a-pulha-' na maku* (EX:188)
  if no he the Pedro no 3SG.SETD-make.ICOMP-IV.AFF the house
  'If it wasn't for Pedro, the house would not have been made.'
  b. *lha ni Ø-hün'ü-'* **si** *kway Ø-ta'* (EX:109)
  no I 3SG.SETC-know.COMP-IV.AFF if FUT 3SG.SETC-come.COMP-IV.AFF
  'It is not known to me if he will come.'

However, in Guazacapán there is some indication of an additional option in forming a conditional clause: via juxtaposition of the two clauses, as illustrated in example 327.

(327) Guazacapán juxtaposition in conditional clauses.
  müya-ka' nalh nen' ün-pahat'a nalh naka (EX:1092)
  help.COMP-2SG.SETA PST I 1SG.SETD-pay.ICOMP PST you
  'If you had helped me, then I would have paid you.'

No examples are attested of conditional clauses in Jumaytepeque being introduced by a Spanish loanword (as seen in examples 325–326). Rather, speakers of this language use an irrealis particle *ma* to form conditional clauses. This particle is always in the protasis—the clause referring to the condition.

(328) Conditional clauses in Jumaytepeque.
  a. *la* **ma** *Pegro la h-yak'a mak'u-h* (EX:293)
  no CON Pedro no 3SG.SETB-make.ICOMP house-3SG.SETE
  'If not for Pedro, he would not have made his house.'
  b. *müya-ka'* **ma** *nin n-pahat'a k'e nak* (EX:296)
  help.COMP-2SG.SETA CON I 1SG.SETB-pay.ICOMP IDUR you
  'If you had helped me, I would have been paying you.'
  c. *lan* **ma** *n-narila naalih lan k'e yamu-hri'* (EX:292)
  no CON 1SG.SETB-teach.ICOMP them no IDUR know.COMP-3PL.SETA
  'If I had not taught them, they would not have known.'

FIVE

Na Mulha Uy

Acceptable use of a language is based on more than grammatical properties, patterns, and constructions. Communicative and social effects accompany every utterance in every language. This chapter is included in this volume to give a sample of the communicative effect of the Xinkan languages and to provide samples of connected utterances that are larger than a clause or constituent. These samples are called *texts*, in line with traditional linguistic nomenclature.

These texts, recorded in the 1970s, represent the speech patterns of the last fully fluent speakers of the language, although the last speakers of Guazacapán understand them and found them entertaining and culturally meaningful. Tables 1.1 and 1.2 list some of the text titles; as mentioned in section 1.4.1, variations of a number of these texts were recorded in different years. Including the variations, a total of 89 texts were recorded and they touch on many different topics, including Xinkan mythology, cultural beliefs, daily life, and Christianity, as well as more general conversations. The majority of these are told in Guazacapán Xinka (81); the remainder are in Jumaytepeque (8). Chiquimulilla texts were recorded also, but they were lost sometime between the 1970s and 2007 when I began collaborating with the Xinkas.

Including all of these texts in this grammar would be a valuable support to understanding the languages and the culture. However, space limitations require me to be selective in which texts I include. Consequently, I have chosen a single text: a mythical story about the birth of Tuuru', one of the cultural heroes of the Xinkas. The story was told by Cipriano Gómez, the main Guazacapán Xinka linguistic consultant during the 1970s, and I chose it because of its cultural value and the breadth of linguistic information it exhibits. A separate volume dedicated specifically to these texts, which will include all of them, is planned for the future in collaboration with the Xinkan community.

This text is called *Na Mulha Uy* 'The Water Lord'. This story was recorded various times over a ten-year period, which resulted in a number of versions, some longer than others. The version presented below, recorded in 1978 by Terrence Kaufman, highlights the grammatical properties of Guazacapán Xinka and represents the essential features of the story. It is used with permission.

The format of the text is intended to aid both students of linguistics and the members of the Xinkan community. The first line, given in italics and numbered, provides the text in Guazacapán Xinka (represented orthographically; see section 2.6). I have tried to introduce line breaks in the places that are most convenient for the presentation and comprehension of the texts. The second line lists the morphemes of each word. The third line provides the meaning of each of these morphemes according the discussions in chapters 3 and 4. The fourth line gives a free translation of the text in English. (The translation will be given in Spanish in the community version of this grammar.) One version of this story was translated by Cipriano Gómez into Spanish; the English translation below is based on his Spanish translation.

5.1   *Na Mulha Uy*

Cipriano Gómez (1979)

1 *nah   na   mulha   uy*
   nah   na   mulha   uy
   he   the   spirit   water
   'He the Water Lord'

2 *taatah   aku'   na'alh   xa   graw'a   xukay'   tenuwa*
   taata-h   a-ku-'   na'alh   xa   graw'a   xuka-y'   tenuwa
   father-3SG.SETE   3SG.SETD-go-IV.AFF   PST   LOC   forest   eat-3SG.SETA   zapote
   'his father went to the forest and he ate zapote'

3 *i   ik'alh   ki'   nalh   tur'ay   utah*
   i   ik'alh   ki'   nalh   tur'a-y   uta-h
   and   one   just   PST   bring-3SG.SETA   mother-3SG.SETE
   'and he brought his mother just one'

4 *kada   vez   ke   aku'   nah   ik'alh   ki'   mutur'a   nah*
   kada   vez   ke   a-ku-'   nah   ik'alh   ki'   mu-tur'a   nah
   each   time   that   3SG.SETD-go-IV.AFF   he   one   just   3SG.SETB-bring   she
   'each time he went, just one he brings her'

5 *entonses   imay'   nah   ay'aalha   "ah   i   hin xan   mas*
   entonses   ima-y'   nah   aya'alha   ah   i   hin xan   mas
   then   say-3SG.SETA   he   woman   ah   and   there is not   more
   'then the woman said to him, "ah isn't there more'

6 *pwes   kon eso   katur'a   pe'   nen'   mas"*
   pues   kon eso   ka-tur'a   pe'   nen'   mas
   well   if so   2SG.SETB-bring   FUT   I   more
   'if so you should bring me more"'

7 *"ah   hin xan   hin xan   man ki'"   imay'   nah*
   ah   hin xan   hin xan   man ki'   ima-y'   nah
   ah   there is not   there is not   that's it   say-3SG.SETA   she
   '"ah there isn't, there isn't, that's it" he said to her'

8   *i*   *ts'ih*   *ki'*   *tupawah*   *'ih*

    i   *ts'ih*   *ki'*   *tupa-wa-h*   *'i-h*

    and quiet just leave-PN-3SG.SETE   REFL-3SG.SETE

    'and the woman just remained quiet'

9   *entonses* *ay'aalha* *uuka'*   *pensar* *ke*

    entonses *ay'aalha* *ø-uuka-'*   *pensar* *ke*

    then   woman   3SG.SETC-be-IV.AFF think that

    'then the woman thought that'

10 *pul'ay*   *ik'alh* *urul'uh*   *xapu* *i* *pul'ay*   *bolah*   *urul'u*

    pul'a-y   *ik'alh* *urul'u-h*   *xapu* *i* *pul'a-y*   *bola-h*   *urul'u*

    make-3SG.SETA a   thread-3SG.SETE cotton and make-3SG.SETA ball-3SG.SETE thread

    'she should make a thread, and she made a ball of thread'

11 *i*   *mats'ay*   *nah* *xa* *musinidor*

    i   *mats'a-y*   *nah* *xa* *mu-sinidor*

    and stick-3SG.SETA it   LOC 3SG.SETB-belt

    'and she stuck it to his belt'

12 *suuku'*   *nalh* *xaminih*

    ø-suuku-'   *nalh* *xamini-h*

    3SG.SETC-tie-IV.AFF PST belly-3SG.SETE

    'which was tied to his waist'

13 *i*   *hin* *nalh* *muuuka'*   *sentir*

    i   *hin* *nalh* *mu-uuka-'*   *sentir*

    and no   PST 3SG.SETB-be-IV.AFF feel

    'and he didn't feel it'

14 *asi* *palh* *ki'* *tuumu'*   *akuh*   *tumuki'*

    asi *palh* *ki'* *ø-tuumu-'*   *a-ku-h*   *tumuki'*

    SO EPIST just 3SG.SETC-finish-IV.AFF 3SG.SETD-go-3SG.SETE entire

    'so when the ball of thread was just about finished unraveling'

15 *bolah*   *urul'u* *waaka'*   *ay'aalha*

    bola-h   *urul'u* *ø-waak'a-'*   *ay'aalha*

    ball-3SG.SETE thread 3SG.SETC-go-IV.AFF woman

    'the woman followed'

16 *kwantas* *vweltas* *munuk'a*   *nah* *huurak* *atüy'ah* *aku'*   *nah*

    kwantas *vweltas* *mu-nuk'a*   *nah* *huurak* *atüy'ah* *a-ku-'*   *nah*

    how many turns 3SG.SETB-give it man there 3SG.SETD-go-IV.AFF she

    'as many turns as the man gave it there she walked'

17 *i*   *pwes* *waxta'*   *palh* *lhük'üy*

    i   *pues* *ø-waxta-'*   *palh* *lhük'ü-y*

    and well 3SG.SETC-enter-IV.AFF EPIST find-3SG.SETA

    'and when she arrived she found'

18   *huuts'uk*   *hutu*   *nalh*   *akuh*   *asük*   *waxta'*   *ay'aalha*
           huuts'uk   *hutu*   *nalh*   *a-ku-h*   *asük*   *ø-waxta-'*   *ay'aalha*
           middle   tree   PST   3SG.SETD-go-3SG.SETE   when   3SG.SETC-enter-IV.AFF   woman
           'he was up in the middle of the tree when the woman arrived'

19   *i*   *hin*   *man*   *paata'*   *lhaara'*
           i   *hin*   *man*   *ø-paata-'*   *lhaara-'*
           and   no   that   3SG.SETC-be.able-IV.AFF   climb-IV.AFF
           'and he couldn't climb [anymore]'

20   *porke*   *uuka'*   *desmayar*   *kikih*
           porke   *ø-uuka-'*   *desmayar*   *kiki-h*
           because   3SG.SETC-be-IV.AFF   faint   REFL-3SG.SETE
           'because he had fainted'

21   *bweno*   *pwes*   *komo*   *paata'*   *lharawah*
           bweno   *pues*   *komo*   *ø-paata-'*   *lhara-wa-h*
           good   well   as   3SG.SETC-be.able-IV.AFF   climb-PN-3SG.SETE
           'well he was able to climb'

22   *porke*   *sam'uy'*   *hutu*   *porke*   *hina'*   *alhteh*   *alhara'*
           porke   *sam'u-y'*   *hutu*   *porke*   *hina'*   *alhte-h*   *a-lhara-'*
           because   grab-3SG.SETA   tree   because   with   penis-3SG.SETE   3SG.SETD-climb-IV.AFF
           'because he grabbed the tree because with his penis he was climbing'

23   *entonses*   *imay'*   *nah*   "*donde*   *ünlhara'*   *na*   *nen'*
           entonses   *ima-y'*   *nah*   *donde*   *ün-lhara-'*   *na*   *nen'*
           then   say-3SG.SETA   he   where   1SG.SETB-climb-IV.AFF   the   I
           'then she said to him "where do I climb?'

24   *weske*   *nen'*   *ik'alh*   *tenuwa*   *na*   *nah*"
           weske   *nen'*   *ik'alh*   *tenuwa*   *na*   *nah*
           throw   I   a   zapote   the   it
           'throw me a zapote"'

25   *tuuyu'*   *xukay'*   *tenuwa*   *i*   *xandiwina*   *ki'*   *muulhuy'a*
           ø-tuuyu-'   *xuka-y'*   *tenuwa*   *i*   *xandiwina*   *ki'*   *mu-ulhu-y'a*
           3SG.SETC-begin-IV.AFF   eat-3SG.SETA   zapote   and   upwards   just   3SG.SETB-fall-CAUS
           'he began to eat zapote and he just made them fall upwards [toward the sky]'

26   *entonses*   *ay'aalha*   *imay'*   "*ah*   *nu'ka*   *nen*   *ik'alh*   *pwes*"
           entonses   *ay'aalha*   *ima-y'*   *ah*   *nu'ka*   *nen*   *ik'alh*   *pues*
           then   woman   say-3SG.SETA   ah   give   I   one   well
           'then the woman said "ah give me one"'

27   "*ah*   *iimaakuh*   *pwes*   *apla*   *xahaka*   *sí*
           ah   *iimaakuh*   *pues*   *apla*   *xaha-ka*   *sí*
           ah   here.it.comes   well   open   mouth-2SG.SETE   yes
           '"okay here comes one, open your mouth'

28 *porke*   *kuy*   *peche'*   *xan*   *xahaka* ”
    porke   *kuy*   *ø-peche-'*   *xan*   *xaha-ka*
    because   FUT   3SG.SETC-smash-IV.AFF   LOC   mouth-2SG.SETE
    'because it will smash on your mouth"'

29 *pwes*   *na*   *ay'aalha*   *lhüknüy'*   *nah*   *ch'arkay'*   *xahah*
    pues   *na*   *ay'aalha*   *lhüknü-y'*   *nah*   *ch'arka-y'*   *xaha-h*
    well   the   woman   obey-3SG.SETA   he   open.mouth-3SG.SETA   mouth-3SG.SETE
    'well the woman obeyed him and opened her mouth'

30 *pwes*   *piichi'*   *ulhuwah*   *tenuwa*   *xan*   *xahah*
    pues   *ø-piichi-'*   *ulhu-wa-h*   *tenuwa*   *xan*   *xaha-h*
    well   3SG.SETC-mash-IV.AFF   fall-PN-3SG.SETE   zapote   LOC   mouth-3SG.SETE
    'and the zapote was mashed when it fell in her mouth'

31 *asük*   *tum'uy*   *ik'alh*   *niway'*   *nah*   *otro*
    asük   *tum'u-y*   *ik'alh*   *niwa-y'*   *nah*   *otro*
    when   finish-3SG.SETA   one   ask-3SG.SETA   he   another
    'when she finished [eating] one she asked him for another'

32 *i*   *imay'*   *nah*   “*iimaakuh*   *otro*   *pwes*
    i   *ima-y'*   *nah*   *iimaakuh*   *otro*   *pues*
    and   say-3SG.SETA   she   here.it.comes   another   well
    'and he said to her "here comes another'

33 *pero*   *apla*   *xahaka*   *xiki*   *porke*   *kuy*   *peche'*   *axiki'* ”
    pero   *apla*   *xaha-ka*   *xiki*   *porke*   *kuy*   *ø-peche-'*   *axiki'*
    but   open   mouth-2SG.SETE   also   because   FUT   3SG.SETC-smash-IV.AFF   also
    'but open your mouth again, because it will be smashed also"'

34 *i*   *par'ay*   *nah*   *mas*   *üra'*   *i*   *na*   *ay'aalha*   *ch'arkay'*   *xahah*
    i   *par'a-y*   *nah*   *mas*   *üra'*   *i*   *na*   *ay'aalha*   *ch'arka-y'*   *xaha-h*
    and   look.for-3SG.SETA   it   more   big   and   the   woman   open.mouth-3SG.SETA   mouth-3SG.SETE
    'and he looked for a bigger one and the woman opened her mouth'

35 *ke*   *si*   *komo*   *hawa*   *na'alh*
    ke   *si*   *komo*   *hawa*   *na'alh*
    that   yes   as   unripe   PST
    'and [the zapote he chose] was not ripe'

36 *i*   *komo*   *uulhu'*   *xan*   *xahah*   *ter'oy*   *na*   *muay'aalha*
    i   *komo*   *ø-uulhu-'*   *xan*   *xaha-h*   *ter'o-y*   *na*   *mu-ay'aalha*
    and   as   3SG.SETC-fall-IV.AFF   LOC   mouth-3SG.SETE   kill-3SG.SETA   the   3SG.SETB-woman
    'and as it fell into her mouth he killed his woman'

37 *hin*   *palh*   *aixi'*   *pwes*
    hin   *palh*   *a-ixi-'*   *pues*
    no   EPIST   3SG.SETD-revive-IV.AFF   well
    'she couldn't be revived'

38   *entonses   así   ke   piriy'   ke   hin palh apelhteme'   ay'aalha*
      entonses   así   ke   piri-y'   ke   hin palh a-pelhteme-'   ay'aalha
      then   so   that see-3SG.SETA   that no EPIST 3SG.SETD-return-IV.AFF woman
      'then he saw that the woman could never return'

39   *akulha'   tur'ay   piocha asadon i   pahniy'   na   wowlhak*
      a-ku-lha'   tur'a-y   piocha asadon i   pahni-y'   na   wowlhak
      3SG.SETD-go-IV.AGT bring-3SG.SETA pickaxe hoe   and dig-3SG.SETA the grave
      'he went and brought a pickaxe and a hoe and he dug a grave'

40   *asi   ke   tumuy'   palh pul'a würülhay'   ay'aalha*
      asi   ke   tumu-y'   palh pul'a würülha-y'   ay'aalha
      so   that finish-3SG.SETA EPIST make carry.away-3SG.SETA woman
      'and when he had finished [digging the grave] he carried the woman'

41   *i   komo uulhu'   tup'away'   i   ukay'   nah   naru*
      i   komo ø-uulhu-'   tup'a-wa-y'   i   uka-y'   nah   naru
      and as   3SG.SETC-fall-IV.AFF leave-PN-3SG.SETA and throw-3SG.SETA she ground
      'and she was in the same position as when she had fallen and he threw dirt on her'

42   *pwes chürükü' pari akulha'   üntüy'   haani' komo chiriwones*
      pues chürükü' pari a-ku-lha'   üntü-y'   haani' komo chiriwones
      well a.little day 3SG.SETD-go-IV.AGT see-3SG.SETA like as cotete
      'well a few days later he went and he saw [creatures] like worms'

43   *hoor'oy'   na mak'uh   peer'e tuur'iilhi*
      hoor'o-y'   na mak'u-h   peer'e tuur'i-ilhi
      have-3SG.SETA the house-3SG.SETE small child-PL
      'the small children had their house'

44   *i   donde piriy'   pe'   akuh   waxta'   naalhik*
      i   donde piri-y'   pe'   a-ku-h   ø-waxta-'   naalhik
      and where see-3SG.SETA from 3SG.SETD-go-3SG.SETE 3SG.SETC-enter-IV.AFF they
      'and he saw that they walked from [the houses]'

45   *lwego xa mak'uh   naalhik*
      lwego xa mak'u-h   naalhik
      later LOC house-3SG.SETE they
      'and then they entered into their houses'

46   *bweno pwes entonses na nah tup'awah   porke nahk'walhin   na'alh*
      bweno pues entonses na nah tup'a-wa-h   porke nahk'walhi-n   na'alh
      good well then the he leave-PN-3SG.SETE because children-1SG.SETE PST
      'well he remained [there] because they were my children'

47   *pwes asi palh üra' pa'alh mas chuüra' waak'a'   uwiy'   ke*
      pues asi palh üra' pa'alh mas chu-üra' ø-waak'a-'   uwi-y'   ke
      well so EPIST big EPIST more DIM-big 3SG.SETC-went-IV.AFF call-3SG.SETA that
      'so when they got bigger and bigger he went and called out [to them]'

48 *aku'*   *hina'   porke   na   nah   taatah*
    a-ku-'   *hina'   porke   na   nah   taata-h*
    3SG.SETD-go-IV.AFF   with   because   the   he   father-3SG.SETE
    'that they should come with him because he is their father'

49 *entonses   t'uuriilhi   imay'*   *nah   naalhik   ke*
    entonses   t'uuri-ilhi   ima-y'   *nah   naalhik   ke*
    then   child-PL   say-3SG.SETA   he   they   that
    'then the children said to him that'

50 "*na   nen'   hin xan   taatan*   *ni   utan*
    na   nen'   hin xan   taata-n   *ni   uta-n*
    the   I   there is not   father-1SG.SETE   no   mother-1SG.SETE
    '"I don't have a father or a mother'

51 *porke   xa   naru   pe'   ixpawan*
    porke   xa   naru   pe'   ixpa-wa-n'
    because   LOC   ground   from   leave-PN-1SG.SETE
    'because I was born from the ground'

52 *xa   naru   pe'   ixpawan* "
    xan   naru   pe'   ixpa-wa-n'
    LOC   ground   from   leave-PN-1SG.SETE
    'I was born from the ground"'

53 *bweno   pwes   entonses   uk'ah*   *naalhik   üraki'*
    bweno   pues   entonses   uk'a-h   *naalhik   ø-üra-ki-'*
    good   well   then   be-3SG.SETE   they   3SG.SETC-big-INCH-IV.AFF
    'well they got bigger'

54 *naalhik   üraki'*   *palh   na'alh*
    naalhik   ø-üra-ki-'   *palh   na'alh*
    they   3SG.SETC-big-INCH-IV.AFF   EPIST   PST
    'and they got bigger'

55 *uuka'*   *naalhik   pensar   ke   kuy   pul'ay*   *naalhik   waya'*
    ø-uuka-'   *naalhik   pensar   ke   kuy   pul'a-y*   *naalhik   waya'*
    3SG.SETC-be-IV.AFF   they   think   that   FUT   make-3SG.SETA   they   corn.field
    'and they thought that they would plant a cornfield;'

56 *kuy   pul'ay*   *naalhik   waya'*
    kuy   pul'a-y   *naalhik   waya'*
    FUT   make-3SG.SETA   they   corn.field
    'they will make a cornfield'

57 *i   tuyuy'*   *naalhik   uuka'*   *rosar*   *kraw'a*
    i   tuyu-y'   *naalhik   ø-uuka-'*   *rosar*   *kraw'a*
    and   begin-3SG.SETA   they   3SG.SETC-be-IV.AFF   clear.ground   forest
    'and they began to clear the ground in the forest'

58
dose	naalhik	huuraklhi	i	manda	tuuru'	hin	nalh	aku'		hina'
dose	naalhik	huurak-lhi	i	manda	tuuru'	hin	nalh	a-ku-'		hina'
twelve	they	man-PL	and	how about	youngest.child	no	PST	3SG.SETD-go-IV.AFF		with

'there were twelve men, and the youngest didn't go with them'

59
oor'o	atüy'ah	xa	maku	nalh	atupa'		xa	mutik'ik waaru
oor'o	atüy'ah	xa	maku	nalh	a-tupa-'		xa	mu-tik'ik waaru
only	there	LOC	house	PST	3SG.SETD-leave-IV.AFF		LOC	3SG.SETB-hammock

'he just remained there in the house in his hammock'

60
i	entonses	muim'a	nah	nah
i	entonses	mu-im'a	nah	nah
and	then	3SG.SETB-say	he	he

'then they said to him'

61
"bweno	pwes	manda	naka	hin	kuy	pul'akan	waya' "
bweno	pues	manda	naka	hin	kuy	pul'a-kan	waya'
good	well	how about	you	no	FUT	make-2SG.SETE	corn.field

'"well how about you aren't you going to make a cornfield?"'

62
"ah	byen	pero	kaa	hi'	chuïnwatal
ah	byen	pero	kaa	hi'	chu-ün-watal
ah	indeed	but	where	TEMP.DUR.3SG	DIM-1SG.SETB-plot

'he said to them "ah okay but where is my plot'

63
watal	harak'u	kuy	uuka'	rosar	man ki' "	muim'a	nah	nah
watal	harak'u	kuy	ø-uuka-'	rosar	man ki'	mu-im'a	nah	nah
plot	chipilín	FUT	3SG.SETC-be-IV.AFF	clear.ground	that's it	3SG.SETB-say	he	he

'the chipilin plot, the ground just needs to be cleared that's it"'

64
i	na	naalhik	amüka'	como	kwalquera	huurak
i	na	naalhik	a-müka-'	como	kwalquera	huurak
and	the	they	3SG.SETD-work-IV.AFF	as	any	man

'and they worked like any other man'

65
i	entonses	na	tuuru'	uuka'	encantar	hüyü naru
i	entonses	na	tuuru'	ø-uuka-'	encantar	hüyü naru
and	then	the	youngest.child	3SG.SETC-be-IV.AFF	changed	gopher

'and then Tuuru' changed [by magic] into gopher'

66
muts'ür'ü	na	maxirah	hutuulhi
mu-ts'ür'ü	na	maxira-h	hutu-ulhi
3SG.SETB-cut	the	root-3SG.SETE	tree-PL

'and cut the trees' roots'

67
i	hin	hünün'	han	hora	xa	süüm'a	como	hopraki'	na	hutu	uulhu
i	hin	hünü-n'	handa'	hora	xa	süüm'a	como	ø-hopra-ki-'	na	hutu	uulhu
and	no	know-1SG.SETE	what	hour	LOC	night	as	3SG.SETC-stack-INCH-IV.AFF	the	tree	fallen

'and I don't know what hour in the night that the fallen trees were stacked'

68	*bweno*	*pwes*	*küüwü'*		*asi*	*ke*	*küüwü'*		*uk'ay*		*na*	*uray*
	bweno	*pues*	*ø-küüwü-'*		*asi*	*ke*	*ø-küüwü-'*		*uk'a-y*		*na*	*uray*
	good	well	3SG.SETC-dry-IV.AFF		so	that	3SG.SETC-dry-IV.AFF		throw-3SG.SETA		the	fire

'well they [the trees] dried and he burned them with fire'

69	*i*	*na*	*dose*	*huuraklhi*	*tal'ay*		*na*	*roosa*	*i*	*tup'ay*	*akani'*
	i	*na*	*dose*	*huurak-lhi*	*tal'a-y*		*na*	*roosa*	*i*	*tup'a-y*	*akani'*
	and	the	twelve	man-PL	burn-3SG.SETA		the	cleared.field	and	leave-3SG.SETA	like.this

'and the twelve men burned the cleared field and they left it like this'

70 | *pwes* | *despwes* | *na* | *tuuru'* | *imay'* | | *nah* | *ke*
--- | --- | --- | --- | --- | --- | --- | ---
 | *pues* | *despwes* | *na* | *t'uuru* | *ima-y'* | | *nah* | *ke*
 | well | later | the | youngest | say-3SG.SETA | | he | that

'well later Tuuru' said to them that'

71 | *"ixik'i* | | *pari* | *kuy* | *tal'an* | | *ünnaru* | | *harak'u*
--- | --- | --- | --- | --- | --- | --- | ---
 | *ixi-k'i* | | *pari* | *kuy* | *tal'a-n* | | *ün-naru* | | *harak'u*
 | revive-ANTIP | | day | FUT | burn-1SG.SETE | | 1SG.SETB-ground | | chipilín

'"the day is dawning and I will burn my chipilin plot'

72 | *kuy* | *pul'an* | | *na* | *malhi* | *'ih* | | *pir'ika'* | | *pe'* | *pwes"*
--- | --- | --- | --- | --- | --- | --- | --- | --- | --- | ---
 | *kuy* | *pul'a-n* | | *na* | *malhi* | *'i-h* | | *pir'i-ka'* | | *pe'* | *pues*
 | FUT | make1SG.SETA | | the | ash | REFL-3SG.SETE | | see-2SG.SETA | | hither | well

'and I will make ash, go watch it"'

73	*uuka'*		*nalh*	*mas*	*teena'*	*roosa*		*ke*	*na*	*dose*	*huuraklhi*
	ø-uuka-'		*nalh*	*mas*	*teena'*	*roosa*		*ke*	*na*	*dose*	*huurak-lhi*
	3SG.SETC-be-IV.AFF		PST	more	a.lot	cleared.field		that	the	twelve	man-PL

'it was bigger than that of twelve men'

74 | *i* | *pat'ay'* | | *kikih* | | *hoor'oy'* | | *nah* | *mas*
--- | --- | --- | --- | --- | --- | --- | --- | ---
 | *i* | *pat'a-y'* | | *kiki-h* | | *hoor'o-y'* | | *nah* | *mas*
 | and | remember-3SG.SETA | | REFL-3SG.SETE | | have-3SG.SETA | | he | more

'and he remembered [lit. enabled himself] that he had more'

75 | *pwes* | *entonses* | *kwando* | *asi* | *uk'ay* | | *palh* | *uray*
--- | --- | --- | --- | --- | --- | --- | ---
 | *pues* | *entonses* | *kwando* | *asi* | *uk'a-y* | | *palh* | *uray*
 | well | then | when | so | throw-3SG.SETA | | EPIST | fire

'well when he already started the fire'

76 | *ki'* | *mutum'u* | | *nah* | *ter'o* | *de* | *kalhi* | *xuy'akalhih*
--- | --- | --- | --- | --- | --- | --- | ---
 | *ki'* | *mu-tum'u* | | *nah* | *ter'o* | *de* | *kalhi* | *xuy'aka-lhi-h*
 | just | 3SG.SETB-finish | | he | die | from | smoke | older.brother-PL-3SG.SETE

'his older brothers died from the smoke'

77 | *porke* | *uk'ay* | | *nah* | *tumuki'* | *kalhi* | *alhi*
--- | --- | --- | --- | --- | --- | ---
 | *porke* | *uk'a-y* | | *nah* | *tumuki'* | *kalhi* | *alhi*
 | because | throw-3SG.SETA | | he | entire | smoke | for

'because they were overcome by all the smoke'

78 bweno pwes entonses uk'ah   na kalhi i   uuka'   naalhik pensar
   bweno pues entonses uk'a-h   na kalhi i   ø-uuka-'   naalhik pensar
   good   well then   be-3SG.SETE the smoke and 3SG.SETC-be-IV.AFF they   think
   'well then there is smoke and they thought'

79 ke   kaa   pe' ki' kuy ixapiy'   ayma neelha na   xawats'a
   ke   kaa   pe' ki' kuy ixapi-y'   ayma neelha na   xawats'a
   that where FUT just FUT remove-3SG.SETA   corn for   the harvest
   'about where they would remove the corn [to] during the harvest'

80 i   entonses akulha'   akuk'i   como tuuru' xa   kraw'a
   i   entonses a-ku-lha'   a-ku-k'i   como tuuru' xa   kraw'a
   and then   3SG.SETD-go-IV.AGT 3SG.SETD-go-INCH   as   youngest LOC forest
   'and then they went and were going like Tuuru' into the forest'

81 i   xa   ik'alh kebrada
   i   xa   ik'alh kebrada
   and LOC a   ravine
   'and in a ravine'

82 lhüküy'   ik'alh pokoko ke   tiik'i nalh hi'
   lhükü-y'   ik'alh pokoko ke   tiik'i nalh hi'
   find-3SG.SETA a   raccoon that sleep   PST   TEMP.DUR.3SG
   'they found a raccoon that was asleep'

83 i   entonses na   pokoko tiik'i nalh hi'
   i   entonses na   pokoko tiik'i nalh hi'
   and then   the raccoon sleep   PST   TEMP.DUR.3SG
   'and then the raccoon was asleep'

84 i   waxta'   xa   nalh hi'
   i   ø-waxta-'   xa   nalh hi'
   and 3SG.SETC-enter-IV.AFF LOC PST   TEMP.DUR.3SG
   'and they entered there'

85 i   suk'uy   müt'alhki nalh hi'   pokoko
   i   suk'u-y   müt'alhki nalh hi'   pokoko
   and tie-3SG.SETA dream   PST   TEMP.DUR.3SG   raccoon
   'and tied up the raccoon that was dreaming'

86 ke   xukay'   ayma muuchi ayma morado ayma sün   ayma tol'o   ayma
   ke   xuka-y'   ayma muuchi ayma morado ayma sün   ayma tol'o   ayma
   that eat-3SG.SETA corn white   corn purple corn black corn yellow   corn
   'which ate the corn: white corn, dark purple corn, and yellow corn'

87 kwando suk'uy   palh na talhi uk'ah   its'iyay   naalhik ki'
   kwando suk'u-y   palh na talhi uk'a-h   its'iya-y   naalhik ki'
   when   tie-3SG.SETA EPIST the nape   be-3SG.SETE wake.up-3SG.SETA   they   just
   'when they had tied [the raccoon] by the neck they just woke it up'

88 *entonses*   *"si*   *hin*   *ka'im'a*   *nen'*   *kaa*   *ka'ixaapi'*   *ka'ayma*
    entonses   *si*   *hin*   *ka'-im'a*   *nen'*   *kaa*   *ka'-ixaapi-'*   *ka'-ayma*
    then   if   no   2SG.SETB-say   I   where   2SG.SETB-leave-IV.AFF   2SG.SETB-corn
    'then "if you don't tell me where you put the corn for you to eat'

89 *neelha*   *ka'xuk'a*   *kuy*   *naka*   *ter'on*   *ya*   *ke*   *ünter'o*   *naka"*
    neelha   *ka'-xuk'a*   *kuy*   *naka*   *ter'o-n*   *ya*   *ke*   *ün-ter'o*   *naka*
    for   2SG.SETB-eat   FUT   you   kill-1SG.SETE   just   that   1SG.SETB-kill   you
    'I will kill you. I will kill you"'

90 *"ay*   *hin*   *nen'*   *ka'ter'o*   *pwes*   *kuy*   *naka*   *iman'*   *kaa*   *hi'*   *ayma*
    ay   *hin*   *nen'*   *ka'-ter'o*   *pues*   *kuy*   *naka*   *ima-n'*   *kaa*   *hi'*   *ayma*
    ay   no   I   2SG.SETB-kill   well   FUT   you   say-1SG.SETE   where   TEMP.DUR.3SG   corn

    '"ay don't kill me I will tell you where the corn is'

91 *kaa*   *hi'*   *ayma*   *pero*   *naka*   *hin*   *ka'ter'o*   *nen'"*
    kaa   *hi'*   *ayma*   *pero*   *naka*   *hin*   *ka'-ter'o*   *nen'*
    where   TEMP.DUR.3SG   corn   but   you   no   2SG.SETB-kill   I
    'but don't kill me"'

92 *"imaka*   *neelhek*   *kaa*   *hi'*   *si"*
    ima-ka   *neelhek*   *kaa*   *hi'*   *si*
    say-2SG.SETA   us   where   TEMP.DUR.3SG   yes
    '"tell us where it is and okay"'

93 *"en fin*   *kuy*   *iman'*   *naka*   *enke*   *hin palh*   *kuy*   *xuk'an*   *ayma*
    en fin   *kuy*   *ima-n'*   *naka*   *enke*   *hin palh*   *kuy*   *xuk'a-n*   *ayma*
    at.last   FUT   say-1SG.SETE   you   even.though   anymore   FUT   eat1SG.SETA   corn
    '"okay I will tell you even though I will not eat corn'

94 *pero*   *hin*   *ka'ter'o*   *nen'"*
    pero   *hin*   *ka'-ter'o*   *nen'*
    but   no   2SG.SETB-kill   I
    'but don't kill me"'

95 *"bweno*   *hin*   *pwes"*
    bweno   *hin*   *pues*
    good   no   well
    '"okay we won't"'

96 *waak'a'*   *naalhik*   *i*   *xa*   *ik'alh*   *chuwoona*   *iipan*
    ø-waak'a-'   *naalhik*   *i*   *xa*   *ik'alh*   *chu-woona*   *iipan*
    3SG.SETC-went-IV.AFF   they   and   LOC   a   DIM-hill   small
    'they went and in a little hill'

97 *uuka'*   *nalh*   *ik'alh*   *kweva*
    ø-uuka-'   *nalh*   *ik'alh*   *kweva*
    3SG.SETC-be-IV.AFF   PST   a   cave
    'was a cave'

98 *i*   *t'en'oy*   *na*   *puh*   *pokoko* *ixapiy'*   *ik'alh* *ayma*

i	*t'en'o-y*	*na*	*pu-h*	*pokoko*	*ixapi-y'*	*ik'alh*	*ayma*
and	insert-3SG.SETA	the	hand-3SG.SETE	raccoon	remove-3SG.SETA	a	corn

'and the raccoon put his hand in and removed an ear of corn'

99 *i*   *tup'ay*   *na*   *ayma* *man*

i	*tup'a-y*	*na*	*ayma*	*man*
and	leave-3SG.SETA	the	corn	that

'and he left the other ears of corn'

100 *i*   *nan'iy*   *i*   *waak'a'*   *pokoko*

i	*nan'i-y*	*i*	*ø-waak'a-'*	*pokoko*
and	release-3SG.SETA	and	3SG.SETC-went-IV.AFF	raccoon

'and they released [it] and the raccoon left'

101 *i*   *waak'a'*   *naalhik* *nah* *axiki'*

i	*ø-waak'a-'*	*naalhik*	*nah*	*axiki'*
and	3SG.SETC-went-IV.AFF	they	he	also

'and they left also'

102 *entonses* *uuka'*   *naalhik* *pensar* *ke*   *han hi'* *kuy* *pul'ay*

entonses	*ø-uuka-'*	*naalhik*	*pensar*	*ke*	*han hi'*	*kuy*	*pul'a-y*
then	3SG.SETC-be-IV.AFF	they	think	that	how	FUT	do-3SG.SETA

'then they thought about how will they do it'

103 *uuka'*   *naalhik* *pensar* *ke*   *hina'* *rayaso* *kuy* *kot'ey*   *woona*

ø-uuka-'	*naalhik*	*pensar*	*ke*	*hina'*	*rayaso*	*kuy*	*kot'e-y*	*woona*
3SG.SETC-be-IV.AFF	they	think	that	with	crack	FUT	break.open-3SG.SETA	hill

'they thought that with a crack they will break open the mountain'

104 *bweno* *pwes* *lhaara'*   *mas*   *üra'* *hin* *kot'ey*

bweno	*pues*	*ø-lhaara-'*	*mas*	*üra'*	*hin*	*kot'e-y*
good	well	3SG.SETC-climb-IV.AFF	more	big	no	break.open-3SG.SETA

'well they climbed a bigger [mountain] but they couldn't break it open'

105 *pero* *naatüükah* *ulhuwah*   *i*   *teero'*

pero	*naatüükah*	*ulhu-wa-h*	*i*	*ø-teero-'*
but	there (far)	fall-PN-3SG.SETE	and	3SG.SETC-kill-IV.AFF

'but it fell and they died'

106 *en fin* *ke*   *como* *pühü* *lhaara'*   *y*   *hin* *nah* *mukot'e*   *woona*

en fin	*ke*	*como*	*pühü*	*ø-lhaara-'*	*y*	*hin*	*nah*	*mu-kot'e*	*woona*
at.last	that	as	bird	3SG.SETC-climb-IV.AFF	and	no	he	3SG.SETB-break.open	hill

'at last they climbed like a bird and they couldn't break open the mountain'

107 *entonses* *muim'a*   *nah* *nah*

entonses	*mu-im'a*	*nah*	*nah*
then	3SG.SETB-say	he	he

'so they said to him ['I'uuru']'

108 *"chüküyün*   *kuriy'a*   *naka*   *chüküyün "*
      chüküyü-n   *kuri-y'a*   *naka*   *chüküyü-n*
      younger.brother-1SG.SETE   leave.there-IMP.IV   you   younger.brother-1SG.SETE
      '"my younger brother get out of here, you are only the younger brother"'

109 *"ha*   *kon*   *ke*   *hin*   *apata'*   *naka*   *ke*   *mas*   *ka'üra'*
      ha   *kon*   *ke*   *hin*   *a-pata-'*   *naka*   *ke*   *mas*   *ka'-üra'*
      ha   with   that   no   3SG.SETD-be.able-IV.AFF   you   that   more   2SG.SETB-big
      '"ha you can't do it either even though you are much bigger'

110 *xik'i pari*   *nen'*   *ke*   *mas*   *ünchürükü' "*
      xik'i pari   *nen'*   *ke*   *mas*   *ün-chürükü'*
      at this moment   I   that   more   1SG.SETB-a.little
      'and right now I am smaller"'

111 *"byen*   *hombre*   *chüküyün*   *kuriy'a*   *naka"*
      byen   *hombre*   *chüküyu-n*   *kuri-y'a*   *naka*
      indeed   friend   younger.brother-1SG.SETE   leave.there-IMP.IV   you
      '"okay just leave my younger brother!"'

112 *al fin*   *pul'ay*   *naalhik*   *mulhükün'ü*   *nah*
      al fin   *pul'a-y*   *naalhik*   *mu-lhükün'ü*   *nah*
      at.last   do-3SG.SETA   they   3SG.SETB-believe   he
      'at last they believed him'

113 *i*   *lhaara'*   *komo*   *tuuru'*
      i   *ø-lhaara-'*   *komo*   *tuuru'*
      and   3SG.SETC-climb-IV.AFF   as   youngest.child
      'and they climbed like Tuuru''

114 *na*   *nah*   *sí*   *kot'ey*   *como*   *yürnay'a*   *woona*
      na   *nah*   *sí*   *kot'e-y*   *como*   *yürna-y'a*   *woona*
      the   he   yes   break.open-3SG.SETA   as   fall-CAUS   hill
      'they indeed broke it open but [the mountain] tumbled down'

115 *i*   *tumuy'*   *yüran'a*   *ayma*   *xa*   *nalh*   *woona*
      i   *tumu-y'*   *yüran'a*   *ayma*   *xa*   *nalh*   *woona*
      and   finish-3SG.SETA   fall   corn   LOC   PST   hill
      'and the corn fell down the mountain'

116 *tumuki'*   *na*   *ayma*   *hoor'oy'*   *woona*
      tumuki'   *na*   *ayma*   *hoor'o-y'*   *woona*
      entire   the   corn   have-3SG.SETA   hill
      'all the corn contained in the mountain'

117 *entonses*   *imay*   *naalhik*
      entonses   *ima-y'*   *naalhik*
      then   say-3SG.SETA   they
      'then they said'

118 "ünta'   siiru'   pwes hin xan kuy tup'ak   nah kumu tuuru'

ün-ta'	ø-siiru-'	pues	hin xan	kuy	tup'a-k	nah	kumu	tuuru'
1SG.SETB-come	3SG.SETC-hurry-IV.AFF	well	there is not	FUT	leave-1PL.SETA	he	as	youngest

'"I will come in a hurry and we will not leave Tuuru'"

119 hin xan   kuy tup'ak   nah"

hin xan	kuy	tup'a-k	nah
there is not	FUT	leave-1PL.SETA	he

'we will not leave him'"

120 bweno pwes   entonses tum'uy   wawüiy'a naalhik tumuki' ayma

bweno	pues	entonses	tum'u-y	wawüiy'a	naalhik	tumuki'	ayma
good	well	then	finish-3SG.SETA	haul	they	entire	corn

'well then they finished hauling away all the corn'

121 i   na   tuuru'   hin nalh a'ixi'

i	na	tuuru'	hin	nalh	a'-ixi-'
and	the	youngest.child	no	PST	3SG.SETD-revive-IV.AFF

'but Tuuru' couldn't be revived'

122 asi ke   tum'uy   lhik wawüiy'a naalhik i   saaka'   kumu tuuru'

asi	ke	tum'u-y	lhik	wawüiy'a	naalhik	i	ø-saaka-'	kumu	tuuru'
so	that	finish-3SG.SETA	PL	haul	they	and	3SG.SETC-lift-IV.AFF	as	youngest.child

'so they finished hauling and Tuuru' was carried'

123 i   pir'iy   ke   hin xan   tuupa'   nah

i	pir'i-y	ke	hin xan	ø-tuupa-'	nah
and	see-3SG.SETA	that	there is not	3SG.SETC-leave-IV.AFF	he

'and he saw that they would not leave him'

124 "ay diabluulhi hin xan   tup'ay   nen'"

ay	diablu-ulhi	hin xan	tup'a-y	nen'
ay	devil-PL	there is not	leave-3SG.SETA	I

'"ay diablos don't leave me"'

125 pwes waak'a'   uw'iy   k'otoro   uw'alh

pues	ø-waak'a-'	uw'i-y	k'otoro	uw'alh
well	3SG.SETC-went-IV.AFF	call-3SG.SETA	zompopo	ant

'well they went and called the ants'

126 i   püpüy'   teena'   kintal aa'u

i	püpü-y'	teena'	kintal	aa'u
and	fill-3SG.SETA	a.lot	quintal	corn

'and filled a lot of quintals of corn'

127 i   kwando uulhu'   uy   waak'a'   naalhik xawats'a

i	kwando	ø-uulhu-'	uy	ø-waak'a-'	naalhik	xawats'a
and	when	3SG.SETC-fall-IV.AFF	water	3SG.SETC-went-IV.AFF	they	planting

'and when the water fell they went planting'

128 *na*   *tuuru'*   *xawxay'*   *muwaya'*   *tahna'*
      na   *tuuru'*   *xawxa-y'*   *mu-waya'*   *ø-tahna-'*
      the   youngest.child   plant-3SG.SETA   3SG.SETB-corn.field   3SG.SETC-grow-IV.AFF
      'Tuuru' planted his cornfield and it grew'

129 *i*   *manda*   *xuy'akalhih*
      i   *manda*   *xuy'aka-lhi-h*
      and   how about   older brother-PL-3SG.SETE
      'and what about his older brothers'

130 *hin* *nalh* *muhün'ü*   *han hi'* *pul'ay'*
      hin *nalh* *mu-hün'ü*   *han hi'* *pul'a-y'*
      no   PST   3SG.SETB-learn   how   do-3SG.SETA
      'they didn't learn how to do it'

131 *muniw'a*   *nalh* *nah* *i*   *imay*   *nah* *ke*
      mu-niw'a   *nalh* *nah* *i*   *ima-y'*   *nah* *ke*
      3SG.SETB-ask   PST   he   and   say-3SG.SETA   he   that
      'they asked him and he told them that'

132 *"ah* *haralhak'i*   " *pwes* *akulha'*   *naalhik* *haralhay'*
      ah *haralha-k'i*   *pues* *a-ku-lha'*   *naalhik* *haralha-y'*
      ah   toasted-ANTIP   well   3SG.SETD-go-IV.AGT   they   toast-3SG.SETA
      '"ah [by] toasting" well they went and toasted [it]'

133 *así* *ke* *haralhay'*   *akulha'*   *pe'* *xawats'a*
      así *ke* *haralha-y'*   *a-ku-lha'*   *pe'* *xawats'a*
      so   that   toast-3SG.SETA   3SG.SETD-go-IV.AGT   FUT   planting
      'so they toasted [it] and they went planting'

134 *i*   *hin* *tahna'*   *hin* *tahna'*   *porke* *haralhay'*   *kikih*
      i   *hin* *ø-tahna-'*   *hin* *ø-tahna-'*   *porke* *haralha-y'*   *kiki-h*
      and   no   3SG.SETC-grow-IV.AFF   no   3SG.SETC-grow-IV.AFF   because   toast-3SG.SETA   REFL-3SG.SETE
      'and it didnt grow, it didn't grow because they toasted themselves'

135 *i*   *entonses* *syempre* *hin* *nalh* *muhün'ü*   *han hi'* *mupul'a*
      i   *entonses* *syempre* *hin* *nalh* *mu-hün'ü*   *han hi'* *mu-pul'a*
      and   then   always   no   PST   3SG.SETB-learn   how   3SG.SETB-do
      'and so they never learn how to do it and he [Tuuru'] said'

136 *i*   *imay'*   *ke*   *"ah* *k'aw'u* *pwes* *hombre* *k'aw'uki'* "
      i   *ima-y'*   *ke*   *ah* *k'aw'u* *pues* *hombre* *k'aw'u-ki'*
      and   say-3SG.SETA   that   ah   boil   well   friend   boil-ANTIP
      '"ah boiling then friend, [by] boiling"'

137 *"ah* *bweno* *pwes"* *imay'*   *naalhik*
      ah *bweno* *pues* *ima-y'*   *naalhik*
      ah   good   well   say-3SG.SETA   they
      '"ah okay then" they said to him'

138 imay'   nah   naalhik   "ünta'   k'aw'uk "
    ima-y'   nah   naalhik   ün-ta'   k'aw'u-k
    say-3SG.SETA   he   they   1SG.SETB-come   boil-1PL.SETA
    'they said to him "we will boil it"'

139 así   ke   k'aw'uy',   waak'a'   naalhik   xawats'a
    así   ke   k'aw'u-y'   ø-waak'a-'   naalhik   xawats'a
    so   that boil-3SG.SETA   3SG.SETC-went-IV.AFF they   planting
    'so they boiled it and they went planting'

140 syempre hin   tahna'   porke   k'aawu'   nalh   chuayma
    syempre hin   ø-tahna-'   porke   ø-k'aawu-'   nalh   chu-ayma
    always   no   3SG.SETC-grow-IV.AFF   because 3SG.SETC-boil-IV.AFF   PST   DIM-corn
    'it would never grow because the little ears of corn were boiled'

141 pwes   entonses   syempre   muniw'a   nah   'ih   ke   han hi'   pul'ay
    pues   entonses   syempre   mu-niw'a   nah   'i-h   ke   han hi'   pul'a-y
    well   then   always   3SG.SETB-ask   he   REFL-3SG.SETE   that howdo-3SG.SETA
    'so they were always asking him how do they do it'

142 "ah   xawxa   akani'   ki' "   a   pwes   akulha'   naalhik   xawats'a
    ah   xawxa   akani'   ki'   a   pues   a-ku-lha'   naalhik   xawats'a
    ah   plant   like.this just   ah   well   3SG.SETD-go-IV.AGT   they   planting
    '"ah plant just like this" and they went planting'

143 a   entonses   sí   tahna'   naalhik   tumuki'   muwaya'
    a   entonses   sí   ø-tahna-'   naalhik   tumuki'   mu-waya'
    ah   then   yes   3SG.SETC-grow-IV.AFF   they   entire   3SG.SETB-corn.field
    'finally their entire cornfield grew'

144 i   uuka'   naalhik   pensar   ke
    i   ø-uuka-'   naalhik   pensar   ke
    and   3SG.SETC-be-IV.AFF   they   think   that
    'and they thought about'

145 kwando   na   tuuru'   üra'   palh   muwaya'   uw'iy   suruur'u
    kwando   na   tuuru'   üra'   palh   mu-waya'   uw'i-y   suruur'u
    when   the   youngest.child big   EPIST   3SG.SETB-corn.field call-3SG.SETA   hurricane
    'when the cornfield of Tuuru' was big and they called a hurricane'

146 tumuki'   wesk'ey'   muwaya'   kumu   tuuru'
    tumuki'   wesk'e-y'   mu-waya'   kumu   tuuru'
    entire   throw-3SG.SETA   3SG.SETB-corn.field as   youngest.child
    'it destroyed Tuuru's entire cornfield'

147 pero   xuuwi'   ki'   tup'awah   hin xan   tuupa'
    pero   ø-xuuwi-'   ki'   tup'a-wa-h   hin xan   ø-tuupa-'
    but   3SG.SETC-sweep-IV.AFF   just   leave-PN-3SG.SETE   there is not 3SG.SETC-leave-IV.AFF
    'it just remained clear and there was nothing left'

148 *tüxk'ü*   *nalh*   *hi'*   *ki'*   *ik'alh*   *ebra*
    tüxk'ü   *nalh*   *hi'*   *ki'*   *ik'alh*   *ebra*
    distance   PST   TEMP.DUR.3SG   just   one   strip
    'there was just one strip in the distance'

149 *entonses*   *tuuru'*   *akulha'*
    entonses   *tuuru'*   *a-ku-lha'*
    then   youngest.child   3SG.SETD-go-IV.AGT
    'then Tuuru' walked [away]'

150 *i*   *par'ay*   *nah*   *ik'alh*   *ts'ama*   *ebra*   *xa*   *xahah*   *kraw'a*   *upuwah*
    i   *par'a-y*   *nah*   *ik'alh*   *ts'ama*   *ebra*   *xa*   *xaha-h*   *kraw'a*   *upu-wa-h*
    and   look.for-3SG.SETA   it   one   good   strip   LOC   side-3SG.SETE   forest   stand-PN-3SG.SETE
    'and looked for one good strip that was standing on the side of the forest'

151 *i*   *wesk'ey'*   *ik'alh*   *ebra*   *upuwah*   *huuts'uk*   *roosa*
    i   *wesk'e-y'*   *ik'alh*   *ebra*   *upu-wa-h*   *huuts'uk*   *roosa*
    and   throw-3SG.SETA   one   strip   stand-PN-3SG.SETE   middle   cleared.field
    'and he threw one strip that was standing in the middle of the field'

152 *i*   *entonses*   *imay'*   *nah*   *par'a*   *ki'*   *na*   *kakerensiya*
    i   *entonses*   *ima-y'*   *nah*   *par'a*   *ki'*   *na*   *ka-kerensiya*
    and   then   say-3SG.SETA   he   look.for   just   the   2SG.SETB-home
    'and then they said to him to just look for a home'

153 *i*   *saaka'*   *tumuki'*   *waya'*
    i   *ø-saaka-'*   *tumuki'*   *waya'*
    and   3SG.SETC-lift-IV.AFF   entire   corn.field
    'and establish his entire cornfield'

154 *i*   *akulha'*   *naalhik*   *uupu'*   *haani'*   *uk'ah*   *na*   *syempre*   *bweno*
    i   *a-ku-lha'*   *naalhik*   *ø-uupu-'*   *haani'*   *uk'a-h*   *na*   *syempre*   *bweno*
    and   3SG.SETD-   they   3SG.SETC-   like   be-3SG.SETE   the   always   good
          go-IV.AGT   stand.up-IV.AFF
    'and they went and stood [or dwelled] as they are always good'

155 *man ki'*
    man ki'
    that's it
    'The end.'

Part 2

The development of the Xinkan languages

Diachronic grammar

SIX

Historical phonology

6.1 Introduction

Previous studies of the general history of the Xinkan languages are very scant indeed, confined to a few remarks in the academic literature. Despite this lack of attention, a number of hypotheses concerning the genetic relationship between the Xinkan languages have been put forth. These suggestions are mentioned in this section, and the historical development of the Xinkan languages is discussed afterwards.

The earliest mentions of the development of Xinkan languages are found in Brinton (1885) and Lehmann (1920). These scholars concluded that Xinkan was related to Lencan. This was mostly based on two facts: first, the languages of both families were dissimilar to any of the languages known at the time; and second, both are found in geographical regions not too distant from one another. Campbell (1979) refutes this claim and shows evidence that the similarities presented as evidence are the result of borrowings between these languages, onomatopoeia, or accident.

Besides arguing against the Xinka-Lenca hypothesis, Campbell hypothesizes that Alagüilac, a language of central Guatemala mentioned in colonial times (about which essentially nothing other than its location is known), may have belonged to Xinkan. This hypothesized relationship was based on two ideas: first, the proximity of Xinkan place names to the assumed Alagüilac-speaking area; and second, the fact that Alagüilac seems not to fit with any of the other language families of the region, including Mayan and Uto-Aztecan. This hypothesis is interesting but untestable. Without information on Alagüilac grammar, the connection can never be substantiated.

In Campbell (1997) the author suggests that Pupuluca—another language mentioned in colonial sources (also about which nothing is known) and said to have been spoken in Conguaco—might be related to Yupiltepeque. This suggestion is based on the geographical proximity of the municipality to Conguaco. However, as with the other hypotheses, this suggestion has not been proven and indeed cannot be unless some words or material from these languages should come to light.

This grammar is not intended as a tool for identifying these relationships. The purpose is to merely show how and why the Xinkan languages are they way they are. This includes the reconstruction of earlier stages of the language and a description of the development from those stages into the four Xinkan languages known today. However, this chapter may contribute to the search for languages possibly related to Xinkan in two ways. First, historically 'Xinka' has been considered a language isolate, although it is in fact a language family with four members. This means that as relationships are suggested in the future, it might be easier to suggest how these fit into this language family. Second, assuring that the comparative language material on Xinkan is published will facilitate further research comparing Xinkan with other languages for theoretical or typological research.

In the following discussion on reconstruction, only native sounds are included. Sounds acquired from borrowings from other languages have been excluded. Section 6.2 provides a brief commentary on the process of language reconstruction. Section 6.3 describes the reconstruction of Proto-Xinkan phonology (summarized in section 6.4). Section 6.5 provides a discussion of the implications of the analysis from section 6.4, along with a discussion on internal subgrouping of the Xinkan family. Section 6.6 offers a conclusion.

6.2 Commentary on the reconstruction of Proto-Xinkan

A few general comments about the historical aspects of this grammar are in order. The purpose of language reconstruction is to use the available data of the most recent stage of a language to hypothesize an earlier stage from which the language developed. This often involves reconstructing a language stage (called a protolanguage) that is common to an entire language family. In the case of this grammar, by comparing the grammars of the four Xinkan languages as discussed in chapters 2 through 4, a reconstruction of Proto-Xinkan is possible. This chapter deals with just the reconstruction of phonology; chapter 7 reconstructs the morphology; and chapter 8 reconstructs the syntactic patterns.

While the reconstruction of the common mother language, Proto-Xinkan, is fairly straightforward, there are at least two sources of complication. First, there are great variations between speakers of an individual Xinkan language and across an individual speaker's utterances. These variations are especially noticeable in the production of sounds, especially glottalized consonants (see section 2.3.1.1). While variation is normal for all languages, the result here is that occasionally the discussion of some elements of grammar are vague and abstract (i.e., hypothetical). I have clarified these sections by describing the most salient linguistic features of each speaker and showing how they relate to those of other speakers.

Second, the quality and extent of the available historical records often leave uncertainties in the exact specifications of sounds, meanings, and functions, especially in the case of Yupiltepeque. Neither of these complications creates insurmountable problems for the reconstruction of Proto-Xinkan grammar, but they are noteworthy because they can limit the amount of information that can be reconstructed. In particular, the lack of data limits the role Yupiltepeque can have in reconstructing Proto-Xinkan grammar. In order to overcome these difficulties as much as possible, I completed an extensive philological analysis and comparison of the information provided by Calderón (1908) and Lehmann (1920). The information about Yupiltepeque in this grammar comes from that analysis, and is presented, where needed, in the orthography of the original sources.

Nevertheless, there are problems with using the Yupiltepeque Xinka data for reconstruction. Specifically, relating the Yupiltepeque Xinkan data to the other three Xinkan languages is problematic. For example, the data found in both Calderón and Lehmann is presented in a prescientific, nonstandard orthography (written before the advent of modern phonetics and the phonemic principle), and consequently it is difficult to consistently determine the phonetic value of the graphemes. This is especially true of words with glottalized sounds in them. For example, in both sources there is no distinction made between /k/ and /k'/, both being represented by the letter ⟨c⟩ (before *a, u, o*). This is an issue because of the extreme importance of distinguishing these sounds throughout the grammar of Xinka. This failure to distinguish these contrasts in the Yupiltepeque Xinka data results in difficulty determining how to compare Yupiltepeque forms with those from the other languages where the contrast between plain and glottalized consonants is clearly distinguished. This means that the Yupiltepeque data provides no reliable witness concerning glottalization in Proto-Xinkan. These Yupiltepeque forms can, however, be useful in highlighting other aspects of the consonants under consideration (such as place and manner of articulation).

A similar problem is found with long and short vowels, which are contrastive in Xinkan languages but are not distinguished in the Yupiltepeque sources. Both vowel quantities are indicated in the sources in the same way—with a single vowel. Furthermore, Calderón lists a few words that begin with ⟨b⟩, but judging from their correspondences in the other languages, they would appear probably to begin with the sounds /p/ or /p'/. Here it is not possible to know whether this is a mistaken recording of /p/, which I suspect, or whether something else was going on that is now unclear.

Consequently, due to these orthographic limitations, it is difficult to give a complete depiction of the subgrouping of the family and Yupiltepeque's position in it. Another example of this issue can be seen in the case of /ɬ/ and /l/ in Xinkan. Proto-Xinkan had a voiceless lateral approximant /ɬ/ that has changed to /l/ in Jumaytepeque in all environments and is retained as [ɬ] in both Guazacapán and Chiquimulilla Xinka. The Yupiltepeque data represents this sound variably as ⟨jl⟩ and ⟨lj⟩ after the low vowel [a] and as ⟨l⟩ elsewhere. Similarly, in some words Proto-Xinkan *l' has changed to /t'/ in Jumaytepeque and ⟨t⟩ in Yupiltepeque.

Taken at face value, because Yupiltepeque and Jumaytepeque share these innovations, it would seem they might be grouped in a single subgroup as descendants of an intermediate common ancestor, itself a daughter of Proto-Xinkan. However, this is uncertain. It can only be a tentative conclusion at best, and the subgroup would need to be supported by other evidence. This matter is considered again in section 6.5. Yupiltepeque is not included in all of the correspondence sets in this chapter because of missing information, but where there is information, it has been included.

There are other internal considerations involving all of the Xinkan languages generally that affect the outcome of the reconstruction of Proto-Xinkan phonology specifically. By internal I mean those morphological and phonological processes of Xinkan that limit the use of consonants and vowels. While in general these do not cause serious problems for reconstruction, they are worth mentioning here as they are commented on throughout the chapter. For example, there is a unique pattern of vowel harmony in Xinkan based on the height of the vowels in a word (see section 2.1.2). Often the changes from Proto-Xinkan to one of its daughter languages appear to be constrained by this limitation.

Additionally, speakers of the Xinkan languages often vary in their use of glottalization (see section 2.3.1.1). In at least one speaker of Jumaytepeque this is due to imperfect learning as a second-language speaker. However, it is generally agreed upon by linguists that although contracting languages are changed due to the imperfect learning of some speakers, there might also be a more general external or internal influence on the language that produces more regular results than the claim from imperfect learning. For example, a (second-language) speaker might tend to simplify the phonology of a language due to imperfect learning; this simplification usually reduces marked elements to unmarked ones (or more difficult ones to less difficult ones, in some meaningful definition of difficulty). However, a common internal change in any language is the move from more marked to less marked phonology.

Consequently, changes such as the simplification of linguistic elements cannot be determined as resulting from one or the other explanation since both are possible at any time in the history of a language. It is difficult in most cases of language change involving moribund or obsolescing languages to ascertain whether a change toward simplification is caused by imperfect learning, by natural internal changes, or both. This issue is brought up throughout the following chapters when required.

A good illustration of this type of 'multiple causation' is found in examples of sound correspondences in which one of the Xinkan languages does not pattern with the others, and the aberrant sound is not motivated by any apparent linguistic phenomenon. For example, often the reflexes for a given protosound, say *p', are glottalized in two languages but not in the third. The absence of glottalization is not predictable; in other words, it does not occur in general across the entire deviant language. If it was predictable, that would offer clear evidence for a sound change. Rather, it occurs randomly in individual lexical items that make up cognate sets. Critically, however, there is never a specific, identifiable linguistic phonetic condition for this change. That is not to say that there are no conditions motivating the change, but it does indicate that any conditions are idiosyncratic in that they reflect the style, preference, or competence of the individual speaker and not general linguistic conditions. For example, it could be that the speaker(s) did not glottalize a consonant because of difficulty in articulatory production. In such a case the motivation for change is sociolinguistic and might indicate a broader shift from *C' to C due to the latter explanation rather than any phonetic environments.

To adequately address the explanations for these differences of pronunciation, there seem to be two competing possible solutions. The first would be to assume, as is common when studying historical linguistics, that languages tend to change in the direction from more marked to less marked—in other words, to assume the change is caused by internal motivations of simplification. Following this it would be appropriate to reconstruct *C′*, postulating a change to a plain consonant in the one language lacking the glottalized sound. The result is merely a language-internal change identified in a few lexical items. Since it is not a general change in the language, it is assumed that it indicates a natural variation in language that can lead to subsequent, more global changes.

However, the other option is to acknowledge the external influences (social and cultural) on this language, to note the imperfect learning of the surviving speakers, and to consider these alongside knowledge of similar problems in the reconstruction of other language families. This acknowledgement might show that it is, sometimes, the least common segment in a correspondence set that is the most conservative and that all other languages being considered underwent the given change. For example, in Romance almost all the modern languages (Spanish, Italian, French, Portuguese, etc.) change *k* to some sort of fricative or affricate—except Sardinian. Nevertheless, because of what is assumed to be plausible in the direction of sound change, *k* is reconstructed and not some fricative or affricate. In the Xinkan example, where all but one language has a glottalized consonant in a given correspondence set, this would mean that it might be appropriate to reconstruct the nonglottalized consonant *C* and posit changes in the other languages. A necessary note would be that the change has proceeded in the direction from less marked to more marked. Fortunately, issues such as the reconstruction of glottalized consonants are not overly problematic; in most cases the reconstruction of Proto-Xinkan sounds is transparent and straightforward. In those situations in which transparency is not the case, careful examination of the data leads to a clear solution.

Note, however, that both of these foregoing suggestions for reconstructions involving glottalized consonants might be accurate representations of the historical development of the Xinkan languages. However, the current state of Guazacapán as spoken by the handful of second-language speakers severely reduces the number of occurrences of glottalized consonants (though not all of them), arguing for a general pattern in the direction of deglottalization (i.e., $C′ > C$). It would be an interesting trend indeed if all of the speakers overgeneralized the glottalization due to imperfect learning. In that case it might be considered a general change in the language—highly unlikely, though, since languages almost never go from $C > C′$ without strong phonetic motivation in the environment of the change. Fortunately, the instances of overgeneralization of glottalization are isolated to one or two speakers and are sporadic occurrences, not regular, and therefore cannot be considered generally relevant for the individual language or language family. This means that unless there is strong evidence to the contrary, it is assumed that in a correspondence set, the most common sound across the related languages is a direct descendent from the protosound.

Furthermore, the reconstruction of the glottalized consonants is made more difficult because of their role in Xinkan morphology. Specifically, verbs can be inflected for either completive or incompletive aspects. In the incompletive, the rightmost consonant of the stem is glottalized, and in the completive it is not. If the root has an underlying glottalized consonant, then it remains unchanged and is glottalized in both aspects. Unfortunately, the extant documentation often records verbs used in only one or the other of the two aspects but not both. This means that if the morphology was the same in the past as it is now, it would be safe to assume that there was an alternation between glottalized and plain variants of the consonants in the aspectual changes in verb roots. In these cases, *C' is always reconstructed for the incompletive aspect.

With these caveats, there are at least three ways that the reconstruction of Proto-Xinkan relates to general issues of historical linguistics: the direction of sound change (traditionally believed to move predominantly from more marked to less marked), the effects of language contact, and implications of the viability of the language to appropriate reconstruction. These issues are discussed in this order, with the language-specific issues being dealt with first, followed by the reconstruction of the Xinkan phonology, and finally a general discussion relating this reconstruction to relevant issues of historical linguistics in general.

As discussed in chapter 1, one of the primary goals of this grammar is to compare synchronic patterns in order to reconstruct the diachronic processes that created those patterns in the Xinkan languages. Thus, the goal of this chapter is to discuss the most plausible reconstruction of the sound system of Proto-Xinkan through a comparison of cognates and sound correspondence in the four Xinkan languages. The examples in this chapter do not use practical orthography, since the object of study is sounds, and these may be more descriptively adequate in conventional linguistic notation (IPA). After a brief introduction, the reconstruction of consonants is given, followed by reconstruction of the vowels. Importantly, no morphology (i.e., words, pronouns, or grammatical affixes) is being reconstructed directly here, only the phonology of Proto-Xinkan.

6.3 Proto-Xinkan phonological reconstruction

In order to be as thorough as possible in this reconstruction of Proto-Xinkan phonology, each proposed reconstruction is supported with a correspondence set, a few examples illustrating the set in the different Xinkan languages, and a reconstructed phoneme. The format for the presentation of the reconstruction is the same throughout the discussion. The reconstructed protosound is given first, followed by the corresponding set of reflexes. These are always given in the same order: Guazacapán, Chiquimulilla, Jumaytepeque, and Yupiltepeque. A question mark is used as placeholder if no information is available for any of the languages. Immediately below the correspondence sets are examples that exemplify the set. The Yupiltepeque forms, where available, are always given in angle brackets to indicate that they represent the source orthography and not necessarily a phonetic value, although in a few cases approximate phonetic values have been included. All the glosses are followed by a code

Table 6.1 **Proto-Xinkan consonants**

		Labial	Alveolar	Alveo-palatal	Retro-Flex	Palatal	Velar	Glottal
Stops	Voiceless	*p	*t				*k	
	Ejective	*p'	*t'				*k'	*ʔ
Fricatives	Voiceless		*s		*ṣ			*h
			(*s')		(*ṣ)			
Affricates	Voiceless			*č				
	Ejective		*ts'	*č'				
Nasal	Plain	*m	*n					
	Glottalized	*m'	*n'					
Liquid	Lateral Plain		*l					
	Lateral Glottalized		*l'					
	Lateral Voiceless		*ł					
	Rhotic Plain		*r					
	Rhotic Glottalized		*r'					
	Glides Plain	*w				*y		
	Glides Glottalized	*w'				*y'		

Table 6.2 **Proto-Xinkan vowels**

		Front	Central	Back and Round
High	Short	*i	*ɨ	*u
	Long	*ii	*ɨɨ	*uu
Mid	Short	*e		*o
	Long	*ee		*oo
Low	Short		*a	
	Long		*aa	

indicating which language each comes from (G = Guazacapán, Ch = Chiquimulilla, J = Jumaytepeque, and Y = Yupiltepeque).

The sounds of Proto-Xinkan phonology are provided in tables 6.1 (consonants) and 6.2 (vowels) to facilitate comparison throughout the discussion. Following tables 6.1 and 6.2, in section 6.3.1, are the reconstructions of all the consonants grouped by place of articulation. Last are the reconstructed vowels in section 6.3.2.

6.3.1   Consonants

6.3.1.1   *Labials*

(329)   *p   *p : p : p : p*

Examples include *haypu* (G, Ch, J), ⟨jaypu⟩ (Y) 'receive'; *paama* (G, Ch), *paaha* (J), ⟨paja⟩ (Y) 'shoulder, wing'. In one word in both Chiquimulilla and Jumaytepeque *p > b: bar < paɬ* 'epistemic modal particle'. No information is available in Yupiltepeque Xinka for this word.

(330)   **p'*   *p' : p' : p' : ?*

Examples include *hap'a* (G, Ch, J) '(to) wait'; *p'eese* (G, Ch, J) 'lizard'; and *p'oyo* (G, Ch), *p'oy'o* (J) 'believe/charge (a price)'. In the verb 'wait' there is an alternation in the glottalized consonant based on the aspect of the verb, so for example *hapa-n* 'I waited' but *in-hap'a* 'I wait'. Only the incompletive form of this word is listed in the data for Jumaytepeque.

There is one instance where Chiquimulilla has /p'/ but where Guazacapán and Jumaytepeque have /p/: *pitz'ɨ* (G), *p'itz'ɨ* (Ch), *pitz'a* (J) 'to add'. These can be viewed as instances of a very common change from marked [p'] to less marked [p] which happened independently in the two languages.[1] Though in this correspondence set this is contrary to the traditional intuition of 'majority wins', the opposite change /p/ > /p'/ goes against the traditional intuition of direction of change. Moreover, the motivation for this change might be a clash in the number of glottalized segments within a word. That is, there may have been a constraint against having a glottalized segment in two adjacent syllables (see section 2.3.1.4). This suggestion is not meant to hypothesize a regular sound change affecting all the words with two glottalized consonants. On the contrary, this change is sporadic, occurring in only this word. What I do suggest is that the dissimilation process actually in the Xinkan phonology was extended to this word as well. (See section 2.3.1.4 for examples of dissimilation involving glottalized consonants.)

(331)   *m   *m : m : m : m*

Examples include *taɬma* (G, Ch), *talma* (J), ⟨taljma⟩ (Y) 'path, road'; and *map'uɬ* (G, Ch), *map'* (J) 'tortilla'. The last example is unattested in Yupiltepeque.

(332)   **m'*   *m' : m' : m' : m*

Examples include *sɨɨm'a* (G, Ch, J), ⟨tz'üöma⟩ (Y) 'night'. The Yupiltepeque form may represent either [m] or [m'], as these are not distinguished in the orthography of the sources.

(333)   *w   *w : w : w : w*

Examples include *šawi* (G, Ch, J), ⟨sahui⟩ (Y) 'hard'; and *wak'i* (G, Ch, J), ⟨guaki⟩ (Y) 'to play'. The Yupiltepeque orthography for these two words follows that of Guatemalan Spanish where the letter combinations ⟨hu⟩ and ⟨gu⟩ both represent the sound [w].

Interestingly, in one word it would appear that [w] > [k'] in Jumaytepeque: *weetan* (G, Ch), *k'eetan* (J) 'large worm'. This is a sporadic change that is missing any contextual motivation, but a general confusion between labial consonants and velar consonants in sound change has been highlighted by Ohala (1993).

(334)   *w'   w' : w' : w' : w

Examples include *uw'ał* (G), *iw'ał* (Ch), *uw'al* (J), ⟨ugua⟩ (Y) 'ant'; *łiw'ɨ* (G), *łiw'a* (Ch), *łɨw'a* (J) 'candy, honey', ⟨lövua⟩ (Y) 'honey'; and *nuw'a* (G, Ch, J) 'son/daughter'. It is not clear why there is a ⟨v⟩ in the Yupiltepeque form for 'honey', but the combination *ua* is meant to represent the sequence [wa]. However, it is conceivable that the ⟨v⟩ was an attempt to reflect a slight difference in the pronunciation of this sound in this context when compared to ⟨w⟩. As /w/ and voiced bilabial fricatives [β] frequently change into one another diachronically, the ⟨vu⟩ sequence probably indicates a slight bilabial frication. It is considered to represent one of the possible realizations of the phoneme /w/ in Yupiltepeque.

6.3.1.2   *Alveolars*

(335)   *t   t : t : t : t

Examples include *til'a* (G, Ch), *tit'a* (J), ⟨tita⟩ (Y) 'salt'; *tuma* (G, Ch, J), ⟨túma⟩ (Y) 'deer'; and *k'ooto* (G: rarely this word was pronounced [k'oot'o], Ch, J), ⟨coto⟩ (Y) 'molar (tooth)'. From the cognate set meaning 'salt' it can be seen that Yupiltepeque and Jumaytepeque have undergone similar changes where a [t] corresponds to a [l'] in the other two languages. It is also assumed, based on the absence of any indication of glottalization of consonants in the Yupiltepeque data, that it is probable that the ⟨t⟩ in the Yupiltepeque word was glottalized but not distinguished from plain /t/ in the orthography used. This change in Jumaytepeque and Yupiltepeque might suggest a shared history—evidence for a subgroup of the family. Even generally lacking the information on glottalization, a general change from a glottalized lateral to an alveolar stop is seen in both Jumaytepeque and can be inferred for Yupiltepeque.

(336)   *t'   t' : t' : t' : t

Examples include *ts'ot'o* (G, Ch, J), ⟨n'sotó⟩ (Y) 'to tire' or 'to scare'; *t'iiši* (G, Ch, J) 'lazy man'; and *t'uuri* (G, Ch, J) 'small young child'. In one word, Guazacapán has [t] and the others have [t']: *tay'a i* (G), *t'ay'a* (Ch, J) 'to kick'. However, in this one word every speaker of Guazacapán showed the same pattern of absence of glottalization, indicating that this might be due to a restriction on the number of glottalized consonants in a word or might show a more general pattern of reduction of marked segments (see section 2.3.7).

(337)   *s   s : s : s : ⟨s⟩

Examples include *mur'us* (G, Ch, J) 'flower bud'; *seema* (G, Ch, J) 'fish'; *saha* (G, Ch, J) 'mouth, side', and ⟨sajá⟩ (Y) 'edge, bank', cf. ⟨sajan⟩ (Y) 'my tooth'. In many Mesoamerican languages the word for 'edge' and 'bank' are related to those with the meaning 'tooth' or 'mouth'.

(338)   *l   l : l : l : l

There is only one example of this set with cognates in all four languages: *elaha* (G, Ch), *eela* (J), and ⟨elay⟩ (Y) 'tongue'. The reason this is not more pervasive throughout the family is due to the other changes affecting the lateral sounds in the phonology. Other examples of /l/ found in only two of the languages include *hulap'i* (G, J) 'tortilla for traveling'; *ololo* (G, Ch) 'white'; and *ipla* (G), *apla* (J) 'to bathe'. While these correspondences allow for a reconstructed voiced lateral *l*, in each case there are arguments that suggest that this sound did not exist in the protolanguage, or was quite marginal, at best. As an example, some Uto-Aztecan languages often have irregularities in the word for 'tongue' involving /l/ or /n/, often involving onomatopoeia. In Xinkan, the [l] in 'tortilla for traveling' might possibly be an underlying /l'/ but is realized unglottalized due to the following glottalized consonant [p']. Similarly the [l] in 'bathe' might be an underlying /l'/ but is realized unglottalized due to the phonotactic constraints of the languages. (See section 2.3.1 for a discussion of the restrictions on glottalized consonants.) What this means is that while the languages exhibit this correspondence set, there is sufficient reason to question /*l/ as a Proto-Xinkan segment. It is included here and in the chart in table 6.2, above, for clarity.

(339)   *l'   l' : l' : l' : ?
                l' : l' : t' : ⟨t⟩

This set (or sets) needs more explanation as it relates to set 340 below. When the voiceless lateral approximant [ɬ] is glottalized due to morphological conditioning connected with verbal aspects, it is always realized as [l'] (voiced glottalized lateral resonant). Furthermore, in Jumaytepeque [l'] appears to have been retained in some instances and to have become [t'] in others, though predictably. Specifically, if the original segment in Proto-Xinkan was /*ɬ/ then it becomes [l'] in glottalizing contexts in Jumaytepeque, even though Jumaytepeque no longer exhibits the segment [ɬ], it having changed to plain voiced /l/ (see 340 below). On the other hand, when the original segment was /*l'/ then it became [t'] in Jumaytepeque (and apparently in Yupiltepeque). The phonetics of this change might seem unusual; consequently, it is significant to comment on the possible motivations of this change.

Glottalized sonorants are produced with a glottal closure either before or after the consonant articulation, rather than simultaneously as is done with the ejectives.[2] Most likely, the glottal closure in this sound was produced before the lateral articulation, and the glottal stop was reinterpreted as a fully contrastive stop. Through assimilation this stop would have assumed the place of articulation of the following lateral to produce [t']. This means that the change in both Jumaytepeque and Yupiltepeque might be seen as a strengthening of the glottal closure portion of the protosegment.

Furthermore, the change from *l' to [t'] is evidence that in these two languages the glottalized alveolar approximant was preglottalized in nonderived situations. However, in derived situations (i.e., where /*ɬ/ becomes [l']), the glottal closure follows the consonant articulation and is not open to the same kind of strengthening. That this change is rare phonetically, though possible, is clear evidence in support of the subgrouping discussed below.

Examples include *hiḻ'a* (G, Ch), *hiṯ'a* (J), ⟨julay⟩ (Y) 'to empty' (original /ḻ'/); *k'ol'o* (G, Ch, J) 'shuck [incompletive]' (original /ɬ/ in a glottalizing context); and *til'a* (G, Ch), *tiṯ'a* (J), ⟨tita⟩ (Y) 'salt' (original /ḻ'/).

(340)   *ɬ   ɬ : ɬ : l : ɬ/l

Examples include *ts'uuɬi* (G, Ch), *ts'uuli* (J) 'ladino'; *eɬa* (G, Ch), *ila* (J), ⟨ila⟩ (Y) 'new'; and *ɬawru* (G), *ɬarw'u* (Ch), *larw'ɨ* (J), ⟨lahuar⟩ (Y) 'to dance'. Interestingly the /r/ segment in Yupiltepeque is in a different position from the other three Xinkan languages. This seems to be an isolated occurrence, though it cannot be asserted as chance due to a lack of data. It might involve metathesis in this form in this language. Furthermore, the /w/ segment is in a different place in Chiquimulilla and Jumaytepeque compared to Guazacapán; a sporadic metathesis occurred here.

One further comment on the correspondence set is in order. There is clear evidence that Yupiltepeque does exhibit the voiceless lateral fricative, but only in a very few words. This means that for the majority of situations the change from *ɬ > /l/ is probable, as indicated above, but that the change is not complete for all words in the language. Calderón (1908) represents this sound [ɬ] in one of two ways ⟨jl⟩ or ⟨lj⟩. Examples of these less common cases include ⟨ajla⟩ (Y), *aɬape'* (G), *aɬawak* (Ch) 'tomorrow'; ⟨ajli⟩ (Y), *aɬ* (G), *aɬi* (Ch), *al* (J) 'over, on'; ⟨avuajla⟩ (Y), *awaɬak'an* (Ch), *aw'al'an* (J); and ⟨májli⟩ (Y), *maaɬi* (G), *maɬi* (Ch), *mali* (J), among others. Fortunately, a pattern emerges that can explain the voiceless laterals in Yupiltepeque. In all but two cases *ɬ is preserved in Yupiltepeque when it immediately follows the low vowel [a]. (The exceptions are ⟨sal⟩ 'good' < *šaɬ 'pretty', and ⟨mali⟩ 'firewood' < *maaɬik 'firewood' < *maɬi 'ash'. The reasons for the exceptions are not apparent.) Lastly, after the change from *ɬ to [l], and the preservation of [ɬ] after [a], a third change took place in Yupiltepeque: namely word-final voiceless laterals were deleted. Thus we get cognates such as the following *tak'aɬ* (G, Ch), *tak'al* (J), ⟨tacá⟩ [taká] (Y) 'six'; *t'ɨɨm'aɬ* (G, Ch), *t'ɨɨmal* (J), ⟨tüöma⟩ [tɨma] (Y) 'louse'; and *uw'aɬ* (G, Ch), *uw'al* (J), ⟨ugua⟩ [uwa] (Y) 'ant'.

(341)   *r   r : r : r : r

As in *nuuru* (G, Ch, J), ⟨nuru⟩ (Y) 'pus, matter'; *hiiru* (G), *iiru* (Ch, J), ⟨iru⟩ (Y) 'monkey'; and *k'ɨri* (G), *k'iri* (Ch), *kɨri* (J), ⟨kurri⟩ (Y) 'to pull out'.

(342)   *r'   r' : r' : r' : r

As in *haar'un* (G), *haar'u* (Ch, J), ⟨jaru⟩ (Y) 'tick'; and *t'ar'u* (G, Ch, J) 'to offer'. As with the other glottalized consonants there is some variation with this set based on verbal inflection and individual speaker patterns.

(343)   *n   n : n : n : n

Examples include *naki* (G, Ch, J), 'chile'; *nim'a* (G, Ch, J), ⟨numa⟩ (Y) 'to eat'; and *kunu* (G, Ch, J), ⟨n'cunu⟩ (Y) 'to buy' (in Yupiltepeque most likely 'I buy (it)').

(344)   **n'*   *n' : n' : n' : n(')?*

This correspondence set is hindered by the Yupiltepeque orthography. As may have been observed in some of the correspondence sets above, there is a letter ⟨n'⟩ used in the Yupiltepeque data; however, the phonetic value of this letter is uncertain. Calderón (1908: 10) gives the following definition: "The sounds *tz'* and *n'* are wounded letters [letras heridas], that is, sounds whose pronunciation permits a short pause to occur in order to continue pronouncing the syllables or letters that these so-called wounded letters follow" (translation mine).[3] This definition is very similar to the articulatory process involved in producing a glottalized resonant,[4] and it seems from this definition that ⟨n'⟩ represents a glottalized alveolar nasal. In addition, this consonant only occurs word initially before another consonant, as in the correspondence set above; this sound is fairly uncommon in the corpus.

However, a cautionary note is in order: because the phonotactics of the other languages restrict the first member of a consonant cluster to nonglottalized consonants, this segment does match well with the other languages. In all of the Xinkan languages, however, the first-person singular possession and incompletive aspect verbal agreement is indicated through a prefix involving an alveolar nasal (see section 3.6.2). So while it is assumed that the grapheme ⟨n'⟩ represents a glottalized consonant it is not clear why only two letters are so indicated in the Yupiltepeque data when Xinkan languages generally have a large number of glottalized segments. Furthermore, it is not immediately clear if the phonotactics of Yupiltepeque allowed cluster initial glottalized consonants.

Examples exhibiting this set include *ts'un'i* (G, Ch, J) 'put into a shirt to carry', and *tan'ik* (G, Ch, J) 'headboard, head (of something)'.

(345)   **ts'*   *ts' : ts' : ts' : ts'* ⟨tz'⟩

Examples include *huuts'uk* (G), *huts'uk* (Ch, J), ⟨jutz'u⟩ (Y) 'center, middle'; *ts'uuma* (G, Ch, J), ⟨tz'uma⟩ (Y) 'to kiss, suck'; *ts'ɨɨwɨ* (G, Ch, J) 'green, unripened corn'; and *sarara'* (G, Ch, J), ⟨tz'arará⟩ (Y) 'cold'. As mentioned in the discussion of set 344, the phonetic nature of the *tz'* grapheme in the Yupiltepeque is defined as being a 'wounded letter' and is consequently most likely a glottalized alveolar affricate. (It is assumed to be so in the comparisons of cognate forms.) However, a few remarks on this segment are in order.

This grapheme ⟨tz'⟩ appears most commonly in word-initial position in the Yupiltepeque data, but there are some exceptions: for example, ⟨tz'antz'a⟩ 'chew' (*č'ahma* 'chew' in Guazacapán and Chiquimulilla and *ts'aama* 'chew' in Jumaytepeque); ⟨kurtz'a⟩ 'comb' (*kɨrša* 'comb' [verb], *kɨrats'a* 'combing' [abstract verbal noun] in Guazacapán, Chiquimulilla, and Jumaytepeque); and ⟨pitz'akila⟩ 'midwife'. It is interesting to note that this is only one of the two consonants that Calderón (1908: 10) identified as glottalized consonants, despite the fact that other languages have a complex system of plain and glottalized consonants (see section 2.2). Furthermore, in some of the cases where this sound is given in noninitial position, it corresponds to the expected [ts'] in the other Xinkan languages, resulting from glottalization process involving verbal aspect (see section 2.3.1 and 3.6.3). It can therefore be assumed, at least in the few examples available, that the same process of glottalization was part of the Yupiltepeque system. For example, ⟨cauki its'u⟩ 'changed' in Yupiltepeque corresponds to *k'iišu* '(ex)change' in the other three languages. In the incompletive aspect this verb would be pronounced [k'iits'u], which resembles the Yupiltepeque form where the sequence ⟨cau…⟩ represents the second-person singular pronominal prefix. Likewise, in some words ⟨tz'⟩ corresponds to [ts'] in all of the Xinkan languages. For example, *ts'orna* 'drip' (G, Ch), ⟨tz'orna⟩ 'drop' [gota] (Y); *ts'oko* (G, J), *ts'ok'ok* (Ch), ⟨tz'oko⟩ (Y) 'grackle'; *ts'ɨp'ɨ* (G, Ch), ⟨tz'opoki⟩ (Y) 'sting'; and *ts'uuma* (G, Ch, J), ⟨tz'uma⟩ (Y) 'to kiss, suck'.

However, in other environments (i.e., word initially), this grapheme corresponds to not only [ts'] in the other languages, but also [š], [s], [k] (in one word only), and [t] (in one word only). The complete list of these correspondences are:

⟨tz'amá⟩ (Y)	*sam'a* (G, Ch)		'dark (nighttime)'
⟨tz'arará⟩ (Y)	*sarara?* (G, Ch)	*sarar'a* (J)	'cold (weather)'
⟨untz'uku⟩ (Y)	*suk'u* (G, Ch, J)		'tie up'
⟨tz'üöma⟩ (Y)	*šɨma* (G, Ch, J)		'rat'
⟨nitz'api⟩ (Y)	*išaapi* (G)	*išapi* (Ch, J)	'remove'
⟨tz'imá⟩ (Y)	*šɨm'a* (G, Ch, J)		'black'
⟨tz'al⟩ (Y)	*k'aɬi* (G, Ch, J)		'smoke'
⟨tz'umiki⟩ (Y)	*t'uhmi-k'i* (G)	*tuhmi-k'i* (Ch, J)	'spit'

These correspondences do not have any apparent environment or linguistic motivation in changing from either a reconstructed alveolar affricate *ts'* or from reconstructed *s*, *š*, *t*, or *k*. That is, there is no evidence to support the claim that either [*ts'] > {[s], [k], [š] [*ts'] [*t]} / #__ in non-Yupiltepeque Xinkan and remained [ts'] in Yupiltepeque, or that {[*s], [*k], [*š] [*ts'] [*t]} > [ts'] / #__ in Yupiltepeque but remained unchanged in the other Xinkan languages. Consequently, the correspondences just given are considered to be the consequence of speaker error, sporadic change, or mistakes in transcription in the original source.

This set also highlights an interesting point: in none of the Xinkan languages is there a surface [s'] or [š'], though there may be one underlyingly (see section 2.3.1 for discussion). Furthermore, there is no surface [ts] in any of the Xinkan languages either. That is, what would be expected to be /s'/ or /š'/ as the result of glottalization of /s/ or /š/ is always realized as [ts'] in Xinkan. This happens only during the glottalization process of verbal aspects discussed in section 3.6.3 in the languages about which we have clear data, Guazacapán, Chiquimulilla, and Jumaytepeque. Consequently there are no surface segments *s'* or *š'* that can be used to reconstruct these segments on the surface of Proto-Xinkan. Although, as discussed above, both of these segments are underlyingly necessary and so can be reconstructed as underlying segments in

Proto-Xinkan. Using internal reconstruction we might hypothesize that Proto-Xinkan had surface glottalized fricatives along with a glottalized alveolar affricate. However, the fricatives would have occurred in word-medial position, while the affricate would have occurred word initially. The changes *s' > [ts'] and *š' > [ts'] could have been motivated by the articulatory difficulty in producing a glottalized fricative, following from which this change occurred as a means of making the production of the sound easier.[5] Another possible explanation for this change might have been the fact that the glottal closure was reanalyzed as an alveolar stop.

Because this alternation of /s/ and /š/ with /ts'/ in glottalizing contexts is true in all of the Xinkan languages, it necessarily must have occurred in the protolanguage before any divergence. That is, ejective fricatives must have been lost, or changed, quite early in the language's history. Examples of cognates with this correspondence set include *huuša-* (G, Ch), *uuša-* (J) 'to blow (completive stem)' versus *huuts'a* (G, Ch), *uuts'a* (J) 'to blow (incompletive root)'.

This alternation, furthermore, indicates a possible source of internal reconstruction. Since this morphological process holds for all the Xinkan languages, it can be hypothesized that there was a language internal change, *{/s'/, /š'/} > [ts'] in all of the Xinkan languages. The articulatory constraints on producing glottalized fricatives might have motivated this change.

6.3.1.3 *(Alveo-)palatals*

(346)   *č   č : č : č : č

It is likely that some of the cases with word-initial [č] involve borrowings from neighboring languages. While this correspondence set is included here, some of the reflexes in the Xinkan language may prove to be artifacts of language contact, while others (like 'a little (bit)' below) are most assuredly native Xinkan. Examples include *čikwit* (G, Ch, J), ⟨chikihuit⟩ (Y) 'basket' (borrowed from Nahua); *čɨrɨkɨ* (G, Ch), *čɨr'ɨkɨ* (J) 'a little (bit)'; ⟨churucujlí⟩ [čurukułí] (Y) 'a little'; and *koočo* (G, Ch, J) 'dirty (clothes)'.

(347)   *č'   č' : č' : č' : ?

Examples include *č'ahma* (G, Ch, J) 'to chew'; *č'oy'e* (G, Ch, J) 'to fold (paper or cloth)'; and *moč'o* (G, Ch, J) 'to wet'. There are no words containing letters that might correspond to this sound in Yupiltepeque or that are cognate with these words from the other languages.

(348)   *š   š : š : š : š/s

Examples include *hatišma* (G, Ch, J), ⟨atisma⟩ (Y) 'to sneeze'; *šɨłɨk* (G, Ch), *šilik* (J), ⟨xili⟩ (Y) 'corncob'; and *kɨšma* (G, Ch, J) 'to give a gift'. Yupiltepeque is the only language that has two reflexes for this reconstructed protoform. In most environments the protosound *š has been changed into [s] in Yupiltepeque. However, when the voiceless alveo-palatal fricative occurs before the high front vowel [i], the sound is retained unchanged from Proto-Xinkan and is written ⟨x⟩ in Calderón. Additionally, there is some indication that Yupiltepeque [s] had a more retroflexed pronunciation, something like [ʂ]. While this cannot be said to be true for all instances of [s] in the data, for one word Calderón indicates the variability: ⟨ruca⟩ and ⟨suca⟩ 'eat, bite'. In the data the letter ⟨r⟩ is used to represent [š] in many of the words in Chiquimulilla in his glossary. (This is most likely due to Spanish influence where /r/ → [š] quite often.) The word for 'eat, bite' above is the only one listed with ⟨r⟩ for Yupiltepeque.

Incidentally, according to the data available for the Xinkan languages in Guazacapán, Chiquimulilla, and Jumaytepeque, the sound corresponding to the letter *x* was pronounced [š], while in both Guazacapán and Chiquimulilla there are indications that the sound corresponding to the letter *s* was pronounced [ʂ] (i.e., with slight retroflection).

(349)   *y   y : y : y : y

Examples include *miya* (G, J), *mihya* (Ch, Y?) 'hen'; *yɨw'aɬi* (G, Ch), *yiw'ali* (J) 'to lose (something)', ⟨yuwán sáma⟩ (Y) 'to forget', literally 'to lose inside'; and *hayu* (G, Ch, J), ⟨nuanjayu⟩ (Y) 'to clean'.

(350)   *y'   y' : y' : y' : y

Examples include *č'oye* (G, Ch, J) 'fold'; *mɨy'a* (G, Ch, J) 'help', ⟨muyay-nen⟩ (Y) 'help me!'; and *tuy'a* (G, Ch, J) ⟨tuyac⟩ (Y) 'to scold'. The Yupiltepeque data does not represent glottalization; therefore it is impossible to know whether the sound was in fact glottalized in this language.

6.3.1.4 *Velars*

(351)   *k   k : k : k : k

Examples include *kama* (G, CH, J), ⟨cama⟩ (Y) 'blood'; *kawi* (G, Ch, J), ⟨cahuiki⟩ (Y) 'to yell/shout'; and *maku* (G, Ch, J), ⟨macu⟩ (Y) 'house'.

(352)   *k'   k' : k' : k' : k

Examples include *k'oočo* (G, Ch, J) 'dirty (clothes)'; *šuk'imaɬ* (G, Ch), *šuk'imal* (J), ⟨sukinali⟩ also ⟨sukinal⟩ (Y) 'coals'; and *tik'iɬa'* (G), *tiik'i'* (Ch), *tik'ila'* (J), ⟨tiki⟩ (Y) 'to sleep'. The sound [k] is represented by the graphemes ⟨k⟩ and ⟨c⟩ in the Yupiltepeque data, the distribution being random; both graphemes signal (presumed) glottalized and nonglottalized velar stops.

Some isolated changes in the Xinkan languages involve only a handful of words, and so they cannot be considered to reflect general patterns of change in the language. In one word in Guazacapán [k'] appears to have been substituted for [p']: *p'isku* (G), *k'isku* (Ch, J) 'to remove'. There does not seem to have been any contextual (i.e., phonetic) motivation for this change. Another isolated change involves a disjunctive set: *k'aɬ* (G), *gar* (Ch), *ar* (J), ⟨nayar⟩ (Y) 'still' (Sp. *'todavía'*). It should be noted that it is very likely that while the glosses are consistent across languages, these words are not cognates; this is especially true for the Yupiltepeque form. However, the sequence *ar* is often used in conjunction with numerals and numeral-like objects in Jumaytepeque and older sources of Xinkan.

Since Xinkan does not have voiced stops, the Chiquimulilla form can be analyzed as having undergone the voicing of the stop, probably because of a former preceding nasal, now lost (e.g., *na kar > n kar > gar). If there ever was a velar consonant in Jumaytepeque it has been deleted entirely. Of course, all of this highlights only possible explanations and should be considered speculation.

Lastly, [k'] is changed to [h] intervocalically in three words in Jumaytepeque: *łiik'a* (G, Ch), *liiha* (J) 'to lower oneself/to climb down'; *hik'a* (G, Ch), *hiha* (J), ⟨jüöca⟩ (Y) 'to sew'; *yik'iša* (G, Ch), *yihiša* (J) 'to mix, stir, swing'. I have no explanation for why this happened in only these three words.

6.3.1.5 *Glottals*

(353) *h   h : h : h : ⟨j⟩

Examples include *hapa* (G, Ch, J), ⟨japá⟩ (Y) 'to wait'; *hayu* (G, Ch, J), ⟨nuanjayu⟩ (Y) 'to clean'; *huuši* (G, Ch, J), ⟨jüsal⟩ (Y) 'head'. Additionally, /h/ is often inserted before high vowels and coronal fricatives in Guazacapán: for example, *hiiru* (G), *iiru* (Ch, J), ⟨iru⟩ (Y) 'monkey'; *huutuk* (G), *uutuk* (Ch, J), ⟨ujutuc⟩ (Y) 'soot'; *nuhšu* (G), *nuušu* (Ch), *uušu* (J) 'to smoke, cure with smoke'; *hiyɨ* (G), *ɨyɨ* (Ch, J) 'gopher'; and *łuhsu* (G), *łuhsu/łisɨ* (Ch), *luusu* (J) 'to bite, sting'.

(354) *ʔ   ʔ : ʔ : ʔ : N/Aʔ

Examples include *huušaʔ* (G, Ch), *uušaʔ* (J) 'be blown' (cf. to blow); *k'iišiʔ* (G, Ch, J) 'be roasted' (cf. 'to roast'); *puułiʔ* (G, Ch), *puuliʔ* (J) 'be washed glass' (cf. 'to wash, clean glass'), ⟨puliy⟩ (Y) 'to wash'; and *meʔe* (G, Ch), *mee* (J) 'green' ⟨meyatí⟩ (Y) 'green, turn green'. In all but the last example the reflexes are of the intransitive affective verb form. Also note that stress placement in Calderón's data indicates that there was also a glottal stop. That is, because stress is consistently placed before the rightmost consonant in Xinkan languages, and often the words in Calderón's glossary have final stress, it might signify a glottal stop that has not been indicated in the orthography: for example, ⟨acú⟩ (Y) 'go' and *akuʔ* (G, Ch, J) 'go.ICOMP'; ⟨čé⟩ (Y), *šeʔ* (G, Ch) 'possum'; ⟨jonó⟩ (Y), *hoonoʔ* (G, Ch, J) 'get.drunk.IV.AFF', among others.

A note about the glottal stop is in order. Phonetically all words in Xinkan that begin with a vowel have a predictable phonetic glottal stop before the vowel. This can make the data seem irregular because these words are not typically written with the initial glottal stops, though Terrence Kaufman (field notes) does represent them with the initial /ʔ/, even though it is phonetically predictable. However, the realization that there is both a predictable phonetic word-initial glottal stop and a contrastive phonemic one makes the data completely regular. The phonemic glottal stop only occurs in two situations: word finally in verbs, usually coupled with a lengthened root vowel to indicate the intransitive affective form of the verb; or word medially between two identical vowels.

6.3.2   Vowel changes

Vowels underwent fewer changes in the four different Xinkan languages, making their reconstruction more straightforward. That is, the protovowels remain largely unchanged in the respective daughter languages. As mentioned in the introduction to this chapter, the synchronic changes in vowel quality are limited by the vowel harmony constraints that are in operation in all four Xinkan languages and that seem to have also characterized the protolanguage. These constraints limit the kinds of the vowels which can co-occur in a polysyllabic word and are based primarily on the height and the centrality of the vowels involved. This means that the only permitted combinations are {/i/, /u/, /a/}, {/e/, /o/, /a/}, or {/ɨ/, /a/} in a single root. Across morpheme boundaries, within a word, the vowels must be either {/i/, /ɨ/, /u/, /a/} or {/e/, /o/, /a/}. For the reconstruction of Proto-Xinkan vowels this means there is a limited number of vowels that a vowel in a suffix can be 'changed into' in order to follow the rule of vowel harmony when suffixes are involved. Or rather, vowels have not been allowed to change in violation of the vowel harmony constraints.[6]

Additionally, while Proto-Xinkan clearly had contrastive vowel length, in some situations the length of the vowel in the protolanguage is difficult to determine. More specifically, sometimes vowel length can differ in the different Xinkan languages without any apparent phonetic explanation. While some instances of vowel lengthening seem to be a consequence of a vowel following a word-initial fricative, at least in Guazacapán, there are other exceptions that do not offer any obvious explanation. This is especially true with cognates containing [u] or [uu]. This issue is discussed in detail following correspondence set 360 below. Moreover, the vowel length changes apply only to nouns, adjectives, and adverbs but not to verbs—in verbs, vowel length is determined by the morphology (i.e., vowels are lengthened in the participle construction, and vowels are lengthened before the plural suffix).

Additionally, as mentioned above, when a word-medial syllable-coda consonant is deleted, the vowel is lengthened. Furthermore, Jumaytepeque appears to lengthen vowels randomly in a number of words that in Guazacapán and Chiquimulilla have only short vowels, though there are often alternative pronunciations with short vowels in Jumaytepeque. Lastly, as mentioned above, the Yupiltepeque data represents vowels with a single vowel letter, and thus does not indicate whether there may have been a length contrast. This makes the latter data unhelpful in determining vowel length (a problem similar to that of the glottalized consonants mentioned above). The same presentation order observed in the consonant reconstructions is followed here in the vowel reconstructions: namely the reconstructed protosound is listed first, followed by the reflexes in the various languages in the order Guazacapán, Chiquimulilla, Jumaytepeque, and Yupiltepeque. Cognates exemplifying the correspondence sets are given in the text immediately following the set itself.

(355)   *i   i : i : i : i

Examples include *čawi* (G, Ch), *šawi/čawi* (J), ⟨sahui⟩ (Y) 'hard'; *čikwit* (G, Ch, J), ⟨chikihuit⟩ (Y) 'basket'; and *ima* (G, Ch, J), ⟨ima⟩ (Y) 'to say, tell'.

(356) *ii   ii : ii : ii : ʔii/i

Examples include *iiti* (G, Ch, J) 'tomato'; *hiiru* (G), *iiru* (Ch, J), ⟨iru⟩ (Y) 'monkey'; and *šiir'an* (G, Ch, J) 'nit'.

(357) *e   e : e : e : e

Examples include *netka* (G, Ch, J) 'to push'; *ter'o* (G, Ch, J), ⟨teroy⟩ (Y) 'to kill'; and *meʔe* (G, Ch), *mee* (J) 'green', ⟨meya-ti⟩ (Y) 'to make/become green'. The mid vowels [e], [ee], [o], and [oo] are rare in general in Xinkan, with the short vowels being more common than their long counterparts. In one word, Guazacapán and Chiquimulilla are grouped together as having [e] while Jumaytepeque and Yupiltepeque both have [i]: *eɬa* (G, Ch), *ila* (J), ⟨ila⟩ (Y) 'new'.

(358) *ee   ee : ee : ee : ʔ

Examples include *seema* (G, Ch, J) 'fish'; *šeeke* (G, Ch, J) 'rib'; *p'eese* (G, Ch, J) 'lizard'; and *weetan* (G, Ch), *k'eetan* (J) 'large worm'.

(359) *u   u : u : u : u
              u : u : ɨ : ʔu

Examples include *naru* (G, Ch, J), ⟨arru⟩ also ⟨narro⟩ (Y) 'land, ground'; *hiiru* (G), *iiru* (Ch, J), ⟨iru⟩ (Y) 'monkey'; *huhuɬ* (G, Ch), *huhul* (J) 'bee, wasp'; *ušu* (G, Ch, J), ⟨usu⟩ (Y) 'fly'; and *uɬka* (G, Ch), *ulka* (J), ⟨ula⟩ (Y) 'to want, love'.

Both correspondence sets in 359 are difficult to reconstruct, though I have put the most apparent reflexes in the correspondence sets given. The [u] vowel has undergone a number of changes in all of the Xinkan languages, which makes the exact specification of its value in the protolanguage uncertain in a few contexts. In Jumaytepeque, for example, [u] became [ɨ] word finally after a labial consonant (i.e., [u] > [ɨ] / [+Labial]__#).[7] For all the words that underwent this change and are attested in the Yupiltepeque data, the letter ⟨u⟩ is the reflex. It would seem then that only Jumaytepeque underwent this change and not any of the other Xinkan languages, though the representation ⟨u⟩ in this Yupiltepeque data might conceivably be a misinterpretation of [ɨ]. Examples include *map'u* (G, Ch), *map'ɨ* (J), ⟨mapu⟩ (Y) 'tortilla'; *tawu* (G, Ch), *tawɨ* (J) 'air, wind'; *šapu* (G, Ch), *šapɨ* (J), ⟨sapu⟩ (Y) 'cotton'; and *hamu* (G, Ch), *hamɨ* (J) 'dirty'.

Meanwhile there are some words with [u] in both Chiquimulilla and Jumaytepeque and with [uu] in Guazacapán. This difference seems to be caused by the presence of a preceding fricative, so [u] > [uu] / [+continuant]__ in Guazacapán. This rule, however, is restricted entirely to nouns and adjectives, because vowel length is fully predictable in the morphology of the verb and the suffixing of the plural morpheme, where the length of the vowel is determined by its morphological context in the Xinkan languages. However, there are a few exceptions that cannot be accounted for with the data available on the languages. Examples include *huurak* (G), *frak* (Ch), *hurak* (J), ⟨jurra⟩ (Y) 'man'; *huuts'uk* (G), *huts'uk* (Ch, J), ⟨jutz'u⟩ (Y) 'center, middle'; *šuunik* (G), *šunih* (Ch, J) 'pan (used for cooking)'; and *šuuruk* (G), *šuruk* (Ch, J) 'staff, cane'; but not *huhuł* (G, Ch), *huhul* (J) 'bee, wasp'; *hulap'i* (G, Ch, J)[8] 'tamale for traveling', among others.

(360)   *uu*   uu : uu : uu : ⟨u⟩

Examples include *nuuru* (G, Ch, J), ⟨nuru⟩ (Y) 'pus, matter'; *łuuri* (G, Ch), *luuri* (J) 'rabbit'; and *puułi* (G, Ch), *puuli* (J) 'to wash one's hands', ⟨puliy⟩ 'wash' and ⟨papulipá⟩ (Y) 'washed'. See the discussion in set 359 for more cognates in Guazacapán with [uu] that do not appear in the other Xinkan languages.

(361)   *o*   o : o : o : o

Examples include *one* (G, Ch, J), ⟨one⟩ (Y) 'child, young (one)'; *ts'oto* (G, Ch, J), ⟨n'soto⟩ (Y) 'to tire, to be tired'; and *ts'ok'o* (G, J), *ts'ok'ok* (Ch), ⟨tz'oko⟩ (Y) 'grackle'.

(362)   *oo*   oo : oo : oo : ⟨o⟩

Examples include *k'oočo* (G, Ch, J) 'dirty (clothes)'; *hoor'o* (G, Ch) 'to take care of, have'; *k'ooto* (G, Ch, J), ⟨cotoay⟩ (Y) 'molar'; and *p'oošo* (G, Ch, J) 'partridge'.

(363)   *i*   i : i : i : ʔi

Examples include *nim'a* (G, Ch, J), ⟨numa⟩ (Y) 'to eat'; *łiw'i* (G, Ch), *liw'i* (J), ⟨lövua⟩ (Y) 'squash'; and *pipi* (G, Ch, J), ⟨pupüöpa⟩ (Y) 'to fill'. The Yupiltepeque data in both Calderón (1908) and Lehmann (1920) make use of umlauts to represent the high central vowel of Xinkan languages. However, they use ⟨ü⟩, ⟨ö⟩, and sometimes ⟨u⟩, seemingly indiscriminately to represent this sound, making it difficult to see how it behaves in this language. That is, while it is clear that Yupiltepeque had a high central vowel /i/, it is not clear if the variation in representing it is linguistic or the result of transcription errors.

(364)   *ii*   ii : ii : ii : ʔii

Examples include *miiri* (G, Ch, J), ⟨müri⟩ (Y) 'to complain'; *šim'a* (G, Ch), ⟨tz'üöma⟩ (Y) 'night'; and *iil'i* (G, Ch), *iit'i* (J) 'back, in back of', ⟨utuy⟩ (Y) 'behind, in back of'.

(365)   *a*   a : a : a : a

Examples include *naru* (G, Ch, J), ⟨arru⟩ also ⟨narro⟩ (Y) 'land, ground'; *naki* (G, Ch, J), ⟨naki⟩ (Y) 'chile'; and *ałi* (G), *ałi* (Ch), *al* (J), ⟨ajla⟩ (Y) 'over, on top of'.

(366)   *aa*   aa : aa : aa : ʔaa/a

Examples include *paama* (G, Ch), *paaha* (J), ⟨paja⟩ (Y) 'shoulder, wing'; *maama* (G, Ch, J), ⟨mamay⟩ (Y) 'ear'; and *šaaru* (G, Ch, J).

6.4   Summary of sound changes

A complete list of the phonological changes discussed above for each of the Xinkan languages is provided below, followed in parentheses by the number of the correspondence set that shows its application in the respective language. The summary in this section does not list any of the sporadic changes or the alternations between plain and glottalized consonants that are a result of speaker performance (see sections 6.2 and 6.3). While these sporadic changes are important to the history of each individual language, they are usually motivated by common limitations on phonetic implementation (see the discussion in section 6.2) and cannot be shown to be generalized to the language in question as a regular sound change, as such is defined. Only those sound changes that have been shown to have a clear linguistic motivation are listed below. Lastly, it is interesting to note that all the regular consonant changes in Xinkan have to do with the more marked sounds in the coronal area of production.

1. *l' > t' in Jumaytepeque in words with original [l'] (set 339)
2. *l' > ⟨t⟩ in Yupiltepeque (set 339)
3. *ɬ > l in all environments in Jumaytepeque (set 340)
4. *ɬ > ɬ / a__ in Yupiltepeque (set 340)
   *ɬ > l / elsewhere
5. [ɬ] > Ø / __# in Yupiltepeque (set 340) — internal reconstruction
6. *š > š / __i in Yupiltepeque (set 348); *š > s and possibly [ṣ] / elsewhere in Yupiltepeque (set 341)
7. *s' > [ts'] in Proto-Xinkan (set 345) — internal reconstruction
8. *š' > [ts'] in Proto-Xinkan (set 345) — internal reconstruction
9. *u > i / [+labial]__# in Jumaytepeque (set 359)
10. *u > [uu] / [+continuant][-sonorant] __ in Guazacapán; there are a few exceptions (set 359)

6.5   Subgrouping

It is beneficial to note what kinds of linguistic information the reconstructions in section 6.2 and 6.3 provide. That is, what does the information presented indicate about subgroups of the Xinkan languages? This is an important aspect of understanding Xinkan linguistic and cultural history. However, due to the limited data available, the subgroups proposed here are at best preliminary, the refinement of which is left for future investigations.

It seems most probable that Jumaytepeque and Yupiltepeque form a subgroup within the Xinkan family. This is supported by a few shared innovations in the development of these two languages, among them: [l'] > [t'] and [e] > [i] exhibited in 339 and 357 above, respectively; both of these innovations are predictable and regular.[9] This evidence points to this subgrouping, which is tentatively proposed, with the caveat that more shared innovations need to be uncovered to support this claim; future grammatical investigations and, perhaps, lexical innovations, may provide necessary additional evidence. However, a few changes do indicate that these two languages have had separate histories. For example, in Jumaytepeque Xinka [u] > [i] / [ı Labial]__#, while no similar change is reported in the Yupiltepeque data.

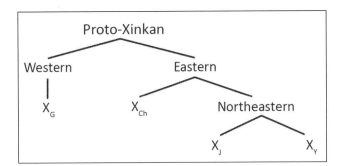

Figure 6.1 Xinkan family tree with posited subgroups

There is also one shared innovation that would group Jumaytepeque and Chiqui-mulilla Xinka: [p] > [b] in *pał* > *bar* 'epistemic modality marker', though this is prob-ably due to the voicing caused by some now-unknown voiced consonant. As this change affects only a single grammatical particle, it would hardly be considered suffi-cient grounds for subgrouping, as a number of possible explanations could account for the form in addition to shared subgrouping. This means that the similarities are most likely due to chance than to shared innovation.

While a single phonological innovation is not ideal in proposing a subgroup of a language family, the uniqueness of the phonetic change involved in the variation seems to be sufficient evidence to at least hypothesize that this subgrouping existed. The information on morphosyntactic reconstruction in chapters 7 and 8 does not provide any indication of shared innovation among the languages. This is unfortu-nate, as shared innovation, as well as any correspondence in the morphosyntax, often provides a stronger prediction of relationship than changes found in the phonology. Due to the lack of morphosyntactic shared innovation, the best possibility is to point out the subgrouping hypothesis and note that with more evidence the picture of the Xinkan family might be refined.

If, on the other hand, we consider this single phonological change that was used to group Jumaytepeque and Yupiltepeque as speculative and inconclusive, the only available option would be to argue for four independent branches diverging from Proto-Xinkan. Figure 6.1 shows the hypothesized family tree for the Xinkan lan-guages, assuming the validity of the phonological shared innovation.

In addition to the implications that the analysis in this chapter might have for his-torical linguistics in general, the phonological reconstruction of Xinkan also points to some interesting typological peculiarities. Proto-Xinkan exhibited a number of sound segments that are rare in the world's languages. For example, the glottalized frica-tives, which I argue here changed to the glottalized alveolar affricates, are very rare cross-linguistically.

Few languages exhibit glottalized fricatives and even fewer have been discussed historically.[10] The changes involving glottalized fricatives discussed in this chapter in-dicate at least one avenue of change that a language has at its disposal, and depending on the type of glottalized fricative, such changes might be considered stop fortition, the avoidance of generally difficult production patterns, or the avoidance of marked segments.

Similarly, there is an interesting gap in the protolanguage phonemic inventory that has been passed on to all of Proto-Xinkan's daughters. The absence of [ts] alongside the presence of [ts'] is interesting for several reasons. First, as is generally thought, and is argued in Maddieson (1984: 98–117), there is an implicational universal which posits that the presence of ejectives in a language presuppose the existence of plain consonants, and a single ejective presupposes its plain counterpart. This is obviously not true of Xinkan; it has an ejective alveolar affricate [ts'], but no plain counterpart. A significant typological consideration is that this gap was present in the protolanguage as well as in the daughter languages. There seems to be no evidence supporting or debunking a claim that the missing [ts] appears to be the result of some historical process (e.g., a merger); it is merely a fact of the language. While the reasons for this gap are unknown, its existence requires that typological claims about glottalized consonants and their implications be revisited.[11]

6.6   Conclusion

This chapter outlines the phonological correspondences in the Xinkan languages and reconstructs the inventory of sounds in the protolanguage. The reconstruction easily confirms the hypothesis that the four languages are related. Furthermore, I argue that there might be evidence for subgrouping two of the languages together—Yupiltepeque and Jumaytepeque—in a Northeastern Xinkan branch. Interestingly, this grouping parallels the oral traditions of the Xinkan peoples, although my subgrouping is based solely on linguistic evidence. Their tradition holds that in the remote past a group of Xinkan-speaking people left Guazacapán (considered the center of Xinkan territory) and divided into two groups. One group went into the mountains (i.e., Jumaytepeque) to avoid the unhealthy climate of the coastal region, while the other settled farther east, closer to El Salvador, on the side of a mountain.[12] While much work must still be done on the historical reconstruction of Xinkan phonology (for instance, the motivation for gaps and the typological implications of Proto-Xinkan sounds considered in light of the changes in the daughter languages), the information presented in this chapter constitutes a first investigation of the historical developments of the phonologies of the four Xinkan languages. See chapter 7 for a discussion of the historical development of Xinkan morphology and chapter 8 for a discussion of the historical development of Xinkan syntax.

SEVEN

Historical morphology

The survey of Xinkan morphology in chapter 3 revealed some very obvious patterns of historical change. This chapter focuses on the reconstruction of the morphology of Proto-Xinkan. That is, the purpose of this chapter is to state explicitly the developmental processes that led to the current Xinkan morphological system in the individual languages. The actual phonetic realizations of the various Xinkan morphemes can be recreated by following the phonological reconstruction discussed in chapter 6. Consequently, this chapter does not provide any new insight into the historical development of Xinkan grammar beyond that indicated above. Rather, this chapter (and the following one) reconstructs the Proto-Xinkan morphosyntactic system — exploring the ways the individual elements form a complete grammatical whole. The benefit of these final chapters is a better understanding of the development of Xinkan morphosyntax, though specific reconstructed morphosyntactic forms are presented below to illustrate the system. The pronouns and pronominal affixes are reconstructed first. Next I address the bound morphemes, followed by the various particle and question words.

The reconstructions all follow the template used in chapter 6, with the actual forms in Xinkan being given in the order Guazacapán, Chiquimulilla, Jumaytepeque, and Yupiltepeque. The gloss of each form being compared is given in the leftmost column, and the reconstructed form is given in the rightmost column preceded by an asterisk. As was the case in previous tables, gaps in the data are indicated by a dash. The Yupiltepeque data presented in this chapter is found in Calderón (1908) and Lehmann (1920).

7.1   Pronouns and pronominal affixes

7.1.1   Pronouns

The pronoun system in the Xinkan language family is largely unchanged from the protosystem, although there are a few significant changes in some of the individual languages in the family. The comparison table and the reconstruction are given in table 7.1.

Table 7.1 Xinkan pronominal reconstruction

	Guaz.	Chiqui.	Jumay.	Yupil.	Proto-Xinkan
1SG	*nen'*	*ni'*	*nin*	*nen/nin*	**nin'* [a]
2SG.FORM	*naka*	*nak*	*nak*	—	**nak(a)*
2SG.INFORM	—	*nay*	*nay*	*nay* [b]	**nay*
3SG	*nah*	*nah*	*nah*	*nah*	**nah*
1PL.INCL	*neelhek*	*nalhki*	*nalki*	*nelek*	**nelhek* [c]
1PL.EXCL	*neelhek 'ay*	—	—	—	—
2PL.FORM	*naka 'ay*	*nalhik*	*nalka/naalik*	*nalika*	**na(a)lhik*
2PL.INFORM	—	*naylhik*	*nayliy*	—	**naylhik*
3PL	*naalhik*	*nalhi(h)*	*naali(h)*	*nah lhik*	**nahlhik*

[a] This is the protoform suggested by the cognates in the four Xinkan languages; however, since the first-person plural form also begins with [ne] **nelhek*, it might be hypothesized that the first-person singular pronoun was **nen'* in Proto-Xinkan.

[b] The gloss as 'informal' for this Yupiltepeque is likely not accurate. That is, it would be rare for a language to have an informal pronoun without a formal one to contrast it with. It is glossed this way to show the relevant cognates in the languages and not as a typological generalization about the language.

[c] An internal reconstruction of this form suggests that it might have developed from *nen-lhe-k* '1SG-PL-?'. This is the basis for suggesting that the first-person singular pronoun might be best reconstructed as **nen'* rather than **nin'*. In fact, all of the plural pronouns can be internally reconstructed as consisting of the formula 'base-plural-k'. Thus, in addition to the first-person plural pronoun, there is **nalhik < na-lhi-k* (second-person plural formal pronoun); **naylhik < nay-lhi-k* (second-person plural informal pronoun); and **nahlhik < nah-lhi-k* (third-person plural pronoun).

The distinction between FORMAL and INFORMAL in the second-person forms is an important issue in the reconstruction of Proto-Xinkan. This distinction exists in both Chiquimulilla and Jumaytepeque but not in Guazacapán. Also, Yupiltepeque has cognates with one or the other form but not both. The reason for this last observation might stem from the lack of data rather than from a difference in the grammatical patterns. This is significant for questions of family subgrouping, as the formal/informal distinction can be, on the one hand, viewed as a shared innovation—thereby grouping Jumaytepeque and Chiquimulilla as a separate branch, with the possibility of Yupiltepeque being part of this group. On the other hand, if this issue is viewed as a shared retention, then the Proto-Xinkan pronominal system had a formal/informal distinction and only Guazacapán (and possibly Yupiltepeque) exhibits an innovated pattern. The specifics are perhaps less important, however, because in either scenario Chiquimulilla and Jumaytepeque will be set apart from Guazacapán (though for different reasons); Yupiltepeque will not fit neatly with any other possible subgroup. Of course, if it is Guazacapán that shows the innovation, then the formal/informal distinction should be reconstructed for Proto-Xinkan; in the alternative scenario, this distinction should not form part of the Proto-Xinkan grammatical system.

7.1.2 Pronominal affixes

This section presents the reconstructed affixes in Proto-Xinkan. The comparative tables in this section follow the same format as in the previous section. In tables 7.2–7.6, where there is insufficient information to determine the exact form of the morpheme or the exact segments in a morpheme, I offer as much information as possible.

Table 7.2 provides the comparison of the SET A transitive verb suffixes. (See section 3.5.2.2 for a discussion of the pronunciation of these forms in Jumaytepeque.) Overall the reconstruction of the suffixes follows directly from the phonological changes observed in the development of the individual Xinkan languages discussed in chapter 6.

Table 7.3 shows the comparison and reconstruction of the SET B prefixes, which are used in conjunction with alienably possessed nouns and transitive verbs marked for the incompletive aspect. Table 7.4 shows the comparison and reconstruction of intransitive verb SET C prefixes, and table 7.5 shows the reconstruction of the intransitive verb SET D prefixes. Table 7.6 shows the SET E nominal possessive suffixes.

Table 7.2 Xinkan verb SET A reconstructed suffixes

	Guaz.	Chiqui.	Jumay.	Yupil.	Proto-Xinkan
1SG	*-n'*	*-n'*	*-n'/-n*	*-n*	**-n'*
2SG.FORM	*-ka'/-kan*	*-kan*	*-ka'/(-ili)*	—	**-kan*
2SG.INFORM	—	*-y*	*-y*	*-y*	**-y*
3SG	*-y'*	*-y'*	*-yi'*	*-i*	**-y(V)'*
1PL	*-k*	*-lhik'*	*-lki'*	*-k*	**-(lhi)k*
2PL.FORM	*-ka ay*	*-lhik*	*-lik*	*-lika*	**-lhika*
2PL.INFORM	—	*-y lhik*	*-liy*	*-y*	**?-y lhik*
3PL	*-y' ay*	*-lhi(h)*	*-hri*	*-i*	**-(C)y(C)*

Table 7.3 Xinkan SET B reconstructed prefixes

	Guaz.	Chiqui.	Jumay.	Yupil.	Proto-Xinkan
1SG	*ün-*	*ün-*	*n-*	*n-*	**ün-*
2SG.FORM	*ka-*	*mük-*	*k-*	—	**k(V)-*
2SG.INFORM	—	*müy-*	*y-*	*(mu)y-*	**y-*
3SG.	*mu-*	*mü-*	*h-*	—	**m(V)*
1PL	*muk-*	*mülhki-*	*lki-*	*muh-*	**mulhki*[a]
2PL.FORM	*ka-...ay*	*mülhik-*	*lka-/lik-*	*lika-*	**ka-*
2PL.INFORM	—	*mülhay-*	*liy-*	—	—
3PL	*mu-...ay (lhik)*	*mülhi(h)-*	*lih-*	*Ø-...ay*	**mu-PL*

[a] This form might have developed internally from *mu-lhi-ki* 'Person-PL-INCH' **mulhki*.

Table 7.4 Xinkan SET C reconstructed prefixes

	Guaz.	Chiqui.	Jumay.	Yupil.	Proto-Xinkan
1SG	*ün-*	*ün-*	*n-*	—	**ün-*
2SG.FORM	*ka'-*	*mük-*	*k-*	—	**k(V)-*
2SG.INFORM	—	*müy-*	*y-*	—	**y-*
3SG	*Ø-*	*Ø-*	*Ø-*	—	**Ø-*
1PL	*muk-*	*mülhki-*	*lki-*	—	**mulhki*
2PL.FORM	*ka- ay*	*mülhik-*	*lka-/lik-*	—	**ka-*
2PL.INFORM	—	*mülhay-*	*liy-*	—	-
3PL	*Ø- ay (lhik)*	*Ø- lhik*	*Ø- lik*	—	**Ø-*PL

Table 7.5 Xinkan SET D reconstructed prefixes

	Guaz.	Chiqui.	Jumay.	Yupil.	Proto-Xinkan
1SG	*ün-*	*ün-*	*n-*	—	**ün-*
2SG.FORM	*ka'-*	*mük-*	*k-*	—	**k(V)-*
2SG.INFORM	—	*müy-*	*y-*	—	**y-*
3SG	*a-*	*a-*	*a-*	—	**a-*
1PL	*muk-*	*mülhki-*	*lki-*	—	**mulhki*
2PL.FORM	*ka- ay*	*mülhik-*	*lka-/lik-*	—	**ka-*
2PL.INFORM	—	*mülhay-*	*liy-*	—	—
3PL	*a- ay (lhik)*	*Ø- lhik*	*a- lik*	—	**a-*PL

Table 7.6 Xinkan SET E reconstructed nominal suffixes

	Guaz.	Chiqui.	Jumay.	Yupil.	Proto-Xinkan
1SG	*-n'*	*-'*	*-n*	*-n*	**-n'*
2SG.FORM	*-ka(ʔ)*	*-k*	*-ka'*	-	**-ka'*
2SG.INFORM	—	*-(a)y*	*-y*	*-y*	**-y*
3SG	*-h*	*-h*	*-h*	*-h*	**-h*
1PL	*-k*	*-lhki'*	*-lki'*	*-k*	**-(lh)ki*[a]
2PL.FORM	*-ka ay*	*-lhik*	*-lik*	*-lika*	**-lhik(a)*
2PL.INFORM	—	*-y lhik*	*-liy*	—	**-y lhik*
3PL	*-h lhik*	*-lhi(h)*	*-hri*	*-h*	**-hCi*

[a] This form might also have developed from the source *-lhi+ki* 'PL+INCH'.

7.2   Bound morphology

This section deals with the reconstruction of the bound morphology in the Xinkan languages, aside from the personal pronominal affixes. That is, this section deals with valency-changing affixes, voice, aspect, and tense. The aspect and voice systems are consistent across the Xinkan languages (see sections 3.6.2 and 3.6.3). Therefore, it can be said that Proto-Xinkan also had a distinction between transitive verbs on the one hand and intransitive agentive and intransitive affective verbs on the other. Furthermore, all verbs can be inflected for two aspects, completive and incompletive.

Specifically, transitive verb roots in Proto-Xinkan used the verbal SET B prefixes and a glottalization process (i.e., glottalization of the rightmost consonant) to indicate the incompletive aspect. The completive aspect was signaled by use of the verbal suffixes only and no glottalization (as it is for all the daughter languages). Intransitive verbs were furthermore inflected for the two aspects by the SET C and SET D prefixes given in tables 7.4 and 7.5. These characteristics are identical within all the daughter languages, as discussed in chapter 3.

Following from the similarities in the verb class system—generally across daughter languages (though not specific class membership)—the same intransitive verb system is reconstructed for Proto-Xinkan. Intransitive verbs have been classified based on semantic criteria as being agentive or affective, though for some words their exact class membership is not known. Intransitive affective verbs were those that had the undergoer (logical patient) of the action as the sole argument, while intransitive agentive verbs were those that had the doer (logical agent) of the action as their sole argument. Intransitive agentive verbs are marked with the suffix *-lha'* while intransitive affective verbs are marked with the suffix *-' [ʔ]*. Furthermore, for intransitive affective verbs, the first vowel in the stem was long except when there were consonant clusters involved (see section 3.6.1). Table 7.7 shows these verb classes, and their characteristics, for Proto-Xinkan.

Table 7.7 Xinkan verb class reconstruction

Intransitive agentive	Intransitive affective
The suffix *-lha'* [-ɬaʔ] used in the completive aspect	Marked by -' [-ʔ] in all grammatical aspects
No change in the root for either aspect	First vowel is lengthened in the completive aspect except in CVCCV roots

Additionally, from the comparison of the valency-changing devices in the Xinkan languages it can be hypothesized that Proto-Xinkan also had these valency changes available. Specifically, all of the Xinkan languages have derivation processes whereby a transitive verb can become an intransitive verb (either agentive or affective), and these processes are identical cross-linguistically within this language family. Therefore, the same patterns can be said to have existed in Proto-Xinkan. These grammatical operations are summarized in table 7.8. The specifics of this operation are discussed in section 3.12.3.2.

Table 7.8 Xinkan valency changes reconstruction

Intransitive verb derivation
TV → IV.AGENTIVE
TV → IV.AFFECTIVE

Importantly, however, each language is unique as to which transitive verbs are allowed to undergo which of the two processes. This means that particular verb forms might be able to be reconstructed if they behave the same in all three languages, but the only generalizable fact that can be reconstructed is the morphosyntactic patterns. For example, the verb 'to yawn' is intransitive agentive in all of the Xinkan daughter languages (*hat'išmalha'* [Guazacapán and Chiquimulilla], *hat'išmala'* [Jumaytepeque]), and so was most probably intransitive agentive in Proto-Xinkan. In contrast, the verb 'to sleep' is intransitive affective in Chiquimulilla *tiik'i'*, and intransitive agentive in both Guazacapán *tik'ilha'* and Jumaytepeque *tik'ila'*. This means that this verb most likely belonged to the intransitive agentive class in Proto-Xinkan with an innovation in Chiquimulilla. However, because class membership is language dependent, this is only an unsubstantiated hypothesis and cannot be reconstructed for Proto-Xinkan with the same degree of certainty as the verb 'to yawn' can be.

Similarly, all of the Xinkan languages have two participle constructions (see section 3.12.3.5). In all three languages the present participle is formed through the use of the suffix *-k'i* and consequently can be reconstructed for Proto-Xinkan. The past passive participle is formed by lengthening the first vowel in the verb root, except for verbs with the phonological shape CVCCV. Table 7.9 shows the comparison of the participles.

Table 7.9 Xinkan participle reconstruction

	Guaz.	Chiqui.	Jumay.	Yupil.	Proto-Xinkan
Present participle	*-k'i*	*-k'i*	*-k'i*	⟨ki⟩	**-k'i* TV→PARTICIPLE
Past participle	Vowel length	Vowel length	Vowel length	—	*Vowel length TV→PARTICIPLE

The valency-increasing processes (see section 3.12.3.4) can likewise be reconstructed, though with less precision. Specifically, there are a number of causative constructions in each of the Xinkan languages. The suffixes involved can be reconstructed, although due to missing and conflicting information the precise semantics of each cannot be. Because the daughter languages show few consistencies in meanings of the verbs derived using these suffixes, as with the verb classes specific meanings cannot be reconstructed. In table 7.10, consequently, the phonological shapes of these suffixes are reconstructed and their presence in Proto-Xinkan grammar is accorded, but not the specific meanings entailed therein.

Table 7.10 Xinkan causative suffixes reconstruction

	Guaz.	Chiqui.	Jumay.	Yupil.	Proto-Xinkan
Causative	-lha	-lha	-la	—	*-lha
Causative	-ha	-ha	-ha	⟨ha⟩	*-ha
Causative	-y'a	-y'a	-yi	⟨ya⟩	*-y'a
Causative	-ka	—	-k'a	—	*k'i + -ha

The only change that should be noted here is that in Jumaytepeque *y'a → [-yi]. It is not common for *i to become [a] in the Xinkan languages, though in this isolated example it has done so. Similarly, the epistemic modal particle also existed in Proto-Xinkan with a similar meaning to that found in the daughter languages. Table 7.11 indicates the modal particle correspondences.

Table 7.11 Xinkan epistemic modal reconstruction

	Guaz.	Chiqui.	Jumay.	Yupil.	Proto-Xinkan
Epistemic modal	palh	bar	bar	—	*palh 'indeed'

The reconstruction of this particle is fairly straightforward. However, a note is in order about the methodology involved. Normally, reconstructed forms represent the simplest feasible path of development. Thus, a hypothesis positing one change is a better than one requiring many changes or changes in different languages. This usually means that the most frequently occurring form or segment across the languages should be reconstructed for the protolanguage. However, as can be seen, I have not chosen the most frequent form across Xinkan languages (i.e., *bar*). Because voiced stops are extremely limited in the phonology of the Xinkan languages, they are almost certainly not part of Proto-Xinkan phonology, while voiceless stops are ubiquitous. Therefore, instead of hypothesizing that *b became [p], except in a few isolated words, a simpler hypothesis changes *p to [b] in only a few exceptional cases. I follow the same argument for the reconstruction of the word-final consonant in this particle (though here it is less compelling, and an original *r is a possibility). Moreover, this hypothesized path of development for both Chiquimulilla and Jumaytepeque, if true, would show that these two languages have a shared innovation and might consequently be grouped together as a branch of Proto-Xinkan.

Lastly, the verbal noun derivations can likewise be reconstructed for Proto-Xinkan with a considerable amount of certainty. (For more detailed information on verbal noun derivations, see section 3.12.1.) There are four constructions that derive nouns from underlying verbs. The first, termed the abstract verbal noun in section 3.12.3.4.1, is the same for all three languages. It is derived by not adding personal pronominal affixes to the incompletive verb form. Consequently, I suggest that it has not changed from the protolanguage system; this same process is reconstructed for Proto-Xinkan.

The other three verb-to-noun derivations require explicit suffixes that can be reconstructed for Proto-Xinkan. The morphological operations entailed in these derivations and their specific meanings are thought to be the same as in the daughter languages. Table 7.12 lists the gloss of the resulting noun and the suffixes involved. The reconstructed Proto-Xinkan is given in the rightmost column.

The patient noun is included in table 7.12 despite it being used only in Guazacapán because it highlights again that Guazacapán Xinka may have innovated away from the other Xinkan languages. Consequently, Guazacapán might be considered an independent branch of the family.

Table 7.12 Xinkan verbal noun reconstruction

	Guaz.	Chiqui	Jumay.	Yupil.	Proto-Xinkan
Abstract noun	Uninflected verb form	Uninflected verb form	Uninflected verb form	N/A	*Uninflected verb form
Agent noun	*-lha*	*-lha*	*-la*	⟨(-ki-)la⟩[a]	*-lha*
Instrument noun	*-k*	*-k*	*-k*	⟨-c⟩[b]	*-k*
Patient noun	*-wa*	—	—	—	—

[a] See for example ⟨cayikíla⟩ 'seller', ⟨chiguakíla⟩ 'player', ⟨cumíkila⟩ 'buyer', ⟨mucala⟩ 'worker', and ⟨sacsla⟩ 'thief' (probably a typo for *sacala*, cf. *sacatz'a* 'steal') in Calderón 1908.

[b] See ⟨kürtz'ac-li⟩ 'comb-PL' (cf. *kürtz'a* 'to comb' in the other Xinkan languages), and ⟨xinac⟩ 'bladder' (cf. *xiin'a* 'to urinate' in the other Xinkan languages).

EIGHT

Historical syntax

8.1   Overview of syntactic reconstruction

One of the major goals of this grammar is to study the diachronic development of the Xinkan languages through a careful reconstruction of Proto-Xinkan grammar, including phonology, morphology, and syntax. However, it must be acknowledged that many linguists believe that the reconstruction of syntax is difficult if not impossible.[1] This means that one contribution to the study of linguistics that I hope to accomplish with this chapter is to convincingly reconstruct Proto-Xinkan syntax. In order to determine if I have achieved this goal, I here provide a brief overview of what syntactic reconstruction is.

To be meaningful, the historical reconstruction of any aspect of a language rests on its ability to provide informative hypotheses about the grammar that speakers of the protolanguage must have used. That is, linguistic reconstruction must have as its initial motivation the 'discovery' of language structure, patterns, sounds, and meanings as they existed in the past and from which the modern language patterns have developed. Consequently, the object of syntactic reconstruction is to hypothesize about the original syntactic patterns from which the syntactic patterns discussed in chapter 4 developed.[2]

Reconstructing patterns alone, of course, constrains what can effectively be reconstructed for the syntax of any protolanguage because syntax is fundamentally different than phonology or morphology. Unlike these other linguistic components of a grammar, the syntax of a language is not limited. For example, there is a closed set of phonemes available to each language as well as a closed set of grammatical morphemes and morphological patterns; languages do not just infinitely make up new sounds or create new morphological paradigms in the same way they generate new utterances.

In one perspective on syntax, sentences are not limited in the same way. Speakers can adjust sentences in novel ways with each utterance. An infinite number of sentences can be produced by the grammar in any given language. However, despite the unbounded nature of syntax, it is possible to discuss bounded patterns and syntactic strategies in a language. This is what chapter 4 accomplished; the general syntactic patterns were outlined for each of the Xinkan languages. These patterns make it possible to comprehend how to structure an utterance, not what every single utterance would look like. Since these patterns are bounded and limited, in this regard they are much like the other linguistic components of a language's grammar (i.e., phonology and morphology). Naturally, the patterns discussed in chapter 4 are surface patterns and do not inform us directly about deep or underlying patterns of language competence, acquisition, or use. Actually, the syntactic patterns discussed in chapter 4 are empirically derived patterns abstracted from surface structures. It is these abstracted empirical patterns that are of concern for Xinkan syntactic reconstruction.

A language exhibiting a finite set of patterns enables us to reconstruct these same surface patterns using the comparative-historical method (although we cannot know individual utterances themselves) The outcome of these reconstructions represents abstract patterns based on surface structures that the speakers of Proto-Xinkan exhibited in their speech and that formed the base from which the modern Xinkan languages derived their syntactic patterns.

However, there are some limitations specific to Xinkan in the application of the comparative method and to the reconstruction of Proto-Xinkan syntax. Specifically, the lack of abundant documentation from the past means that the reconstructions are hypothetical (as, of course, all reconstructions are). That is, while the materials available reflect the patterns available to Proto-Xinkan speakers, there is no immediate way of knowing what actual sentences the speakers of Proto-Xinkan may have uttered based on these patterns—in other words, no way to reconstruct actual utterances. Additionally, as mentioned throughout this grammar, often linguistic information is missing or contradictory, and the reconstructions are contingent upon the information available.[3]

8.2 Xinkan syntactic reconstruction

Within these limitations, this chapter presents a syntactic reconstruction of Proto-Xinkan through a comparison of the four Xinkan languages' grammatical patterns. The correspondence sets are presented in much the same way as in previous chapters: the material compared from each language in the reconstruction is separated by a colon. The reconstructed form is given immediately following each correspondence set separated by an asterisk, and where necessary a short discussion of each reconstruction and historical development is given. The order of the correspondence sets is also the same as previously: Guazacapán, Chiquimulilla, Jumaytepeque, and Yupiltepeque (where possible).

8.2.1 Syntactic alignment

The syntactic alignment of the individual Xinkan languages was discussed in detail in section 4.1. Here I simply repeat that all of the Xinkan languages exhibit NOMINATIVE-ACCUSATIVE alignment in basic sentences. Since in all of the daughter languages this alignment was indicated by subject-verb agreement in person and number (and linear order of constituents), I argue that such was the strategy employed in Proto-Xinkan as well. That is, Proto-Xinkan required subjects to agree with their verbs in person and number. Lastly, it can also be hypothesized that since none of the daughter languages exhibits overt morphological case marking, case was likewise not present in Proto-Xinkan morphology. Table 8.1 indicates the relevant patterns that can be reconstructed for Proto-Xinkan.

Table 8.1 Xinkan syntactic patterns reconstruction

Guazacapán	Chiquimulilla	Jumaytepeque	Yupiltepeque	Proto-Xinkan
NOM/ACC	NOM/ACC	NOM/ACC	NOM/ACC	*NOM/ACC
SUBJ AGR	SUBJ AGR	SUBJ AGR	SUBJ AGR	*SUBJ AGR
NO CASE	NO CASE	NO CASE	NO CASE	*NO CASE

8.2.2   Verb classes

The verb classes can likewise be reconstructed for Proto-Xinkan based on the fact that all of the daughter languages with sufficient documentation exhibit them. Recall section 3.6.1, which describes three verb classes in Xinkan: neutral (transitive), intransitive agentive (intransitive), and intransitive affective (intransitive). Due to the consistency of these patterns in general across the language family, but not necessarily specific group membership within those classes, Proto-Xinkan most likely also had the same system of verbal classes. Table 8.2 shows the reconstruction of the Xinkan verb classes.

Table 8.2 Xinkan verb classes reconstruction

Guazacapán	Chiquimulilla	Jumaytepeque	Yupiltepeque	Proto-Xinkan
3 verb classes:	3 verb classes:	3 verb classes:	—[a]	*3 verb classes:
TV, IV.AGT,	TV, IV.AGT,	TV, IV.AGT,		TV, IV.AGT, and
and IV.AFF	and IV.AFF	and IV.AFF		IV.AFF

[a] Note that Calderón 1908 offers isolated examples that show suffixes in Yupiltepeque that are cognate to the intransitive agentive and intransitive affective markers in the other three languages, but since the available information is scarce, it is not clear whether Yupiltepeque also had three classes or merely exhibited the remnants of these classes.

Section 3.6.1 shows that the phonological shape of an intransitive agentive verb was identical to that of a transitive verb, while the phonological shape of an intransitive affective verb required a lengthened vowel (targeting the first vowel in the root). It is assumed that this was also true for Proto-Xinkan.

8.2.3   Word order

The discussion of word order in chapter 4, and of noun phrases in section 3.4, indicates word-order patterns that can be reconstructed for Proto-Xinkan. For the basic word order of a sentence, the reconstruction is fairly straightforward: table 8.3 shows the word-order correspondences.

Table 8.3 Xinkan word-order reconstruction

Guazacapán	Chiquimulilla	Jumaytepeque	Yupiltepeque	Proto-Xinkan
VOS	VOS	VOS	VOS (?)	*VOS

Calderón (1908) records a number of sentences (though most are with pronouns—few have two full noun phrase arguments), some of which suggest VOS, although many others with SVO word order appear to be direct translations of Spanish. For example, the following three examples indicate VOS word order: ⟨tz'opojí nen naj urumúhui⟩ [bite me the snake] 'la culebra me mordió'; ⟨mi sukí nen pelu⟩ [bite me dog] 'el perro me muerde'; ⟨sukí nen pelu⟩ [bite me dog] 'el perro me mordió'. For this reason alone, it is assumed that VOS order was basic for Yupiltepeque.

However, the preposing of nominal arguments in the Xinkan language is an optional strategy. While explicitly shown for Guazacapán, it was only marginally shown for Chiquimulilla and Jumaytepeque (see section 4.4).[4] It is undesirable to reconstruct a Proto-Xinkan syntactic pattern on the basis of a single language's patterns. Consequently, the optional preposing strategy is left unreconstructed, though it was probably a pattern available for the speakers of Proto-Xinkan, perhaps for topicalization, focus, or emphasis.

There are three patterns that can be reconstructed for noun phrases. These reconstructions, like most of those in this chapter, are quite transparent. These patterns serve to show that little has changed from Proto-Xinkan in terms of the word-order patterns in the daughter languages. Table 8.4 gives the noun phrase reconstruction. In noun phrases, adjectives occur on the left of the nouns they modify, while for both demonstrative and genitive constructions the head of the phrase is to the left with the modifier to the right. In the correspondence sets in table 8.4, the head is always N and thus N-GEN = N (HEAD) of GEN; and N-DEM = N (HEAD) DEM.

Table 8.4 Xinkan noun phrase reconstruction

Guazacapán	Chiquimulilla	Jumaytepeque	Yupiltepeque	Proto-Xinkan
ART-N-DEM	ART-N-DEM	ART-N-DEM	—	*ART-N-DEM
ADJ-N	ADJ-N	ADJ-N	ADJ-N	*ADJ-N
N-GEN	N-GEN	N-GEN	—	*N-GEN

Similarly, the syntactic patterns of verb phrase and predicate constituents can be reconstructed for Proto-Xinkan grammar. The most basic pattern, observed in chapter 4, is that in both sentences with a verb and sentences without, the predicate is most commonly placed before the subject. Table 8.5 shows the correspondence of, and reconstructs, the verbless sentence patterns.

Table 8.5 Xinkan verbless sentence pattern reconstruction

Guazacapán	Chiquimulilla	Jumaytepeque	Yupiltepeque	Proto-Xinkan
PRED-SUBJ	PRED-SUBJ	PRED-SUBJ	PRED-SUBJ	*PRED-SUBJ

This is observed in the VOS basic word order and in verbless sentences such as the null-copula constructions. In the former case the predicate of the clause is VO and the subject is S, while in the latter instance the predicate is the characterization indicated for the subject as the nominal argument thus modified (see section 4.2). For complex sentence constructions table 8.6 shows the patterns that can be observed and reconstructed in Proto-Xinkan grammar.

Table 8.6 Xinkan complex sentence pattern reconstruction

Guazacapán	Chiquimulilla	Jumaytepeque	Yupiltepeque	Proto-Xinkan
N [REL] VP	N [REL] VP	N [REL] VP	—	*N [REL] VP
VP [COMP] S	VP [COMP] S	VP [COMP] S	—	*VP [COMP] S
[V-S V]$_{VP}$	[V-S V]$_{VP}$	[V-S V]$_{VP}$	—	*[V-S V]$_{VP}$
XP [CONJ] XP	XP [CONJ] XP	XP [CONJ] XP	—	*XP [CONJ] XP

The first correspondence set represents the patterns in relative clauses. In this pattern the head noun is to the left followed by the relativizer and the relative clause to the right. Importantly, however, the phonological form of the relativizer varies in the languages, as discussed in section 4.6.3. Juxtaposition is the only strategy employed in all the Xinkan languages, where there is a null (phonologically zero) relativizer. This strongly suggests that this strategy of relative-clause formation was available to the speakers of Proto-Xinkan.

The second correspondence set represents the patterns exhibited in complement clauses in the Xinkan languages. The matrix clause consistently appears to the left, followed by the complementizer and the embedded clause. This pattern is, consequently, reconstructed for Proto-Xinkan. It can further be suggested that juxtaposition with a null complementizer is the only non-Spanish influenced strategy available for these constructions. This means that the speakers of Proto-Xinkan would have exhibited the null-complementizer pattern and would have most likely used this same strategy of juxtaposition to form complement clauses.

The third correspondence set is the patterns available in the Xinkan languages for serial verb constructions. These constructions, as discussed in section 4.6.2, include two verbs within a single verb phrase. This is illustrated in the correspondence set by the square brackets labeled as a single verb phrase. In all of the Xinkan languages this type of construction requires that the leftmost verb be inflected for person, number, and aspect, but that the rightmost member of the chain be left in its basic morpho-phonological form, not bearing inflectional morphology.

The final correspondence set indicates the patterns in syntactic constituents that are conjoined. The 'XP' in this set stands for any type of constituent or phrase available in the syntax of the language. Constituents are conjoined in the Xinkan languages with one of the three conjunctions (see section 4.6.1). However, juxtaposition is also the only strategy that is not Spanish-influenced that all of the Xinkan languages exhibit. Consequently, this suggests that juxtaposition was a strategy for conjoining constituents available to the speakers of Proto-Xinkan.

8.2.4   Nominal syntax reconstruction

Lastly, some noun morphology might also be reconstructed for Proto-Xinkan. Specifically the noun possession strategies can be reconstructed fairly straightforwardly.

Recall that nouns are possessed in two different ways: inalienable nouns are possessed using suffixes, while alienable nouns are possessed using prefixes. The individual morphemes were reconstructed in section 7.1, but here the general patterns are reconstructed for Proto-Xinkan. Table 8.7 gives the possession pattern reconstruction.

Table 8.7 Xinkan noun possession pattern reconstruction

	Guazacapán	Chiquimulilla	Jumaytepeque	Yupiltepeque	Proto-Xinkan
Noninherent possession	-N	-N	-N	-N	*-N
Inherent possession	N-	N-	N-	N-	*N-

Despite the drawbacks to the reconstruction of Proto-Xinkan syntax, from the available data it has been possible to reconstruct a number of syntactic patterns. Additionally, when coupled with the phonological and morphological reconstructions of the Xinkan languages, a strong hypothesis of actual sentences uttered by Proto-Xinkan speakers can be made. For example, if one reconstructs the *sounds* of an adjective and a noun that are both cognates across the languages, then it is feasible that the actual adjective or noun can be reconstructed. (See the phonological reconstruction in chapter 6.) Furthermore, knowing the phonological shape of Proto-Xinkan words as well as the syntactic patterns into which they were organized allows one to reconstruct actual sentences in Proto-Xinkan, though not necessarily the actual proto-grammar that produced these utterances.

Important to the discussion of diachronic syntax is the notion that these reconstructed utterances are mere surface patterns and that there may have been multiple grammars capable of producing them. This means that these patterns only indicate a small portion of the grammar of Proto-Xinkan. The way that grammar was organized depends largely on the theoretical machinery one uses to adequately explain these patterns. This chapter concludes that syntactic reconstruction is possible, when it is approached with the proper assumptions and definitions.

Looking forward

This book has described the grammar of four related Xinkan languages and presented what is known about how they developed from a common protolanguage. In light of the disappearance of the world's linguistic diversity in general, and of the paucity of documentation of the Xinkan languages in particular (see chapter 1), I hope this book has scientific value for scholars and community members. However, a language is never used in a bubble—in isolation from social and cultural factors. Neither does an empirical description exist in a scientific bubble. Rather, this grammar exists within both a cultural context and a scientific one. It is framed by the science of linguistics on the one hand and by Xinkan cultural history and resurgence on the other. This chapter will briefly discuss how this grammar fits into these contexts.

The American linguist Charles Hockett remarked that "linguistics is a classificatory science".[1] Other linguists have supported this view; classification is often considered one of the most important aspects of modern linguistic activity. Language can also act as a badge of identity, as an artifact of culture, and as a mutually developed (and developing) sociocultural code of communication. This means that there is more to a linguistic description than complex observations about patterns and grammatical rules. Linguistic descriptions provide the basis for a number of meaningful classifications of the languages described. These classifications can, in turn, tell us how each language fits into the world—how each linguistic pattern has value in the global human experience.

Linguistic classifications are scientifically and culturally appropriate labels given to an entire language or to parts of languages. In general, these classifications are trivial unless we use them as a point of comparison between various languages. These comparisons allow us to gather some languages into meaningful groups. For example, if we classify a linguistic code using a specific name (such as English), we create two broad (and ultimately uninteresting) groups: the group of codes called English and the group of codes called something else. This type of lower classification is found throughout the discipline of linguistics: some sounds are grouped according to the phonetic feature [+/- voice]; words are grouped according to various grammatical properties, resulting in classifications like *noun* and *verb*; and we group syntactic constituents in terms of their properties and functions, resulting in labels like *noun phrase* or *adjective phrase*.

There are more interesting classifications available for various aspects of a linguistic code, but they all crosscut more than a single language. These higher (and more interesting) classifications lead to conclusions about the world around us and the place of language in that world. One example of this type of higher classification is the observations that many (if not all) languages can be grouped into the class of languages that distinguishes nouns and verbs. This classification reveals something about language: humans have a need to distinguish between actions and nonactions (to put it simply). These higher classifications are built upon empirical descriptions of the world's languages compared across many languages. They will most often refer to the concepts listed below.

- Grammatical properties (including sounds, morphemes, and utterances)
- Lexical similarities (such as color terminology or kinship terms)
- Cross-generational development (in other words, the language's history)
- Social and cultural factors of use

According to these concepts, languages can be classified into cross-linguistic groups based on the criteria listed below.

1. Genetic affiliation (at least between the languages described)
2. Typological characteristics
3. Vitality (i.e., the level of endangerment)
4. Geographical context

Considered in light of the information and descriptions contained in this volume, many classifications are available for the Xinkan languages. This chapter will discuss how the four broad classifications listed above relate to the data analyzed in this book.

9.1 Genetic affiliation

Genetic affiliation refers to a shared development over time of two or more languages with a common linguistic ancestor. The genetic classifications of the Xinkan languages have been considered throughout this grammar. Specifically, chapters 6 through 8 show that internally these languages evidence very little divergence, though various speakers of the languages report mutual unintelligibility.

From this divergence the languages can be thought of as having unique and independent developments. Often language change, and divergence, is based on social, cultural, and/or political factors. The social and historical factors that induced change among the Xinkan languages are unknown, but their consequences are seen in the unique development of each of the languages.

As discussed in chapter 1, the development of the Xinkan language family does not point to a relationship with any other known languages. The Xinkan languages have a shared a common story of origin, but each developed individually, isolated from all other known languages. Of course, the Xinkan languages have not existed in a social or cultural bubble; they have inevitably been in contact with other languages (see below). However, none of the other known languages in Mesoamerica have diverged from a protolanguage that is shared with the Xinkan languages. Consequently, the Xinkan family of languages can be classified as an isolate.

9.2   Typological characteristics

Typological classifications seek to identify cross-linguistic similarities and differences in the world's languages. These classifications are typically very broad and include many languages in each type. The classifications are made based on ideas such as word order, phonemic inventory, valency changes, morphological patterns, and syntactic patterns (among many other parameters).

The typological classifications relevant to the Xinkan languages are highlighted throughout this grammar. However, they are left largely unexplored in terms of cross-linguistic comparisons. For example, while Xinkan languages exhibit vowel harmony (chapter 2), nothing has been said about how this feature compares to other languages that employ vowel harmony. The typological facts of Xinkan indicate that there are many implications from these languages for our understanding of language in general. These comparisons have been left for subsequent work, as they are not an essential part of the descriptive adequacy required in a reference grammar. However, to aid in these types of comparisons, the typological index at the end of the book lists the most salient topics for easy reference.

9.3   Vitality: Xinkan as a family of endangered languages

Classifying a language as 'endangered' is predicated on other specific and quantifiable classifications. For many linguists, an endangered language is a secondary classification based on: (1) language demographics; (2) language and cultural shift; (3) intergenerational transmission; (4) the amount of descriptive documentation; or (5) human rights violations affecting its speakers. Of course, in reality a language can be classified as endangered for any single one of these factors or for a combination of them.

As mentioned in chapter 1, there are very few remaining speakers of any of the Xinkan languages, though there is a large community of heritage Xinkans, who are defined in terms of ancestry or cultural history. In this sense, Xinkan languages are severely endangered and perhaps already extinct. However, the cultural identity of Xinkan and its individual heritage are currently undergoing a resurgence of interest. This makes the Xinkan culture and community somewhat less endangered than the language.

For the last one hundred years, Spanish has been the predominant public language in Xinkan communities. This language shift has resulted in there being very few people with knowledge about the languages or the cultural behaviors of the original communities. A strong, politically backed cultural shift has been in place for perhaps longer. This cultural shift (called *ladinization* locally) is, for outsiders, perhaps one of the defining features of the Xinkan communities. Nevertheless, the current cultural resurgence is aimed at negating the outcomes of ladinization by preserving some aspects of the Xinkan cultural identity and language.

Starting with the 1996 peace accords that ended the Guatemalan civil war, the Xinkan community has been officially recognized as an indigenous population in Guatemala. However, this recognition comes with a number of social and political conflicts. Most Guatemalans think the only native communities that still exist speak one of the Mayan languages; the others (including the Xinkans) are assumed to have been completely assimilated into the dominant culture, leaving only memories behind. Like the Xinkans, the Mayans are active in preserving and revitalizing their language and culture, resulting in a skewed perspective of legitimacy in some people's eyes. Lastly, because of the severe social and political turmoil in the Xinkan communities, and because the Xinkans never seem to have had a centralized government, the definition of what it means to be Xinkan is under constant negotiation.

There are no new speakers of any of the Xinkan languages growing up in the communities. The children of the last native speakers of the language were not encouraged to use the language (the shift mentioned above). In this sense Xinkan is already extinct. The community has recently started language classes for adults and children in the hope of creating interest in Xinkan identity, but as of yet no new speakers of any of the languages are being reared. New speakers in this type of scenario might end up speaking something patterned after their ancestors but not identical to the source languages; this is the consequence of interrupted intergenerational transmission. The goal should never be to recreate the past, but to use the past to inform the future.

Xinkan languages have been documented sporadically since 1770. However, the depth of these descriptions is not encouraging. The works by German linguist Frauke Sachse and this volume represent the most thorough documentation of the Xinkan languages. In this regard Xinkan is severely endangered. Not enough research is being done on this clearly relevant language. The descriptions above all point to a number of important scientific implications it offers in the field of linguistics.

The Xinkan communities have been subject to a number of very harsh social and political abuses. These abuses have gone on since the arrival of the Europeans in Guatemala—and most likely before then under the hands of the Mayans. These human rights violations are coming to an end, but they have created an atmosphere of denial, and shame, for those who identify as Xinkan or speak the languages. This results in another way these languages are endangered.

However the Xinkan languages are classified, the conclusion leads to extreme language shift, language loss, and consequently, endangerment. Looking forward, the community must decide how important the language is to their identity and what steps to take to preserve and revitalize their linguistic heritage.

9.4   Geographical context: Xinkan as a consequence of Mesoamerican geographical contact and history

The Xinkan languages do not exist in isolation, nor have they ever. They have been influenced by many languages all around them, including Spanish, Mayan, Uto-Aztecan, Jicaque, Misumalpan, and possibly Chibchan languages. There is evidence of this influence in every aspect of each language to varying degrees. Vocabulary has been added, morphemes have been altered, word order has been affected, and other syntactic structures have been changed. Nobody would ever doubt that the Xinkan languages are and were spoken in Mesoamerica, but it can be helpful to indicate the ways this location has affected their development and use. The influence from other languages that is observed in the Xinkan languages helps place them in the Meso-american cultural and linguistic area.

Some of the traits that Xinkan languages share with other Mesoamerican languages (and must have acquired through contact with them) are listed below.

1. *A specific nominal possession structure.* Mesoamerican languages share the abstract structure discussed in section 3.1.1. This Mesoamerican structure typically has the form 'possession-noun₁ the noun₂', meaning 'the noun₂'s noun₁': the example below shows the Guazacapán Xinka structure.

    (mu-)müüm'ü toktok
    (3SG.POSS-)song mocking.bird
    'song of the mockingbird'

    It is interesting to note that due to the alienablity parameter in Xinkan, the possessive affix can occur on either side of the noun—unlike other Mesoamerican languages. Similarly, as mentioned in chapter 3, this is not the only way of indicating possession in the Xinkan languages.
2. *Relational nouns.* Described in section 3.7, relational nouns are a pan-Mesoamerican feature. These are shared among all Mesoamerican languages, indicating language contact. However, it is interesting to note that relational nouns in Xinkan can also be used as prepositions and in conjunction with the alienability of noun possession. These are unique to the Xinkan languages.
3. *Non–verb-final basic word order.* This has been noted as a significant parameter in the Mesoamerican linguistic area. In basic declarative clauses, the Xinkan languages do seem to follow suit. However, as discussed in chapter 4, a number of possible word orders are present in the Xinkan languages. It is interesting to note the amount of this type of variation.
4. *Semantic calques.* Mesoamerican languages have a set of specific idiomatic structures to refer to culturally identifiable items. For example, Xinkan languages (and other Mesoamerican languages) refer to the 'edge of something' as its 'mouth' (*xaha* in Xinkan) and a 'thumb' as the 'mother of the hand' (as in Chiquimulilla Xinkan *u'ta pu'* 'mother (of) hand'), among many other examples.

All of these linguistic traits help place Xinkan languages in Mesoamerican history. For these shared traits to have existed in all four of the Xinkan languages, their speakers must have been in contact with many other Mesoamerican languages for a considerable amount of time.

Similarly, a number of geographical place names throughout Guatemala have been identified as having possible Xinkan origins.[2] For example, Lyle Campbell suggested that the following are possible Xinkan place names: *Ipala*, from the Xinkan word *ipal'a* 'bath'; and Sanarate, from the Xinkan word *xan* 'LOCATIVE' + *arat'ak* 'maguey', among many others. This indicates that while the Xinkans were never a cohesive social group, they must have occupied places throughout Mesoamerica for a very long time. In fact, these place names suggest that the original dispersion of people speaking a Xinkan language was much larger than its current parameters.

A reference grammar such as this one is a linguistic tradition dating back many hundreds of years. Over the years the incentive to publish these grammars has changed. In the past there were social, political, and religious motives for producing this kind of linguistic documentation. Currently, however, the motivation to produce a reference grammar is fueled by the field of scientific linguistics. As such, this volume represents a contribution to the growing scientific knowledge of described languages.

Hopefully, however, this book is significant for more than its contributions to scientific knowledge. I hope that the descriptions of the Xinkan languages here have cultural, historical, social, and linguistic implications. This means that while linguistic inquiry provided the initial motivation to write this book, I hope that its broader applications for humanity, and for Xinkan humanity specifically, may be of lasting value.

Appendix

Regular verb conjugation

There are different conjugation paradigms for transitive and intransitive verbs respectively. They are surveyed here. There is one conjugation pattern for transitive verbs that requires the rightmost consonant be glottalized in the incompletive aspect (applying vacuously to underlying glottalized consonants). If this creates an ungrammatical consonant cluster, a vowel is epenthesized to split the cluster; this is necessary only in the case of transitive verbs with the phonological shape CVCCV. A complete listing of possible transitive verb shapes is included for each language, both for reasons of clarity and to offset the extreme lack of documentation of the Xinkan languages.

(367) Guazacapán transitive verb inflection.

	waki	'play'
	Completive	**Incompletive**
1SG	waki-n'	ün-wak'i
2SG	waki-ka'	ka-wak'i
3SG	waki-y'	mu-wak'i
1PL	waki-k	mülhki-wak'i
2PL	waki-ka ay	ka-wak'i ay
3PL	waki-y' ay	mu-wak'i ay (lhik)

	hük'a	'sew, weave'
	Completive	**Incompletive**
1SG	hük'a-n'	ün-hük'a
2SG	hük'a-ka'	ka-hük'a
3SG	hük'a-y'	mu-hük'a
1PL	hük'a-k	mülhki-hük'a
2PL	hük'a-ka ay	ka-hük'a ay
3PL	hük'a-y' ay	mu-hük'a ay (lhik)

	wiiixa	'shake out'
	Completive	**Incompletive**
1SG	wiiixa-n'	ün-wiiitz'a
2SG	wiiixa-ka'	ka-wiiitz'a
3SG	wiiixa-y'	mu-wiiitz'a

1PL	*wüüxa-k*	*mülhki-wüütz'a*
2PL	*wüüxa-ka ay*	*ka-wüütz'a ay*
3PL	*wüüxa-y' ay*	*mu-wüütz'a ay (lhik)*

	hawka	'empty'
	Completive	**Incompletive**
1SG	*hawka-n'*	*ün-hawak'a*
2SG	*hawka-ka'*	*ka-hawak'a*
3SG	*hawka-y'*	*mu-hawak'a*
1PL	*hawka-k*	*mülhki-hawak'a*
2PL	*hawka-ka ay*	*ka-hawak'a ay*
3PL	*hawka-y' ay*	*mu-hawak'a ay (lhik)*

(368) Chiquimulilla transitive verb inflection.

	axi	'burn'
	Completive	**Incompletive**
1SG	*axi-n'*	*ün-atz'i*
2SG.FORM	*axi-kan*	*mük-atz'i*
2SG.INFORM	*axi-y*	*müy-atz'i*
3SG	*axi-y'*	*mü-atz'i*
1PL	*axi-lhik'*	*mülhki-atz'i*
2PL.FORM	*axi-lhik*	*mülhik-atz'i*
2PL.I	*axi-y lhik*	*mülhay-atz'i*
3PL	*axi-lhi(h)*	*mülhi(h)-atz'i*

	mütz'a	'bury'
	Completive	**Incompletive**
1SG	*mütz'a-n'*	*ün-mütz'a*
2SG.FORM	*mütz'a-kan*	*mük-mütz'a*
2SG.INFORM	*mütz'a-y*	*müy-mütz'a*
3SG	*mütz'a-y'*	*mü-mütz'a*
1PL	*mütz'a-lhik'*	*mülhki-mütz'a*
2PL.FORM	*mütz'a-lhik*	*mülhik-mütz'a*
2PL.INFORM	*mütz'a-y lhik*	*mülhay-mütz'a*
3PL	*mütz'a-lhi(h)*	*mülhi(h)-mütz'a*

	huuxa	'blow'
	Completive	**Incompletive**
1SG	*huuxa-n'*	*ün-huutz'a*
2SG.FORM	*huuxa-kan*	*mük-huutz'a*
2SG.INFORM	*huuxa-y*	*müy-huutz'a*
3SG	*huuxa-y'*	*mü-huutz'a*
1PL	*huuxa-lhik'*	*mülhki-huutz'a*
2PL.FORM	*huuxa-lhik*	*mülhik-huutz'a*
2PL.INFORM	*huuxa-y lhik*	*mülhay-huutz'a*
3PL	*huuxa-lhi(h)*	*mülhi(h)-huutz'a*

	netka/nelhka	'push'
	Completive	**Incompletive**
1SG	*nelhka-n'*	*ün-nelhak'a*
2SG.FORM	*nelhka-kan*	*mük-nelhak'a*
2SG.INFORM	*nelhka-y*	*müy-nelhak'a*
3SG	*nelhka-y'*	*mü-nelhak'a*
1PL	*nelhka-lhik'*	*mülhki-nelhak'a*
2PL.FORM	*nelhka-lhik*	*mülhik-nelhak'a*
2PL.INFORM	*nelhka-y lhik*	*mülhay-nelhak'a*
3PL	*nelhka-lhi(h)*	*mülhi(h)-nelhak'a*

(369) Jumaytepeque transitive verb inflection.

	wixuyi'	'hit'
	Completive	**Incompletive**
1SG	*wixu-n'/n*	*n-wixu*
2SG.FORM	*wixu-ka'*	*k-wixu*
2SG.INFORM	*wixu-y*	*y-wixu*
3SG	*wixu-yi'*	*h-wixu*
1PL	*wixu-lki'*	*lki-wixu*
2PL.FORM	*wixu-lik*	*lka-wixu*
2PL.INFORM	*wixu-liy*	*liy-wixu*
3PL	*wixu-hri*	*lih-wixu*

	yoch'oyi'	'wash'
	Completive	**Incompletive**
1SG	*yoch'o-n'/n*	*n-yoch'o*
2SG.FORM	*yoch'o-ka'*	*k-yoch'o*
2SG.INFORM	*yoch'o-y*	*y-yoch'o*
3SG	*yoch'o-yi'*	*h-yoch'o*
1PL	*yoch'o-lki'*	*lki-yoch'o*
2PL.FORM	*yoch'o-lik*	*lka-yoch'o*
2PL.INFORM	*yoch'o-liy*	*liy-yoch'o*
3PL	*yoch'o-hri*	*lih-yoch'o*

	k'iixuyi'	'(ex)change'
	Completive	**Incompletive**
1SG	*k'iixu-n'/n*	*n-k'iitz'u*
2SG.FORM	*k'iixu-ka'*	*k- k'iitz'u*
2SG.INFORM	*k'iixu-y*	*y-k'iitz'u*
3SG	*k'iixu-yi'*	*h-k'iitz'u*
1PL	*k'iixu-lki'*	*lki-k'iitz'u*
2PL.FORM	*k'iixu-lik*	*lka-k'iitz'u*
2PL.INFORM	*k'iixu-liy*	*liy-k'iitz'u*
3PL	*k'iixu-hri*	*lih-k'iitz'u*

	p'urxiyi' 'singe'	
	Completive	**Incompletive**
1SG	*p'urxi-n'/n*	*n-p'uratz'i*
2SG.FORM	*p'urxi-ka'*	*k-p'uratz'i*
2SG.INFORM	*p'urxi-y*	*y-p'uratz'i*
3SG	*p'urxi-yi'*	*h-p'uratz'i*
1PL	*p'urxi-lki'*	*lki-p'uratz'i*
2PL.FORM	*p'urxi-lik*	*lka-p'uratz'i*
2PL.INFORM	*p'urxi-liy*	*liy-p'uratz'i*
3PL	*p'urxi-hri*	*lih-p'uratz'i*

Intransitive verb stems can be inflected for completive and incompletive aspects, but there are significant differences when compared to transitive verbs. Specifically, in the completive aspect pronominal suffixes are not used with intransitive verbs, while pronominal prefixes are used in both aspects, with a small but significant change in third-person singular agreement. With third person only, the completive aspect of the prefix is null, while the incompletive aspect of the prefix is *a-*.

The conjugation patterns of intransitive verbs are similar to those of transitive verbs in that the phonological shape of the verb root (its syllable structure, see section 3.6) affects the surface form of the verb. These will be discussed below, and examples can be found in section 4.2. In an intransitive agentive verb root of the shape CVCV, the rightmost consonant is glottalized in the incompletive aspect (i.e., is realized as CVC'V). A vowel is epenthesized between the two consonants of a cluster if the intransitive verb root has the shape CVCCV—in other words, if it contains a word-internal consonant cluster. Section 2.2.5.4 discusses the phonetic realization of the vowel to be inserted. There are a couple of irregular intransitive agentive verbs that have the incompletive base formed with a word-final glottal stop. These are rare and include words such as *-müka',* 'work'.

Intransitive affective verbs are similar in their conjugational patterns. They use the modified set of pronominal prefixes discussed above, and both verbal aspects have a word-final glottal stop. In the completive aspect, verb roots of the shape CVCV (including CVC'V) have the first vowel lengthened (i.e., CVVCV-ʔ for both roots). In cases where there is a consonant cluster, the vowel is not lengthened; the word-final glottal stop is suffixed (i.e., CVCCV-ʔ). In the incompletive aspect, the vowel is not lengthened; an underlying short vowel remains short and an underlying long vowel stays long. (This is especially relevant for transitive verb derivations: see section 3.12.3.2.) An epenthetic vowel is inserted to break up any consonant clusters caused by the glottalization of the rightmost consonant.

(370) Guazacapán intransitive agentive conjugation.

	yanalha' 'be ashamed'	
	Completive	**Incompletive**
1SG	*ün-yanalha'*	*ün-yan'a*
2SG	*ka-yanalha'*	*ka-yan'a*
3SG	*Ø-yanalha'*	*a-yan'a*
1PL	*muk-yanalha'*	*muk-yan'a*
2PL	*ka-yanalha'*	*ay ka-yan'a ay*
3PL	*Ø-yanalha' lhik*	*a-yan'a lhik*

(371) Guazacapán intransitive affective conjugation.

	saaka' 'get up, be lifted'	
	Completive	**Incompletive**
1SG	*ün-saaka'*	*ün-saka'*
2SG	*ka-saaka'*	*ka-saka'*
3SG	*Ø-saaka'*	*a-saka'*
1PL	*muk-saaka'*	*muk-saka'*
2PL	*ka-saaka' ay*	*ka-saka' ay*
3PL	*Ø-saaka' lhik*	*a-saka' lhik*

(372) Chiquimulilla intransitive agentive conjugation.

	k'iixu' 'exchange'	
	Completive	**Incompletive**
1SG	*ün-k'iixulha'*	*ün-k'iitz'u*
2SG.FORM	*mük-k'iixulha'*	*mük- k'iitz'u*
2SG.INFORM	*müy-k'iixulha'*	*müy-k'iitz'u*
3SG	*ø-k'iixulha'*	*a-k'iitz'u*
1PL	*mülhki-k'iixulha'*	*mülhki-k'iitz'u*
2PL.FORM	*mülhik-k'iixulha'*	*mülhik-k'iitz'u*
2PL.INFORM	*mülhay-k'iixulha'*	*mülhay-k'iitz'u*
3PL	*ø-k'iixulha' lhik*	*a-k'iitz'u lhik*

(373) Chiquimulilla intransitive affective conjugation.

	haama' 'ripened'	
	Completive	**Incompletive**
1SG	*ün-haama'*	*ün-hama'*
2SG.FORM	*mük- haama'*	*mük-hama'*
2SG.INFORM	*müy- haama'*	*müy-hama'*
3SG	*ø- haama'*	*a-hama'*
1PL	*mülhki- haama'*	*mülhki-hama'*
2PL.FORM	*mülhik- haama'*	*mülhik-hama'*
2PL.INFORM	*mülhay- haama'*	*mülhay-hama'*
3PL	*ø- haama' lhik*	*a-hama' lhik*

(374) Jumaytepeque intransitive agentive conjugation.

	wixt'ala' 'hiss' (to get someone's attention)	
	Completive	**Incompletive**
1SG	*n-wixtala'*	*n-wixat'a*
2SG.FORM	*k-wixtala'*	*k-wixat'a*
2SG.INFORM	*y-wixtala'*	*y- wixat'a*
3SG	*ø-wixtala'*	*a-wixat'a*
1PL	*lki-wixtala'*	*lki-wixat'a*
2PL.FORM	*lka-wixtala'*	*lka-wixat'a*
2PL.INFORM	*liy- wixtala'*	*liy-wixat'a*
3PL	*ø-wixtala' lik*	*a-wixat'a lik*

(375) Jumaytepeque intranstive affective conjugation.

	yooko' 'float'	
	Completive	**Incompletive**
1SG	*n-yooko'*	*n-yoko'*
2SG.FORM	*k-yooko'*	*k-yoko'*
2SG.INFORM	*y-yooko'*	*y-yoko'*
3SG	*ø-yooko'*	*a-yoko'*
1PL	*lki-yooko'*	*lki-yoko'*
2PL.FORM	*lka-yooko'*	*lka-yoko'*
2PL.INFORM	*liy-yooko'*	*liy-yoko'*
3PL	*ø-yooko' lik*	*a-yoko' lik*

Irregular verb conjugation

There are a few irregular verbs in the Xinkan languages that do not follow the patterns described in the foregoing sections. The conjugation patterns of these verbs are given here in full. Unfortunately, however, for some of these verbs the data is incomplete. That is, there are gaps in the data available such that for some person and number combinations there is no information available. These gaps are indicated below by a dash (—) as a place marker. These verbs are considered irregular because they do not follow the same general patterns of conjugation as indicated above. For example, the verb *ta'* 'to come' in Guazacapán has a lengthened root in the completive aspect but does not follow regular intransitive affective alternations in the incompletive aspect.

(376) Guazacapán irregular verb conjugations.

	ta' 'to come'	
	Completive	**Incompletive**
1SG	*ün-daayi'*	*n-da' (pe')*
2SG	*ka-taayi'*	*ka-ta' (pe')*

3SG	Ø-taay'i	a-ta' (pe')
1PL	muk-taayi'	muk-ta' (pe')
2PL	—	—
3PL	—	—

y'a 'to be'

Completive/Incompletive
1SG	y'a-n'
2SG	y'a-ka'
3SG	hi'
1PL	y'a-k
2PL	y'a-ka' 'ay
3PL	lhik/hi' nahlhik

aku'/ku' 'go, walk'

	Completive	Incompletive
1SG	n-gulha	n-gu'/n'-aku'
2SG	ka-kulha	ka-ku'/ka'-aku'
3SG	—	'a-ku'
1PL	muk-kulha	muk-ku'/muk-aku'
2PL	—	—
3PL	—	—

Verbal noun	**Imperative**
ku'	'aku-y'a
Antipassive	
aku-k'i	

waak'a' 'go'

Completive
1SG	n-waak'a'/ünwaak'a
2SG	ka-waak'a'
3SG	Ø-waak'a'
1PL	muk-waak'a'
2PL	ka-waak'a' 'ay
3PL	Ø-waak'a' lhik

(377) Chiquimulilla irregular verb conjugations.

ya' 'to be'

Completive/Incompletive
1SG	ya'
2SG.FORM	ya-ka'
2SG.INFORM	ya-y
3SG	'a-yi'/'ay'
1PL	ya-lhki'

2PL	*ya-lhka'*	
3PL	*'ay' lhik*	
	Completive	**Incompletive**
1SG	*n-da'ilha'/ n-daawi'*	*n-da'*
2SG	*mük-taawi'*	*mük-ta'*
3SG	*ta'ilha/taawi'*	*a-ta'*
1PL	—	*mülhki-ta'*
2PL	—	—
3PL	—	—
	Verbal noun	
	ta'	

---

ku' 'go, walk'

	Completive	**Incompletive**
1SG	*n-gulha*	*n-gu'*
2SG	—	*mük-ku'*
3SG	—	*a-ku'*
1PL	—	*mülhki-ku'*
2PL	—	—
3PL	—	—
	Imperative	**Antipassive**
	'akuy' t'ah/'akuy' p'eh	*'akuk'i*

---

wak'a' 'go' intransitive verb

	Completive	**Incompletive**
1SG	*n-waak'a/n-walha'*	*n-wak'a'*
2SG	*mük-waak'a*	—
3SG	*waak'a/walha'*	*a-wak'a'*
1PL	—	—
2PL	—	—
3PL	—	—

(378) Jumaytepeque irregular verb conjugations.

ayaw'a' 'to be'

	Completive/Incompletive
1SG	*ayaw'a-n*
2SG.FORM	*ayaw-ka'*
2SG.INFORM	*ayaw'a-y*
3SG	*ayi'*
1PL	*ayaw'a-lki'*
2PL.FORM	*ayaw'a-lka'*
2PL.INFORM	*ayaw'a-liy*
3PL	*ay-ili*

	ta' 'come'	
	Completive	**Incompletive**
1SG	*n-ti'/n-taayi'*	*n-ta' (p'eh)*
2SG	*k-taayi'*	*k-ta' (p'eh)*
3SG	*taayi'*	*a-ta' (p'eh)*
1PL	*lki-ti'/lki-taayi'*	*lki-ta' (p'eh)*
2PL	*lka-taayi'*	—
3PL	*taayi-lik'i*	—

Verbal noun
ta'

	aku' 'go, walk'	
	Completive	**Incompletive**
1SG	*n-'aaku'*	*n-'aku'*
2SG	*k-'aaku'*	—
3SG	*'aaku'*	*a-'aku'*
1PL	*lki-'aaku'*	—
2PL	—	—
3PL	—	*a-aku-lik'i*

Verbal noun   **Imperative**
ku'   *'akuy' (p'eh)/kuy' (p'eh)*

Antipassive
aku-k'i-la/'aku-la'

	wak'a 'go'	
	Completive	**Incompletive**
1SG	*n-waak'a'*	*n-k'a/n-wak'a'*
2SG	*k-waak'a'*	*k-k'a/k-wak'a'*
3SG	*waak'a/wa*	*a-wak'a*
1PL	*lki-waak'a'*	*lki-wak'a*
2PL	*waak'a-lik'i*	—
3PL	*wa-lik'i*	*a-wak'a naalih*

Notes

Chapter 1: Introduction to the languages and their speakers

1   See Maldonado 1770 for the earliest mention of this name. See also Rogers 2016 for a description of the current cultural and linguistic efforts in the community and the importance of the term 'Xinkan' in these efforts.

2   A neighboring Uto-Aztecan language, Pipil, has a word *xinka* meaning 'dregs, grounds, or sediment'. The Xinkan languages have borrowed elements from Pipil, indicating contact between the two groups. This suggests one possible source for the label, which, if correct, clearly reflects part of the nature of the contact. Unfortunately, this suggestion is merely speculative. In fact in the earliest documentation of the Xinkan languages (Maldonado 1770) the label used, 'Szinca', might possibly have been pronounced with a retroflex voiceless alveolar fricative [ʂinka], rather than the current practice of using a voiceless alveopalatal fricative [šinka] (as in the Pipil word). This suggests that Pipil might not have been the ultimate source of this ethnonym.

3   See Campbell 1997b.

4   See Lehmann 1920 and Calderón 1908 for the only extant materials on these Xinkan varieties.

5   See Sharer 2006: 190–236.

6   The exact time frame of language loss for Yupiltepeque Xinka is unknown. The only reliable information on the language comes from Calderón 1908, who offers a short grammatical sketch with a useful word list. That information was repeated in Lehmann 1920 without the addition of new information. There were no longer any speakers of this language by the 1960s (Otto Schumann 1967) or the 1970s (Lyle Campbell and Terry Kaufman, pers. comm.).

7   Lehmann 1920: 727, 767 (probably relying on Brinton 1885: 96) suggested a relationship with Lencan, and Calderón 1908: 6 suggested a relationship with a Mixe-Zoquean language. All of these have been soundly refuted by Campbell 1972 & 1979.

8   See Campbell 1972 & 1978: 603; Kaufman 1977: 67; and Sachse 2010 for clear examples of loanwords in Xinkan.

9   See Campbell, Kaufman & Smith-Stark 1986 and Sachse 2010 for a discussion on the Mesoamerican Linguistic Area and for evidence of the influence of Xinkan on some Mesoamerican languages.

10   The original source of this example is Campbell 1972, but there are many others throughout this grammar.

11   See Campbell, Kaufman & Smith-Stark 1986.

12   See Campbell 1978 and Sharer 2006: 193 for more information.

13 I find labels like 'semi-speaker' and 'rememberer', which are often used in the literature on language endangerment, to be inexact; in addition, they can be perceived as derogatory by language communities and speakers. I prefer to simply refer to individuals as speakers of the language. In the Xinkan community, in fact, the last speakers are considered 'speakers'. However, they do have varying fluencies in the languages: some recall only memorized lexical items or idiomatic expressions, while others can produce novel utterances and understand recorded speech from the 1970s. All of the data used here (and information on the differences between the languages) has been recognized by these final speakers as legitimate Xinkan ways of speaking.

14 In a few cases the current last speakers of the Xinkan languages had known the people recorded in the 1970s, and they commented that it was like hearing from a very good friend after a long absence.

15 Some community members have expressed the opinion that COPXIG (housed in the town of Chiquimulilla) was attempting to refer to this grammar as a grammar of Chiquimulilla Xinka (pers. comm.). The community is often quite politicized, but I see no reasonable explanation for this perspective.

16 See Rogers 2016.

17 Speakers both past and present remark that they are unable to understand the majority of the other Xinkan varieties (Terry Kaufman and Lyle Campbell pers. comm.). Similarly, the last speakers of these languages do not understand the varieties once spoken in towns not their own.

18 This is an observation from my time in the community. I hope that this grammar will be seen as a complement to the community one.

19 See Sapper 1904; Stoll 1886 & 1958; Rambo 1965; Campbell 1979; and Termer 1944.

20 See Termer 1944 and Sachse 2010: 36.

21 See Campbell 1978 for preliminary comments on Xinkan place names and Sachse 2010: 36 for an expanded discussion. There are a number of potential Xinkan place names not mentioned in either of these sources, however, and this possibly would be a very rewarding area of future research.

22 Instituto Nacional de Estadísticas. 2002. http://web.archive.org/web/20080605011453 /http:/www.ine.gob.gt/Nesstar/Censo2002/survey0/dataSet/dataFiles/dataFile1/var26 .html (in Spanish). Archived from www.ine.gob.gt/Nesstar/Censo2002/survey0/dataSet /dataFiles/dataFile1/var26.htm (accessed on 6-5-2008).

23 Schumann 1967: 11.

24 MacArthur 1966.

25 Saville 1918: 1.

26 Calderón 1908: 6.

27 See Sachse 2010: 35–38 for a good overview of the historical census figures of the Xinkan population.

28 Brinton 1885: 1.

29 Calderón 1908: 6.

30 See Sharer 2006.

31 See Sharer 2006: 190–236; Nash 1967; Vogt 1969; Olson 1991; Estrada-Belli & Kosakowsky 1996; and Ichon & Grignon 1998.

32 Nash 1967; Vogt 1969; Olson 1991: 404; Estrada Belli & Kosakowsky 1996: 29; and Ichon & Grignon 1998: 327.

33 See Rogers 2016.

34 See Rogers 2016 for a discussion of the revitalization goals of the community.

Chapter 2: Phonology

1 See Ladefoged 1997 and Ladefoged & Maddieson 1996 for examples.

2 Crothers 1978 and Boer 2001 have suggested that absence of the mid-central vowel in this type of inventory is due to the optimization of the vowel space for needed linguistic contrasts. Vowels tend to be maximally distant from one another to enhance perception, called 'maximum differentiation'.

3 Note that for other phonological shapes this vowel lengthening process is not required. For example, CVCCV is realized as CVCCV-ʔ, and CVCVCV is derived as CVCVCV-ʔ. This phenomenon was originally discussed by Campbell 1972 but under a different set of analytical assumptions.

4 See Crothers 1978; Ladefoged & Maddieson 1996; and Boer 2001.

5 See Maddieson 1984: 136 and Crothers 1978 for discussions of peripheral vs. nonperipheral vowels as an important distinction in the world's languages.

6 See Greenberg 1970 and Maddieson 1984 & 2005.

7 See Campbell 1973b and Santos Nicolás et al. 1997: 14–15 for more details.

8 This is a relatively recent change in the language. The /b/ phoneme is confined to a few new words and some borrowed words from Spanish.

9 In the data this sound is sometimes given by native speakers of the language as /ɸ/ and sometimes as /f/. It is easy to see the connection between the two in articulatory and perceptual terms. The change is most likely conditioned by the loss of the intervening long vowel /uu/. See chapter 6 for further discussion.

10 This difference between the languages is a consequence of the sound change *ɬ > l in Jumaytepeque but not in the other varieties.

11 See Rogers 2010.

12 See Campbell & Muntzel 1989.

13 See Campbell & Muntzel 1989.

14 There is no formal distinction between a verb in the incompletive aspect and a verbal noun except that the verbal noun bears only nominal affixes and the verb bears only verbal affixes (see section 4.3.3.2.1).

15 This quite abstract, and underlying, segment [ɬ'] is posited on the same grounds as [s'] and [š'] were above. Namely, in deglottalization processes some underlying glottalized consonants must be assumed to accurately predict the nature of the process (see section 3.3.1).

16 This areal trait is discussed in Campbell, Kaufman, & Smith-Stark 1986.

17 In Jumaytepeque this alternation does not include /ɬ/ since it is absent from this language's consonant inventory.

18 See Tozzer 1921.

19 The difference between a nucleus with a short vowel and one with a long vowel is in the finer organization of the nucleus itself. A long vowel nucleus has two moras, while a short vowel nucleus has a single mora.

20 This means that there are no Xinkan words with the syllabic structure of **CCV(V) or **CVCC except in loans from Spanish.

21 See Kaufman 1970 and Oxlajuuj Keej Maya' Ajtz'iib' 1993.

Chapter 3: Morphology

1 In Rogers 2010 I opted to conflate nouns and adjectives and called them, collectively, 'nominals'. This was largely because I was paying more attention to their surface morphological similarities than to the differences in their semantics. In Xinkan languages, nouns and adjectives have distinctly different morphological and syntactic properties. However, they also share a few characteristics. Because I consider the differences to be more significant than the similarities, instead of combining them into a single grammatical category, such as 'nominal', they are discussed as two separate grammatical categories. Table N1 summarizes the properties to be discussed below.

**Table N1 Morphological and syntactic properties
of Xinkan nouns and adjectives**

	Possession	Inchoative	Modified by Determiners	Number	Arguments of Verb	Modifier of Noun
Nouns	Yes	Yes	Yes	Yes	Yes	No
Adjectives	Fused head noun	Yes	Fused head noun	No	No	Yes

2 This is similar to the English classifications for nouns.

3 When inflected for possession, mass nouns have the meaning of 'possessed quantity of noun.' For example, *in-uy* means 'my quantity of water' in Guazacapán Xinkan.

4 Unfortunately, noun class membership is largely unknown in Yupiltepeque.

5 In Guazacapán and Chiquimulilla that diminutive clitic might be a grammaticalization of the *chür'ükü* 'little, small'. This, however, is not the case for the Jumaytepeque diminutive.

6 See Kaufman & Campbell's unpublished field notes; Sachse 2010; and Maldonado 1770.

7 The word order in this example might have been influenced by calquing from Spanish due to the presence of the Spanish adjective.

8 This means that it is plausible to suggest that the Xinkan vowel harmony system has either eroded or was being extended due to speaker error. This grammar does not consider either to have happened, but I point it out for the sake of completeness. Section 2.1.2 details vowel harmony.

9 'Grados comparative y superlativo no existen en ninguno de los idiomas en cuestión'.

10 See Campbell 1987.

11 It is possible that the indefinite article is the result of interference from Spanish *un/una*. However, all bare nominals (those that are not modified by a determiner) have a definite meaning. Thus, *maku* in Guazacapán means 'house' or 'the house' but never 'a house'. On these grounds it might be argued that the indefinite article behaves as such and does not merely mean 'one'.

12 Note that the absence of most numbers, except for the lower ones, is found in many Latin American indigenous languages. In these cases, as in Xinkan, the higher numbers have been replaced by Spanish.

13 See Calderón 1908 and Sachse 2010: 79–385 for information and data sources for numbers in Chiquimulilla Xinka.

14 Calderón 1908: 4–6.

15 It could be argued that some of the pronouns have derived historically from the combination of pronouns with inflection categories like number or with the definite article. For example *naka* 'you' in Guazacapán could be derived historically from *na* 'definite article' + *ka-* 'your',

both of which are components of the current morphological system. However, there is little evidence to support this speculation and so this line of development is not pursued here.

16 The system described for Cupeño in Hill 1969 & 2005 and Jacobs 1976, or the discussion of verb classes in Aikhenvald 2000 is similar to the organization of the Xinkan system. The consequence of this system is similar to what has been called semantic alignment. See Klaiman 1991; Mithun 1991a; Payne 1997: 144–162; Song 2001: 150–153; and Donahue & Wichmann 2008.

17 As discussed in section 3.6.4, the glottalization of the rightmost consonant of a verb stem is a marker of the incompletive aspect in roots in which it is not glottalized in the lexicon (underlyingly). In this verb the form does not change because the rightmost consonant is glottalized in the underlying form of the verb, and the process of glottalization is applied vacuously. See section 2.3.1 for information on glottalization.

18 Note that all of the forms that follow are given in the second-person singular. There is no data to attest to imperative verb forms in any other person or number, and current speakers of Xinkan do not produce such.

19 It is possible that the Chiquimulilla and Jumaytepeque past-tense markers are related historically either with the loss of [wi] or its addition. There is no empirical evidence that would support either of these analyses, and so it is felt that a descriptively adequate account would not argue for further morphological complication.

20 See Klaiman 1991: 228–245; Berinstein 1985; and Dayley 1985: 13; and the references in each.

21 Campbell 1977 & 2000 and Robertson 1992.

22 Split-intransitive systems are about the lexical marking and organization of intransitive verbs; active-stative alignment systems are about the morphological case on nouns; and split-S systems are about the subject agreement markings on verbs. See Rogers 2014 for the details as they relate to Xinkan languages.

23 Note, though, that even most Mayan languages have at least one preposition *tiʔ/chiʔ* 'to, at' (derived ultimately from 'mouth').

24 See Bakker 2013.

25 I speak of incorporation here and not of borrowing, because it is not clear if the Spanish verbs have become part of the Xinkan lexicon in any linguistic sense. It is most likely the case that speakers of Xinkan who have trouble recalling a native verb can substitute the Spanish verb in its place using this construction without this verb forming part of the grammar of Xinkan. Consequently, incorporation seems more appropriate than borrowing.

26 It is obvious that the word *kumu* is phonetically similar to the Spanish word *como* 'like, as'. However, I am not convinced that this is a borrowing from Spanish. There are subtle meaning differences between the two. The Spanish word is one of similarity or equalness between to entities, *el hombre es **como** la mujer* 'the man is **like** the woman'. The meaning of the Xinkan word is less about equality of characteristics and more about role in discourse: *nah **kumu** tuuru* 'He **the one acting the role of** tuuru'. This difference in meaning does not rule out Spanish as a source for the word, of course, but I do not think there is sufficient evidence to say one way or the other. I have opted to treat it as an integral part of the Xinkan grammar because of its unique function in the language.

27 It is a historical accident that the Chiquimulilla form resembles Spanish *hay* 'there is'.

28 See König, Siemund & Töpper 2013 for information about the typological distribution and properties of intensifiers.

29 Smith-Stark 1978.

30 An alternative hypothesis would be to suggest that all of the present participle forms are really antipassive verb forms and that subject-verb agreement is made using the nominal possession affixes with these verbs only. This would clear up the ambiguity between the antipassive verbs and the present participles. However, there is not sufficient evidence to support this hypothesis. Furthermore, it might be suggested that both the antipassive and the present participle are really just inchoative verbs with reanalyzed meanings. Thus, the antipassive and the present participle would be something like 'to do VERB'. While this hypothesis cannot be proven definitively, this does seem to be a very likely source of historical development for the word forms involving the suffix -*k'i*.

Chapter 4: Syntax

1 I am grateful to Frauke Sachse (pers. comm.) for mentioning that the similarity in syntax across the four languages (in light of the assumed time frame for diversification of twelve to seventeen centuries) might a be a consequence of contact with Spanish. Campbell 1978: 36 mentions a lexicostatistic distance of twelve mean centuries for the Xinkan languages, something that Terry Kaufman agrees with (pers. comm.). Scientifically, I do not find value in the dates estimated through the methodology of glottochronology, but it is often used as a general heuristic when estimating language diversification. If this dating schema is assumed to be accurate, there would have been sufficient time for the syntax of the various languages to have changed. In light of this depth of time, the absence of differentiation would be inconsistent. Relatively recent contact with Spanish, it can be argued, provides a possible explanation. However, while there are clear similarities in Xinkan languages to Spanish syntax (mentioned below in note 2), there are also clear differences. I do think that Spanish syntax has been borrowed into Xinkan, but it is unclear if this is the sole reason for the high similarity across the four languages.

2 In other languages (e.g., the Mayan languages) these nonsubject nominals might be signaled overtly through verbal affixes or nominal case assignments that indicate their relationship to the verb. However, nonsubject nominals are not so marked in the Xinkan languages. Relational nouns come the closest to case marking in the Xinkan languages (see section 3.7). However, these indicate spatiotemporal relationships between two noun phrases rather than marking grammatical functions and relationships between a noun phrase and a verb.

3 The term 'oblique' is used to refer to nominal arguments that are not core arguments of the verb. Oblique nominal arguments can be used with either transitive or intransitive verbs.

4 See Campbell, Kaufman, & Smith-Stark 1986.

5 See Dixon 1979: 85.

6 Presumably, this means that indefinite subjects cannot be preposed.

7 As it is for most of the other languages in Mesoamerica.

8 See Thompson & Kaufman 1988 and Campbell & Harris 1995 for a discussion about the difference and relationship between lexical borrowing and syntactic change.

9 See Campbell 1987 for a discussion of a similar process involving the neighboring Pipil language of El Salvador.

10 There is an apparent cognate in Yupiltepeque *uc(a)* 'hacer', listed in Calderón's 1908 glossary. This might mean that a possible interpretation is 'to do verb', or rather that the person is doing the verb being used.

11 Note that this particle is only accidentally similar to Spanish '*hay*' despite the similarity in content and function.

12 See Campbell 1985 and England 1989.

13 This is, of course, a controversial definition, since in some theoretical approaches verbs that take complement clauses are considered to be different from verbs that do not take complement clauses, and in these cases their complements are not considered to be objects. Thus, in the sentence 'John believes that it will rain', some would say 'that it will rain' is the object of 'believe', but others have an entirely different syntactic descriptions for the latter clause. I have opted to refer to complement clauses as arguments of a higher-order predicate simply because within the Xinkan languages there is no evidence to do otherwise.

14 This is ignoring, for the moment, such hypothetical adverbial clauses as in 'When John may sing, the chickens might join in.' These are ignored here precisely because there is no data confirming these types of structures, although it is assumed that something similar might be possible.

Chapter 6: Historical phonology

1 An alternate analysis suggests that the change has gone from [p] to [p'], but there is no motivation to suggest that this may be the case. However, a change from [p'] to [p] is preferred, because throughout the history of these languages glottalized consonants become their plain counterparts, thus making it a general pattern of change. Additionally, there is phonetic motivation for deglottalization (i.e., ease of articulation), while there is no such evidence supporting a claim for glottalization.

2 See Bird et al. 2008.

3 "Los sonidos *tz'*, *n'* son ⟨letras heridas⟩, es decir, sonidos que en la pronunciación dejan pasar corto tiempo para seguir pronunciado las sílabas ó letras que á esas llamadas ⟨letras heridas⟩ siguen."

4 See Howe & Pulleyblank 2001: 45–47.

5 Note that there are potentially two types of glottalized fricatives. The first might be extremely rare and require the simultaneous gestures of continuous airflow and glottalization; this type occurs in languages such as Tlingit. The other type, which is slightly easier to vocalize, would be produced in a manner similar to glottalized resonants, in which two nonsimultaneous gestures of a glottal-stop closure occur together with a fricative. Thus, the latter might be produced as [ʔs] or [sʔ] instead of [s']. The argument in favor of difficulty would be supported only by the latter type of glottalized fricative, and not the former. This is because in the first instance [sʔ] is a affricative glottal stop sequence, whereas [s'] is a simultaneous fricative and glottalic movement.

6 See Rogers 2008 for an in-depth description of Xinkan vowel harmony.

7 The change of [u] to [ɨ] after a word-final labial consonant supposes that the reason for the change is to differentiate between the two labial sounds: the consonant and the vowel. Perhaps a better solution is to posit that the [ɨ] became [u] after a labial in Guazacapán and Chiquimulilla due to assimilation of the labial feature; this would be a phonetically natural change. However, there are a number of words in these two languages that exhibit the sequence of a labial consonant followed by a [ɨ]: for example, *pɨɨmɨ* (G, Ch) 'mute', and *kɨɨwɨ* (G, Ch) 'shin'. There is no conditioning environment that would motivate the change to [u] in some words but not in others. Furthermore, the change from [u] to [ɨ] in Jumaytepeque

in this context is extremely regular. There are no Jumaytepeque words with a word-final [u] after a labial consonant.

8 One cognate set that seems to be related to this is *huuši* (G, Ch, J), ⟨jüsal⟩ (Y) 'head'. There is some indication that ⟨ü⟩ might either represents /ɨ/ or /uu/. Without knowing the exact phonetic value of this letter, it difficult to show how this cognate set fits into Xinkan reconstruction.

9 Note that Jumaytepeque and Yupiltepeque do not share a common rule *ɬ > *l*, since it is in every phonetic context in Jumaytepeque, but it is conditioned to all instantiations not following a low vowel in Yupiltepeque.

10 Maddieson 1984: 98.

11 Note, of course, that highly marked glottalized fricatives that otherwise would have been produced in the processes that glottalize consonants in particular morphological environments are avoided through the use of /ts'/ as the glottalized counterpart of the fricatives; thus, while this results in the otherwise unexpected gap (/ts'/ but no /ts/), it nevertheless contributes to the languages' being able to avoid the highly marked glottalized fricatives.

12 PAPXIG, pers. comm.

Chapter 8: Historical syntax

1 See, for example, Lightfoot 1983 & 2002 and Ferraresi & Goldbach 2008a & 2008b.

2 See Harris & Campbell 1995; Campbell & Harris 2002; and Campbell 1990 & 2004.

3 The drawbacks to the syntactic reconstruction of Proto-Xinkan mentioned in this paragraph are, of course, true of all linguistic reconstructions. That is, no matter how rich is the corpus of available material, the reconstructions are merely hypotheses. Similarly, any linguistic reconstruction is only as good as the materials available on which it is based. I mention these well-known drawbacks here, however, because of the controversial nature of syntactic reconstruction and the often misunderstood claims and goals of such reconstruction.

4 There is some indication that this word order was available to Yupiltepeque speakers also, but it is not clear if this was simply interference from Spanish.

Chapter 9: Looking forward

1 Hockett 1942: 3.

2 A preliminary discussion of Xinkan place names is found in Campbell 1986, where these examples were first cited. Ongoing work suggests many more than those Campbell mentions. This work should be published in the future.

Bibliography

Aikhenvald, Alexandra Y. 2000. *Classifiers: A typology of noun categorization devices.* Oxford: Oxford University Press.

Bakker, Dik. 2013. Person marking on adpositions. In Matthew S. Dryer & Martin Haspelmath (eds.), *The world atlas of language structures online.* Leipzig: Max Planck Institute for Evolutionary Anthropology. http://wals.info/chapter/48 (accessed 8-27-2014).

Berinstein, Ava. 1985. *Evidence for multiattachment in K'ekchi Mayan.* New York: Garland.

Bird, Sonya, et al. 2008. Oral laryngeal timing in glottalised resonants. *Journal of Phonetics* 36. 492–507.

Boer, Bart de. 2001. *The origins of vowel systems* (Studies in the Evolution of Language 1). Oxford: Oxford University Press.

Bowern, Claire. 2008. Syntactic change and syntactic borrowing in generative grammar. In Gisella Ferraresi & Maria Goldbach (eds.), *Principles of syntactic reconstruction*, 187–216. Amsterdam: Benjamins.

Brinton, Daniel G. 1885. On the language and ethnologic position of the Xinca Indians in Guatemala. *Proceedings of the American Philosophical Society* 22. 89–97.

Calderón, Eustorjio. 1908. *Estudios lingüísticos.* Volume 1, *Las lenguas (Sinca) de Yupiltepeque y del barrio de norte de Chiquimulilla en Guatemala.* Guatemala: Tipografía Sánchez.

Campbell, Lyle. 1972. Mayan loan words in Xinca. *International Journal of American Linguistics* 38. 187–190.

Campbell, Lyle. 1973a. On glottalic consonants. *International Journal of American Linguistics* 39(1). 44–46.

Campbell, Lyle. 1973b. The philological documentation of a variable rule in the history of Pokom and Kekchi. *International Journal of American Linguistics* 39(3). 133–134.

Campbell, Lyle. 1977. Quichean linguistic prehistory (University of California Studies in Linguistics [UCPL] 81). Berkeley: University of California Press.

Campbell, Lyle. 1978. Quichean prehistory: Linguistic contributions. In Nora England (ed.), *Papers in Mayan linguistics* (Miscellaneous Publications in Anthropology 6), 25–54. Columbia: Dept. of Anthropology, University of Missouri.

Campbell, Lyle. 1979. Middle American languages. In Lyle Campbell & Marianne Mithun (eds.), *The languages of Native America*, 902–1000. Austin: University of Texas Press.

Campbell, Lyle. 1985. *The Pipil language of El Salvador.* Berlin: Mouton de Gruyter.

Campbell, Lyle. 1987. Syntactic change in Pipil. *International Journal of American Linguistics* 53. 253–280.

Campbell, Lyle. 1990. Syntactic change in Finno-Ugric. In Henning Andersen & Konrad Koerner (eds.), *Historical linguistics 1987: International Conference on Historical Linguistics* (8. ICHL), 51–94. Amsterdam: Benjamins.

Campbell, Lyle. 1997a. The linguistic prehistory of Guatemala. In Jane Hill, P. J. Mistry & Lyle Campbell (eds.), *Papers in honor of William Bright*, 183–192. Berlin: Mouton de Gruyter.

Campbell, Lyle. 1997b. *American Indian languages: The historical linguistics of Native America*. Oxford: Oxford University Press.

Campbell, Lyle. 2000. Valency-changing derivations in K'iche'. In R. M. W. Dixon & Alexandra Y. Aikenvald (eds.), *Changing valency: Case studies in transitivity*, 236–281. Cambridge: Cambridge University Press.

Campbell, Lyle. 2004. Historical linguistics: An introduction, 2nd edn. Cambridge, MA: MIT Press.

Campbell, Lyle & Alice Harris. 1995. *Historical syntax in cross-linguistic perspective*. Cambridge: Cambridge University Press.

Campbell, Lyle & Alice Harris. 2002. Syntactic reconstruction and demythologizing 'myths and the prehistory of grammars'. *Journal of Linguistics* 38. 599–618.

Campbell, Lyle & Marianne Mithun. 1981. Syntactic reconstruction priorities and pitfalls. *Folia Linguistica Historica* 1. 19–40.

Campbell, Lyle & Martha Muntzel. 1989. The structural consequence of language death: Investigating obsolescence. In Nancy Dorian (ed.), *Studies in language contraction and death*, 181–196. Studies in the Social and Cultural Foundation of Language 7. Cambridge: Cambridge University Press.

Campbell, Lyle, Terrence Kaufman & Thomas C. Smith-Stark. 1986. Meso-America as a linguistic area. *Language* 62(3). 530–570.

Comrie, Bernard. 1989. *Language universals and linguistic typology: Syntax and morphology*. Chicago: University of Chicago Press.

Consejo del Pueblo Xinka de Guatemala (COPXIG). 2004. *Gramática y diccionario xinka: Una descripción e introducción al idioma*. Chiquimulilla and Santa Rosa, Guatemala: CECI.

Crothers, John. 1978. Typology and universals of vowel systems. In Joseph Greenberg (ed.), *Universals of human language*, vol. 2, 93–152. Stanford, CA: Stanford University Press.

Dayley, Jon Phillip. 1985. Voice and ergativity in Mayan languages. *Journal of Mayan Linguistics* 2(2). 3–82.

Dixon, Robert M. W. & Alexandra Y. Aikenvald (eds.). 2000. *Changing valency: Case studies in transitivity*. Cambridge: Cambridge University Press.

Dixon, Robert M. W. 1979. Ergativity. *Language* 55(1). 59–138.

Dixon, Robert M. W. 2000. A typology of causatives: Form, syntax and meaning. In Robert M. W. Dixon & Alexandra Y. Aikenvald (eds.), *Changing valency: Case studies in transitivity*, 30–79. Cambridge: Cambridge University Press.

Donohue, Mark & Søren Wichman. 2008. *The typology of semantic alignment*. Oxford: Oxford University Press.

Dorian, Nancy D. 1993. Internally and externally motivated change in language and contact settings: Doubts about dichotomy. In Charles Jones (ed.), *Historical linguistics: Problems and perspectives*, 131–155. New York: Longman Group.

Edmonson, Barbara. 1996. How to become bewitched, bothered, and bewildered: The Huastec versive. *International Journal of American Linguistics* 61(44). 378–395.

England, Nora. 1989. Comparing Mam (Mayan) clause structures: Subordinate versus main clauses. *International Journal of American Linguistics* 55(3). 283–301.

Estrada Belli, Francisco, Laura Kosakowsky, Marc Wolf & D. Blank. 1996. Patrones de asentamiento y uso de la tierra desde el preclásico al postclásico en la costa del Pacífico de Guatemala: La arqueología de Santa Rosa, 1995. *Mexicon* 18(6). 110–115.

Fant, Gunnar. 1973. *Speech sounds and features*. Cambridge, MA: MIT Press.

Fernández, Jesus. 1938. Diccionario del Sinca. *Anales de la Sociedad de Geografía e Historia de Guatemala* 15. 84–95, 359–366.

Ferraresi, Gisella & Maria Goldbach (eds). 2008a. *Principles of syntactic reconstruction*. Amsterdam: Benjamins.

Ferraresi, Gisella & Maria Goldbach. 2008b. Syntactic reconstruction: Methods and new insights. In Gisella Ferraresi & Maria Goldbach (eds.), *Principles of syntactic reconstruction*, 1–26. Amsterdam: Benjamins.

Gavarett, D. Juan & Sebastian Valdez. 1868. *Vocabularios de la lengua Xinca de Sinacantan y de Yupiltepeque y Jalapa*. Philadelphia: Berendt Linguistic Library.

Gildea, Spike. 1998. *On reconstructing syntax: Comparative Cariban morphosyntax*. Oxford: Oxford University Press.

Good, Jeff. 2004. The descriptive grammar as a (meta)database. In *E-MELD Workshop on Linguistic Databases and Best Practice*. http://emeld.org/workshop/2004/jcgood-paper.html.

Greenberg, Joseph. 1970. Some generalizations concerning glottalic consonants, especially implosives. *International Journal of American Linguistics* 36(2). 123–145.

Harris, Alice. 2008. Reconstruction in syntax: Reconstruction of patterns. In Gisella Ferraresi & Maria Goldbach (eds.), *Principles of syntactic reconstruction*. Amsterdam: Benjamins.

Harris, Alice & Lyle Campbell. 1995. *Historical syntax in cross-linguistics perspective*. Cambridge: Cambridge University Press.

Hill, Jane H. 1969. *A grammar of the Cupeño language*. Los Angeles: University of California dissertation.

Hill, Jane H. 2005. *A grammar of Cupeño*. Los Angeles: University of California Press.

Hock, Hans Heinrich. 1985. Yes, Virginia, syntactic reconstruction is possible. *Studies in the Linguistic Sciences* 15. 49–60.

Hockett, Charles F. 1942. A system of descriptive phonology. *Language* 18(1). 3–21. DOI:10.2307/409073.

Hogan, John T. 1976. An analysis of the temporal features of ejective consonants. *Phonetica* 33. 275–284.

Howe, Darin & Douglas Pulleyblank. 2001. Patterns and timing of glottalization. *Phonology* 18. 45–80.

Ichon, Alain & Rita Grignon. 1998. El título de Ixhuatán y el problema xinca en Guatemala. In *Memorias del segundo congreso internacional de Mayistas, Mérida, Yucatán, 1992*, 327–338. Mexico: UNAM, Instituto de Investigaciónes Filológicas, Centro de Estudios Mayas.

Ingram, J. & B. Rigsby. 1987. *Glottalic stops in Gitksan: An acoustic analysis*. Talin, Estonia: International Congress of Phonetic Sciences (ICPhS).

Klaiman, M. H. 1991b. Control and grammar. *Linguistics* 29. 623–651.

Jacobs, Roderick A. 1976. Syntactic reconstruction and the comparative method: A Uto-Aztecan case study. In Archibald A. Hill, Mohammad Ali Jazayery, Edgar C. Polomé & Werner Winter (eds.), *Linguistics and literary studies in honor of Archibald A. Hill*. Amsterdam: Benjamins.

Johnson, Keith. 1997. *Acoustics and auditory phonetics*. Cambridge, MA: Blackwell.

Kaufman, Terrence. 1970. *Proyecto de alfabetos y ortografías para escribir las lenguas mayances*. Antigua, Guatemala: Proyecto Lingüístico Francisco Marroquín (PLFM).

Kaufman, Terrence. 1976. New Mayan languages in Guatemala: Sacapultec, Sipacapa, and others. In Marlys McClaran (ed.), *Mayan linguistics*, vol. 1, 67–89. Los Angeles: American Indian Studies Center, University of California.

Kaufman, Terrence. 1977. Areal linguistics and Middle America. In T. A. Sebeok (ed.), *Native languages of the Americas*, vol. 2, 63–87. New York: Plenum.

Kingston, John Clayton. 1984. *The phonetics and phonology of the timing of oral and glottal events*. Berkeley: University of California dissertation.

Klaiman, M. H. 1991. *Grammatical voice*. Cambridge: Cambridge University Press.

König, Ekkehard, Peter Siemund, with Stephan Töpper. 2013. Intensifiers and reflexive pronouns. In Matthew S. Dryer & Martin Haspelmath (eds.), *The world atlas of language structures online*. Leipzig: Max Planck Institute for Evolutionary Anthropology. http://wals.info/chapter/47 (accessed 8-7-2014).

Kramer, Martin. 2003. *Vowel harmony and correspondence theory*. The Hague: Mouton de Gruyter.

Krause, Michael. 1992. The world's languages in crisis. *Language* 68(1). 1–42.

Ladefoged, Peter. 1997. Linguistic phonetic descriptions. In W. Hardcastle & J. Laver (eds.), *The handbook of phonetic sciences*, 589–618. Oxford: Blackwell.

Ladefoged, Peter. 2006. *A course in phonetics*, 5th edn. Boston: Thomson Wadsworth.

Ladefoged, Peter & Ian Maddieson. 1996. *The sounds of the world's languages*. Cambridge, MA: Blackwell.

Lass, Roger. 1993. How real(ist) are reconstructions? In Charles Jones (ed.), *Historical linguistics: Problems and perspectives*, 156–189. New York: Longman.

Lehmann, Walter. 1920. *Zentral-Amerika*. Berlin: D. Reimer.

Lightfoot, David W. 1983. On reconstructing a proto-syntax. In Irmengard Rauch & Gerald F. Carr (eds.), *Language change*, 128–142. Bloomington: Indiana University Press.

Lightfoot, David W. 2002. More myths. *Journal of Linguistics* 38. 619–626.

Lindau, Mona. 1984. Phonetic differences in glottalic consonants. *Journal of Phonetics* 12. 147–155.

Longobardi, Giuseppe. 2008. Foreword. In Gisella Ferraresi & Maria Goldbach (eds.), *Principles of syntactic reconstruction*. Amsterdam: Benjamins.

Lyons, Christopher G. 1978. A look into the Spanish future. *Lingua* 46. 225–244.

Maddieson, Ian. 1984. *Patterns of sounds*. Cambridge: Cambridge University Press.

Maddieson, Ian. 2005. Glottalized consonants. In Martin Haspelmath et al. (eds.), *The world atlas of language structure*, 34–37. Oxford: Oxford University Press.

Maldonado Matos, Manuel de. ~1770. *Arte de la lengua Szinca con algunas reflexiones criticas al Arte K'akchiquel*.

McArthur, Harry. 1966. Xinca. In M. K. Mayers (ed.), *Languages of Guatemala*, vol. 23, 309–312. The Hague: Mouton de Gruyter.

McQuown, Norman A. 1948. *Vocabulario Xinca recopilado en Chiquimulilla del 29 al 30 de noviembre (1948) con Mauricio García y Desiderio García González*. Microfilm collection of manuscripts on cultural anthropology no. 296, series 56. University of Chicago Library, 1977.

McQuown, Norman A. 1967. History of studies in Middle American linguistics. In Norman McQuown (ed.), *Handbook of Middle American Indians*. Volume 5, *Linguistics*, 3–7. Austin: University of Texas Press.

McQuown, Norman A. 1976. American Indian linguistics in New Spain. In Wallace. L. Chafe (ed.), *American Indian languages and American linguistics*, 105–127. Lisse: Peter de Ridder.

Mithun, Marianne. 1991a. Active/agentive case marking and its motivation. *Language* 67(3). 510–546.

Mithun, Marianne. 1991b. A functional approach to syntactic reconstruction. In Elizabeth C. Traugott, R. LaBrum & S. Sheperd (eds.), *Fourth international conference on historical linguistics*, 87–96. Amsterdam: Benjamins.

Nash, Manning (ed.). 1967. *Handbook of Middle American Indians.* Volume 6, *Social Anthropology.* Austin: University of Texas Press.

Norman, William M. & Lyle Campbell. 1978. Toward a Proto-Mayan syntax: A comparative perspective on grammar. In Nora England (ed.), *Papers in Mayan linguistics* (Miscellaneous Publications in Anthropology 6), 136–156. Columbia: Dept. of Anthropology, University of Missouri.

Ohala, John. J. 1993. The phonetics of sound change. In Charles Jones (ed.), *Historical linguistics: Problems and perspectives*, 237–278. London: Longman.

Olson, James S. 1991. *The Indians of Central and South America: An ethnohistorical dictionary.* Westport, CT: Greenwood Press.

Oxlajuuj Keej Maya' Ajtz'iib'. 1993. *Maya' Chii': Los idiomas Mayas de Guatemala.* Guatemala: Cholsamaj.

Payne, Thomas. 1997. *Describing morpho-syntax.* New York: Cambridge University Press.

Pires, Acrisio & Sarah G. Thomason. 2008. How much syntactic reconstruction is possible? In Gisella Ferraresi and Maria Goldbach (eds.), *Principles of syntactic reconstruction.* Amsterdam: Benjamins.

Plauché, Madelaine C. 1988. Glottalied sonorants in Yowlumne (Yawelmani). *Texas Linguistic Forum* 41. 133–145. Austin: University of Texas Linguistics Society.

Plauché, Madelaine C., et al. 1998. Glottalized sonorants: A phonetic universal? *Berkeley Linguistics Society* 24(1). 318–389.

Prince, Alan & Paul Smolensky. 2004. *Optimality theory: Constraint interaction in generative grammar.* Malden, MA: Blackwell.

Pye, Clifton & Pedro Quixtan Poz. 1988. Precocious passives (and antipassives) in Quiché Mayan. *Papers and Reports on Child Language Development* 27. 27–80.

Rambo, A. Terry. 1965. Urgent research in Guatemala: Xinca Indian villages and Xinca language recommended for intensive study. *Bulletin of the International Committee on Urgent Anthropological and Ethnological Research* 7. 105.

Roberts, Ian. 2007. *Diachronic syntax.* Oxford: Oxford University Press.

Robertson, John S. 1992. *The history of tense/aspect/mood/voice in the Mayan verbal complex.* Austin: University of Texas Press.

Rogers, Chris. 2008. Una descripción de la gramática de los idiomas Xinkas. Unpublished manuscript.

Rogers, Christopher. 2010. *A comparative grammar of Xinkan.* Salt Lake City: University of Utah dissertation.

Rogers, Chris. 2014. Xinkan verb categorization: Morphosyntactic marking on intransitive verbs. *International Journal of American Linguistics* 80(3). 371–398.

Rogers, Chris. 2016. Indigenous authenticity as a goal of language documentation and revitalization: Addressing the motivations in the Xinkan community. In Gabriela Pérez-Báez, Chris Rogers & Jorge Emilio Rosés Labrada (eds.), *Latin American contexts for language documentation and revitalization.* Berlin: Mouton de Gruyter.

Rogers, Chris & Lyle Campbell. 2011. *Endangered languages.* Oxford Bibliographies Online. www.oxfordbibliographies.com/view/document/obo-9780199772810/obo-9780199772810-0013.xml?rskey=PhHMt2&result=1&q=endangered+languages.

Sachse, Frauke (ed.). 2004. *Manuel Maldonado de Matos: Arte de la lengua Szinca: Estudio introductorio y edición del texto* (Fuentes Mesoamericanas 5). Markt Schwaben, Germany: Saurwein.

Sachse, Frauke. 2010. *Reconstructive description of eighteenth-century Xinka grammar* (LOT Dissertation Series 254). Utretch, Netherlands: Landelijke Onderzoekschool Taalwetenschap (LOT).

Santos Nicolás, José Fernando, A. Cervantes López, M. M. Gómez & Jose Benito. 1997. *Gramática del idioma Poqomam*. Antigua, Guatemala: Proyecto Lingüístico Francisco Marroquín (PLFM).

Sapir, Edward. 1938. Glottalized consonants in Navaho, Nootka, and Kwakiutl (with a note on Indo-Euorpean). *Language* 14(4). 248–274.

Sapper, Karl. 1904. *Der gegenwärtige Stand der ethnographischen Kenntnis von Mittelamerika.* Archiv für Anthropologie N.F. 3, 1–38.

Saville, Marshall H. (1918). A grammar and vocabulary of the Szinca language of Guatemala. *American Anthropologist* 20(3). 999–340.

Schumann Gálvez, Otto. 1967. *Xinca de Guazacapán*. Mexico, DF: Escuela Nacional de Antropología e Historia.

Sharer, Robert J., with Loa P. Traxler. 2006. *The ancient Maya*. Stanford, CA: Stanford University Press.

Smalley, William A. 1989. *Manual of articulatory phonetics*. New York: University Press of America.

Smith-Stark, Thomas. 1978. The Mayan antipassive: Some facts and fictions. In Nora England (ed.), *Papers in Mayan linguistics* (Miscellaneous Publications in Anthropology 6), 169–187. Columbia: Dept. of Anthropology, University of Missouri.

Song, Jae Jung. 2001. *Linguistic typology: Morphology and syntax*. London and New York: Routledge.

Stoll, Otto. 1886. *Guatemala-Reisen und Schilderungen aus den Jahren 1878–1883*. Leipzig: F. A. Brockhaus.

Stoll, Otto. 1958. *Etnografía de Guatemala* (Seminario de Integración Social Guatemalteca 8). Guatemala: Editorial del Ministerio de Educación Pública.

Termer, Franz. 1944. Ein Besuch bei den Xinca-Indianern in Südostguatemala. *Ethnos* 9(3–4). 97–117.

Thomason, Sarah Grey & Terrence Kaufman. 1988. *Language contact, creolization, and genetic linguistics*. Berkeley: University of California Press.

Tozzer, Alfred M. 1921. *A Maya grammar*. Cambridge, MA: Peabody Museum.

Tujab, Gloria. 1987. Lenguas indígenas que se encuentran en vias de extinción. *América Indígena* 47(3). 529–533.

Vincent, N. & Ian Roberts. 1999. Remarks on syntactic reconstruction. Deutsche Gesellschaft für Sprachwissenschaft, University of Constance, February 1999.

Vogt, Evon Z. (ed.). 1969. *Handbook of Middle American Indians*. Volume 7, *Ethnology*, part 1. Austin: University of Texas Press.

Warner, Natasha. 1996. Acoustic characteristics of ejectives in Ingush. *International Conference on Spoken Language Processing* (ICSLP) 96(3). 1525–1528.

Wright, Richard, Sharon Hargus & Katherine Davis. 2002. On the categorization of ejectives: Data from Witsuwit'en. *Journal of the International Phonetic Association* 32(1). 43–77.

Typological Index of Cross-Linguistic Terms

The typological significance of a language is a rewarding area of study. Typology requires cross-linguistic comparisons between a specific language and other languages spoken in a geographical area, as well as languages spoken throughout the world. The result is a better understanding of what makes the languages unique and how it represents the general human language faculty.

This smaller index includes a short list of typological parameters that can be used to compare the Xinkan languages with languages in Mesoamerica and beyond. It is noticeably shorter than the general index. I have opted only to represent those parameters that are important for the study of Xinkan languages. All of these have influenced my thinking about Xinkan grammar and the representation of the information in this book. The goal of this index being to highlight the salient typological features without making the reader hunt for them — or guess which ones would be relevant. Other topics of interest may be found in the general index.

General Index

absolutive antipassive, 119

abstract quantifiers, 79–80

abstract verbal nouns, 128–29

adjectives, 59, 88; comparative and superlative, 73–74; inchoative verbs and, 116–18; and *ki*, 72–73; as noun modifiers, 70–72

adverb order, 72–73

adverbial clauses, 164–65, 245n.14

affixes, 122, 244n.2; possessive, 64–65; pronominal, 209, 211–12; subject-verb agreement, 94–95

agent nouns, 129–30

agent noun suffixes, 25, 120–21, 130

agents, 139

AILLA. *See* Archive of the Indigenous Languages of South America

Alagüilac, 187

alienable nouns, 61–62

alignment patterns, 7

allomorphy: of glottalization, 43–47

alternation: vowel-length, 23

Alvarado, Pedro de, 9

alveolars: ejective affricate, 32–33; Proto-Xinkan, 195–200

(alveo-)palatals: Proto-Xinkan, 200–201

antipassive: construction of, 119–21; and verb agreement, 139–40

Archive of the Indigenous Languages of South America (AILLA), 8

Arte de la lengua Szinca (Maldonado), 7

articles, 74–75, 242n.11

assimilation, 26; vowel harmony, 29–31

beneficiaries, 139

bisyllabic roots, 56

body parts: relational nouns and, 104

bound morphology: Proto-Xinkan, 213–16

Brinton, Daniel, 10, 187

Calderón, Eustorjio, 7, 10

Campbell, Lyle, 13, 14, 187, 228; fieldwork, 5–6, 8

case marking, 102, 105

causative construction, 125–28

causative verbs, 24; construction of, 125–28

central vowels, 30

Chalchuapa (El Salvador), 6

Chiquimulilla Xinka, 4, 5, 7, 8, 11, 243n.27; adjectives, 71; adverbs in, 72, 165; alienable possession, 62; antipassive, 119, 120, 121, 140; causative constructions, 127; complement clauses, 164; conditional clauses, 166; conjunctions and disjunctions, 159; consonants, 33, 34(table), 35, 36, 37, 38, 40, 43, 55–56, 189, 194, 197, 201, 202; demonstratives, 75–76, 77; diminutive construction, 69, 242n.5; directional particle, 106; direct object, 110, 111; example sentences, 14; existential sentences, 150–51; genitives in, 66; glottalization in, 32, 44, 45, 46, 47–48, 54; grammatical mood, 103–4; inalienable possession, 63; inchoative verbs, 117; intransitive verbs, 24, 48–49, 89, 91–92, 93, 97, 122, 123, 124, 233; irregular verbs, 235–36; and Jumaytepeque, 207; labials in, 245–46n.7; lenition to [h] in, 52; lexical items, 13; long vowels, 22; mood particle, 104; nasal assimilation, 51; negative sentences, 157–58; nouns, 68, 105, 115, 130; null-copula sentences, 148–49; numbers in, 77, 78; participles, 133; preposing in, 156;